MAS

1st

WBSS

MAS

Peaks and Pioneers
The Story of Mountaineering

PEAKS AND PIONEERS

The Story of Mountaineering

Francis Keenlyside

Preface by Lord Hunt of Llanvair Waterdine

Elek London

ISBN 0 236 31042 9

Designed by Harold Bartram and produced
by Paul Elek Ltd

First published in Great Britain 1975 by
Paul Elek Ltd
54-58 Caledonian Road
London N1 9RN

and simultaneously in Canada by
Griffin House
461 King Street West
Toronto M5V 1K7

Filmset in England by Photocomp Ltd, Birmingham
Printed in France by Maison Mame

Title page: an engraving of
1851 exaggerates the perils of
negotiating the crevasses of
Mont Blanc.

Contents

Chamouni

A watercolour by John Ruskin
(1891): the village of Chamonix
at the foot of Mont Blanc.

Preface

I learned to climb as a teenager in the western Alps, at the hands of professional guides, some of whose forebears were among the pioneers in the Golden Age of mountaineering in the latter half of the nineteenth century: men with names such as Rodier at the western end of the range and Klucker in the eastern Alps.

Perhaps this is one reason why I have felt a link with those beginnings of our sport which may not be shared by the modern generation of brilliant young climbers. In the old Promontoire hut beneath the southern flank of the Meije on a night in August 1928, my youthful thoughts were with de Castelnau who with his guides, Gaspard *père et fils*, had dared to tackle the famous rock wall which bears his name, and whose problems on the morrow so daunted an eighteen-year-old 50 years after the first ascent. A few years later, struggling up the Mummery crack on the Grépon during my first guideless season, I marvelled at the skill of the greatest amateur climber of his day; even more did I wonder at his prediction that this classic route would, one day, be adjudged 'an easy day for a lady'. Alfred Mummery was very much in my mind many years further on as I followed in his footsteps on Dyktau in the Caucasus, which he had first climbed with his guide Zurfluh at a speed which is deemed astonishing even by Soviet climbers of the present day. On these and other great climbs, it was those early pioneering achievements against a background of primitive equipment and skills, without the convenience of modern roads and transport, let alone the benefit of high-placed mountain huts, which have fired my imagination.

It may, therefore, easily be understood with what delight I attended the celebrations in Chamonix in September 1974 to mark the centenary of the Club Alpin Français. Here, in that Mecca of mountaineering, were displayed the archives, the artefacts, the portraits and the paintings dating from the first ascent of Mont Blanc in 1786 to the present day.

It is one thing to write about men and mountains but it is far better to let those rugged and often amusing characters tell their own story. It is this alternative which my friend Francis Keenlyside has wisely taken in this book, a history of mountaineering told as far as possible in the words of those who made the history. In this way, it really conjures up the past and, for those who climb today, contrasts it with the present.

Reading it, some may well conclude that mountaineering, which our modern tyros sometimes call a 'game', is rather more than a sport. It may be seen as a struggle with nature and a relationship between human beings of a very special quality. If so, Mr Keenlyside has rendered a service to a much wider readership than only to those who climb.

JOHN HUNT

1 Darkness to Dawn

... through many a dark and dreary vale
They passed, and many a region dolorous,
O'er many a Frozen, many a Fiery Alp,
Rocks, Caves, Lakes, Fens, Bogs, Dens and shades of death,
A Universe of death, which God by curse
Created evil. . . .

John Milton

Mountaineering is an elaboration of the simple experience of walking up or down hill. The elaboration has developed into a game, a skill, an adventurous art, and has nourished a full and fascinating literature. It is surprising that this development is so recent: the history of mountaineering begins only two hundred years ago. Of course, some men had at times found themselves among, even on top of, mountains at earlier dates, but they were not mountaineers any more than the first child to strike a stone with a stick was a cricketer.

The reason for this late development was that mountains were outlandish, desert and dangerous. Being useless, they were unknown; and being unknown they were feared.

The custom of worshipping on sacred mountains is widespread, and its origin lost in the mists of unrecorded antiquity. The ancient attitude to mountains is clear enough in the Bible. They were held in awe and were the appropriate setting for divine manifestations. Moses received the tables of the law on Mount Sinai; Christ was transfigured after he had led Peter and James and John up into an high mountain. The classical world felt similarly; the official pantheon dwelt on Mount Olympus and mountains were the proper place for sacred and terrible mysteries. Aphrodite Urania, Queen of the Mountain, after mating with the sacred king on a mountain top, destroyed him as the queen bee destroys the drone. Supernatural beings of various kinds, nymphs and satyrs, were to be found in all unfrequented spots, and mountains were the least frequented of all. Most of these gods, demigods and demi-semi-gods had their gracious as well as their savage side, and there is no reason to suppose that mountains were altogether a place of horror to the rational Greek spirit.

The terror came later as a result of the policy of the early church. Finding belief in supernatural powers and beings infesting all wild places to be unshakable, the church deemed it easier to twist than to destroy this rural faith; the creatures of pristine poetic fancy were converted into demons, dragons or other agents of the devil, though a few of the favoured were promoted into saints. The mountains having become outposts of Satan's forces, the Christian had good cause to shun them. This attitude, supreme throughout the Dark Ages, lingered on well into the eighteenth century. But, as the fear of monsters waned in the Age of Reason, other grounds still put mountains beyond the pale of civilised man. Their agricultural production was meagre; they interrupted communications; they 'obstructed prospects', were a 'uniformity of barrenness'; they were dangerous by reason of tempest, stonefall and icefall; they were the refuge of outlaws. As they were both useless and dangerous, mankind, by a common confusion, found them ugly.

In the latter part of the eighteenth century two new and liberating influences began to make themselves felt: the growth of natural science and the stirring of Romanticism. The scientists wanted to learn about alpine plants, geological structure, the movement of glaciers and the rarefaction of the air; a few even penetrated the mountains to find out. The early Romantics found mountains grand and sublime but attempted no close inspection. Some of them visited the more accessible valleys and crossed unglaciated highway passes. Rousseau, Shelley and Byron, like Ruskin later, worshipped strictly at their idols' feet. Wordsworth, on the other hand, did know his lakeland fells.

During the long centuries of mountain ostracism, many passes were in occasional or regular use, not only for trade, but as military or pilgrim routes.

Opposite: a view across the northern slopes of Mont Blanc, the highest mountain in the Alps; its summit was the goal of the first mountaineers.

Above: a dragon, reportedly seen in 1660, from J. J. Scheuchzer's study of alpine natural history typifies the long-held view of mountains as the haunt of ferocious creatures.

Hannibal took his army, elephants and all, across a high and snow-bound alpine pass.[1] Pompey, Hasdrubal and Caesar all crossed the Alps and Augustus built a road, to be repaired by Napoleon, over the Grand St Bernard. The Théodule Pass, between Zermatt and Breuil, and other passes now glaciated were in regular use in the Middle Ages, but these routes were interrupted by increased glaciation from the fifteenth century onwards. (The glaciers only began their present withdrawal in the nineteenth century.) Apart from medieval travellers over such easy passes, the only people to venture above the snowline before the dawn of mountaineering were the chamois hunters, the crystal-seekers and the smugglers. The same man often pursued all three of these occupations, according to season and opportunity. There was a boom in smuggling when Napoleon was trying to exclude British products from Europe with his 'continental system'. Smugglers certainly used glacier passes but for trade reasons did not publish their routes.

Very occasionally during the Middle Ages modest climbs were made in exceptional circumstances or by exceptional or eccentric individuals. Late in the thirteenth century, King Peter III of Aragon claimed the solitary ascent of Canigou (9,144 feet) in the Pyrenees; he reported that he had roused a dragon by throwing a stone into a lake at the top–but there is no lake anywhere near the top. Petrarch and his brother climbed Mont Ventoux (6,273 feet) near Avignon in 1335. Two decades later Rotario d'Asti, a knight, made the first recorded climb of a snow peak when, in fulfilment of a vow, he carried a triptych to the summit of Rocciamelone (11,605 feet), a southern outpost of the Graians. The triptych may still be seen in the cathedral at Susa. Leonardo da Vinci ascended one of the outliers of Monte Rosa above Alagna, and a more rigorous climb, that of Mont Aiguille (6,880 feet), south of Grenoble, was made in 1492 when Antoine de Ville was ordered by King Charles VIII of France to make the ascent, which he duly did.

In the New World, when Cortes was advancing on Montezuma's capital in 1519, his route took him between Popocatapetl and Iztaccihuatl. In order to show the Indians that 'no achievement was beyond the dauntless daring of his followers', he encouraged some of his officers to attempt Popocatapetl (17,888 feet). Now a picnic resort near Mexico City, it was then still an active volcano. Diego Ordaz led the party; they got high but did not reach the summit, 'being nearly blinded and suffocated by the volumes of smoke, sparks and cinders which were belched forth'. The account given by W. H. Prescott in his classic, *The Conquest of Mexico*,[2] continues:

The general was not satisfied with the result. Two years after he sent up another party, under Francisco Montano, a cavalier of determined resolution. The object was to obtain sulphur to assist in making gunpowder for the army. The mountain was quiet at this time, and the expedition was attended with better success. The Spaniards, five in number, climbed to the very edge of the crater, which presented an irregular ellipse at its mouth, more than a league in circumference. Its depth might be from eight hundred to a thousand feet. A lurid flame burned gloomily at the bottom, sending up a sulphurous steam, which, cooling as it rose, was precipitated on the sides of the cavity. The party cast lots, and it fell on Montano himself to descend in a basket into this hideous abyss, into which he was lowered by his companions to the depth of four hundred feet. This was repeated several times, till the adventurous cavalier had collected a sufficient quantity of sulphur for the wants of the army. This doughty enterprise excited general admiration at the time. Cortes concludes his report of it, to the Emperor, with the judicious reflection that it would be less inconvenient, on the whole, to import their powder from Spain.

The Alps were the natural cradle of mountaineering. They stand in the heart of densely populated Europe whereas all the other great ranges rise in areas that are, or at least were until recently, remote from any con-

centrations of mankind. It was equally natural that the first men to study and visit the mountains in a true mountaineering spirit were Swiss humanists, and this was in the middle of the sixteenth century. Two such were Conrad Gesner and Josias Simler, who wrote of their mountains, modest eminences though they were, with an understanding and enjoyment very much more modern in spirit than did any of their successors for two hundred years. This budding school, with so much else of value, was snuffed out by the religious and civil turmoil of the seventeenth century and medieval attitudes lived on. Even in the Age of Enlightenment it was still necessary for bishops to exorcise glaciers. In 1708 J. J. Scheuchzer, then the leading authority on the Alps and a Fellow of the Royal Society, classified the alpine dragons with scientific care. Some progress, however, had been achieved; the dragons had largely dropped their medieval attributes and become kindly and hospitable.

The peasants living among the mountains, Rousseau's heroes, took little interest in the higher regions; they were content to wrest their living from the highland meadows (strictly 'alp' means highland meadow) or to cross such simple passes as served their domestic purposes. The mountaineering impulse which stirred in the late eighteenth century was found entirely among educated townsmen and the better educated village priests.

In 1744 Hess, Waser and two other monks of Engelberg climbed the Titlis (10,627 feet) 'at the beginning of the hay month',[3] while the Genevese brothers Deluc climbed the Brevent (8,288 feet) in 1754 and the Buet (10,201 feet) in 1770. The Delucs were keen amateur scientists; when they climbed these two viewpoints near Chamonix they duly recorded the atmospheric pressure and the temperature at which water boiled. For at least two generations thereafter thermometers and barometers were standard mountaineering equipment; though often carried from genuine scientific interest, they were sometimes merely taken to give an air of respectability to an activity regarded as daft in itself.

In these very early days the botanists were foremost. Albert von Haller travelled in his native Alps to supervise the labour of his plant collectors who were responsible for much early exploration. He also wrote a poem, *Die Alpen*, which became a best-seller and did much to draw attention to the mysterious mountains. Pierre and Abraham Thomas, father and son, were the best known of his collectors and were the most experienced alpine travellers of their day.

The history of mountaineering proper–that is, mountain travel with the intention of reaching a summit–begins with Mont Blanc. This happened partly because it is the culminating point of the Alps, partly because of the attention drawn to it by early travellers (such as Windham and Pococke in 1741), but mainly because the necessary men were there, de Saussure in Geneva and Paccard in Chamonix.

On his first visit to Chamonix in 1760, Horace-Benedict de Saussure fell under the spell of the mountain and offered a prize to the guides for the dis-

covery of a route to its summit. De Saussure was an ambitious man of science, well-known and respected, and indeed, after his marriage, the richest man in Geneva. For more than thirty years after this first visit he was a keen and active mountain traveller. Although he travelled on mule-back whenever possible and generally kept to the valley tracks and the grassy passes, he had a sensitive feeling for mountains and their scenery; it is this enthusiastic devotion rather than any technical expertise that earned him his place as a father of mountaineering.

The hope of winning de Saussure's prize did, after a time-lag, stimulate some efforts. The route generally favoured was via the Dôme du Goûter, and this was the route attempted by Couteran, the son of Widow Couteran who kept the inn at Chamonix. With three guides, he did get to the top of the Dôme (14,121 feet) in 1775, the first time a major snow mountain had been climbed.

JOHANNES JACOBUS SCHEUCHZERUS
Med. D. Helvetio-Tigurinus SOC. Reg. Lond. et Acad. Nat.
Cur. dictus ACARNAN Nat. IV. Non. Aug. 1672.

In the same year a young Scot, Thomas Blaikie, was sent to the Alps by two distinguished British botanists to collect specimens. They could not have chosen a better man, tough, determined and an excellent walker. His first excursions were in the Jura, where he had the originality and imprudence to loiter on the summit of the Dôle to see the sun set. Turning to the Alps, he soon called on the Thomases at Bex, with the younger of whom he crossed the Pass of Cheville to Sion. He made a solitary excursion above the Gemmi to a point which Montagnier identifies as on the ridge of the Felsenhorn. On a visit to the glaciers of Grindelwald his guide would not venture on the ice so Blaikie 'went along the sides of the rock'. After other journeyings he walked to Chamonix from Geneva, arriving from Sallanches in time for lunch. 'After refreshing at a publick house went with my letter I had for Mr Paccard, found him at home; he seems to be a man of respect in this place, he has three sons, very genteel young men.'[4] The youngest of these three was Michel-Gabriel, then eighteen. That same afternoon Blaikie crossed the Mer de Glace with two of the Paccard sons. Next day, with Michel-Gabriel, he reached a point some distance above the Lac du Plan de l'Aiguille and descended to sleep at the chalet of Blaitière-dessus. On the following day they made the first guideless attempt on Mont Blanc; they crossed the Glacier des Bossons and the Taconna Glacier and reached a point high on the slopes of the Aiguille du Goûter, if not its actual summit. This remarkable expedition took place seven weeks after Couteran's

Histoire Naturelle, Fig.1. *Glacier de Savoye.*
Fig 2. *Glacier de Gottemberg dans le Canton de Berne.*

Most eighteenth-century alpine travellers went to the mountains to investigate their amazing rock structure and their strangely moving rivers of ice. Above: an illustration from Hacquet's *Mineralogische-Botanische Lustreise* (1779–81); above right: drawings of glaciers published in Paris in 1768.

ascent of the Dôme du Goûter. The next two days were spent in climbing the Brévent and visiting the Jardin de Talèfre. After packing up the plants he had collected, Blaikie set off for Geneva straight over the mountains by himself, a most daring undertaking during which he had to fly for his life across country by night. Revisiting the Thomases, he made another long excursion above the Rhône valley before returning home. Although this was his only season, Blaikie

established himself as the first British mountaineer.

There were stirrings elsewhere. Lorenz Willnötzer climbed Triglav (9,393 feet) in the Julian Alps in 1778, and the next year the Abbé Murith, a canon of the Great St Bernard, climbed the Velan (12,247 feet). Besides being a reputable botanist, the abbé must have been a competent mountaineer; the Velan is harder than any peak so far reached. He hired two incompetent men as guides but had to cut the steps himself and finally drag his two professionals up a steep ice-slope to the top. He never climbed another peak but continued to travel among the mountains and to explore glaciers. Another priest, J. M. Clement of Val d'Illiez, climbed the Dents du Midi (10,696 feet) in 1788. And in 1793, penetrating where few British travellers even now venture, Robert Townson made the first certain ascent of Lomnica (8,642 feet) in the Polish Tatra.

The first ascent of Mont Blanc

Over the years Michel-Gabriel Paccard, now a doctor, continued to study Mont Blanc through a telescope from Chamonix and from the Brévent and by a series of penetrating reconnaissances. He thus evolved an original route of his own; up the Taconna Glacier to the Grand Plateau, then by the lower *ancien passage* between the two lines of Rochers Rouges. On August 8, 1786, he reached the summit (15,771 feet) by this route accompanied by one porter, Jacques Balmat.

Unfortunately, apart from a record of his barometer

and thermometer readings (now in the British Museum) and the briefest of mentions in his Notebook (now at the Alpine Club), Paccard left no written account of his climb. Equally unfortunately, Balmat gave several versions to different persons over a long period, quite inconsistent one with another and more fiction than history. The best, and only immediate, account is in the *Journal* of Baron von Gersdorff. The Baron had watched the later stages of the climb through a telescope and interviewed Dr Paccard within a few hours of his return. De Saussure has also left an account derived from a conversation with Paccard thirteen days later, on his return from his first attempt to follow the doctor's route.

At 9 pm on August 7, Paccard and Balmat bivouacked some 850 feet below the top of the Montagne de la Côte. Apart from bread and meat and blankets they had scientific instruments, pen, ink and notebook and long glacier poles. Next morning the doctor read his instruments and they set out at 4.15. They had no ladder and no rope and had difficulty threading the crevasses of the Jonction, an area of tumbled ice where the Taconna and Bossons glaciers meet. The night had been too warm and four times one or other of them broke through the snow covering; when this happened they threw themselves forwards with pole horizontal and crawled out. As they mounted the north wind blew more strongly. The passage across the Grand Plateau was laborious for laden men breaking through the snow crust into the

soft deep snow below. At about 3 pm, Balmat refused to go on, probably shaken by the discovery that Paccard was following a new route and not that taken by the guides earlier. In spite of the late hour, the cold wind and the untrodden distance still to go, Paccard did not falter but rallied his porter and they went on. The lower stretch of the *ancien passage* up steepish ice was the only remaining technical obstacle. The doctor led, chipping steps with his iron-shod pole. There were still some 1,200 feet to go over an easy but windy snow ridge. Pausing from time to time for Dr Paccard to examine rocks and collect specimens, they pushed on. At 6.12 they were seen from the valley, Dr Paccard going straight up and Balmat zigzagging to the left; it must have been almost a race, so fast were they going. At 6.23 they were on top. Readings were taken of all the instruments and they sought for shelter; finding none, they set out on a night descent. The full moon helped them down to the top of the Montagne de la Côte where they bivouacked. Both had slight frostbite in one hand and the doctor was snow-blind; he reached his father's house at 8 am and went to bed.

Here is Gersdorff's account:[5]

They had moved on again at daybreak; had several times met moderate difficulties at crevasses and slippery places; had climbed slowly, and had finally paused every 100 steps; had been tired to a certain extent by sinking deep in the new snow, and for this reason had often interchanged the leading; had

Top: the Dents du Midi, first climbed by a Swiss priest, J. M. Clément, in 1788.

Above: Horace Benedict de Saussure, the scientist whose passion for Mont Blanc led him to offer a reward to the first guide to find a route to the summit.

Top: the Aiguille du Géant, an illustration from de Saussure's *Voyages dans les Alpes* (1803).

Above: de Saussure fulfilling his ambition of climbing Mont Blanc in 1787, when he reached the top accompanied by 18 guides and his valet.

suffered no bad effects from the thin air, but on the contrary had felt unusually fit; had been equipped with alpenstocks, crampons and nails in their shoes, and had worn gaiters. But on the summit they had a strong west wind and, at a temperature of $-6°$ Reaumur [$-18·5°$ F], their hands were soon frozen. The fingers of the Herr Doctor's right hand are still feelingless in spite of much rubbing with snow. The roast meat they had was nearly frozen, and they were unable to eat it. They thought they saw the sun set whilst they were on the summit, but here they were mistaken according to my own exact observation yesterday. During the descent at night they fell several times up to the waist into snow-covered crevasses, but because of their horizontally held alpenstocks they were fortunately able to get out again each time. At open crevasses they laid their two alpenstocks across and crawled over on all fours. . . . The Herr Doctor lost his hat above. He tied a red handkerchief to a stick and planted it on the summit, and we saw it both yesterday and today.

If anyone is the father of mountaineering, it is the quiet and dignified village doctor of Chamonix.

As soon as he heard that the mountain had been climbed, de Saussure made an abortive attempt to follow Paccard's route. The next year he went about it more thoroughly; he arranged for two huts to be built and for the condition of the mountain to be watched. In the course of these duties, two of the guides, J. M. Cachat and A. Tournier, with Jacques Balmat, made the second ascent. Four weeks later, de Saussure's classic caravan of twenty made the third ascent. Within six days Mark Beaufoy made the fourth.

The Col du Géant to the east of Mont Blanc was first reached from Courmayeur by Thomas Ford Hill, probably looking for a route to the top of Mont Blanc, in either August or September of 1786. It was not crossed until the next year by J. M. Cachat and A. Tournier; they were seeking a route for Charles-François Exchaquet, who made the crossing on the following day with J.-M. Tournier and J.-M. Couttet, in ignorance that they had been preceded. The third crossing was made, also in 1787, by Marc-Théodore Bourrit with his son and four guides. Characteristically he wrote, 'The difficulties of Mont Blanc are nothing compared to the difficulties of this passage'; equally characteristically he suppressed the fact of Exchaquet's previous crossing. Next year de Saussure encamped for sixteen days on the Col and left a

Above left: the porter Jacques Balmat (left) and the Chamonix doctor Michel-Gabriel Paccard (right), the first to ascend Mont Blanc.

Left: the Col du Géant to the east of Mont Blanc, first reached by Thomas Ford Hill in 1786 and given its present name by de Saussure.

Below: an engraving by Marc Théodore Bourrit, a poor artist, of the Glacier des Bossons. Bourrit, jealous of Paccard's achievement, falsified the story of his ascent.

memorable account of the adventure.

Bourrit was much involved in the events around Chamonix in these years, but through the energy of his pen rather than of his limbs. He had a good voice and was precentor of the cathedral of St Pierre in Geneva. He was a poor painter and worse writer, but his alpine writings and sketches became remunerative as the flow of tourists swelled. He was insanely jealous, a liar, a snob and a bore. Yet in a way he must have loved mountains, to which he was self-appointed publicity agent. For fifty years he travelled in the Alps but his climbing ambitions were nearly always defeated by his timidity and incompetence. His attempts on Mont Blanc and the Aiguille du Goûter petered out feebly; he did get up the Buet and his best achievement was the crossing of the Col du Géant. Today he is remembered as the first of the many misguided or untruthful persons who foisted on the world the story that the brave and brilliant Balmat had dragged the reluctant doctor up the route which Balmat had designed. Bourrit's part was deliberately untruthful as well as misguided. The fiction held the field for a century and a quarter, gradually fraying under the evidence collected by many careful historians[6] and finally blown away by Graham Brown and Gavin de Beer in 1957.

2 The Exploration of the Alps

And Time flowed on till all the realm forgot
The great King lying in the limestone hills;
Only the busy water dripping through
His hard white bones knew of him lying there.
                                    W. J. Turner

The wave of military aggression that followed the French Revolution came hard on the heels of the Mont Blanc successes. It checked but did not stop the advance.

Father Placidus da Spescha worked quietly away in the Bündner Oberland (Grisons) in spite of the trouble which his suspect habit of mountaineering caused him with his brother monks as well as with the invaders, first French, who stole his collections, and then Austrian, who put him in prison. His many first ascents[1] between 1788 and 1824 were quite outstanding for the period; his list of climbs and explorations is longer and much more impressive than de Saussure's and, had he possessed the latter's resources, would certainly have surpassed him in fame. When he was 72, he watched his hunters reach the Todi (11,857 feet), the culminating point of the Glarus Alps, though he himself had to halt at what is now called the Porta da Spescha.

Meantime, things were happening in the eastern Alps. Count von Salm, Prince-Bishop of Gurk, stimulated and organised the attack on the Gross Glockner (12,461 feet); he finally reached the summit in 1800.[2] The highest Austrian mountain, the Ortler (12,793 feet), engaged the attention of the Archduke John, an unlucky general but a persistent alpine traveller from 1800 until his death in 1859. He ordered Dr Gebhard to explore and climb the peak. The doctor organised a number of attacks; eventually a chamois hunter, Joseph Pichler, took over the leadership and with Gebhard's Zillertal men climbed the mountain in 1804. Gebhard himself made the climb next year. Later Archduke John interested himself in the Gross Venediger (12,008 feet) and took part in the first attempt in 1828. The peak was not climbed until 1841 when the forester Rohregger, who had led the early exploration, reached the summit with a large party.

Peter Carl Thurweiser, Professor of Oriental Languages at Salzburg, was the first mountaineer (in the sense of one who made a practice of climbing mountains) in the Tyrol. Between 1820 and 1847 he made some seventy climbs, including first ascents of Strahlkogel (10,794 feet), Fernerkogel (10,827 feet), Gross Morchener (10,785 feet), and Schrammacher (11,208 feet). One of his companions was Prince Frederick

von Schwarzenberg, who also made some good expeditions on his own account.

In the Western Alps, apart from Chamonix and Grindelwald, the valleys which were to become famous climbing centres were only slowly penetrated by travellers. Another of Haller's plant collectors, Ricou, was at Zermatt in 1766; de Saussure traversed the Italian valleys of Monte Rosa on his way from Macugnaga to the Théodule; Murith, with the Thomases, son and grandson, botanised extensively, reaching Zermatt, Saas, Evolena and Zinal; but no assault on the great peaks of the Valais, apart from Monte Rosa, was made until much later.

Monte Rosa, as the second peak of the Alps after Mont Blanc, was the next natural objective. Moreover, it is clearly visible from much of north Italy, including Milan. The siege of this great mountain lasted 77 years, from 1778 until 1855. In the former year seven men from Gressoney, perhaps seeking the legendary lost valley beyond, reached the Rock of Discovery (14,325 feet) just west of the Lysjoch. The attack was renewed spasmodically over the years, the subsidiary summits of the complex of peaks which constitute the mountain falling one by one[3] until, in 1855, a large party consisting of two of the Smyth brothers, E. J. Stevenson, Charles Hudson, J. Birkbeck and four guides climbed to the highest point, the Dufourspitze (15,204 feet).

The first half of the century saw much, if intermittent, activity in the Bernese Oberland. Before 1800 nothing much had been achieved, though the Hangendgletscherhorn (10,798 feet) had been climbed by J. E. Muller, one of the surveyors employed by Weiss in compiling his excellent atlas. This atlas had been financed by Johann Rudolf Meyer of Aarau, who had himself climbed the Titlis in 1787 and one of his sons had crossed the Tschingel Pass in 1790. Members of his family were soon to carry out the most astonishing and successful explorations in the heart of the Oberland.

In 1811 Johann Rudolf Meyer II and his brother Hieronymus, with three family servants and a porter from Gutannen, crossed the Grimsel, went down the Rhône valley to somewhere near Fiesch whence, in a single day, they crossed the Aletsch glacier, ascended the Ober Aletsch glacier to the Beich Pass, which they crossed to Gletschertafel. There they picked up two chamois hunters and started next day at 5 am. They crossed the Lötschenlücke, where the three servants turned back, and bivouacked on the Grosser Aletschfirn. Next morning they set out to climb the Jungfrau

Above: Father Placidus da Spescha, a monk of the seventh-century Benedictine monastery of Disentis in the Grisons. His first ascents included the Stockgron and the Rheinwaldhorn, both over 10,000 feet.

Opposite top left: a fourteenth-century painting of Moses on Mount Sinai.

Opposite top right: 'The Bard' by the English Romantic painter John Martin.

Opposite bottom: 'Hannibal Crossing the Alps' by J. M. W. Turner.

16

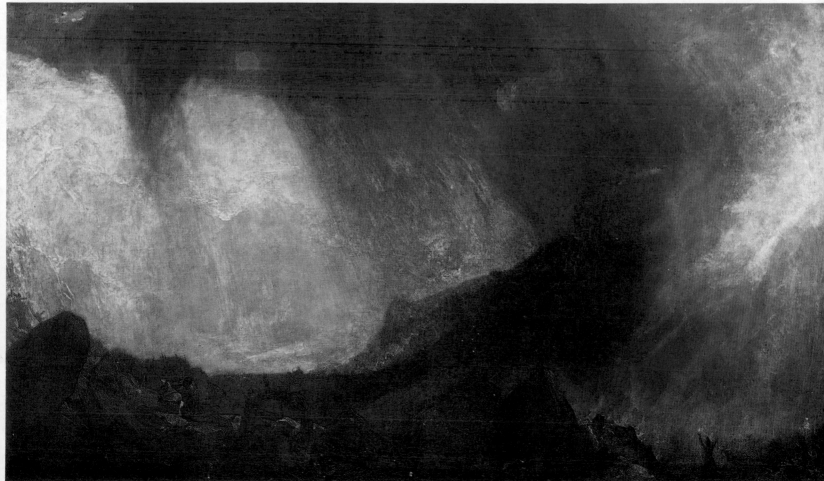

but were turned back by bad weather and spent the afternoon in reconnaissance; no doubt they climbed the Kranzberg, a good and accessible viewpoint. They then moved camp and, starting at dawn next day, reached the summit of the Jungfrau (13,642 feet) at 2 pm, getting back to camp as night fell.[4]

Next year the Meyers, this time Johann Rudolf III and Gottlieb, the sons of J. R. Meyer II, crossed the Oberaarjoch with their uncle Hieronymus and Dr Thilo, a teacher at Aarau. At their second attempt on the Finsteraarhorn Johann Rudolf III had to stop exhausted at about 12,000 feet, at the point now known as Meyer's Peak, but three of the guides (Alois Völker, Joseph Bortis and Arnold Abbühl) went on as far as the Vorgipfel (13,469 feet). Next day they crossed the Grünhornlücke but ran into bad weather. Within three weeks, Gottlieb returned from the Märjelenalp with Völker and Bortis and made the second ascent of the Jungfrau. On the same day Johann Rudolf III made the first certain crossing of the Strahlegg Pass from the Unteraar to Grindelwald. From then on, we hear no more of the Meyers, but on the record of those two years, they remain unsurpassed as mountain explorers. (They were also very modern; they carried no barometers and boiled no water.)

In 1828 F. J. Hugi tried the Jungfrau from the Rothtal and a fortnight later Yeats Brown and Frederick Slade tried the same route. Hugi went on to attack the Finsteraarhorn from the west, but bad weather stopped the party on the Hugisattel. In the same month Caspar Rohrdorf from Berne crossed

Opposite top: the Glacier de Lauteraar from *Vues Remarquables des Montagnes de Suisse* (1836).

Opposite bottom: 'Ascending a cliff' from Sir C. Fellowes, *Ascent of Mont Blanc* (1827).

Left: the Jungfrau (left centre) and the Aletschhorn (far right). The Jungfrau was first climbed by Johann Rudolf Meyer II and his brother in 1811, two of a family of notable early mountaineers.

Below: the Gross Aletschgletscher from the slopes of the Jungfrau. The Meyers crossed the lower slopes of this glacier on their ascent of the Jungfrau.

both the Unter- and the Ober-Mönch Joch; a few days later some of his Grindelwald men made the third ascent of the Jungfrau. Next year Hugi made another attempt on the Finsteraarhorn and two of his guides reached the summit (14,019 feet).

Louis Agassiz and Edouard Desor were two scientists keenly interested in glacier movement. In order to test Agassiz' theories, they established themselves in their famous 'Hôtel des Neuchâtellois' on the Unteraar glacier. The Hotel was under a rock, with gaps plugged by makeshift walls; it was draughty, wet and miserably uncomfortable. Nevertheless these men and their friends spent weeks there every year from 1840 to 1845. Life at this icy camp no doubt advanced their science; it certainly developed a deep love of mountains. Agassiz and Desor climbed the Jungfrau in 1841; next year Desor tried for the Schreckhorn but in fact climbed the Gross Lauteraarhorn which, at 13,262 feet, is about a hundred feet lower. The year after, he reached the Rosenhorn peak (12,100 feet) of the Wetterhörner and his guides climbed the Hasli Jungfrau point (12,140 feet) of the same mountain, an ascent which Agassiz repeated a year later. The highest rock of the Wetterhörner, the Mittelhorn (12,149 feet), fell to Stanhope Templeman Speer in 1845.

Another scientist deeply interested in geology and glaciers was the Scot J. D. Forbes, who was with Agassiz and Desor on their Jungfrau climb. A man of frail physique and indifferent health, he yet had the stamina and determination to walk and scramble over great distances. He was one of the great pioneers of the Alps, not so much for the peaks he climbed as for his extensive travels in remote valleys and over unrecorded passes. His book, *Travels in the Alps*,[5] reflecting the unaffected charm of his character, was deservedly popular and did much to direct the efforts of the ensuing generation of climbers who completed the ascents of all the major alpine peaks. Let him tell us of his ascent of the Stockhorn (a very minor eminence) and crossing of the Col d'Hérens.[6]

The crossing of the Col d'Hérens
from J. D. Forbes, *Tour of Mont Blanc*
I soon after returned to the hut to supper. As might be expected, the cheer was not great, but cheerfully given. There could not be much less comfort than at Evolena; but it was at least freely offered. There was no temptation to prolong a stay within doors, unless to sleep. I retired early with my guides to the lodging prepared for us with the aid of the hay which we had brought. It was a small shed, about six feet square, and four high, attached to the principal hut, entered by a doorway through which one could creep with difficulty, and which was shut up with a piece of cloth. I was placed next the wall, and the others slept beside me. The shepherds themselves slept in a separate hut a little way removed. Before we went to rest, it was agreed that they should call us at 3 am, that we might be on foot before day, for all reports agreed, that whatever might be the difficulties of the journey, it was, at least, a very long one. In order to awaken us at the right time, they begged to have my watch with

them for the night, a request which, in some other countries, might have been suspicious (it was a valuable gold chronometer), but which here I granted as readily as it was undoubtingly asked. As we lay down I was struck by the conduct of Pralong, who knelt down on the hay and said his prayers shortly, and without form or pretension of any kind; and we had not been long composed to rest, before we heard a solemn, and not unmusical voice proceeding from the neighbouring apartment. On enquiry of Pralong, I found that the practice of evening prayer is kept up amongst the assembled shepherds; a rare but touching solemnity amongst men of the common ranks,– for no women usually live in the higher châlets,– separated during so large a part of the year from the means of public worship.

I passed a sleepless, though far from an uncomfortable night. Pralong had spoken doubtingly of the weather in the evening, and I well knew that anything like uncertainty in that respect could not be hazarded on such an expedition, for which I felt more and more disposed as I got better acquainted with the scenery of this interesting chain. Every change of direction of the moon's rays falling through the open walls and roof of our shelter I mistook for a cloud, and felt fresh anxiety lest the hour of rising should be overpast, as it had been at Prarayon. I was up before the rest, and whilst the stars were shining bright, the moon having set, I performed my hasty toilet. It was some time before breakfast could be got ready, and, as usual, an hour and a quarter elapsed before we were fairly under way, exactly at a quarter to five. . . .

It will be recollected that, besides Pralong, the guide of Evolena, I had the trusty Biona of Val Biona, and Tairraz of Chamouni, as my attendants. The provisions, and my personal effects, made a burden so light for each, that even an Eringer could not reasonably complain; and taking leave of our hosts with thanks and remuneration, we hastened at a good pace to gain the glacier. But this was not the work of a moment. I have already said that the châlets of Abricolla stand on a shelf many hundred feet above the glacier; and, what is always disagreeable, our first step to mounting was a steep and uncomfortable descent. We had not left the châlets ten minutes when we found a foaming torrent to be crossed. Now, a plunge up to the knees in a river even ice-cold is a trifle in ordinary travelling, and might be considered a refreshing commencement of a long day's walk; but when that walk is to be of ten or twelve hours on a

Above: a chamois-hunter, an illustration from Sazerac's *Un Mois en Suisse* (1825). Until de Saussure's time, chamois-hunters were among the few brave enough to venture into the mountains.

Below left: an early climbing iron (1809). Some form of crampon had been used by mountain peasants since the Middle Ages, but they fell out of use.

Opposite: the Macugnaga face of Monte Rosa, the second peak of the Alps. The mountain's highest point, the Dufourspitze, was first climbed in 1855.

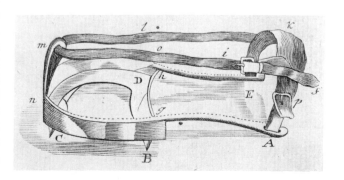

glacier, and over snows 11,000 or 12,000 feet high, such a freak might endanger life or limb. Accordingly, while Pralong and Biona spluttered through, I sought an easier passage higher up, which I at length found, and was followed by the wary Savoyard. Without difficulties worth mentioning we gained the surface of the ice, having lost, however, in level, a height of perhaps 1,000 feet; we then patiently and warily proceeded on our march . . .

We were now close under the rocks which bordered the glacier on our left, beneath the lofty peak of the Dent Blanche. Before us was the Motta Rotta, the rocky precipice already described as rising through the ice. At length the glacier became much crevassed, and we had a choice of difficulties, either to skirt the precipitous rocks on our left, or to make for the centre of the glacier on our right, with the chance of crevasses yet more impassable. Pralong, indeed, broached the notion of attempting the ascent of the glacier between the Motta Rotta and the Mont Miné, which, he said, would lead us more directly to the col; but he did not know that such a passage had been attempted, and as, upon examination with the telescope, I perceived an enormous *Berg-Schrund*, or well-defined crevasse, which separated the higher summits from the glacier steep, I preferred pursuing the direction in which he had already passed. [A *bergschrund* is the crevasse between a glacier and its retaining rock wall.] We accordingly made for the rocks, and scrambled along and up them for a considerable way. We were preceded by a whole troop of chamois, eleven in number, which we startled upon the ice, and which took immediately to the cliffs. At length it became difficult to say whether the rock or the glacier was the more formidable opponent, and we regained, with some difficulty, the surface of the latter, being now more than on a level with the châlets which we had left.

The sun was only now rising behind the ridge of the Dent Blanche, the ice was still hard frozen and slippery. The glacier was very steep and rugged, but the crevasses were exposed and the walking was more difficult than dangerous, although once I was only withheld by my companions from slipping into a chasm. But the snow line was soon gained, and the surface being still crisp, our footing was sure, and the bed of snow too thick to create any risk from crevasses. We were on the north or shady exposure, always the easiest to mount, and had a fatiguing climb up dazzling snow fields, about 30° of elevation abreast of the Motta Rotta, which was on our right. Pralong took the lead manfully, and was now quite recovered from his indisposition. The heights of the Motta Rotta gained, the col might be said to be reached, for although snow fields of great extent separated us from it, they evidently presented no difficulty. It is, perhaps, only in this part of the Alps that such a prodigious extent of comparative tablelands of snow are to be found at such an elevation. New peaks began to rise before us, and especially the Mont Cervin, or Matterhorn, and the Dent d'Erin, whilst to the westward, the summits of Mont Collon, and the neighbouring chains, peeped over the wilderness of snow and ice. The col or pass lay now, Pralong told me, considerably to the right, but seeing just before us a snowy summit, which alone concealed from us the view of Monte Rosa, and the great chain of Alps in that direction, I proposed, as we had gained this height at a very early hour, and with far less difficulty that I expected, to climb to the top of it to enjoy the view. Now, Pralong was not one of those teazing, pedantic guides who will never listen to any opinion, and who make it a point to thwart a proposition merely to show their consequence, the more so if it offer a chance of delay. I liked him for his confidence and good temper. He admitted that a traveller's opinion might be taken, at least as to the course which would please him best; accordingly, we walked right over towards the precipice stretching from the Dent Blanche to the Stockhorn. As we approached it, I caught one of those glorious bursts of scenery of which all description must ever fail to realize the incommunicable grandeur, and one sight of which at once and instantly repays the traveller for days of toil and sleepless nights. Wandering on alone, as near the verge of the snow-crowned precipice as I dared venture (for there an unseen fissure in the compacted snow, some yards from the very ledge, might readily occasion the detachment of a mass, by the traveller's weight, into the abyss), I gained the summit of the Stockhorn, of which I had considerably overrated the height from where I first proposed the deviation, and was seated on its top exactly at nine o'clock. . . .

Of all the views which I have seen in the higher Alps,

Above: J. D. Forbes, the Scottish scientist who travelled extensively in the Alps. His writings and lectures helped to foster British interest in mountaineering.

Right: early nineteenth-century climbers (from F. J. Hugi's *Naturhistorische Alpenreise*, 1830). Two climbers have alpenstocks with crooks, two have an early form of ice-axe, while one carries a hammer and a rope slung on a sack.

none can compare with that from the Stockhorn of the Col d'Erin (as I propose to call this pass, which has not yet received a name). The unequalled view of Monte Rosa, and the centrical position with respect to three summits of the second (if not of the first) order, the Mont Cervin, Dent Blanche, and Dent d'Erin, which seem all so near as almost to be tangible, are sufficient to mark its character. The Weisshorn and the Cima di Jazi, as well as Mont Cervin, all border on 15,000 feet; so that, counting all the peaks of Monte Rosa but as one, we see at once at least five distinct mountains higher than the Finsteraarhorn, long esteemed the highest in Switzerland proper. Compared to the Col du Géant, the view is here more vast and savage, and the individual objects finer and closer; though the distant view of the chain of the Alps gives to the former a delightful and peculiar charm. . . .

Stretched upon the snow, we made a hearty meal; and the hour and a half which I spent here in observing my instrument, taking magnetic bearings of the principal objects, sketching the outline of Monte Rosa, and trying effectually to impress upon my memory a scene which I scarcely expect ever to see equalled or under circumstances so favourable, went quickly by, when Pralong modestly invited me to depart, as our task was far from accomplished; indeed, as it appeared, the most difficult part was to come.

Our object was now to descend upon the glacier of Zmutt, of which, as I have endeavoured to explain, the lower or more level part swept along the base of

Top: the Finsteraarhorn, whose summit Hugi failed to reach. The mountain was first climbed by two of his guides in 1829.

Left: the cover illustration to *Die Besteigung des Jungfrauhorns durch Agassiz* (1842). The Swiss naturalist Louis Agassiz (above), like Forbes, explored the Alps for scientific reasons but also came to feel a genuine love of mountains.

Above: John Ball, the first president of the Alpine Club and editor of the first in the classic series *Peaks, Passes and Glaciers* (1859), the forerunner of the *Alpine Journal.*

Above right: Forbes measuring a glacier during one of his scientific expeditions to the Alps.

the Mont Cervin and Dent d'Erin, whilst a higher stage of it rose to the foot of the lofty precipice above which we stood. Now, whilst the *top* of this precipice sunk from the summit of the Stockhorn, westwards to the col, and then rose a little, the glacier and the *foot* of the precipice rose rapidly and continuously to the westward, so that the top and bottom of the precipice became at length blended together, under a snowy sheet. To reach this point, however, would have been a long *détour*, and the glacier appeared dangerously crevassed. Having, therefore, descended from the Stockhorn to the col (which was not a great deal lower), Pralong proposed to attempt descending the cliff, by which he recollected to have passed when he last crossed, and to have successfully reached the glacier below. We began cautiously to descend, for it was an absolute precipice: Pralong first, and I following, leaving the other guides to wait about the middle, until we should see whether or not a passage could be effected. The precipice was several hundred feet high. Some bad turns were passed, and I began to hope that no insurmountable difficulty would appear, when Pralong announced that the snow this year had melted so much more completely than on the former occasion, as to cut off all communication with the glacier, for there was a height of at least thirty vertical feet of rocky wall, which we could by no means circumvent. Thus, all was to do over again, and the cliff was re-ascended. We looked right and left for a more feasible spot, but descried none. Having regained the snows above, we cautiously skirted the precipice, until we should find a place favourable to the attempt. At length, the rocks became mostly masked under steep snow slopes, and down one of these, Pralong, with no common courage, proposed to venture, and put him-

self at once in the place of danger. We were now separated by perhaps but 200 feet from the glacier beneath. The slope was chiefly of soft deep snow, lying at a high angle. There was no difficulty in securing our footing in it, but the danger was of producing an avalanche by our weight. This, it may be thought, was a small matter, if we were to alight on the glacier below; but such a surface of snow upon rock rarely connects with a glacier without a break, and we all knew very well that the formidable 'Bergschrund,' already mentioned, was open to receive the avalanche and its charge, if it should take place. We had no ladder, but a pretty long rope. Pralong was tied to it. We all held fast on the rope, having planted ourselves as well as we could on the slope of snow, and let him down by degrees, to ascertain the nature and breadth of the crevasse, of which the upper edge usually overhangs like the roof of a cave dropping icicles. Were that covering to fail, he might be plunged, and drag us, into a chasm beneath. He, however, effected the passage with a coolness which I have never seen surpassed, and shouted the intelligence that the chasm had been choked by previous *avalanches*, and that we might pass without danger. He then (having loosed himself from the rope) proceeded to explore the footing on the glacier, leaving me and the other two guides to extricate ourselves. I descended first by the rope, then Biona, and lastly Tairraz, who, being unsupported, did not at all like the slide, the termination of which it was quite impossible to see from above. We then followed Pralong, and proceeded with great precaution to sound our way down the upper glacier of Zmutt, which is here sufficiently steep to be deeply fissured, and which is covered with perpetual snow, now soft with the heat of the morning sun. It was a dangerous passage, and required many wide circuits. But at length we reached in a slanting direction the second terrace or precipice of rock which separates the upper and lower glacier of Zmutt, and which terminates in the promontory called Stöckhi. When we were fairly on the debris we stopped to repose, and to congratulate ourselves on the success of this difficult passage.

Gottlieb Studer of Berne was the foremost mountaineer around the mid-century. His climbing extended from 1823 to 1883 and included 643 expeditions, many of them new. His *Uber Eis und Schnee*, a very full history of mountaineering in the Swiss Alps, came out in four volumes between 1869 and 1883. He travelled much with Melchior Ulrich, the most prominent of the Zurich school, whose great contribution was the exploration of the glaciers around Zermatt. J. J. Weilenmann of St Gall, whose 350 peaks and passes included the second ascent of Monte Rosa, was the first to make a practice of high climbing solo.

Although his career ran well on into the next phase, John Ball falls into this chapter because his greatest work belongs to the exploration of the Alps rather than the climbing of peaks. He did collect first ascents, such as the Pelmo (10,397 feet), on which he had to leave his guide behind and complete the ascent alone, and the Cima Tosa (10,420 feet), but as a botanist and topographer he preferred passes to peaks and, like Forbes, was primarily a mountain traveller. By 1863, the year in which he brought out the first volume of his *Alpine Guide*, he had crossed the main chain of the Alps 48 times by 32 different passes, plus traversing nearly a hundred lateral passes. His knowledge of the whole of the Alps was unrivalled and he was very properly made the first president of the Alpine Club.

By the mid-1850s the main work of exploration had been done; in the next decade the great peaks fell like ninepins. Leadership had lain with the Swiss, but for the next fifty years the British were in the van. In the present century the game has become truly international and much more specialised, with the lime-light shifting uncertainly from this school or group to another under the influence of technical innovations and dominant individuals.

It is interesting, though probably vain, to consider how this sudden British predominance arose. Some writers have found an easy answer in that the British were richer, took longer holidays (i.e. were idler) and could afford guides. Like most easy answers, this doesn't get us far. The margin of affluence between the professional classes (who supplied all the climbers) in Britain and in the rest of Western Europe was not great, and easily cancelled by the greater difficulty and expense of getting to the Alps. Nor were the British, in the nineteenth century, idle. The answer is much more complex because the strands are multiple and various. The most important strand is probably the tradition of athletic pedestrianism which had existed since the Peninsular War. The high stakes which Charles James Fox would play at Brooks's were almost equalled by the wagers laid on a walk from London to Edinburgh or the distance to be covered in 24 hours; walking was a minor national sport. When the existence of the Alps and the opportunities of travel afoot which they offered became publicised, it was apparent to discerning souls that to

walk on a gradient over ice, snow and rock would be more interesting than bashing the highroad on the flat. Furthermore, travel in the Alps offered all the joys of polar exploration with most of the trials omitted. The same urge that took Mungo Park, Speke and Baker to Africa took the pioneers to the Alps.

Professor Forbes's book was a considerable influence but probably the popular lectures of Albert Smith[7] on Mont Blanc were even more important in firing the imagination of young people. Communications had, of course, improved immensely and it was very much easier, cheaper and quicker to get to Zermatt or Chamonix than it had been twenty years earlier. But whatever the causes or motives, a greatly increased number of men and women took to visiting the Alps in the second half of the century with the aim of mountaineering enjoyment and most of these people were British.

We have seen earlier that the first four ascents of Mont Blanc followed each other quickly; Beaufoy's, the fourth, was made a year after Paccard's. In the next 66 years 41 further ascents were made, or roughly two every three years. In 1854, no less than 16 attempts were successful, involving 21 amateurs; 16 British, two American, two Savoyard and one French.[8] This burst of activity marked the arrival of the Golden Age of alpine climbing.[9]

Left: breakfast on a snow-bridge, an illustration to a popular guide to Mont Blanc published in 1835.

Above: Albert Smith faces a packed audience at the Egyptian Hall in 1852. His entertainment, in which he described his ascent of Mont Blanc with the aid of slides, patter-songs and St Bernard dogs, ran for six years and enormously boosted alpine travel.

3 The Golden Age

The leaves fall and the flowers and the seasons,
The flickering of a wheel, darkness and light, life
And the summer leaves, the opening bud, the petals;
Rigid in frosty dawn, the new rope sparkles, and the axe
Rings on the final slope.

Michael Roberts

The typical climber of the Golden Age was a don, barrister or clergyman. He climbed with guides who were reaching a much higher standard of competence. Some, like Melchior Anderegg, Michel Croz, J. A Carrel, Christian Almer, were outstanding mountaineers. They did not have the technique of the next generation, of Alexander Burgener, the Lochmatters, Joseph Knubel, but nor did their employers have the climbing skills of Mummery or Young. The time was not ripe to venture into places where these skills were needed.

The climber now seldom pretended that he went to the hills out of scientific curiosity; he climbed because it was his greatest happiness, the perfect foil and counterpart to a chairborne life of intellectual grind. The best restorative for a hard-working man was not idleness but a complete change of activity. With all the vigour and confidence of the Victorian age, he set out to reach the heights that man had shunned through all his troubled history.

Club huts had not yet been built conveniently at the foot of climbs. The pioneers either slept out with a blanket or walked through the night from a valley inn. There were no specialised artificial aids but nobody rejected a ladder where it might be useful; its use was then as natural in the Alps as it is today in, say, the Khumbu icefall below Everest. Controversy continued as to whether an alpenstock or an ice-axe were the more useful tool. A rather primitive safety technique involving the rope was slowly being established, but many guides were still somewhat backward in this. The mountaineering game was still too young for any firm conventions.

The number of peaks first climbed in the quarter century covered by this chapter is far too great to allow separate mention of each; a few examples must suffice, but Appendix I (p. 232) gives a list of all Alpine peaks over 13,000 feet with the dates of their first ascents. There are 74 in this list but, as there can be no hard and fast objective criterion of what constitutes a separate peak, the number must not be accepted as absolute. How distinctive does a point on a ridge have to be to count as a peak? For example, I have given both Point Walker and Point Whymper of

the Grandes Jorasses; another might quite reasonably include only the highest point, the Walker, while yet another might include also the Points Young, Margharita, Helena and Croz.

It will be seen that out of the 74, 51 were first climbed during the period covered by this chapter. Thirteen were climbed earlier and ten later; these last ten are all in some degree subsidiary. Mont Maudit, the Dôme and Aiguille de Rochefort, the Aiguille du Géant, the Aiguille Blanche de Peuterey, Pic Luigi Amadeo and Mont Brouillard are all subsidiary to Mont Blanc; the Bieshorn is the northern bulwark of the Weisshorn; the Mominghorn an eminence on the north ridge of the Zinal Rothorn; the Stecknagelhorn a not very well discriminated point on the long ridge descending northward from the Dom. It is therefore fair to say that this chapter sees the conclusion of the phase when the great Alpine peaks were first climbed.

The first significant climb at the start of the Golden Age, the heyday of the guided climber, was quite untypical in that it was guideless.

In 1855, most of the party that had achieved the first ascent of the highest point of Monte Rosa (see Chapter 2) crossed over to Mont Blanc. They tried to climb the mountain from Courmayeur but turned back when the weather worsened. During this essay Charles Hudson made the first ascent of Mont Blanc du Tacul by himself.[1] They all then went round to St Gervais to try the ascent from there. (Hudson had already explored the route as far as the Aiguille du Goûter in March 1853, an early example of winter mountaineering.) They climbed over the Aiguille to the Dôme du Goûter, where their two chasseurs left them at about 7 am. They had the choice of proceeding over the then unclimbed Bosses du Dromedaire or of joining the ordinary Chamonix route on the Grand Plateau. They—that is, Charles Hudson, E. S. Kennedy, Charles Ainslie and the brothers Christopher and Grenville Smyth—thought the Bosses ridge looked practicable,[2] but fearing that the ridge would be very cold in the wind, they dropped down to the Grand Plateau. From there they reached the summit of Mont Blanc at 12.35 pm.

The Schreckhorn (13,379 feet) had resisted two attempts by Eustace Anderson and by Desor. The former had reached the Klein Schreckhorn (11,460 feet) in 1857; the latter, with Escher von der Linth, had got to the lower, more southerly summit in 1842, but there was still a quarter mile of awkward ridge to go, which they judged impracticable. Leslie Stephen describes the first ascent:[3]

Above: the Rev. Charles Hudson, a notable climber of the Golden Age. He was one of the casualties of Whymper's tragic Matterhorn expedition in 1865.

Opposite: Mont Blanc du Tacul, first climbed by Hudson alone in 1855.

The ascent of the Schreckhorn

from Leslie Stephen, *The Playground of Europe*

On the night of August 13, 1861, I found myself the occupant of a small hole under a big rock near the northern foot of the Strahleck. Owing to bad diplomacy, I was encumbered with three guides–Peter and Christian Michel, and Christian Kaufmann–all of them good men, but one, if not two, too many. As the grey morning light gradually stole into our burrow, I woke up with a sense of lively impatience– not diminished, perhaps, by the fact that one side of me seemed to be permanently impressed with every knob in a singularly cross-grained bit of rock, and the other with every bone in Kaufmann's body. Swallowing a bit of bread, I declared myself ready. An early start is of course always desirable before a hard day's work, but it rises to be almost agreeable after a hard night's rest. This did not seem to be old Peter Michel's opinion. He is the very model of a short, thick, broad mountaineer, with the constitution of a piece of seasoned oak; a placid, not to say stolid, temper; and an illimitable appetite. He sat opposite me for some half-hour, calmly munching bread and cheese, and meat and butter, at four in the morning, on a frozen bit of turf, under a big stone, as if it were the most reasonable thing a man could do under the circumstances, and as though such things as the Schreckhorn and impatient tourists had no existence. A fortnight before, as I was told, he had calmly sat out all night, half-way up the Eiger, with a stream of freezing water trickling over him, accompanied by an unlucky German, whose feet received frost-bites on that occasion from which they were still in danger while old Michel had not a chilblain.

And here let me make one remark, to save repetition in the following pages. I utterly repudiate the doctrine that Alpine travellers are or ought to be the heroes of Alpine adventures. The true way at least to describe all my Alpine ascents is that Michel or Anderegg or Lauener succeeded in performing a feat requiring skill, strength, and courage, the difficulty of which was much increased by the difficulty of taking with him his knapsack and his employer. If any passages in the succeeding pages convey the impression that I claim any credit except that of following better men than myself with decent ability, I disavow them in advance and do penance for them in my heart. Other travellers have been more independent: I speak for myself alone. Meanwhile I will only delay my narrative to denounce one other heresy–that, namely, which asserts that guides are a nuisance. Amongst the greatest of Alpine pleasures is that of learning to appreciate the capacities and cultivate the good will of a singularly intelligent and worthy class of men. I wish that all men of the same class, in England and elsewhere, were as independent, well-informed, and trustworthy as Swiss mountaineers! And now, having discharged my conscience, I turn to my story.

At last, about half-past four, we got deliberately under weigh. Our first two or three hours' work was easy enough. The two summits of the Schreckhorn form as it were the horns of a vast crescent of precipice which runs round a secondary glacier, on the eastern bank of the Grindelwald glacier. This glacier is skirted on the south by the ordinary Strahleck route. The cliffs above it are for the most part bare of snow, and scored by deep trenches or gullies, the paths of avalanches, and of the still more terrible showers of stones which, in the later part of the day, may be seen every five minutes discharged down the flank of the mountain. I was very sanguine that we should reach the *arête* [sharp ridge or spine] connecting the two peaks. I felt doubtful, however, whether we could pass along it to the summit, as it might be interrupted by some of those gaps which so nearly stopped Desor's party. Old Michel indeed had declared, on a reconnoitring expedition I had made with him the day before, that he believed, *'steif und fest'*, that we could get up. But as we climbed the glacier my faith in Michel and Co. began to sink, not from any failing in their skill as guides, but from the enormous appetites which they still chose to exhibit. Every driblet of water seemed to be inseparably connected in their minds with a drop of brandy, and every flat stone suggested an open-air picnic. Perhaps my impatience rather exaggerated their delinquencies in this direction; but it was not till past seven, when we had deposited the heavy part of our baggage and, to my delight, most of the provisions on a ledge near the foot of the rocks, that they fairly woke up, and settled to their task. From that time I had no more complaints to make. We soon got hard and steadily at work, climbing the rocks which form the southern bank of one of the deeply-carved gullies of which I have spoken. It seemed clear to me that the summit of the Schreckhorn, which was invisible to us at present, was on the other side of this ravine, its northern bank being in fact formed by a huge buttress running straight down from the peak. This buttress was cut into steps, by cliffs so steep as to be perfectly impracticable; in fact, I believe that in one place it absolutely overhung. It was therefore necessary to keep to the other side; but I felt an unpleasant suspicion that the head of the ravine might correspond with an impracticable gap in the arête.

Meanwhile we had simply a steady piece of rock-climbing. Christian Michel, a first-rate cragsman, led the way. Kaufmann followed, and, as we clung to the crannies and ledges of the rock, relieved his mind by sundry sarcasms as to the length of arm and leg which enabled me to reach points of support without putting my limbs out of joint–an advantage, to say the truth, which he could well afford to give away. The rocks were steep and slippery, and occasionally covered with a coat of ice. We were frequently flattened out against the rocks, like beasts of ill repute nailed to a barn, with fingers and toes inserted into four different cracks which tested the elasticity of our frames to the uttermost. Still our progress though slow was steady, and would have been agreeable if only our minds could have been at ease with regard to that detestable ravine. We could not obtain a glimpse of the final ridge, and we might be hopelessly stopped at the last step. Meanwhile, as we looked round, we could see the glacier basins gradually sinking, and the sharp pyramid of the

Christian Almer, a famous guide of the period, who climbed with, among others, Leslie Stephen and Coolidge. His first ascents included the Mönch (1857) and the Eiger (1858).

Finsteraarhorn shooting upwards above them. Gradually, too, the distant ranges of Alps climbed higher and higher up the southern horizon. From Mont Blanc to Monte Rosa, and away to the distant Bernina, ridge beyond ridge rose into the sky, with many a well-remembered old friend amongst them. In two or three hours' work we had risen high enough to look over the ridge connecting the two peaks, down the long reaches of the Aar glaciers. A few minutes afterwards we caught sight of a row of black dots creeping over the snows of the Strahleck. With a telescope I could just distinguish a friend whom I had met the day before at Grindelwald. A loud shout from us brought back a faint reply or echo. We were already high above the pass. Still, however, that last arête remained pertinaciously invisible. A few more steps, if steps is a word applicable to progression by hands as well as feet, placed us at last on the great ridge of the mountain, looking down upon the Lauteraar Sattel. But the ridge rose between us and the peak into a kind of knob, which allowed only a few yards of it to be visible. The present route, as I believe, leads to the ridge at the point further from the summit of the mountain. We were, however, near the point where a late melancholy accident will, it is to be hoped, impress upon future travellers the necessity of a scrupulous adherence to all recognised precautions. The scene was in itself significant enough for men of weak nerves. Taking a drop of brandy all round, we turned to the assault, feeling that a few yards more would decide the question. On our right hand the long slopes of snow

Left: Whymper's equipment (1865). This is more or less standard for the time, except the crampons, which were not generally used.

Below: some British climbers with their guides: back row: Melchior Anderegg, R. J. S. Macdonald, F. C. Grove, Jakob Anderegg, 'young' Peter Taugwalder; front row: Leslie Stephen, W. F. Short, E. N. Buxton, R. Liveing, F. F. Tuckett. All the amateurs were members of the Alpine Club.

ASCENT OF THE ROTHHORN.

THE

PLAYGROUND OF EUROPE.

BY

LESLIE STEPHEN,

LATE PRESIDENT OF THE ALPINE CLUB.

VALLEY OF LAUTERBRUNNEN.

'We complain of the mountains as rubbish, as not only disfiguring the face of the earth, but also to us useless and inconvenient; and yet, without these, neither rivers nor fountains nor the weather for producing and ripening fruits could regularly be produced.'
Abp. KING *On the Origin of Evil*.

LONDON:
LONGMANS, GREEN, AND CO.
1871.

Above: the frontispiece and title-page to *The Playground of Europe* by Leslie Stephen, the philosopher and critic.

Below: an illustration to 'An Autumn Tour in Switzerland', published in *The Graphic*, October 1874. Note the use of a ladder to cross a crevasse.

ran down towards the Lauteraar Sattel, as straight as if the long furrows on their surface had been drawn by a ruler. They were in a most ticklish state. The snow seemed to be piled up like loose sand, at the highest angle of rest, and almost without cohesion. The fall of a pebble or a handful of snow was sufficient to detach a layer, which slid smoothly down the long slopes with a low ominous hiss. Clinging, however, to the rocks

which formed the crest of the ridge, we dug our feet as far as possible into the older snow beneath, and crept cautiously along. As soon as there was room on the arête, we took to the rocks again, and began with breathless expectation climbing the knob of which I have spoken. The top of the mountain could not remain much longer concealed. A few yards more, and it came full in view. The next step revealed to me not only the mountain top, but a lovely and almost level ridge which connected it with our standing-point. We had won the victory, and, with a sense of intense satisfaction, attacked the short ridge which still divided us from our object. It is melancholy to observe the shockingly bad state of repair of the higher peaks, and the present was no exception to the rule. Loose stones rattled down the mountain side at every step, and the ridge itself might be compared to the ingenious contrivance which surmounts the walls of gaols with a nicely balanced pile of loose bricks—supposing the interstices in this case are to be filled with snow. We crept, however, cautiously along the parapet, glancing down the mighty cliffs beneath us, and then, at two steps more, we proudly stepped (at 11.40) on to the little level platform which forms the *allerhöchste Spitze* of the Schreckhorn.

I need hardly remark that our first proceeding was to give a hearty cheer, which was faintly returned by the friends who were still watching us from the Strahleck. My next was to sit down, in the warm and perfectly calm summer air, to enjoy a pipe and the beauties of nature, whilst my guides erected a cairn of

NIGHT BEFORE THE START—OUTSIDE THE HOTEL

THROUGH THE SNOW

SO FAR AND NO FARTHER

INTERIOR OF HUT, GRAND MULETS

RUBBING BOOTS ON THE TOP OF GRAND MULETS

SIGNALLING TO CHAMOUNIX

stones round a large black flag which we had brought up to confute cavillers. Mountain tops are always more or less impressive in one way – namely, from the giddy cliffs which surround them. But the more distant prospects from them may be divided into two classes: those from the Wetterhorn, Jungfrau, or Monte Rosa, and other similar mountains, which include on one side the lowland countries, forming a contrast to the rough mountain ranges; and those from mountains standing, not on the edge, but in the very centre of the regions of frost and desolation. The Schreckhorn (like the Finsteraarhorn) is a grand example of this latter kind. Four great glaciers seem to radiate from its base. The great Oberland peaks – the Finsteraarhorn, Jungfrau, Mönch, Eiger, and Wetterhorn – stand round in a grim circle, showing their bare faces of precipitous rock across the dreary wastes of snow. At your feet are the 'urns of the silent snow', from which the glaciers of Grindelwald draw the supplies that enable them to descend far into the regions of cultivated land, trickling down like great damp icicles, of insignificant mass compared with these mighty reservoirs. You are in the centre of a whole district of desolation, suggesting a landscape from Greenland, or an imaginary picture of England in the glacial epoch, with shores yet unvisited by the irrepressible Gulf Stream. The charm of such views – little as they are generally appreciated by professional admirers of the picturesque – is to my taste unique, though not easily explained to unbelievers. They have a certain soothing influence like slow and stately music, or one of the strange opium dreams described by De Quincey. If his journey in the mailcoach could have led him through an Alpine pass instead of the quiet Cumberland hills, he would have seen visions still more poetical than that of the minster in the 'dream fugue'. Unable as I am to bend his bow, I can only say that there is something almost unearthly in the sight of enormous spaces of hill and plain, apparently unsubstantial as a mountain mist, glimmering away to the indistinct horizon, and as it were spell-bound by an absolute and eternal silence. The sentiment may be very different when a storm is raging and nothing is visible but the black ribs of the mountains glaring at you through rents in the clouds; but on that perfect day on the top of the Schreckhorn, where not a wreath of vapour was to be seen under the whole vast canopy of the sky, a delicious lazy sense of calm repose was the appropriate frame of mind. One felt as if some immortal being, with no particular duties upon his hands, might be calmly sitting upon those desolate rocks and watching the little shadowy wrinkles of the plain, that were really mountain ranges, rise and fall through slow geological epochs. I had no companion to disturb my reverie or introduce discordant associations. An hour passed like a few minutes, but there were still difficulties to be encountered which would have made any longer delay unadvisable. I therefore added a few touches to our cairn, and then turned to the descent. . . .

The Schreckhorn, first climbed in 1861 by Leslie Stephen with guides Peter and Christian Michel and Christian Kaufmann.

The Weisshorn (14,780 feet), the reigning beauty of the Alps, had, says Professor John Tyndall, 'been tried on various occasions and on different sides by brave and competent climbers, but all efforts had been hitherto unavailing'. In August, 1861, Tyndall, with Bennen and Wenger, bivouacked on the rocks below the east ridge. Here is his account of the next day.[4]

The ascent of the Weisshorn

from John Tyndall, *Hours of Exercise in the Alps*
We rose at 2.15 am, consumed our coffee, and had to wait idly for the dawn. A faint illumination at length overspread the sky, and with this promise of the coming day we quitted our bivouac at 3.30 am. No cloud was to be seen; as far as the weather was concerned we were sure to have fair play. We rounded the shingly shoulder of the mountain to the edge of a snow-field, but before entering upon it I disburthened myself of my strong shooting jacket, leaving it on the mountain-side. The sunbeams and my own exertion would, I knew, keep me only too warm during the day. We crossed the snow, cut our way through a piece of entangled glacier, reached the Bergschrund, and passed it without a rope. We ascended the frozen snow of the couloir by steps, but soon diverged from it to the rocks at our right, and mounted them to the end of the eastern *arête* of the mountain.

A snow saddle separated us from the higher rocks. With our staff-pikes at one side of the saddle, we pass by steps cut upon the other. We find the rocks hewn into fantastic turrets and obelisks, while the loose chips of this sculpture are strewn confusedly upon the ridge. Amid these we cautiously pick our way, winding round the towers or scaling them amain. The work was heavy from the first, the bending, twisting, reaching, and drawing up calling upon all the muscles of the frame. After two hours of this work we halted, and, looking back, saw two moving objects on the glacier below us. At first we took them to be chamois, but they were men. The leader carried an axe, and his companion a knapsack and an alpenstock. They followed our traces, losing them apparently now and then, and waiting to recover them. Our expedition had put Randa in a state of excitement, and some of its best climbers had urged Bennen to take them with him. This he did not deem necessary, and now here were two of them determined to try the thing on their own account, and perhaps to dispute with us the honour of the enterprise. On this point, however, our uneasiness was small.

Resuming our gymnastics, the rocky staircase led us to the flat summit of a tower, where we found ourselves cut off from a similar tower by a deep gap bitten into the mountain. The rope was here our refuge. Bennen coiled it round his waist; we let him down along the surface of the rock, until he fixed himself on a ledge, where he could lend me a helping hand. I followed him, and Wenger followed me. By a kind of screw motion we twisted ourselves round the opposite tower, and reached the ridge behind it. Work of this kind, however, is not to be performed by the day, and, with a view of sparing our strength, we quitted the ridge and endeavoured to get along the southern slope of the pyramid. The mountain was scarred by long couloirs, filled with clear hard ice. The cutting of steps across these couloirs proved to be so tedious and fatiguing that I urged Bennen to abandon them and try the ridge once more. We regained it and worked along it as before. Here and there upon the northern side the snow was folded over, and we worked slowly upward along the cornice snow. The ridge became gradually narrower, and the precipices on each side more sheer. We reached the end of one of its subdivisions, and found ourselves separated from the next rocks by a gap about twenty yards across. The ridge has here narrowed to a mere wall, which, however, as rock, would present no serious difficulty. But upon the wall of rock was placed a second wall of snow, which dwindled to a pure knife-edge at the top. It was white, of very fine grain, and a little moist. How to pass this snow catenary I knew not, for I did not think a human foot could trust itself upon so frail a support. Bennen's practical sagacity, however, came into play. He tried the snow by squeezing it with his foot, and to my astonishment began to cross it. Even after the pressure of his feet the space he had to stand on did not exceed a hand-breadth. I followed him, exactly as a boy walking along a horizontal pole, with toes turned outwards. Right and left the precipices were appalling. We reached the opposite rock, and an earnest smile rippled over Bennen's countenance as he turned towards me. He knew that he had done a daring thing, though not a presumptuous one. 'Had the snow,' he said, 'been less perfect, I should not have thought of attempting it; but I knew after I had set my foot upon the ridge that we might pass without fear.' . . .

After this we found the rocks on the ridge so shaken that it required the greatest caution to avoid bringing them down upon us. With all our care, moreover, we sometimes dislodged vast masses, which leaped upon the slope adjacent, loosened others by their shock, these again others, until finally a whole flight of them would escape, setting the mountain in a roar as they whizzed and thundered along its side to the snow-fields 4,000 feet below us. The day was hot, the work hard, and our bodies were drained of their liquids as by a Turkish bath. To make good our loss we halted at intervals where the melted snow formed liquid veins, and quenched our thirst. A bottle of champagne, poured sparingly into our goblets over a little snow, furnished Wenger and myself with many a refreshing draught. Bennen feared his eyes, and would not touch champagne. We, however, did not find halting good; for at every pause the muscles became set, and some minutes were necessary to render them again elastic. But for both mind and body the discipline was grand. There is scarcely a position possible to a human being which, at one time or another during the day, I was not forced to assume. The fingers, wrist, and forearm were my main reliance, and as a mechanical instrument the human hand appeared to me this day to be a miracle of constructive art.

For the most part the summit was hidden from us, but on reaching the successive eminences it came frequently into view. After three hours spent on the *arête*–about five hours, that is, subsequent to starting–we saw the summit over another minor summit, which gave it an illusive proximity. 'You have now good hopes,' I remarked, turning to Bennen. 'I do not allow myself to entertain the idea of failure,' he replied. Well, six hours passed on the ridge, each of which put in its inexorable claim to the due amount of mechanical work; and at the end of this time we found ourselves apparently no nearer to the summit than when Bennen's hopes cropped out in confidence. I looked anxiously at my guide as he fixed his weary eyes upon the distant peak. There was no confidence in his expression; still I do not believe that either of us entertained for a moment the thought of giving in. Wenger complained of his lungs, and Bennen counselled him several times to remain behind: but this the Oberland man refused to do. At the commencement of a day's work one often feels anxious, if not timid; but when the work is very hard we become callous, and sometimes stupefied by the incessant knocking about. This was my case at present, and I kept watch lest my indifference should become carelessness. I repeatedly supposed a case where a sudden effort might be required of me, and felt all through that I had a fair residue of strength to fall back upon should such a call be made. This conclusion was sometimes tested by a spurt; flinging myself suddenly from rock to rock, I proved my condition by experiment instead of relying on surmise. An eminence in the ridge which cut off the view of the summit was now the object of our exertions. We reached it; but how hopelessly distant did the summit appear! Bennen laid his face upon his axe for a moment; a kind of sickly despair was in his eye as he turned to me, remarking, *'Lieber Herr, die Spitze ist noch sehr weit oben'*.

Lest the desire to gratify me should urge him beyond the bounds of prudence, I told my guide that he must not persist on my account; that I should cheerfully return with him the moment he thought it no longer safe to proceed. He replied that, though weary, he felt quite sure of himself, and asked for some food. He had it, and a gulp of wine, which mightily refreshed him. Looking at the mountain with a firmer eye, he exclaimed, *'Herr! wir müssen ihn haben'*, and his voice, as he spoke, rung like steel within my heart. I thought of Englishmen in battle, of the qualities which had made them famous: it was mainly the quality of not knowing when to yield–of fighting for duty even after they had ceased to be animated by hope. Such thoughts helped to lift me over the rocks. Another eminence now fronted us, behind which, how far we knew not, the summit lay. We scaled this height, and above us, but clearly within reach, a silvery pyramid projected itself against the blue sky. I was assured ten times over by my companions that it was the highest point before I ventured to stake by faith upon the assertion. I feared that it also might take

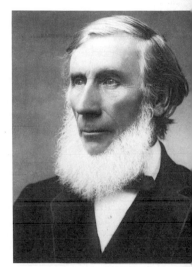

Opposite: the Matterhorn, the Weisshorn and Dent Blanche in the Pennine Alps. The Weisshorn, regarded by Professor John Tyndall (above) as 'the noblest of all the Alps', was climbed by him in 1861.

Above: the Eiger, the Mönch and the Jungfrau, three giants of the Bernese Oberland.

Opposite top: 'In the region of the séracs' from E. T. Coleman, *Scenes from the Snowfield* (1859).

Opposite bottom: 'Leaving the Grand Mulets' from George Baxter, *The Ascent of Mont Blanc* (1853).

rank with the illusions which had so often beset our ascent, and I shrunk from the consequent moral shock. A huge prism of granite, or granitic gneiss, terminated the *arête*, and from it a knife-edge of pure white snow ran up to a little point. We passed along the edge, reached that point, and instantly swept with our eyes the whole range of the horizon. We stood upon the crown of the redoubtable Weisshorn.

The long-pent feelings of my two companions found vent in a wild and reiterated cheer. Bennen shook his arms in the air and shouted as a Valaisian, while Wenger raised the shriller yell of the Oberland. We looked downwards along the ridge, and far below, perched on one of its crags, could discern the two Randa men. Again and again the roar of triumph was sent down to them. They had accomplished but a small portion of the ridge, and soon after our success they wended their way homewards. They came, willing enough, no doubt, to publish our failure had we failed; but we found out afterwards that they had been equally strenuous in announcing our success; they had seen us, they affirmed, like three flies upon the summit of the mountain. Both men had to endure a little persecution for the truth's sake, for nobody in Randa would believe that the Weisshorn could be scaled, and least of all by a man who for two days previously had been the object of Philomène the waitress's constant pity, on account of the incompetence of his stomach to accept all that she offered for its acceptance. The energy of conviction with

which the men gave their evidence had, however, proved conclusive to the most sceptical before we arrived.

Bennen wished to leave some outward and visible sign of our success on the summit. He deplored having no suitable flag; but as a substitute for such it was proposed that he should use the handle of one of our axes as a flagstaff, and surmount it by a red pocket-handkerchief. This was done, and for some time subsequently the extempore banner was seen flapping in the wind. To his extreme delight, it was shown to Bennen himself three days afterwards by my friend Mr Francis Galton, from the Riffelberg hotel.

Every Swiss climber is acquainted with the Weisshorn. I have long regarded it as the noblest of all the Alps, and most other travellers share this opinion. The impression it produces is in some measure due to the comparative isolation with which it juts into the heavens. It is not masked by other mountains, and all around the Alps its final pyramid is in view. Conversely, the Weisshorn commands a vast range of prospect. Neither Bennen nor myself had ever seen anything at all equal to it. The day, moreover, was perfect; not a cloud was to be seen; and the gauzy haze of the distant air, though sufficient to soften the outlines and enhance the colouring of the mountains, was far too thin to obscure them. Over the peaks and through the valleys the sunbeams poured, unimpeded save by the mountains themselves, which sent their

shadows in bars of darkness through the illuminated air. I had never before witnessed a scene which affected me like this one. I opened my note-book to make a few observations, but soon relinquished the attempt. There was something incongruous, if not profane, in allowing the scientific faculty to interfere where silent worship seemed the 'reasonable service'. . . .

In this same year Edward Whymper[5] made his first attempt on the Matterhorn (14,689 feet); he returned to the attack five times in 1862, again in 1863 and, finally in 1865. J.-A. Carrel, who lived on the Italian side of the mountain, had started his own campaign in 1858 and continued it, sometimes with Whymper, sometimes with the backing of influential compatriots, until he reached the summit by the Italian ridge two days after Whymper had reached it by the Hörnli (Zermatt) ridge. All earlier attempts had been by the Italian ridge except for two guideless forays by the Parker brothers and one by T. S. Kennedy in *January* 1862.

The Hudson-Whymper party of 1865 was too large, being a fortuitous combination of three parties: Hudson and Hadow, with Croz; Douglas with the Taugwalders; and Whymper, who had been left guideless. Even more fatal, there was no acknowledged leader. It was far from a weak party; Hudson and Whymper in the front rank of amateurs; Michel Croz, 'the equal of Jakob Anderegg in daring, of Melchior and Almer in executive ability': Taugwalder, *père*, had shown himself a first-rate guide, while his son's career proved him at least better than average and he must have been already a useful man at twenty-two; Hadow's inexperience has been unfairly stressed. He was, in Captain Farrar's words, 'one of those active young Englishmen capable, with experienced companions, of going anywhere'[6]: Douglas had several enterprising expeditions behind him; he had just made the first ascent of the Gabelhorn from Zinal. Here is Whymper's account of the climb.[7]

The ascent of the Matterhorn
from Edward Whymper, *Scrambles amongst the Alps*
We started from Zermatt on the 13th of July 1865, at half-past five, on a brilliant and perfectly cloudless morning. We were eight in number—Croz, old Peter [Taugwalder] and his two sons, Lord F. Douglas, Hadow, Hudson, and I. To ensure steady motion, one tourist and one native walked together. The youngest Taugwalder fell to my share, and the lad marched well, proud to be on the expedition, and happy to show his powers. The wine-bags also fell to my lot to carry, and throughout the day, after each drink, I replenished them secretly with water, so that at the next halt they were found fuller than before! This was considered a good omen, and little short of miraculous.

On the first day we did not intend to ascend to any great height, and we mounted, accordingly, very leisurely; picked up the things which were left in the chapel at the Schwarzsee at 8.20, and proceeded thence along the ridge connecting the Hörnli with the Matterhorn. At half-past eleven we arrived at the base of the actual peak; then quitted the ridge, and clambered round some ledges, on to the eastern face. We were now fairly upon the mountain, and were astonished to find that places which from the Riffel, or even from the Furggen Glacier, looked entirely impracticable, were so easy that we could *run about*.

Before twelve o'clock we had found a good position for the tent, at a height of 11,000 feet. Croz and young Peter went on to see what was above, in order to save time on the following morning. They cut across the heads of the snow-slopes which descended towards the Furggen Glacier, and disappeared round a corner; but shortly afterwards we saw them high up on the face, moving quickly. We others made a solid platform for the tent in a well-protected spot, and then watched eagerly for the return of the men. The stones which they upset told us that they were very high, and we supposed that the way must be easy. At length, just before 3 pm, we saw them coming down, evidently much excited. 'What are they saying, Peter?' 'Gentlemen, they say it is no good.' But when they came near we heard a different story. 'Nothing but what was good; not a difficulty, not a single difficulty! We could have gone to the summit and returned to-day easily!'

We passed the remaining hours of daylight—some basking in the sunshine, some sketching or collecting; and when the sun went down, giving, as it departed, a glorious promise for the morrow, we returned to the tent to arrange for the night. Hudson made tea, I coffee, and we then retired each one to his blanket bag; the Taugwalders, Lord Francis Douglas, and myself, occupying the tent, the others remaining, by preference, outside. Long after dusk the cliffs above echoed with our laughter and with the songs of the guides, for we were happy that night in camp, and feared no evil.

We assembled together outside the tent before dawn on the morning of the 14th, and started directly it was light enough to move. Young Peter came on with us as a guide, and his brother returned to Zermatt. We followed the route which had been taken on the previous day, and in a few minutes turned the rib which had intercepted the view of the eastern face from our tent platform. The whole of this great slope was now revealed, rising for 3,000 feet like a huge natural staircase. Some parts were more, and others were less, easy; but we were not once brought to a halt by any serious impediment, for when an obstruction was met in front it could always be turned to the right or to the left. For the greater part of the way there was, indeed, no occasion for the rope, and sometimes Hudson led, sometimes myself. At 6.20 we had attained a height of 12,800 feet, and halted for half an hour; we then continued the ascent without a break until 9.55, when we stopped for fifty minutes, at a height of 14,000 feet. Twice we struck the north-east ridge and followed it for some little distance,—to no advantage, for it was usually more rotten and steep, and always more difficult than the face. Still, we kept near to it, lest stones perchance might fall.

Opposite: Albert Smith's board game based on a journey from Piccadilly to the summit of Mont Blanc.

Below: Edward Whymper, illustrator turned mountaineer, who was determined to scale the Matterhorn.

Bottom: an illustration from Whymper's book *Scrambles Amongst the Alps* (1871) depicts a *bergschrund* (the crevasse between a glacier and its retaining rock wall).

Above: a view of the Matterhorn showing, right, the east face and the Hörnli ridge (skylined), along which Whymper reached the summit.

Right: an illustration by Gustave Doré of a camp set up during Whymper's first attempt on the Matterhorn in 1861.

Far right: an engraving by Whymper of the east face of the Matterhorn and the village of Zermatt.

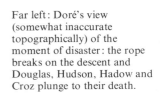

Far left: Doré's view (somewhat inaccurate topographically) of the moment of disaster: the rope breaks on the descent and Douglas, Hudson, Hadow and Croz plunge to their death.

Left: the Italian guide Jean-Antoine Carrel, Whymper's rival in the race to climb the Matterhorn. He reached the summit by the Italian ridge two days after Whymper.

Centre left: the *Führerbuch*, a guide's book of testimonials, of 'young' Peter Taugwalder. The reference for the Matterhorn climb is missing as Lord Francis Douglas, Taugwalder's employer, was one of those killed.

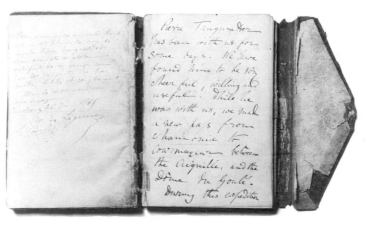

The French guide Michel-August Croz, a portrait based on a photograph. Croz toured with A. J. Moore (opposite) through the Dauphiné Alps in 1864.

We had now arrived at the foot of that part which, from the Riffelberg or from Zermatt, seems perpendicular or overhanging, and could no longer continue upon the eastern side. For a little distance we ascended by snow upon the arête – that is, the ridge – descending towards Zermatt, and then, by common consent, turned over to the right, or to the northern side. Before doing so, we made a change in the order of ascent. Croz went first, I followed, Hudson came third; Hadow and old Peter were last. 'Now,' said Croz, as he led off, 'now for something altogether different.' The work became difficult and required caution. In some places there was little to hold, and it was desirable that those should be in front who were least likely to slip. The general slope of the mountain at this part was *less* than 40°, and snow had accumulated in, and had filled up, the interstices of the rockface, leaving only occasional fragments projecting here and there. These were at times covered with a thin film of ice, produced from the melting and refreezing of the snow. It was the counterpart, on a small scale, of the upper 700 feet of the Pointe des Ecrins, – only there was this material difference; the face of the Ecrins was about, or exceeded, an angle of 50°, and the Matterhorn face was less than 40°. It was a place over which any fair mountaineer might pass in safety, and Mr Hudson ascended this part, and, as far as I know, the entire mountain, without having the slightest assistance rendered to him upon any occasion. Sometimes, after I had taken a hand from Croz, or received a pull, I turned to offer the same to Hudson; but he invariably declined, saying it was not necessary. Mr Hadow, however, was not accustomed to this kind of work, and required continual assistance. It is only fair to say that the difficulty which he found at this part arose simply and entirely from want of experience.

This solitary difficult part was of no great extent. We bore away over it at first, nearly horizontally, for a distance of about 400 feet; then ascended directly towards the summit for about 60 feet; and then doubled back to the ridge which descends towards Zermatt. A long stride round a rather awkward corner brought us to snow once more. The last doubt vanished! The Matterhorn was ours! Nothing but 200 feet of easy snow remained to be surmounted!

You must now carry your thoughts back to the seven Italians who started from Breuil on the 11th of July. Four days had passed since their departure, and we were tormented with anxiety lest they should arrive at the top before us. All the way up we had talked of them, and many false alarms of 'men on the summit' had been raised. The higher we rose, the more intense became the excitement. What if we should be beaten at the last moment? The slope eased off, at length we could be detached, and Croz and I dashing away, ran a neck-and-neck race, which ended in a dead heat. At 1.40 pm the world was at our feet, and the Matterhorn was conquered. Hurrah! Not a footstep could be seen.

As is well known, disaster overtook the party on the descent and Hudson, Douglas, Hadow and Croz perished. No other mountain accident attracted so much publicity and controversy until the 1930s. Every aspect of popular interest was present; the unexpectedly easy success after years of siege; the defeat of the Italian party in the race for the summit; the euphoria of victory dashed by the sudden death of four men; the cruciform Brocken spectres thrown on the sky in spectacular memorial; the search for the bodies; the Zermatt enquiry; the correspondence in *The Times* and the melodramatic speculations of the ignorant. Nevertheless it is not true, as has been asserted, that the disaster 'checked the progress of mountaineering for a decade'. The check lay only in the disappearance of two such outstanding performers as Hudson and Croz and so promising a young man as Douglas. Whymper, too, gave up serious climbing.

On the very next day, 15 July, A. W. Moore's party (himself, Horace Walker, Frank Walker, G. S. Mathews with Melchior and Jakob Anderegg) climbed Mont Blanc by the Brenva glacier. They bivouacked at about 9,400 feet and set out at 2.45 am. Moore continues:[8]

The ascent of Mont Blanc by the Brenva glacier
from A. W. Moore, *The Alps in 1864*
Julien Grange volunteered to go with us to learn the way, but his companion, not seeming to see how, unaided, he was to carry all the *impedimenta* down to the valley, our friend had to curb his desire, which Melchior afterwards cruelly suggested would not have been so ardently expressed, had he not foreseen the obstacle which would arise to its gratification. The rocks on which we had slept are connected with others higher up by a series of snow-slopes, up which we went in Melchior's steps of the previous day, keeping rather to the left. At 3.15 the rope was put on, and then, bearing still more to the left, we made our way, by 3.35, to the edge of the ice-fall, which had so much excited Melchior. Had our purpose been different, we might, by keeping a more straightforward course, have gained the upper névé of the glacier above the fall without any difficulty at all, but, when there, we should have been above the buttress we had to steer for, and quite out of our proper direction. [A *névé* is a permanent snowfield not yet transformed to glacier.] From the head of the glacier, a pass, worth attention, might be easily made over the low ridge west of La Tour Ronde to the Glacier du Géant. It was still dark when we started, but now, as our difficulties were commencing, there were signs of dawn. Gorgeous as had been the sunset, the sunrise was more gorgeous still, the gradations of colour over the eastern horizon before the appearance of the luminary being indescribably beautiful, while, as the sun rose, the great wall of precipices before us glowed again as its beams crept down them. This ice-fall certainly was worthy of Melchior's respect and admiration, for a grander and more broken one I have rarely seen, but, when we fairly attacked it, we got on with less difficulty than had been feared. Of course, there was the usual up and

down sort of work, but, in spite of one or two checks, we progressed steadily, and, finding ourselves more than half-way across, were about to indulge in a crow of exultation, when we came to what looked like a full stop. We had worked ourselves into a position from which there appeared, after several trials, to be no way of extrication except by returning in our footsteps, always a disheartening proceeding. We pottered about for some time without result, and then Melchior cast off the rope, and went alone to seek out a way, leaving us in rather a blank state of mind. We shivered miserably, but were finally rejoiced by a distant cry, which evidently meant 'come on'. The ground in front did not look promising, but, following in Melchior's steps, we gradually left the worst bit behind, and struck a broad causeway between two huge chasms which led us out of the labyrinth to where he was waiting for us.

One of the doubtful points in connection with our expedition was thus happily solved. The glacier was crossed, and all was plain sailing in front as far as the base of our buttress, which was not far above us. A smooth slope of snow between the foot of the cliffs on our left and the ice-fall offered an easy line of march, but, as we went, we had ocular evidence of the propriety of keeping out of the way of the hanging glaciers already spoken of, as a large mass of ice from one in front fell before our eyes, its débris rolling right across our path. At 5.30 we were at the base of the buttress. The rocks were approached by a steep slope of hard snow, intersected by the usual bergschrund. The latter gave us little trouble, and we were soon hard at work with the rocks. For nearly two hours we were engaged in a scramble, which, though not difficult, was sufficiently severe to be interesting, some care being required in places where snow was lying. At first we kept straight up, but later bore away to the left, ascending diagonally, until, at 7.20, when not far from the crest of the buttress, we halted for breakfast. We had risen very rapidly, and must have been at an elevation of more than 12,000 feet. Our position, therefore, commanded an extensive view in all directions–but details would be uninteresting.

The guides were in a hurry, so, cutting our halt shorter than would have been agreeable, we resumed our way at 7.55, and, after a few steps up a slope at an angle of 50°, found ourselves on the crest of the buttress, and looking down upon and across the lower part of a glacier tributary to the Brenva, beyond which towered the grand wall of Mont Maudit. We turned sharply to the left along the ridge, Jakob leading, followed by Mr Walker, Horace Walker, Mathews, Melchior, and myself last. We had anticipated that, assuming the possibility of gaining the ridge on which we were, there would be no serious difficulty in traversing it, and so much as we could see ahead led us to hope that our anticipations would turn out correct. Before us lay a narrow, but not steep, arête of rock and snow combined, which appeared to terminate some distance in front in a sharp peak. We advanced cautiously, keeping rather below the top of the ridge, speculating with some curiosity on what lay

beyond this peak. On reaching it, the apparent peak proved not to be a peak at all, but the extremity of the narrowest and most formidable ice arête I ever saw, which extended almost on a level for an uncomfortably long distance. Looking back by the light of our subsequent success, I have always considered it a providential circumstance that, at this moment, Jakob, and not Melchior, was leading the party. In saying this, I shall not for an instant be suspected of any imputation upon Melchior's courage. But in him that virtue is combined to perfection with the equally necessary one of prudence, while he shares the objection which nearly all guides have to taking upon themselves, without discussion, responsibility in positions of doubt. Had he been in front, I believe that, on seeing the nature of the work before us, we should have halted and discussed the propriety of proceeding, and I believe further that, as the result of that discussion, our expedition would have then and there come to an end. Now in Jakob, with courage as faultless as Melchior's and physical powers even superior, the virtue of prudence is conspicuous chiefly from its absence, and, on coming to this ugly place, it never for an instant occurred to him that we might object to go on, or consider the object in view not worth the risk which must be inevitably run. He, therefore, went calmly on without so much as turning to see what we thought of it, while I do not suppose that it entered into the head of any one of us to spontaneously suggest a retreat. On most arêtes, however narrow the actual crest may be, it is generally possible to get a certain amount of support by driving the pole into the slope below on either side. But this was not the case here. We were on the top of a wall, the ice on the right falling vertically (I use the word advisedly), and on the left nearly so. On neither side was it possible to obtain the slightest hold with the alpenstock. I believe, also, that an arête of pure ice is more often encountered in description than in reality, that term being generally applied to hard snow. But here, for once, we had the genuine article–blue ice, without a speck of snow on it. The space for walking was, at first, about the breadth of the top of an ordinary wall, in which Jakob cut holes for the feet. Being last in the line, I could see little of what was coming until I was close upon it, and was, therefore, considerably startled on seeing the men in front suddenly abandon the upright position, which, in spite of the insecurity of the steps, and difficulty of preserving the balance, had been hitherto maintained, and sit down à cheval. The ridge had narrowed to a knife edge, and for a few yards it was utterly impossible to advance in any other way. The foremost men soon stood up again, but, when I was about to follow their example, Melchior insisted emphatically on my not doing so, but remaining seated. Regular steps could no longer be cut, but Jakob, as he went along, simply sliced off the top of the ridge, making thus a slippery pathway, along which those behind crept, moving one foot carefully after the other. As for me, I worked myself along with my hands, in an attitude safer, perhaps, but considerably more uncomfortable, and, as I went, could

A. W. Moore, who climbed regularly in the Alps from 1860 to 1881; he was the first to climb Mont Blanc by the Brenva Glacier in 1865.

not help occasionally speculating with an odd feeling of amusement, as to what would be the result if any of the party should chance to slip over on either side – what the rest would do – whether throw themselves over on the other or not – and if so, what would happen then. Fortunately the occasion for the solution of this curious problem did not arise, and at 9.30 we reached the end of the arête, where it merged in the long slopes of the broken névé, over which our way was next to lie. . . .

At 9.40 we started up the slopes of the névé which rose with ominous steepness in front of us, and for the next two hours and a half the work was rather monotonous. There was no particular difficulty beyond what arose from the extreme steepness of the slope, necessitating almost continuous step-cutting, the labour of which fell upon the two guides, who, naturally enough, did not consider the way easy. Sometimes there was snow enough to help us, but as often as not it was too thin and powdery to give secure footing, and I suppose that altogether about every other step had to be cut in ice. The Corridor all the time was hidden, but we knew it to lie far away to our right, and, therefore, worked generally in that direction. Two ridges of rock, running parallel to each other, but separated by a broad expanse of ice, crop out from the face of the slope. We passed underneath the first, and cut our way across to the second, and, on reaching it, ascertained our exact position. On our right below was the upper part of the lateral glacier so often mentioned, beyond which was the wall of the Mont Maudit, the depression marking the head of the Corridor being apparently at about the same level as we were. There was our goal in full view, but between us and it was a great gulf, which there was no obvious way of crossing. Beneath the Corridor the glacier falls away very rapidly. At the foot of the Mur de la Côte the difference of level is but a few feet, but, under the Mont Maudit, a precipice of some two thousand feet intervenes. It is, therefore, only practicable to pass from one to the other at the former point. Unfortunately *we* were nearly opposite the Mont Maudit, and the glacier lay at a corresponding depth below us. From where we were standing it was not possible to descend on to it, nor, if it had been possible, would it have been profitable, as, just above the point we must have struck, was a great wall of ice running right across, and completely barring the way upwards. Our position was, in fact, rather critical. Immediately over our heads the slope on which we were terminated in a great mass of broken séracs, which might come down with a run at any moment. It seemed improbable that any way out of our difficulties would be found in that quarter. But where else to look? There was no use in going to the left – to the right we *could* not go – and back we *would* not go. After careful scrutiny, Melchior thought it just possible that we might find a passage through these séracs on to the higher and more level portion of the glacier to the right of them, and, there being obviously no chance of success in any other direction, we turned towards them. The ice here was steeper and harder than it had yet been. In spite of all

Melchior's care the steps were painfully insecure, and we were glad to get a grip with one hand of the rocks alongside which we passed.

Melchior had steered with his usual discrimination, and was now attacking the séracs at the only point where they appeared at all practicable. [A *sérac* is an ice tower caused by the splitting of a glacier.] Standing over the mouth of a crevasse, choked with débris, he endeavoured to lift himself on to its upper edge, which was about fifteen feet above. But to accomplish this seemed at first a task too great even for his agility, aided, as it was, by vigorous pushes *a tergo*. At last, by a marvellous exercise of skill and activity, he succeeded, pulled up Mr Walker and Horace Walker, and then cast off the rope to reconnoitre, leaving them to assist Mathews, Jakob, and myself in the performance of a similar manoeuvre. We were all three still below, when a yell from Melchior sent a thrill through my veins. 'What is it?' said we to Mr Walker. A shouting communication took place between him and Melchior, and then came the answer, 'He says it is all right.' That moment was worth living for. But every man here can realise without anything further from me what our feelings after so many hours of alternate hopes and fears. Our difficulties were indeed over. Before us was a narrow shelf of névé, stretching from the base of a perpendicular wall of ice, fifty feet high or more, to the edge of a huge crevasse, or rather dislocation, in the glacier. Over our heads was an immense projecting fringe of icicles, but we paid no heed to them, and, hurrying along as fast as was consistent with not slipping into the gulf below, emerged in a few minutes upon gently sloping snow-fields, – the same upon which, in 1864, I had looked so longingly from the Mur de la Côte. From here we might have struck the top of the Mur, or, as I believe, the actual summit of Mont Blanc. But the adoption of either course would have involved an amount of step-cutting to which, after their already arduous labours, we should have been scarcely justified in exposing our two men. Besides which, we were all heavily laden, and the idea of depositing our burdens at the foot of the Mur was too alluring to be resisted. The intervening distance was traversed at a trot, and at 1.20 we stepped on to the head of the Corridor. The height of the Corridor, according to the French Survey, is 4301 mètres, or 14,112 feet. We had, therefore, made the highest as it is certainly the grandest, pass across the chain of Mont Blanc. No one's satisfaction at our success was more profound than that of dear old Melchior, notwithstanding that his predictions had been falsified, and the expedition shown *not* to be 'eine miserable Dummheit' after all. Of the behaviour of both him and Jakob it is impossible to speak too highly. But to sing Melchior's praises is needless, while of Jakob it is enough to say that, upon this as upon many previous occasions, he had proved himself worthy of his name.

I have not much to add. We reached the summit at 3.10, and found ourselves safe at Chamouni at 10.30. . . .

Opposite: the Brenva Glacier with Mont Blanc behind. The Peuterey Ridge leads up from the left.

43

This climb was ahead of its time and still maintains a very respectable reputation.

The Macugnaga (east) face of Monte Rosa is the highest sweep of ice and rock in the Alps, and perhaps the most beautiful. There are now several routes up it, none easy, some very dangerous and difficult. The first and standard route was made in 1872 by W. M. and R. Pendlebury and C. Taylor with Ferdinand Imseng, Gabriel Spechtenhauser and Giovanni Oberto. This climb for long preserved a great reputation; it is now generally considered somewhat easier but more dangerous than Moore's 'old' Brenva route. When Hermann Buhl (see Chapter 10) came to Zermatt in 1955 to attend the centenary celebrations of the first ascent of Monte Rosa, he chose appropriately to enter Switzerland by this route, which was selected by Jean Couzy as marking the shift of interest from reaching a summit to the quality and difficulty of the climb. The Pendlebury party crossed the Marinelli couloir, climbed up the rocks on its south bank, up the ice to the Grenzgipfel and then along the main ridge to the highest summit (Dufourspitze).

Imseng, of Saas, was the great expert on the Macugnaga side of Monte Rosa and took part in many first ascents. When he was with Damiano Marinelli's party attempting the third ascent of this face in 1881 they were all swept away by an avalanche. The great couloir, 'the greatest avalanche trough in Europe', has since borne Marinelli's name and the rib of rocks on the couloir's right bank is called Imsengrücken.

The climbers and guides of those days were primarily interested in reaching the summits and naturally chose the easiest, or what seemed the easiest, way. This was nearly always on snow and ice; the guides were at home on this terrain and it was on snow and ice that the amateurs learned to climb. (In fact, they would sometimes have escaped difficulty if they had ventured off ice onto neighbouring rock as, indeed, Tyndall had insisted on the Weisshorn.) So it was that the great rock playgrounds of later generations were neglected and the rockier peaks were the later to fall.

The Aiguille du Dru (12,316 feet) towers above the Mer de Glace, a prominently visible and obvious challenge. Clinton Dent attacked this mountain with resolute persistence; others like Oakley Maund, E. R. Whitwell and J. Birkbeck came and went. In 1875 Dent succeeded on his nineteenth attempt, accompanied by J. Walker Hartley, Alexander Burgener and Kaspar Maurer.

By now all the great alpine peaks had been climbed, save one. There were, of course a multitude of lesser mountains, needles and Dolomite towers still untrodden; indeed some very difficult points, particularly among the Chamonix aiguilles, remained unclimbed even after the first war but mopping-up operations were then soon concluded in the Alps. New routes on familiar mountains are still being made today, but of great severity or danger, or both.

The one great peak outstanding was the Meije (13,068 feet) in Dauphiny. It was naturally the object of determined attacks by the best mountaineers. The

Baron Emmanuel Boileau de Castelnau, who at the age of 20 climbed the Meije (opposite) with Pierre Gaspard and his son in 1877. It was the last of the great alpine peaks to be ascended.

Central Peak had been reached by Coolidge[9] and his capable aunt, Miss Brevoort, in 1870, but it was not until 1877 that a young Frenchman, the Baron Emmanuel Boileau de Castelnau, climbed the highest summit with Pierre Gaspard and his son. Here is a translation of the account he wrote in the *Annuaire* of the Club Alpin Français:[10]

The ascent of the Meije
from Boileau de Castelnau, *Annuaire du Club Alpin Français*, Vol. IV.
By 14th August I was well enough to move to Bourg-d'Oisans in pouring rain. On 15th I took a carriage to Venose, whence I left immediately for St Christophe. Gaspard and his son were awaiting me with impatience. We lost too much time in preparations, so it was night when we reached la Bérarde.

Anxious to lighten our loads and fearing we might have to leave someone behind to stand by a rope en route, we thought it best to take on a third guide. We chose Jean-Baptiste Rodier who was soon ready to start.

Having completed our provisions, the four of us set out at 11.0 pm. It was a black night, and we missed our way several times before we arrived by lantern-light at le Châtelleret at 2.0 in the morning. We were heavily loaded, for besides a great deal of provisions we carried 350 feet of rope.

It was still too early to go further. We stretched out by a good fire; the guides warmed up some of that coffee for which I do not care, it being more solid than liquid.

At 4.20 we resumed our way by the first light of dawn. We reached the Shoulder at 7.30. We rested for half-an-hour before crossing the Glacier des Etançons without difficulty. So far we had roped up at about 13 foot intervals; now we doubled this distance to give us more freedom. We also cut the loads down to a single sack, and climbed reasonably fast up the route of our first attempt.

At 9.15 we reached M. Duhamel's cairn, where we stopped for breakfast, continuing the climb at 9.25. The rope we had left in place helped us to get up the pitch we had found so dangerous before. The rest of the wall still offered serious enough difficulties. We could only move one at a time to reduce the number badly placed at any one moment. We also lost much time in hauling the axes which we had to keep detaching from the line in order to use them.

Our advance was desperately slow; we could not relax precautions as the wall was still vertical. We got ourselves into a couloir from which we couldn't escape and saw ourselves momentarily having to beat a retreat; morale began to suffer. I cannot describe in detail the route we followed nor the difficulties we had to surmount in climbing this 500-foot wall. I can only record that, without taking a moment for rest, we took 2 hours 45 minutes to get to the top and reach the Glacier du Doigt. We had at once to leave the glacier on our right to rejoin the W. ridge. From here we could see the houses and meadows of La Grave. To rejoin the glacier we had to go back a few steps and slide down onto the névé, where we stopped 40 minutes for lunch. Rodier, the guide from la Bérarde, had been the main cause of our slowness. Unaccustomed to climbing such steep rocks, he was not only unable to help us but in places we had to haul him up; he thus added to the difficulties and danger. Unfortunately he had also dropped my axe, which landed in pieces at the foot of the Meije. As I could not do without an axe on the glacier, I borrowed Rodier's; he stayed where he was, at about 11,880 feet, to await our return.

At 12.45, Gaspard, his son and I continued on our way. The glacier had a uniform slope and no crevasses. The angle, about 45°, was steep enough but offered no serious obstacles. We had to cut steps for the three-quarters of an hour it took us to cross, and with particular care in the upper part where it was bare ice. At the top of the glacier we found ourselves on a col from which we could see the valley of La Grave, towards which fell a vertical couloir of ice. Turning to the right and keeping always on the S. face of the mountain, we climbed the rocks of the peak proper very fast and without difficulty. Victory seemed ours when, only some 30 feet from the summit, an unexpected obstacle made us doubtful of success. The summit rocks overhung on all sides; in other words the slope was a curve and we were in its concavity. Our efforts were at first fruitless. Gaspard *père* got up about twelve feet and found himself unable either to advance or return. He called for help which I was able to supply by standing on his son's shoulders, but only just in time as his strength was giving out. I then tried, but met with no greater success. Gaspard *fils* succeeded in getting a little higher, but he put us in such danger helping him down that I was ready to order the retreat. He was so exhausted by his efforts that on his

The Meije.

return he could not move his limbs, and the nervous stress had been so great that he dissolved in tears. All three of us were pale and trembling and took a moment to rally ourselves. The biting cold paralysed our forces. The weather had been deteriorating for the last hour. We were enveloped in clouds whipped across by a violent wind which threatened to tumble us. We descended a little way, ready to retreat after having been within twenty feet of the summit, when Gaspard, furious at finding his efforts ineffective, proposed that we try to turn the obstacle on the N. face. With much difficulty we crossed a horrible section, and this time our perseverance was rewarded by success. At 3.30 we set foot on the summit after spending two hours in climbing the last few feet. 'Foreign guides haven't got this one,' cried Gaspard in triumph. All the same, what gave him greatest pleasure was to find enough stones to build a cairn there. Throughout the day he had expressed his fears on this score, always repeating that no-one would believe our story unless a cairn was there to prove it.

The summit of the Meije is bare of snow and is a narrow crest running E.-W. The crest and N. face are rotten, but the rocks of the S. face are quite solid.

While Gaspard and his son collected stones and built two cairns about 5 feet high, I got out of the wind some six feet below them on the La Grave side. The thermometer showed two degrees below zero (Centigrade). The barometer gave a corrected height of 13,124 feet, only 43 feet above the true height.

It was all very well to have climbed the Meije, but we had to get down. This thought was neither pleasant nor reassuring. We set off at 3.55.

The difficulties were many and frightening. The pitch immediately below the top was impossible; we had to fix one of our ropes to a spike of rock and slide down it until we could find a stance on a ledge. This ledge was sixty-five feet lower; we had to cut the rope and abandon this length. Once past this section, we descended to the Glacier du Doigt without too much trouble; but after crossing the glacier, picking up Rodier, and regaining the W. ridge, the difficulties reappeared; a fixed rope was again necessary and another 65 feet had regretfully to be abandoned.

Night was falling; the vertical rocks, scarcely practicable by daylight, became more and more dangerous in the dark. We got down another two or three very difficult pitches, almost without seeing them, but when only 60 feet above M. Duhamel's 'damp rock', we were stopped on a shelf and found ourselves unable to proceed. We had to resign ourselves to awaiting the morning on this narrow rock landing. A rock, conveniently placed by Gaspard *père*, served as parapet; huddled together against the cold, we prepared for a long and terrible night.

We all reknotted the rope to which we were tied for fear of being carried away by the wind. We passed another rope round our backs with a running knot; the end of this rope was anchored to our axes fixed in the rocks a little above us. Thus strung up on a shelf too narrow to allow us either to sit down or to stand up, we awaited the dawn. We had to endure intense cold unable to move, for there was no room to do so; squalls of snow and hail were most painful to our numbed limbs.

Towards 10 o'clock, our clothes showed a curious phenomenon of frost; the falling snow was thawed by our bodily warmth and then refrozen into a coat of ice, so that we could hardly move our arms. We tried to get rid of this icy crust with knives, but in vain. Naturally none of us thought to close an eye during the night. Gaspard did not let go of me for a moment; we stayed with arms enlaced round each other's bodies or knees throughout the storm. The strength of our safety rope was suspect and we knew that there was a drop of nearly two thousand feet below us. Nobody spoke, except occasionally to ask the time, a question which none of us could answer, or to ask a companion to steady him on the rope while he changed position to avoid cramp. We had nothing to help us endure the wind and the cold. Our provisions were long since finished and the last of the brandy had been shared out at the beginning of our vigil. Gaspard *fils* wanted to smoke, but his hands refused him service and he could not fill his pipe. I had fixed my minimum-thermometer a little above us; it recorded a temperature of eleven degrees below zero.

About 2 the weather abated a little and the wind dropped; at about 4, having waited for the first glimmers of light, Gaspard wanted to get on our way. The first effort was most painful; we found ourselves all but incapable of movement. Gaspard ordered us to crouch down again, huddled together, for two more hours. We tried to restore the circulation in our half-frozen limbs by beating each other. We relied on sunrise, but it was the snow that came.

At 6, it was snowing hard and blowing a gale. It was absolutely necessary to move and descend. The rocks, covered with hail and verglas, offered no sure hold so that to reach the 'damp rock' we had to rope down for the third time.

'This was the last pitch to give us trouble,' wrote Gaspard *père* in the simple and modest account which he sent in to the Club, fearing that my military duties might prevent me from recording the climb, 'the rest of the descent was easy. As we passed M. Duhamel's Rock, we wished him a hearty good morning and rejoined the ordinary path.'

'The weather did not improve. However, we were much cheered by the sight of the sack we had left by the rocks the night before. We descended to le Châtelleret at the double. By nine, once more in our old hotel, we built a good fire under the rocks out of the rain, and ate with terrible appetite.'

Our meal over, we regained la Berarde in pouring rain. It was midnight on our happy return.

Little was known of Boileau until Mlle Engel published her researches.[11] Of an ancient family, he accumulated a remarkable alpine record while still a boy, but after the Meije, he never climbed again.[12] The last of the great peaks of the Alps had fallen to a most picturesque and stimulating figure. The Golden Age was over.

4 High Summer

Place me somewhere in the Valais, mid the mountains west of Binn,
West of Binn and east of Savoy, in a decent kind of inn,
With a peak or two for climbing, and a glacier to explore,–
Any mountain will content me, though they've all been climbed before–
    Yes, I care not any more
    Though they've all been done before,
And the names they keep in bottles may be numbered by the score!
                        A. D. Godley

All the great peaks of the Alps had been climbed when Boileau succeeded on the Meije; a few of them, Mont Blanc, Monte Rosa, the Matterhorn, by more than one route but most of them only by the route that seemed the easiest. What remained for the adventurous mountaineer to do?

First, he might go farther afield; to the eastern Alps where many peaks, lower but very steep, remained to be climbed; to the Caucasus whose mountains overtop Mont Blanc; to the Himalaya, to the Andes, to the Rockies or to New Zealand.

Second, he could concentrate on finding new and harder routes on mountains already climbed, or on finding minor points and needles neglected in the Golden Age. Indeed, nearly all the more sporting climbs available to the modern alpinist were first done after the Golden Age.

Third, he could climb without guides, a practice frowned on by most of the founding fathers. In 1870, A. G. Girdlestone had published his *The High Alps without a Guide*, which provoked the Alpine Club into one of the aberrations to which the august are liable, a resolution condemning guideless climbing. The authors of the resolution forgot, for example, that Charles Hudson had climbed without guides when it suited him, and that the three Parker brothers had a fine list of guideless expeditions. Within a few years many of the leading members of the Club were regularly climbing without guides and this was practically standard practice among German climbers in the eastern Alps.

Going guideless can be taken a step further by going alone. Here German-speaking climbers took, and retain, the lead. Even in the midst of the Golden Age, J. J. Weilenmann, a Swiss, made many solo pioneer ascents in the Otztal and Hermann von Barth, a Bavarian, did the same, mainly in the Karwendel and the Wetterstein. Even Tyndall climbed Monte Rosa by himself, but was rather shy about it.

A further variation was to climb in winter. It was not altogether new. Here Charles Hudson had been a pioneer in the Mont Blanc district in 1853, Hugi had reached the Strahlegg Pass in January 1832, T. S.

Kennedy had attempted the Matterhorn in January 1862. In December 1866, Moore and Horace Walker had set out from Grindelwald, crossed the Finsteraarjoch and returned across the Strahlegg. In 1874, Coolidge and Miss Brevoort, as usual with Christian Almer, had climbed both the Jungfrau and the Wetterhorn in winter. In 1867 Miss Straton, with Jean Charlet and two other guides, had climbed Mont Blanc in January. Vittorio Sella traversed the Matterhorn in March 1882. Paul Güssfeld made winter ascents of the Grandes Jorasses and the Gran Paradiso in the 1890s. There were, of course, others but Coolidge is the admitted father of winter climbing as a regular practice and, after him, the Swiss, G. A. Hasler, who climbed most of the Oberland peaks in the first winters of this century.

Another and more fundamental change was taking place at the turn of the Golden Age, an increasing emphasis on rock-climbing. The pioneers, and more particularly, their guides, preferred to climb snow or ice rather than rock. Those who spent their summer holidays in the Alps now began to spend weekends on their home rocks; in this way, they gained much more confidence going guideless on steep rock. Similarly, the greater attention paid to the limestone ranges of the eastern Alps, where there is much steep rock and little snow, and the popularity of the granite of the Chamonix aiguilles both led to a great advance in the standard of rock-climbing.

The first striking example of the new phase was the attempt to find a route from Courmayeur to Mont Blanc over Mont Blanc de Courmayeur. This was seeking a new route on an 'old' mountain, climbing adventure for its own sake, as Professor Graham Brown puts it. It involved making a way out of the Innominata basin, itself difficult of access, by the impending Innominata face or by one of its bounding ridges, the Brouillard or the Peuterey.

W. A. B. Coolidge and his aunt, Meta Brevoort. Coolidge devoted a large part of his life to the Alps, where he made 1700 expeditions. He was also an authority on alpine history and a pioneer of winter mountaineering. With his aunt, who had introduced him to the Alps, he climbed both the Jungfrau and the Wetterhorn in winter.

Although John Birkbeck, junior, had been half-way up the couloir descending from Col Emile Rey in 1864, and the Marchese Agostino Durazzo had climbed and christened Punta Innominata (12,231 feet) in 1872, the collective effort really began the next year when T. S. Kennedy and Garth Marshall climbed the Mont Noir de Peuterey to prospect and were discouraged by what they saw. Two days later A. G. Girdlestone and W. E. Utterson-Kelso, with Julien le Grange and Séraphin Henry, tried for the Innominata face and reached a point on the ridge of Pic Eccles above the Col du Fresnay. In 1874 Kennedy, this time with Thomas Middlemore, projected a route from the head of the Fresnay glacier. With Johann Fischer and Ulrich Almer, they bivouacked on the ridge of Pic Eccles; they went forward next morning and were turned back by a thunderstorm, but not before Kennedy was convinced that the route was feasible.

Six weeks later, after Kennedy had departed for home, Garth Marshall took up the task with Johann Fischer and Ulrich Almer. From their bivouac they proceeded over Pic Eccles (13,248 feet), making its first ascent, and were stopped at 4 pm at the foot of the third step on the Innominata rib,[1] high up on the now standard Innominata route established by Oliver and Courtauld in 1919. Returning in darkness, the party fell into a crevasse at midnight, only Almer surviving. It was Marshall's third season. Like Henri Cordier and Georg Winkler,[2] he was a meteor that shot brilliant across the sky to early extinction.

Next season James Eccles, after careful examination with his telescope, decided on the Brouillard ridge via Col Emile Rey, but turned back on account of the danger of falling stones.[3] From the top of Pic Eccles he decided that this side of the mountain was hopeless. This opinion was only upset during the winter when Eccles happened to see, in a shop in the Strand, a photograph of the Peuterey ridge in profile showing it to be less steep than he supposed. Returning to the attack, he was repulsed by bad weather in 1876, but in July 1877 he set out with M. C. Payot and Alphonse Payot. After spending the night on the rocks of Pic Eccles (as it is now known), the party started out just before three, skirted the upper basin of the glacier, went up the couloir which strikes the Peuterey ridge well above the Col du Peuterey, and climbed the upper part of the ridge and over Mont Blanc du Courmayeur to the summit of Mont Blanc.

Eccles' climb was the first solution of the problem of Mont Blanc from the south. Up to 1939, it was only repeated twice.[4] The courage of these early explorers can be gauged from the fact that until 1927 (when the Peuterey route over the Aiguille Blanche was first accomplished from the Gamba alp) only five parties reached Mont Blanc from the Innominata basin.

The attentive reader may have noticed that Eccles' climb actually took place just before Boileau's ascent of the Meije; apart from this strictly chronological point, Eccles' feat was as definitely the first of the new, as Boileau's was the last of the old, phase, in that it was the ascent of the last major alpine peak.

Of all the figures of this new period, A. F. Mummery was the most striking. To many of his contemporaries he was wholly heterodox, even revolutionary. Today all his heterodoxies have become orthodox; even his very unclassical economic theories have passed into the body of Keynes' *General Theory*. With and without guides, he overcame difficulties believed insuperable, he took risks (as on the Col du Lion) still regarded as excessive, and he wrote one of the most influential climbing books. *My Climbs in the Alps and Caucasus*[5] has probably brought as many young people to the hills as Whymper's *Scrambles*. His partnership with Alexander Burgener, and his guideless group with Norman Collie, G. Hastings and W. C. Slingsby, were alike unsurpassed. His first notable climb was the first ascent of the Zmutt ridge of the Matterhorn, with Alexander Burgener, J. Petrus and A. Gentinetta in 1879 when he was 23; he disappeared on Nanga Parbat when he was 39. In between he laid a tradition and founded a school which is still influential.

After attempting the Grépon (11,421 feet) by the Mer de Glace face (not climbed till 1911, by G. W. Young, H. O. Jones, R. Todhunter with J. Knubel and H. Brocherel), Mummery turned his attention to the Nantillons face of this aiguille. He had with him Alexander Burgener and Benedikt Venetz. He describes the climb as follows:[6]

The ascent of the Nantillons face of the Grépon
from A. F. Mummery, *My Climbs in the Alps and Caucasus*

It turned out that Burgener had to be in Martigny the next morning but one, so, to give him time on our return from the Grépon, to drive over the Tête Noire, we resolved to go up to Blaitière-dessous that evening and make an early start. The tailor duly accomplished his labours and released Venetz, and about four o'clock, with the addition of a porter, we strolled up to the chalet.

We got under weigh at two o'clock the next morning, and, following the route just described, reached the base of the first summit. Passing to the right of this we dropped down a fifteen-feet step and crawled up a smooth rock to the edge of the great cleft which divides the summit ridge into two equal sections. After a careful examination, as there did not appear any other method of descent, we fixed our spare rope, having first tied two or three knots at suitable intervals. Venetz went down first, and after he had made a short inspection he called on us to follow. Burgener descended next, and I brought up the rear in company with the knapsack and an ice-axe. I found the first twenty feet very easy, then I began to think that the Alpine Club rope is too thin for this sort of work, and I noted a curious and inexplicable increase in my weight. To add to these various troubles the axe, which was held by a loop round my arm, caught in a crack and snapped the string. Luckily, by a convulsive jerk, I just managed to catch it in my left hand. This performance, however, greatly excited Burgener, who, unable to see what had happened, thought his Herr and not merely the ice-axe was contemplating a rapid descent on to the Mer de Glace. Having restored our spirits by a quiet consideration of the contents of a certain flask, we set off in pursuit of Venetz, who had carried away our only remaining rope. A convenient flake had split from the mountain on the Nantillons side and offered a fairly easy zigzag path to the top of the tower, which shuts in the great cleft on this side.

We here found one of the many excellences of the Grépon peculiarly well developed. On the Mer de Glace face, from ten to twenty feet below the ridge, a broad road suitable for carriages, bicycles, or other similar conveyances, led us straight along to an obvious chimney by which the last gap was easily attained, thus obviating the necessity of following the ridge and climbing up and down its various irregularities. It is true that this desirable promenade was only to be reached by rounding a somewhat awkward corner, which my companion professed to think difficult, and its continuity was interrupted at another point by a projecting shoulder, which pushed one's centre of gravity further over the Mer de Glace than was wholly pleasant; but, the passage of these minor obstacles excepted, we were able to walk arm in arm along a part of the mountain which we had expected to find as formidable as anything we had encountered. Reaching the last gap, we rejoined Venetz and proceeded to examine the final tower.

It was certainly one of the most forbidding rocks I have ever set eyes on. Unlike the rest of the peak, it was smooth to the touch, and its square-cut edges offered no hold or grip of any sort. True, the block was fractured from top to bottom, but the crack, four or five inches wide, had edges as smooth and true as a mason could have hewn them, and had not one of those irregular and convenient backs not infrequently possessed by such clefts. Even the dangerous help of a semi-loose stone, wedged with doubtful security, between the opposing walls, was lacking. Added to all this a great rock overhung the top, and would obviously require a powerful effort just when the climber was most exhausted.

Under these circumstances, Burgener and I set to work to throw a rope over the top, whilst Venetz reposed in a graceful attitude rejoicing in a quiet pipe. After many efforts, in the course of which both Burgener and I nearly succeeded in throwing ourselves over on to the Mer de Glace, but dismally failed in landing the rope, we became virtuous, and decided that the rock must be climbed by the fair methods of honourable war. To this end we poked up Venetz with the ice-axe (he was by now enjoying a peaceful nap), and we then generally pulled ourselves together and made ready for the crucial struggle.

Our rope-throwing operations had been carried on from the top of a sort of narrow wall, about two feet wide, and perhaps six feet above the gap. Burgener, posted on this wall, stood ready to help Venetz with the ice-axe so soon as he should get within his reach, whilst my unworthy self, planted in the gap, was able to assist him in the first part of his journey. So soon as Venetz got beyond my reach, Burgener leant across

Above: Alexander Burgener, guide and partner of A. F. Mummery on many notable climbs, including the first ascent of the Zmutt ridge of the Matterhorn in 1879.

Opposite: the Chamonix Aiguilles, to which mountaineers began to turn after all the great peaks had fallen. The problems encountered on their bare and precipitous surfaces led to a great advance in rock climbing.

the gap, and, jamming the point of the axe against the face of the rock, made a series of footholds of doubtful security whereon Venetz could rest and gain strength for each successive effort. At length he got above all these adventitious aids and had to depend exclusively on his splendid skill. Inch by inch he forced his way, gasping for breath, and his hand wandering over the smooth rock in those vague searches for non-existent holds which it is positively painful to witness. Burgener and I watched him with intense anxiety, and it was with no slight feeling of relief that we saw the fingers of one hand reach the firm hold offered by the square-cut top. A few moments' rest, and he made his way over the projecting rock, whilst Burgener and I yelled ourselves hoarse. When the rope came down for me, I made a brilliant attempt to ascend unaided. Success attended my first efforts, then came a moment of metaphorical suspense, promptly followed by the real thing; and, kicking like a spider, I was hauled on to the top, where I listened with unruffled composure to sundry sarcastic remarks concerning those who put their trust in tennis shoes and scorn the sweet persuasion of the rope.

The summit is of palatial dimensions and is provided with three stone chairs. The loftiest of these was at once appropriated by Burgener for the ice-axes, and the inferior members of the party were bidden to bring stones to build it securely in position. This solemn rite being duly performed, we stretched ourselves at full length and mocked M. Couttet's popgun at Chamonix

with a pop of far more exhilarating sort.

The aged narrative from which I have been quoting ends abruptly at this point. Before, however, quitting the summit of one of the steepest rocks in the Alps, I may perhaps be permitted to ask certain critics whether the love of rock-climbing is so heinous and debasing a sin that its votaries are no longer worthy to be ranked as mountaineers, but are to be relegated to a despised and special class of 'mere gymnasts'.

It would appear at the outset wholly illogical to deny the term 'mountaineer' to any man who is skilled in the art of making his way with facility in mountain countries. To say that a man who climbs because he is fond of mountaineering work is not a mountaineer, whilst a man who climbs because it is essential to some scientific pursuit in which he is interested, is a mountaineer, is contrary to the first principles of a logical definition, and I trust will never become general. It may be freely admitted that science has a higher social value than sport, but that does not alter the fact that mountaineering is a sport, and by no possible method can be converted into geology, or botany, or topography. That the technique of our sport has made rapid progress is alleged against us as a sort of crime, but I venture to say, in reality, it is a matter, not for regret, but for congratulation. To emulate the skill of their guides was the ideal of the early climbers, and I trust it will still be the ideal that we set before ourselves. A terminology which suggests that as a man approaches this goal, as he increases in mountaineering skill he ceases to be a mountaineer, stands self-condemned, and must be remorselessly eliminated from the literature of our sport.

Probably most mountaineers would agree that the charm of mountain scenery is to be found in every step taken in the upper world. The strange interfolding of the snows, the gaunt, weird crags of the ridges, the vast, blue, icicle-fringed crevasse, or the great smooth slabs sloping downwards through apparently bottomless space, are each and all no less lovely than the boundless horizon of the summit view. The self-dubbed mountaineers, however, fail to grasp this essential fact. To them the right way up a peak is the easiest way, and all the other ways are wrong ways. Thus they would say, to take an instance from a well-known peak, if a man goes up the Matterhorn to enjoy the scenery, he will go by the Hörnli route; if he goes by the Z'Mutt ridge, it is, they allege, merely the difficulties of the climb that attract him. Now, this reasoning would appear to be wholly fallacious. Among the visions of mountain loveliness that rise before my mind none are fairer than the stupendous cliffs and fantastic crags of the Z'Mutt ridge. To say that this route with its continuously glorious scenery is, from an aesthetic point of view, the wrong way, while the Hörnli route, which, despite the noble distant prospect, is marred by the meanness of its screes and its paper-besprinkled slopes, is the right, involves a total insensibility to the true mountain feeling.

The suspicion, indeed, sometimes crosses my mind that the so-called mountaineer confounds the pleasure

he derives from photography or from geological or other research, with the purely aesthetic enjoyment of noble scenery. Doubtless, the summit of a peak is peculiarly well adapted to these semi-scientific pursuits, and if the summit is the only thing desired, the easiest way up is obviously the right way; but from a purely aesthetic standpoint, the Col du Lion, the teeth of the Z'Mutt ridge, or Carrel's Corridor, whilst affording as exquisite a distant prospect, combine with it the dramatic force of a splendid foreground of jagged ridge, appalling precipice, and towering mist-veiled height.

The importance of foreground cannot, I think, be overrated, and it is obvious that the more difficult an ascent the bolder and more significant will usually be the immediate surroundings of the traveller. In other words, the aesthetic value of an ascent generally varies with its difficulty. This, necessarily, leads us to the conclusion that the most difficult way up the most difficult peaks is always the right thing to attempt, whilst the easy slopes of ugly screes may with propriety be left to the scientists, with M. Janssen at their head. To those who, like myself, take a non-utilitarian view of the mountains, the great ridge of the Grépon may be safely recommended, for nowhere can the climber find bolder towers, wilder clefts, or more terrific precipices; nowhere, a fairer vision of lake and mountain, mist-filled valleys, and riven ice.

Eleven years later Mummery made the first guideless ascent of the Grépon (only the fifth in all) with Hastings, Collie and Charles Pasteur. It was to the chapter on the Grépon in his book that Mummery gave the famous title 'An Inaccessible Peak – the Most Difficult Climb in the Alps – An Easy Day for a Lady'.

The Aiguille du Géant had for long seemed an impractically perpendicular pillar; its conquest in 1882 involved the most prolonged and systematic use of artificial aids since 1492, the date of Antoine de Ville's ascent of Mont Aiguille, when he clearly used every engineering device available to contemporary ingenuity. The three Sella brothers, Alessandro, Alfonso, Corradino had with them their cousin Gaudenzio and Jean-Joseph, Battiste and Daniel Maquinaz. For the four preceding days they had been busy hammering in pitons and fixing ropes. Here is Alessandro's account:[7]

The ascent of the Dent du Géant
Alessandro Sella, the *Alpine Journal*, Vol. XI
We made the ascent July 29, 1882, starting from the hut on the Col du Géant. In two hours we found ourselves at the foot of the peak, at the spot where an attempt had formerly been made to throw a rope over the summit by means of rockets. Here we remained some time to allow the rocks to get warmed by the sun. At this spot we left all our traps with our provisions.

A short distance from here we reached the face of the peak, which overlooks the Montenvers. The difficulties begin at the point at which Mr Mummery stopped, and which is about a hundred mètres from

the summit, and not twenty or thirty mètres, as this gentleman says on a visiting card which I found at the foot of the Dent.

With the aid of ropes we got up the terrible slippery wall of rocks which had hitherto stopped everyone, although we were obliged to excavate (or mine) the rock in two places in order to gain the edge *(spigolo)* which overhangs a terrible vertical wall of rocks of about five hundred mètres in height. At times we were suspended in mid-air with a hold for our feet only on small ledges of rock. We then traversed the whole of this face of the peak, where we were obliged again to excavate the rock in order to gain the ridge overhanging the spot from which we had started; at this point we found three steep gullies in succession, so that in order to fix the rope (which was double for better security) we were forced to form a ladder by means of our ice-axes. We then gained the crest which leads to the summit without much difficulty, where we were obliged to sit astride.

I think it right to mention that having employed all the rope which we had with us in order to facilitate our descent, by leaving it on the rocks, our party of seven persons was so pressed together through want of space that from prudential motives we thought it better to divide it. Two of us mounted first with two guides, and the others awaited our return with the third guide, and then completed the ascent by the aid of the other two guides. The ascent from the foot of the peak took us about three hours, and the descent about two.

I should likewise mention that the guides worked altogether four days in driving iron stanchions in the rocks for fixing the ropes and excavating (mining) the rocks, which was possible only in places where it was brittle *(sottile)*. We left 100 mètres of rope: it is impossible to descend without it.

Our guides were Jean Joseph Maquinaz of Valtournanche, with his nephew Daniel and his son Battiste. Their conduct was above all praise, and to judge of it rightly you should have seen them at work.

I was accompanied by my brothers Corradino and Alfonso (the latter only seventeen years of age), and my cousin Gaudenzio.

The ascent is certainly very difficult, but not dangerous. At a single point the slope is 60°, generally from 75° to 80°, and in some parts absolutely vertical. The last ridge which leads to the top is, however, not extraordinarily steep.

It was impossible for us, owing to lack of time and rope, to make the ascent of the point nearest the Jorasses. The guides, however, the day before had almost conquered it *(l'avevano quasi superata)*. I understand that later a party from Chamonix succeeded in scaling it.

The Aiguille has a forked summit. The Sellas had climbed the south-western prong (13,150 feet). The ascent of the slightly higher north-eastern prong (13,163 feet) was made three weeks later by W. W. Graham with Alphonse Payot and Auguste Cupelin. The best route on the Aiguille, the only one which permits an entirely 'free' climb, was opened in 1900 by

Opposite: views of the Dolomites: top left, Tre Cime di Lavaredo; top right, the north face of the Civetta; bottom, the peaks of Vajolet.

T. Maischberger, H. Pfannl and F. Zimmer.

Julius Kugy, an Austrian from Trieste, was the great explorer of the Julian Alps (in Yugoslavia) and later a tireless climber in the massifs of Monte Rosa and Mont Blanc. He wrote *Alpine Pilgrimage (Aus dem Leben eines Bergsteiger)*,[8] as beautiful a book as has ever been written about mountains. In it he describes how, coming over the Théodule with Alexander Burgener, they met a tall Englishman riding up to the Schwarzsee Hotel. 'He cut a most unknightly figure

on the mule, sitting all hunched up, with his long legs almost trailing on the ground. I was amused at this mule-rider with his ice-axe. "Who's that poor fellow?" I asked Burgener, who had greeted him with enthusiasm. "That's Mummery," he replied, "he climbs better than I do." '

Kugy also relates how his friend, G. Bolaffio, had dreamed of the Neuvaz side of Mont Dolent (12,540 feet), on which he saw a possible route. 'I had myself examined it from the Grand Luis, but I should never have suspected the possibility of an ascent of Mont Dolent among the formidable gullies and ice-cliffs of this remote S.W. corner of the Neuvaz basin.' They tried it at once but conditions were against them; returning in 1904 they succeeded in climbing the mountain by the east face, finishing along the north-north-western ridge. Their guides were Joseph Croux and Cyprien Savoye. 'A few days later Croux asked me if I had noticed anything from the north ridge of Mont Dolent. "Certainly I noticed something," I replied, "the possibility of climbing Mont Dolent from the Argentière glacier." Yes, that was his idea too: it would be harder than the Neuvaz route, but in his view it was the greatest and worthiest problem which the Mont Blanc range could still offer.'[9] Two years later the opportunity came.

The ascent of Mont Dolent by the Argentière glacier
from Julius Kugy, *Alpine Pilgrimage*

We started at 1 am, and by dawn were at the bergschrund. It was not so large here as we had found it beneath the col, but it was not far behind it. Steep, black ice above led to the rocks. We had crossed the schrund almost directly below the Brèche de l'Amône, from which a steep, narrow, slabby rock-couloir ran down, opening straight above us. Here we took to the rocks. The couloir being apparently impassable, we kept to its right. At first all went well; then a smooth slab, quite seventy feet high, rose so steep that it defied our efforts to climb it unaided. Croux tried a bold manoeuvre with the rope. With left hand grasping a poor hold, hanging to the rocks with legs outspread, and his body bent back, he endeavoured with his right hand to throw one end of the rope round a small tooth above him to the right, while I was to hold the other end firm. If the rope caught, he was to swing with its help across the slab. He threw at least ten times, and each time the rope slid off. The situation became critical; he was clinging high above us in a fearfully exposed place, and it seemed superhuman that he could hold on so long. Below us was the abyss, the dark ice-wall, and the gaping crevasse. Again and again, with an iron determination, he drew in the rope, aimed and threw.

'Croux,' I called up, 'don't risk too much. I can't hold you if you fall!'

'Si vous commencez déjà à avoir peur maintenant, qu'est-ce que ce sera plus tard?' came the gruff answer. Then I understood that we would go to our uttermost. Chamonix versus Courmayeur!

The rope held. 'Attention!' I heard from above. A

swing, a quick scraping on the rock, and Croux had conquered the slab.

The rocks grew easier, with stretches of scree, and we made height rapidly somewhat to the left. The gap of the Brèche de l'Amône was now close at hand. We reached a niche, shut in by a semicircle of vertical cliffs, above the head of the couloir. Here our enterprise threatened to fail; there was no visible chance of scaling the final wall. Our only hope was a narrow, partly-glazed chimney, into which we could not see properly, as it faced the precipice. Croux called me to his side, and climbed from my shoulders into the chimney. He disappeared behind a bluff, and no sound came for half an hour. Only now and then, we noticed from the movements of the rope that he was at work. No answer came to our questions. At last his 'Venez!' rang out, clear and encouraging. When I climbed round the corner, I saw him high above me; he had overcome the final wall, and was standing two-thirds of the way up, on a well-defined ledge. At his side was a small belay in the wall, set there as if by Providence, to which he had fastened the spare rope. The wall below him was of granite, russet-coloured and vertical, with holds far apart from each other, like mushrooms. Even with the aid of the spare rope, it was difficult enough to reach them, but once grasped, they were as safe as iron stanchions. Nevertheless, the climbing of this splendid wall was a first-class feat. The highest third is set in steps, and here the rocks lie back. A look of wild triumph was on Croux's face. The Brèche de l'Amône was won, and from now onward the ground was familiar.

It was already late, and Croux urged us to hasten. 'Je ne veux pas bivaquer,' he called back, when we moved too slowly for his taste. We were soon beside the bottle we had left on our previous visit. On the ice-slope, Proment did not work quick enough for him; very tired as he was, Croux again took the lead, and cut all the steps still needed before the traverse on the west face. It was 4.45 pm when we reached the summit of Mont Dolent.

The last years before 1914 were largely dominated, at least in the western Alps, by Geoffrey Winthrop Young and V. J. E. Ryan. Ryan always climbed with guides, Franz and Joseph Lochmatter, or sometimes Joseph and Gabriel Lochmatter, and the Alps are littered with Ryan-Lochmatter routes. Ryan never carried anything on a climb, he never cut a step and his routes seem to have been designed by the Lochmatters; hardly the complete mountaineer but nevertheless a superb climber. He recorded nothing; what is known about his climbs was extracted in conversation from his guides. Young, like Mummery, climbed sometimes with and sometimes without guides; his great partner was Joseph Knubel. He delighted in the design of elegant routes and he described them in polished and efficient prose; he was also a poet. Young and Knubel sometimes joined forces with Ryan and the Lochmatters, most notably on the south face of the Täschhorn. They overcame this terrible wall in storm and driving snow; in these conditions,

Franz Lochmatter's lead up the overhang, in nailed boots, no artificial aids, remains unsurpassed. Young's account is justly famous and is in all the anthologies. No *cassecou* climb has been better recorded.

Here we shall give Young's account of a less nerve-racking performance, as an example of the good guideless climbing that was going on at this time. It was 1909. Young had long had designs on the long south-eastern ridge of the Nesthorn. This had been descended by the Hopkinsons and Slingsby in 1895

The Aiguille du Géant, first climbed by four of the Sella family and three guides in 1882, an ascent preceded by four days of preparation, hammering in pitons and fixing ropes.

but never ascended. Young was at Belalp with George Mallory and Donald Robertson; it was evening before the weather improved, so that a night approach was necessary for any climb the next day. After wasting some hours trying to find a local man to help with the night march, it was 3 am before they started up towards the Unterbachen glacier without any particular plan. Out of the fog the day broke late but with signs of promise, so they climbed the Unterbachhorn. They then decided to attempt the ridge to the Nesthorn. Here is Young's description of the last part of the climb:[10]

The ascent of the south-eastern ridge of the Nesthorn
from G. W. Young, *On High Hills*

At last we found ourselves at the foot of the dark tower which shows conspicuously on the skyline, as the last great obstacle upon the ridge. To us below, its summit had all the appearance of yet another independent spire, overhanging on all its three visible sides. But we knew that this Titan also must be propping his shoulders against the supporting arête behind. The ridge above would be ours if we could but grip him within his guard, and tug him by the red beard, and finally get some hold upon his nodding fringe of snowy curls.

Leaving Donald as our anchor in a rock ingle at the foot of the bulging north wall, George and I clambered twenty feet up the edge of the tower and on to a triangular bracket that broke its precipitous profile. Above us, the slabs shot up sheer, and ended under a hopeless penthouse of projecting rock. I craned round the edge and looked across the southern face of the tower. Downward, the fluted red-rent crags rushed into nothingness: over the rim of the shelf upon which we stood the eye plunged disconcertingly, until it met the gleam of the glacier far and deep below in the Gredetschthal. Upward, the crags of this southern face rose vertically for twenty feet, and then all further sight of them was cut off by the cornice jutting above our heads against the wind-speed of the clouds.

Discouraged upon this side, I leant round the other corner of the slabby edge and looked across the darker northern face of the tower. For some ten feet above our heads the shattered organ-pipes on the face looked practicable; but there, just where the rock began to give back, a huge mass of snow, or probably snow-ice, had attached itself to the roughness of the face, like a lump of ivy on an old church tower or a great fungoid growth on a tree-trunk. It was far too big to be cleared away, and its face or outside surface was undercut, the steepest snow wall I have seen except upon the broken upper lip of a bergschrund. Supposing that the face of this mass could be climbed, and that the mass held to the wall, it looked possible to creep along its sloping upper surface to the foot of a small icy chimney between some higher organ-pipes; and, by this, mount to the edge of the ridge again, where it emerged from under the rear helmet-peak of the tower. There seemed, indeed, to me to be more 'supposing' than support upon this northern face. I had been working in the lead for some ten hours with-

out halt, and hesitated before the bold effort of strength and faith which the insecure snow wall would clearly require.

Meanwhile, George had been making his own examination of the flutings on the south face, and on my return to the mantelpiece he remarked confidently that he thought it would go. The effortless ease with which he wound up rocks which reduced me to convulsive struggling gave me reason to hope that he might be right. It was for emergencies such as this that the younger and more brilliant cragsmen of the party had been so far, somewhat selfishly, kept in reserve upon the rope. And selfishness had still another share in the decision; because a change of leader at this point would mean some useful rest before we began the race with darkness down the crevassed glaciers of the north face: a last lap, for which every hoarded faculty and every pound of energy and experience might be needed.

We changed places on the rope. At about my shoulder level, as I leaned against it, there was a nick on the extreme south corner of the slab. Across this I could pass George's rope, and as my footing was good and my two hands could hold and spring the rope conveniently on either side of the nick, I felt certain of keeping the belay sufficiently 'indirect' to be sound. George traversed out from our shelf, moving subtly across the red rib and hollow of the vertical face; then he disappeared behind a farther volute. I could hear him; but the rope ceased to run out. The minutes passed. He was trying for some possible line up the smooth flutings, clinging to the wall, and with the overhang above checking each attempt. The long-continued effort must have been exhausting, for the holds over all this wall were few and inadequate, up to the level at which they ceased altogether. It was a relief to see him returning into sight, swinging agilely across

the cliff on a broken line of finger-holds.

But, unexpectedly, when he reached the scoop between the two nearest upright slats, about ten feet away from me, I saw him glance upward, pause, and then begin to wrestle up it. The sight of my shelf, recalling our dangerous alternative route up the north face, may have suggested to him a last attempt on the south wall as a preferable course. So far as I could see, he had no real holds at all; but he fought his way up magnificently, until all that remained below the rock cornice, which cut off everything else above from my sight, was his two boots. They were clinging, cat-like, and continued to cling for long seconds, to almost imperceptible irregularities on the walls of the rift. The mere sight of them made me breathless; and I tightened every muscle, ready to spring the rope on its nick. For, on such foot-hold no climber would choose to wait long, were his hand-holds adequate for a lift; and if George's hand-holds were *not* adequate—!

Anyway, they did not serve for the gymnastic backward swing, outward and upward, which he was forced to risk. I saw the boots flash from the wall without even a scrape; and, equally soundlessly, a grey streak flickered downward, and past me, and out of sight. So much did the wall, to which he had clung so long, overhang that from the instant he lost hold he touched nothing until the rope stopped him in mid-air over the glacier. I had had time to think, as I flung my body forward on to the belayed rope, grinding it and my hands against the slab, that no rope could stand

such a jerk; and even to think out what our next action must be – so instantaneous is thought. The boots had been standing some fifteen to twenty feet above me, so that the clear fall could not have been much less than forty feet. But the rope held, springing like an elastic band, and cracking under my chest and hands on the rock. We were using that year a then rather popular Austrian woven rope, since entirely condemned. Whenever, in later years, I have looked back at the tabulated rope-tests, which show that this rope is warranted to snap like straw under the jerk of a man's weight falling from, I think, five feet, I have thought again of the transfigured second in which I realized that the rope had, miraculously, held. The fact being, I suppose, that two rather abnormally resilient anatomies at either end of a rope may introduce a confusing element into the nicest theory of strains.

At first there was nothing to do but hold on, and watch the pendulum movement of a tense cord straining over the edge and down into space. My first cautious shouts were unanswered. Then there came, from nowhere, a tranquil call to let out more rope, and to 'lower away'. So soon as I was convinced that, owing to the good fortune of a clear fall, he had not even been hurt, I complied. The short visible length of rope slackened, and then began to jerk along the edge of the shelf on which I stood. George had spied a line of possible holds across the face of the cliff below him. As I lowered him on the rope, he coolly hooked himself in to them with his axe, and proceeded to make his way along the invisible cliff underneath me. Presently he appeared up a slanting groove, and rejoined me on the mantelshelf, apparently entirely undisturbed. He had not even let go of his axe during the fall.

The whole incident had passed so swiftly and un-

emotionally—I had almost said with such decorum—that Donald, twenty feet below us, and round the corner on the north face, remained unaware that anything unusual had happened. Nor did we enlighten him at the time. Immediate action was of importance, so as to waste not one of our precious moments and to leave no time for the reaction that has sometimes as ill an effect upon a party as the crisis itself. Without waiting to alter the order, I called to both end men to look after their ropes to me—which gave me a two-fold anchor—and set to work on the north face of the tower, only vexed with myself for having allowed it to frighten me before.

Not that I liked it. The crawl up and over the baffle of the snow-fungus was an anxious performance. In angle and character of hold it was not unlike that very strenuous problem, the climb up the loose, higher part of the cut wall of a haystack. Its protrusion pushed me out of balance; and I had to try for a pick-hold at arm's-length over its crest and trust to toe-holds kicked timorously up its indurating snow face. I heard myself grunt with relief as I got a friction arm-hold over the edge, on the sloping snow-shelf above. I wriggled my chest up on to the slant of the shelf, and then swung up my legs, so that I lay along the narrow snow. A few caterpillar coilings, and then at last I found a finger-hold on the smooth rock wall behind my snow-fungus. This reduced my interest in the question of the stability of the whole jerry-built attachment. I wormed along the shelf on my chest, with finger-holds on the wall and feet kicking in air, until I could force my shoulders into the lower end of the ice-chimney between the higher organ-pipes, and so stand upright on a solid once again, and pant comfortably. A few seconds later I was up the chimney, and sitting astride of the sharp snowy neck that joined the head of our tower to the backbone of the main ridge. If only the severe but short and well-protected effort had not been shirked a long half-hour before, what nerves and minutes we might have saved!

With our remainder of daylight and of vigour now still further diminished, we had to economize both, if we were yet to make a way down the north face before night. I determined at once to follow a course which I held to be the most suitable, theoretically, in such an emergency. Mallory was unhurt and unshaken; so was our confidence in him. The continuance of the ridge above us looked stern in the falling dusk, but seemed moderately free of snow. So, again our finest and fastest rock climber passed ahead on the rope.

He appeared, through the shadows, to float like a thistle-down up the last abrupt steps: up and up, through always denser cold and closer darkness. Now and again my eye was half-caught by a splash of light like an aureole that came and went over his stir of shadow moving above me. And then I saw that this was George's long hair, roughed out by the wind and catching or losing as he climbed the level of the last sunlight lifting above the ridge. Even the austerity of the final brow, which arched smoothly and darkly upward against the summit snows and frowned sullenly out upon the evening, gave him no pause. The un-

mistakable feel of the wind that tells us there is nothing now between us and open skies met our faces. A short race along the icy crest, and over rock bosses that spiked like huge red horse-chestnuts out of the snow, and we stood together on the silver tip of the highest cone.

Seven o'clock by the watch. Twelve hours since our start up the rocks of the Unterbächhorn, and with hardly a halt or longer relaxation than an occasional glance round at the promise of the weather.

The last phase of sunset seemed to have been waiting for us, and greeted our eyes across the summit with a long horizon of copper-coloured surf. The breakers of light were beating upon the far sides of the Bietschhorn and of the western Oberland peaks. They sprayed round the mountain edges and across the passes towards us in spurts of gold, and ran in a spent wash of silvery bronze up the nearer snows to our feet. Behind us, to the east, the sunward slopes of the Aletschhorn, of the Finsteraarhorn, and of their white neighbours were beginning to deflect the warm and coloured lighting from their facets in a colder order of tones; and already the pallor of alpine sleep was creeping upon their great snow faces and chilling through the ruddy reflections.

There are evenings in the Alps when the sunset pours out its whole colour-box on to the sky above us, but when the snow peaks, the glaciers, and the rock walls about us will have none of it. They remain colourless, ghostly, and unreceptive; as we may see the forms and faces of sleepers in a dark room startled only in outline and a resentful pallor by the passage of a candle. And there are evenings when every corner of rock, every snow prism, and every ripple of falling glacier, catches fire and colour, and contributes its own varied light to the illumination.

Our few moments of triumph on the summit were transfigured by this blaze of sympathetic celebration. The nearer rock spires reached up towards us their late glowing torches. The recession of snow peaks along the Oberland bore each its dying beacon, ash-red at the heart and hurrying gold at the edges. The uneven snow on the northern slopes descending from our feet caught the shallow waves of retreating colour, and threw them back lower and fainter at each instant as the sun sank. Until the interrupting rock crests of the north ridge hemmed the rays finally beyond our sight; and the snows about us took shelter from the cold inrush of darkness under a uniform monotony of steely disregard.

We were, in fact, in time to overtake the last message of the sunset, but we had no leisure even for food. Very rarely have we been so late upon a peak, and never, elsewhere, but of intention. In a sense we had won; but at a price. We had bought the thrill of victory somewhat dearly, with the sacrifice of the most precious moments of a mountaineering day, the mid-day moments when we can rest relaxed and apart from each other in sunshine, and abandon ourselves to the realization of a purpose happily fulfilled, and to the mere irrational rapture of unthinking and un-troubled well-being.

Franz Lochmatter, whose lead up the Täschhorn with Ryan and Young remains unsurpassed. He climbed mainly with Ryan and seems to have designed most of his routes.

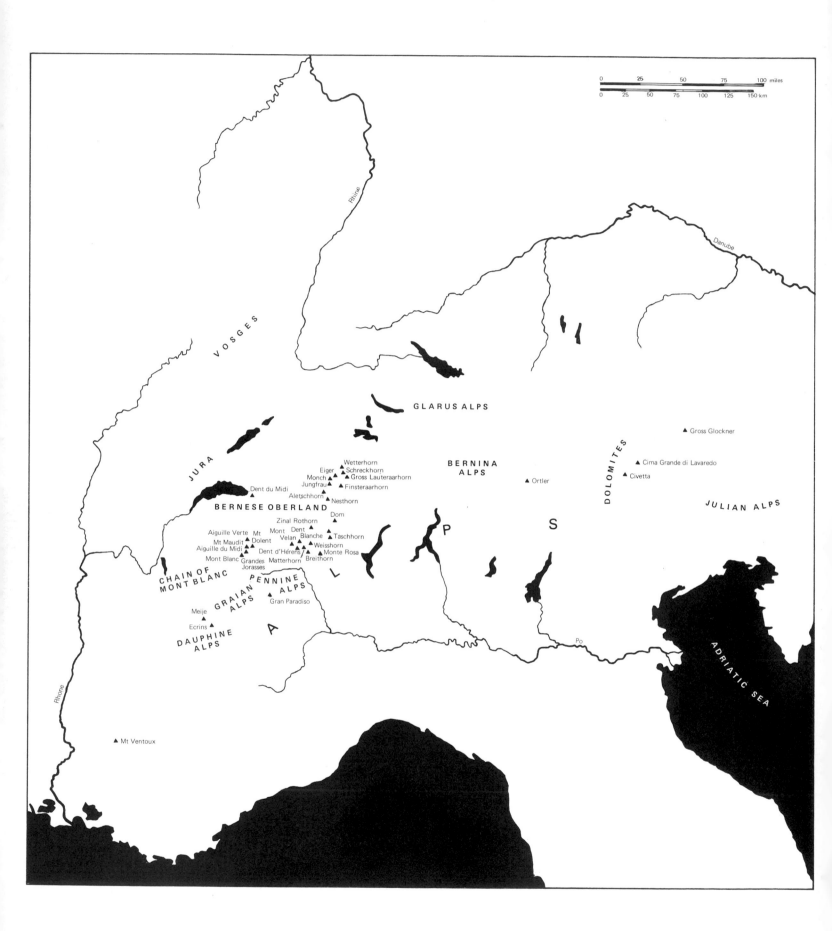

VOSGES

Rhine

Danube

GLARUS ALPS

JURA

BERNINA
ALPS

▲ Gross Glockner

DOLOMITES

▲ Cima Grande di Lavaredo

Wetterhorn
Eiger ▲ Schreckhorn
Monch ▲ ▲ ▲ Gross Lauteraarhorn
Jungfrau ▲ ▲ Finsteraarhorn
Dent du Midi ▲ Aletschhorn
▲ Nesthorn

▲ Ortler

▲ Civetta

JULIAN ALPS

BERNESE OBERLAND

Dom
Zinal Rothorn ▲
Aiguille Verte Mt ▲ Mont Dent ▲ Taschhorn
Mt Maudit ▲ ▲ Dolent Velan Blanche ▲
Aiguille du Midi ▲ ▲ ▲ ▲ Weisshorn
Mont Blanc ▲ Dent d'Hérens ▲ ▲ Monte Rosa
Grandes Matterhorn Breithorn
Jorasses

CHAIN OF
MONT BLANC

PENNINE
ALPS

A   L   P   S

GRAIAN
ALPS

Meije ▲
▲ Gran Paradiso

Ecrins ▲

A

DAUPHINE
ALPS

Po

ADRIATIC SEA

Rhone

▲ Mt Ventoux

0   25   50   75   100 miles
0   25 50 75 100 125 150 km

Women climbers

Throughout this period women came increasingly into the picture. While it is true that Maria Paradis (1808) and Henriette d'Angeville (1838) had climbed Mont Blanc earlier, the first woman to make a regular and successful practice of mountaineering was Lucy Walker (1835-1916). Her father, Frank, and her brother, Horace, were both leading mountaineers; in 1858 they took Lucy with them to the Théodule and then to the Monte Moro, a pass leading from Saas to Macugnaga. Thus she, too, became an enthusiast. For twenty years she climbed regularly with the family and, almost always, with Melchior Anderegg. In this way Lucy collected a very respectable tally of main alpine peaks. In 1871, three days after climbing the Weisshorn, she was the first woman on top of the Matterhorn, an exploit which earned her some admiring verses in *Punch*. Apart from this suspect eccentricity, she was in every way a model Victorian lady. She generally climbed in a print dress, but more usually ladies wore long heavy skirts, their hats bound on with veils; the more dashing wore riding breeches under their skirts, which they removed when they had passed the last chalets.

Some of those hard on Miss Walker's heels had more distinguished records. Meta Brevoort, with her nephew Coolidge and Christian Almer, made many fine expeditions, including the first ascent of the Pic Centrale of the Meije (1870) and the first winter ascents of the Wetterhorn and the Jungfrau. Kathleen Richardson, who often climbed with Mary Papillon, had a record including the first traverses of Les Ecrins from south to north (1888) and of the Petit and Grand Dru (1889). Mrs E. P. Jackson did 140 *grandes courses*, including a winter traverse of the Jungfrau (1888). Slightly later was Lily Bristow, probably the first woman to climb on level terms with competent male guideless climbers; on the second guideless ascent of the Grépon, as Mummery records, 'Miss Bristow showed the representatives of the Alpine Club the way in which steep rocks should be climbed'; she was the lady for whom the Grépon was an 'easy day'.

The founder and first President of the Ladies' Alpine Club was Elizabeth Hawkins-Whitshead (1861-1934), whose career is sometimes confusing to follow as she turns up successively as Mrs Burnaby, Mrs Main and Mrs Aubrey le Blond, though generally remembered under the last name. Well-born, with striking looks and beautiful manners, she was able to do daring things with smooth assurance. Sent to the Engadine for her health in 1879, she walked one day up to the Diavolezza Pass, was entranced by the view, took up mountaineering and climbed regularly until 1900. She did most of the classic routes, specialised in the Bernina and in winter climbing. She started her winter career by crossing the Col du Tacul, which had never been crossed even in summer. She made the first winter ascent of the Disgrazia in 1896 from the Forno hut with Martin Schocher, a very long expedition.

Others of prominence were the great arabist Gertrude Bell, Mrs Norman Neruda, Paola Weisinger and

Opposite: a map of the Alps.

Below left: Henriette d'Angeville inspecting her guides (1838) before setting out to climb Mont Blanc.

Below: Mrs Aubrey le Blond, who climbed regularly until 1900. The founder and first president of the Ladies' Alpine Club, she specialised in the Bernina and winter climbing.

J. Hébert.
1838.

63

Mary Varale. The first manless climb seems to have been the Cima Grande di Lavaredo in 1907 by the Baronesses Rolanda and Illona Eötvös. Eleanor Noll-Hasenclever was on the first guideless traverse of the Drus in 1911; she descended the Macugnaga face of Monte Rosa in 1919 and, with Hans Pfann and Welzenbach, made the two-day traverse of the Matterhorn and the Dent d'Hérens in 1923. She was killed on the Weisshorn in 1925.

In the 1920s and subsequently the number of women climbers increased rapidly. Some credit for this advance should be given to the Groupe de Haute Montagne who admitted men and women equally on climbing qualification. (This is no longer true; latterly the GHM has made a distinction in the qualifications required from men and women.) Climbing among friends in the GHM many women developed their natural ability to a high degree. Among the many distinguished women climbers of the last half century may be mentioned Una Cameron, Miriam Underhill (née O'Brien), Dorothy Richards (née Pilley), Alice Damesme, Micheline Morin, Nea Morin (née Barnard), Claude Kogan, Signorina N. Pietrasanta, Loulou Boulaz, Sonia Livanos, Christine de Colombel, Simone Badier.

It is interesting to note that the ladies took a particularly prominent place in the development of winter mountaineering of which Miss Brevoort, Mrs Jackson, Mrs Charlet-Straton and Mrs le Blond were all pioneers.

The climbers of this period before 1914 were still almost wholly from the professional classes. Their equipment would seem laughable to the young men and women of today. They had no tools beyond rope, axe and crampons; many indeed still looked on crampons as an unfair innovation. (Crampons, steel claws strapped to the boots to improve security on ice, had in fact been used by peasants since the Middle Ages but had dropped out of use in later years.) Boots were leather-soled with iron or steel nails; clothes were the same as those used for, say, a day's shooting in the country, a Norfolk jacket of hard-wearing tweed, no windproofs or duvets. Nights out had become less usual as club huts were built high above the villages. Rope, of course, was manilla or, occasionally, silk. The ice-axe had finally displaced the alpenstock.

The Matterhorn and the Dent d'Hérens. The two-day traverse of both mountains was first achieved by Eleanor Noll-Hasenclever with Hans Pfann and Wello Welzenbach in 1923.

Left: instructional illustrations from Dent's *Mountaineering* (1892), left, and Zsigmondy's *Die Gefahren der Alpen* (1885). They show the conventional mountaineering wear of the period and also a very early piton being used, with karabiner or sling, as a running belay.

5 The Alps between the Wars

After the legshows and the brandies
And all the pick-me-ups for tired
Men there is a feeling
Something more is required.
                    Louis MacNeice

The strategy of attrition so successfully pursued by all the general staffs meant that a new generation came to the hills after the first world war. This no doubt made easier the spread of new attitudes and new techniques. The great feature of this period was the adoption and elaboration of methods of artificial climbing; that is, climbing with the use of pitons and the rope technique that they make possible. A *piton* is a metal peg consisting of a blade at one end, which is hammered into a crack in the rock, and a ring at the other, into which a *karabiner* (or snap-link) is clipped.

The first use of a piton was for security on a stance where a natural belay is lacking. (A *belay* is a rock feature round which a rope can be run or hitched to pro-

Right: traversing on rock with the aid of pitons. The interwar period was remarkable for the introduction and refinement of artificial climbing with pitons and ropes.

Opposite: the Spigolo Giallo in the Tre Cime di Lavaredo in the Dolomites on whose sheer limestone cliffs Germans, Austrians and Italians pioneered new techniques and new routes.

tect a stationary climber; it can also be ice hewn into a knob, an ice-axe jammed in a fissure or driven deep into the snow.) A piton can also be used, generally with a karabiner and a sling, as an artificial hold where nature provides none. A leader can protect himself on a long run-out or a 'thin' pitch by passing the rope between himself and his second through a rope sling or karabiner attached to a piton; this is a 'running belay'.

It was soon realised that, if the leader threaded his rope through a karabiner clipped to a piton inserted above him, he could actually secure an upward pull from his second below him. By climbing on two ropes and using pitons above him alternately to his right and left, this upward pull from below can be applied consecutively to maintain upward progress. Pitons can, of course, also be inserted in overhangs to enable a climber to proceed out and over an impending 'roof'. The other main device is an *étrier*, which is a very short rope ladder for clipping into a piton-held karabiner, thus providing reasonably comfortable footholds.

Obviously a climber practised in the use of this equipment can surmount all sorts of obstacles which are quite unclimbable free, i.e. without such equipment. Yet it would be wrong to jump to the conclusion that all rock faces, however steep, overhanging or holdless, can be overcome by this type of artificial climbing. Given unlimited time and inexhaustible engineering resources, it may be true that nothing would be unclimbable; on an actual climb time and resources are always limited. Cracks suitable for the insertion of pitons may be absent; artificial climbing is strenuous and time-consuming; the sheer weight of equipment required for prolonged artificial climbing is a severe handicap. And ideally every piton put in by the leader is removed by the last man, involving the expenditure of further time and energy. This is not always done and is, in some instances, impracticable. There are now many climbs with a more or less permanent ladder of pitons in place.

Where cracks are too wide for pitons, wooden wedges are used. Where there are no cracks at all, holes can be drilled and expansion bolts placed, but these consume even more time than pegs and cannot be removed by the last man. *Mutatis mutandis*, the same techniques can be applied on ice as on rock, the appropriate piton being much longer and often in the form of a tube or screw of aluminium alloy. A simpler artificial aid is a pebble jammed in a crack, thereby improvising a hold or a belay. This must have been resorted to very early; in British hills it played its part from the 1920s. Nowadays climbers commonly carry a selection of steel nuts of different sizes which are used in place of stones.

These new techniques were tried out tentatively by a few Germans and Austrians, notably Dülfer, before 1914, but the systematic development of the new tools and new methods was carried out by the Munich school in the early 1920s. (Their final development to date has been by the Americans in the Yosemite Valley, who have pioneered a radical change of method—see Chapter 9.) The Munich school soon achieved hitherto impossible successes in the vertical and overhanging limestone cliffs of the Bavarian Alps and the Dolomites. Most outstanding amongst them, perhaps, was Emil Solleder; his routes, such as the direct line on the north-west face of the Civetta, still retain their awe-inspiring reputation.

The Italians, in close contact with the Germans and Austrians in the Dolomites, were the next to adopt artificial techniques and soon showed their successful mastery by a number of startling new routes. According to Riccardo Cassin, the first Dolomite climb in which pitons were systematically used as an aid to progress was the north wall of the Cima Grande di Lavaredo, climbed by Comici and the Dimai brothers in 1933. The Italian school centred on Emilio Comici at Lecco. Like Dülfer before him, Comici was a pianist who looked on mountaineering in artistic terms. He sought the most elegant line up a mountain; this is often the *direttissima*, a direct straight line vertically up the face ending exactly on the summit. That such a man was an outstanding exponent of artificial climbing shows that such techniques are not necessarily unaesthetic. Nevertheless, almost all climbers, including the greatest, prefer to climb free. As Hermann Buhl (see Chapter 10) wrote: 'There is no pleasure like that of balancing up and up, lightfooted and unburdened, free of all mechanical aids.'

The new artificial methods were much criticised as being steeple-jacking rather than mountaineering. The critics overlooked the fact that artificial aids were as old as the sport itself. The pioneers carried ladders almost as standard equipment; Whymper devised and used a grapnel; as did Winkler; Tyndall took, not only a collapsible ladder, but long iron nails and a hammer for his second assault on the Matterhorn; the Sella climb of the Dent du Géant required four days' engineering work with pegs and ropes.

It was only in the late 1930s that the French began to use artificial aids, and the British were later still. In Britain they long lay taboo, vaguely unsporting. Mainly for this reason the interwar years seem to have been dominated by German and Italian climbers, at least in the Alps. This is also because the three climbs that attracted most attention in the press, namely the north face of the Matterhorn, the Eigerwand and the north face of the Grandes Jorasses, all fell to German or Austro-German parties and the best and highest northern spur of the Jorasses to Italians. This publicity was not wholly due to the intrinsic merits of the climbs; it was partly a result of the sensationalism that

The north-west face of the Civetta, climbed in a direct line in the 1920s by Emil Solleder, an outstanding member of the Munich School.

Opposite: The north face of the Dent d'Hérens, climbed by Finch in 1923. His route crosses the glacier terrace from right to left before joining the east ridge.

surrounded them not only because they involved disaster and death but also because they generated a spirit of competitive nationalism. These climbs became a sort of Olympic Games with all the distasteful by-products that that implies. All three climbs are very steep, beset by falling stones and ice, and all invoked artificial aids though not continuously.

The climbing revolution did not seriously reach the western Alps until the 1930s. While it raged in the eastern Alps in the 1920s, French, Swiss and British parties were still putting up notable climbs in the older tradition. For example, George Finch brought off in 1923 a climb which he had studied with meticulous care; this was the ascent of the north face of the Dent d'Hérens. Here is the central part of his account:[1]

The ascent of the north face of the Dent d'Hérens
from G. I. Finch, *Alpine Journal*, Vol. XXXV.
At a quarter to midnight, on August 1-2, we left the Schönbühl hut. The moon was hidden behind the Matterhorn, which was silhouetted against its light with almost startling clearness, and it was not until we had gained the moraine of the Stockje that we were able to dispense with the lantern. [A *moraine* is an accumulation of debris carried down by a glacier.] Walking rapidly, and finding our way through the ice-falls without hesitation, we arrived in the upper basin of the Tiefenmatten glacier at a point below the N.W. ridge just where the slopes steepen up towards the bergschrund. Here, sheltered from the cold wind

behind a huge block of fallen ice, we halted (2.30 to 3 am, August 2) to adjust climbing-irons, breakfast, and rearrange knapsacks. I had the pleasure of handing mine over to Peto. We re-lighted the lantern and climbed up to the bergschrund, to find the steps cut two days before quite usable. Once over the bergschrund a steep ice-slope lay between us and the nearest rocks of the N.W. ridge, now about 200 yards away. Alpine literature contains many examples of that looseness of description which permits the raconteur to describe, as ice, a slope covered with inches of good firm snow. But here in front of us was the real thing. On warm days water from the ice-cliffs perched on the rocks above flows down over this slope, not in well-defined channels, but fanwise, so as to leave bare ice. What the angle of the slope is I cannot say, as I had no clinometer, but where we cut across, always keeping about 100 to 150 feet above the upper lip of the bergschrund, it was very steep. Higher up, the inclination was somewhat more gentle; but for two reasons we chose to cross the slope at its steepest – in the first place, fewer steps would bring us to the ridge, and in the second, should stray stones or odd blocks of ice fall in spite of the early hour and the intense cold, there would be much more chance of such missiles going over us than if we were standing on the less steep slopes higher up. The order of the party was as follows. I led, untrammelled by a knapsack, Forster came in the middle, and Peto brought up the rear. How Peto would manage was rather uncertain, as this was his

first serious essay with climbing-irons. Forster was to look after both my rope and Peto's, and would, in the event of a slip on the part of the latter, have to hold him – a task of which I knew he was fully capable if only the steps were well cut and reasonably large. Just as we began to cut our way across the slope a fierce gust of wind blew out the candle; and henceforth, though it was still rather dark, as the light of the moon did not reach the secluded spot directly, we decided to dispense with artificial light. I cut the steps as quickly as possible without wastage of blows, but very carefully. Always the same method – left-handed cutting, for we were traversing from right to left; six or seven medium blows marking out the base, twice as many heavy blows to break down the roof of each step, half a dozen dragging hits to make floor and wall meet well inside, a scrape or two with the adze to make sure that the floor was clean and slanting into the slope, and another of the many steps was ready. But while I was steadily cutting out my first rope's length from Forster, he and Peto were getting the worst of it in a heated difference of opinion with the lantern. Now a lantern which is not burning should be folded up and put away. But this particular sample proved stubborn. Peto's struggles to make it behave being unavailing, he very considerately passed it on to Forster, by which time I was already straining at the rope to cut a next step. Having only two hands, both of which were wanted on more important business, Forster thrust the lantern between his teeth, came up a few steps, and so gave me sufficient rope to proceed. After a further desperate but vain effort to fold the lantern up – with the candle still in it! – and handicapped by his limited number of hands, he at last solved the difficulty by biting the candle in two, and eventually succeeded in stowing away the very refractory and useless article

in his pocket. From then onwards we really got into our stride. I worked away in a perfectly straight, almost horizontal, line towards the rocks of the N.W. ridge; my comrades moved one at a time, Peto evidently enjoying the slope in spite of its appearance – particularly formidable with darkness surrounding us and the ever-increasing drop beneath.

It was very cold, and from time to time the fierce gusts of a fresh wind made us pause in our labours and crouch well down on to the slope to retain our balance. At a quarter past four the last step had been cut and the rocks of the N.W. ridge gained at a point a little above the bergschrund. We immediately crossed over to the N. face, where the rocks were more broken. They were well plastered up with ice and snow, but nevertheless we all tucked our axes into the rope at our waists and, with both hands free, moved upwards at a good pace. Our mode of advance consisted in my going out the full 60-foot length of rope between myself and Forster and finding good standing-ground or reliable belay; whereupon the other two, moving together with a taut rope between them, would climb up to me. There was much verglas on the rocks, and everything was buried in fresh snow; but I steadfastly refrained from using the axe, utilising hands and fists to clear doubtful places and relying as much as possible on the climbing-irons. To use the axe on this kind of ground before it is absolutely necessary invariably results in the loss of valuable time. We kept to the N. side of the ridge, only twice touching the crest, and, after one and a half hour's climbing at full pressure, arrived at a point high up above the lower end of the great terrace where a feasible way of gaining it at last appeared. Between the terrace and the rocks of the northern flank of the N.W. ridge lies an immense gully, at the narrowest point of which we now stood. It was extremely steep, as the ice had run and formed a sort of bulge. Forster and Peto having stowed themselves firmly away on the last little island of rock, I started to cut across it. After some heavy step-cutting in extraordinarily steep ice, I arrived in the middle of the gully, only to see about 100 feet lower down a better means of gaining the terrace. So I returned and, joining the others, descended these hundred feet and once more set out to cross the gully. It was not very wide, being only some 80 feet from the last of the rocks to the terrace itself, but the work was certainly hard. After about twenty minutes' step-cutting, I found myself standing in the bergschrund formed by the terrace and the ice-slopes above, and there Forster and Peto soon joined me. By following the lower lip of the bergschrund for a short distance and leaving it at a point where it curved abruptly upwards, it would have been possible to make a horizontal traverse of about 300 feet across a steep snow-slope to where the terrace was more gently inclined. Unfortunately, owing to the state of the snow, such tactics could not be indulged in. The slope was heavily covered with an accumulation of new snow, much of which had fallen down from the steeper slopes above. The old snow underneath had a smooth surface and was hard frozen, and the fresh snow was of that

powdery, non-cohesive quality which already possessed the thin, dangerous, wind-formed crust so respected by the winter mountaineer. To traverse such a slope would be simply asking for trouble: there was almost certain danger of our treading loose a snow shield and being swept down by it across the terrace and over the cliffs below. The only alternative lay in descending for a distance of about 200 feet and then crossing the slope at its very foot, where it was no longer steep, hard up against the lower edge of the corridor where it breaks away in the vast ice-cliffs overhanging the Tiefenmatten glacier. It was here that our spare rope proved most valuable. We cut out a large block of snow in the lower lip of the bergschrund and laid our doubled spare rope over the improvised belay. With Peto going first, we then went straight down the dangerous slope towards another suitable belay lying about 100 feet below and consisting of a large stone which had fallen from the Dent d'Hérens and was now firmly embedded in the old snow. By means of this second belay we descended another hundred feet, and then arrived at the very foot of the slope, where its angle eased off so rapidly that in spite of the great masses of powdery snow, it was at last possible to cross, in safety and without fear of loosening a snow shield, over to the great terrace.

The angle of the ground where we now found ourselves was gentle–sometimes no more than 20°; but, under the threat of ice falling from the hanging glacier above, Forster and I urged Peto, who still led, to move forward with all haste until clear of the danger zone. At one place our way passed through an extensive field of ice-blocks–débris from the cliffs above. That practically the whole of this particular fall of ice had been arrested on the terrace will indicate how easy is the gradient at this point. 7.30 am saw us more than halfway along the terrace at a point where it appears almost level. We were more or less directly below the summit. Close to the edge of the ice-cliff in which the terrace breaks away, we were at last in perfect safety. Nothing falling from above could reach us now; for the gentle slopes of the terrace between us and the final wall of the mountain provided an efficient trap for all stones tumbling down from the summit rocks.

It was with a sense of complete security that we sat down to another breakfast and to enjoy a well-earned rest; for, since crossing the bergschrund four and a half hours ago, we had been working at high pressure. The spot must be one of the wildest and most solitary in the Alps: behind us a rampart of precipitous cliffs, before us at our feet a few yards of gently sloping snow, then nothing until the eye rested on the Stockje, a mile and a half distant and nearly 3,000 feet below. Several parties were toiling up the Tête Blanche, but halted upon hearing our exuberant yells of delight as we settled down to our meal. It was cold; the wind was still strong and blowing snow-dust about, and, though all wore extra clothing and windproof overalls, we were by no means overburdened with warmth.

Shortly after eight o'clock we again set off. The slopes of the terrace now steepened up rapidly, and soon we were once more cutting steps–this time in good hard snow–up to the bergschrund separating us from the upper end of the terrace. Just before gaining the lower lip we heard the rattle of falling stones, and a generous avalanche from the gully between the great gendarme on the E. arête and the summit crashed down straight towards us. During one of my reconnaissance trips I had watched through the telescope stones falling down this gully, and had observed that they were all caught by the lower lip of the schrund. Indeed, it was precisely this fact that had led me to the conclusion that the lower lip must protrude very much beyond the upper, which would therefore form a serious barrier in our path. On this occasion again every stone of the avalanche was swallowed up by the bergschrund, without the slightest danger to us. As soon as all was quiet we resumed work and, on gaining the lower lip, moved down along it to the left, where it approached more under the upper lip. The obstacle we now faced was assuredly a difficult one. It appeared to me that the upper lip could be attacked, with fair prospects of success, at its lowest part by cutting steps up about twelve feet of very steep ice and then drilling one's way through a cornice formed of hard frozen snow, some three feet thick, extending from the edge of the upper lip. An alternative way lay in making a difficult traverse still further to the left across the ice-face leading to a fault or notch in the cornice, affording access to the slopes above. At first I chose the former way. Forster anchored himself well and, holding both my rope and Peto's, let us across the débris-choked floor of the bergschrund to the foot of the steep pitch. I was soon cutting my way up this, while Peto held me steady, so as to avoid the necessity of making hand-holds. Now out of arm's reach, but jammed against the ice by his axe, I began to drill through the cornice. I succeeded in driving my axe through into daylight, but only after a great effort, and was forced to return for a rest. Forster then followed up in my steps, but, not liking the idea of laboriously enlarging the hole in the cornice, returned to investigate the possibilities of the alternative traverse to the left. For some distance Peto was able to support him with his axe, but for the last ten or twelve feet Forster had to cut with his left hand, relying on his right to help him retain his balance. By a brilliant piece of ice-work he wormed his way through the fault in the cornice out on to the slopes above. As soon as he had obtained good standing-ground and driven his axe to the head into the snow, I followed quickly, and together we gave Peto the necessary aid to enable him to join us.

Once more I took the lead. We were now aiming straight for the eastern extremity of the level section of ridge lying immediately to the E. of the great gendarme. Everywhere the ground was so steep that steps had to be cut, but four or five blows with the axe were always sufficient, as the snow was hard and of good quality. To gain the foot of the gendarme over the slopes directly above us was out of the question on account of the impassability of an intervening bergschrund. Further to the E., however, this schrund was well bridged, and we crossed without difficulty. Here the snow changed. It was still good, but no longer so hard. Roped on to our 200-foot length of sash-line, Forster now took the lead and kicked his way right up on to the ridge, while Peto and I enjoyed a welcome, if brief, respite from our activities. At eleven o'clock we were all sitting together on a great flat slab on the E. ridge overlooking the Val Tournanche, protected from the wind and revelling in the warm sunshine. We had won. From here to the top was merely a question of time and patience.

Finch had taken great pains to plan a route up the face which minimised the danger of falling ice and stones; this involved taking a somewhat zigzag course. Two years later W. Welzenbach and E. Allwein climbed the north face direct, i.e. in an almost straight line to the summit, an illustration of the changes taking place; greater elegance of line is now bought at the price of greater danger. Marcel Kurz describes Finch's route as 'very interesting, but long and dangerous', and Welzenbach's as 'also very interesting, but even longer and more dangerous'.[2]

In France the leading spirits had formed the Groupe de Haute Montagne, and GHM members, men and women, were soon putting up first-class climbs all over the Alps. Their free climbing was of a class not before achieved anywhere except by isolated individuals of extraordinary talent and daring. Their habits and style (elegance was their watchword) were widely adopted by leading climbers in Switzerland and elsewhere. Mummery was their patron saint.

Here is Tom de Lépiney's account of adventure on the north-east wall of the Aiguille Verte in 1924.[3]

An ascent and descent of the Aiguille Verte
from Tom de Lépiney, *Climbs on Mont Blanc*
Since the first days of acrobatic climbing the Aiguille Verte, most beautiful amongst the beautiful, has never ceased to exercise its disturbing fascination. Since the ascent by Whymper in 1865 many climbers have explored new routes on the flanks of the proud peak: Kennedy, Hudson, Hodgkinson, Mummery, Gugliermina, Canzio, Lampugnani, to cite only the most notable conquerors whose names are recorded in history, whilst those of its victims live only in the memory of a few friends.

Our ambition was no less keen than that of our glorious predecessors. Fired by the ascent of the N.E. wall, successfully carried out on the 31st July, 1876, by Henry Cordier, J. Oakley Maund, and Thomas Middlemore, under the leadership of the guides Jakob Anderegg, Johann Jaun, and Andreas Maurer, we wished in our turn to scale these wild precipices which no one has mastered since then, giving it almost the attraction of the unknown, which stimulated our desire. We knew that the expedition was one of the most serious ever accomplished in the Alps; that the slope of the wall was formidable, that on the bed of the narrow couloirs stones bounded down night and day, that imposing barriers of séracs might collapse at any moment. What did it matter! We should know how to avoid the most critical dangers and that we should conquer.

Bad weather intervened and they made the first ascent of the Pointe Lagarde before returning to their project on the Verte. After a hard climb they duly got up the north-east wall, reaching the summit at 11.30 am. De Lépiney continues:

During this last ascent we hardly paid any attention to the ledges of the Aiguille Carrée nor to the lofty towers of the Montets arête. Admiring as we might have been of the splendours of the high mountain, the circumstances that day did not lend themselves to such. Hardly had we cast a glance at the Aiguille Sans Nom, a small mass of rock at the extremity of a knife-edge arête, than the wind drove us away, depriving us of a good halt on the summit, where, enjoying our victory, we should have liked to enjoy the delights of a long rest.

Retreat became obligatory. It was a question of reaching the Couvercle refuge, which seemed terribly far away.

The bad condition of the snow and the stones furrowing the Whymper Couloir dissuaded us from taking that route and we proceeded towards the Moine arête. With the first steps, we felt the need of recuperating our strength. Meeting with a dry rock, we stayed there for a long while and ate. Moreover, those few metres of descent had already brought home to us that the remaining task was not negligible and that it would exact vigour and skill.

Refreshed by the halt, we resumed the descent, but the very slow pace to which we were condemned by the abundance of new snow almost covering all the rocks caused us to anticipate that a bivouac could hardly be avoided. Several passages required great care and we expended precious time in crossing them. Sometimes the leader had to knock away a too fragile portion of the arête which formed a dangerous cornice, or else it was necessary to clear a slab before grasping the necessary holds. We knew quite well that the descent would not be equally bad from one end to the other, but two hours of continued effort had not gained much, and we were still at a height of 4,000 metres. The arête now bristled with smooth-faced gendarmes; we ought, according to de Ségogne, to have turned to the Talèfre face.

We then took the course of remounting to the start of a couloir by which we would quit the arête. On this very steep wall with unstable snow, the traverse presented real danger. Hesitations, discussions, led us to the conclusion that a direct descent to the Whymper Couloir could alone avoid a bivouac. The desire to sleep on the mattresses of the Couvercle determined us to accept the risk of falling stones, of which, however, the sinister noise during our nocturnal ascent on the Cordier Couloir still echoed in our ears; but at that time our minds were simply bent on going on without pause and we hardly gave a thought to the possibility of the now imminent bad weather.

No one could contemplate without anxiety the

prospect of a night of storm at such a height—an eventuality particularly to be feared by exhausted climbers. To avoid this danger even at the cost of some more immediate risks was definitely an act of prudence on our part.

We descended by the rocks, giving each other mutual aid in order to gain time, and we foresaw pretty exactly the moment at which we should arrive on the snow a little above the great couloir. But the storm broke suddenly with extreme violence; the

hailstones whipped our faces, snow fell in large flakes, the clash of thunder dominated everything and re-echoed on all sides; an awe-inspiring and prodigious spectacle in which all the terrible power of the mountain was manifested, but we should have preferred to admire it from a somewhat greater distance.

The lightning, striking the adjacent spurs, detached boulders which precipitated themselves down the couloir.

Accustomed to the worst traps which the Alps know

The Aiguille Verte, Charpoua face. The twin points on the left are the Petit and Grand Drus; the saw edge in the middle of the skyline are Les Droites.

how to set for climbers, we continued our labours, which circumstances rendered exceptionally severe. Of one accord as to the necessity of going as quickly as possible, no one proposed discarding their ice-axes to avoid attracting the lightning; it would have meant condemning ourselves to an immobility of which the drawbacks would soon become formidable.

Once on the snow, profiting by fugitive bright intervals, we increased our pace still farther. The leaders were held on the rope, while they in turn kept an eye on the descent of the third, checking him when necessary. We lost height rapidly, and each in his own mind congratulated himself on not being marooned on the Moine arête, battered by lightning and wind. Round us the walls ran with water; we descended on almost liquid snow, which, soaking our clothes, made us more and more uncomfortable. Then came the Whymper Couloir, which we took diagonally. Through a deep furrow dug out by stones descended a foaming torrent of snow; no one could have withstood its strength and we crossed it by a leap, which was facilitated by the slope. Shortly afterwards we reached the rocks on the right bank of a secondary couloir, leading us to the bergschrund. Deliverance seemed at hand.

Encouraged by the sight of the Glacier de Talèfre some hundred metres beneath us, we resumed the descent by the snow without stopping for a minute. Suddenly, at the same time that a flash of lightning rent the sky, a terrible noise resounded, and a few seconds later a mass of snow and stones caught my comrades, who had already been struck by electric discharges. One metre away from the trajectory of the missiles, and incapable of resisting the eventual strain of the rope, I was an anxious eye-witness of the scene. Lagarde had been struck on the calf, but it was nothing serious. Our descent, now somewhat sheltered by the cliffs of the Grande Rocheuse, could be resumed.

It was barely more than 6 pm when we approached our last obstacle, the bergschrund, from which an easy and not very long walk led to the Couvercle, safe from the wild elements. The bergschrund, almost entirely blocked up, could be crossed easily, and in a few minutes we should be in security on the other side.

The wall forming the upper lip of the bergschrund was extremely steep and the snow unstable. It would have meant a very long and, moreover, insecure task to make good steps. Emboldened by my companions, who, whipped by the squalls, ardently longed for the end of their troubles, I let myself slide and fell on to soft snow. But I found it impossible to stand up! Imprisoned to the hips with my body lying downwards, I had caused the collapse of a mass of snow of which a portion passed to one side but the rest fell on top of me, aggravating my already very painful position. This new trial was the hardest of all.

Then de Ségogne descended in his turn; rendered careful by my adventure, he took the greatest precautions. In vain! He could not avoid burying himself. With his feet held as if in a vice, he was, like myself, unable to move in spite of his efforts.

Our only hope lay now in Lagarde; evening was drawing in and deliverance became a vital necessity. Fatality! All the care which he exercised in his manoeuvre failed to preserve him from being sucked in like ourselves! At sunset we were all three enclosed in the traitorous snow of the bergschrund!

What thoughts could have crossed our minds during those tragic minutes? Perhaps fatigue, numbing the brain as well as the muscles, spared us too gloomy reflections. With the whole of his energy each one struggled to escape from the fatal grip, Lagarde being the first to succeed, and then he extricated us one after the other. We were saved!

Then in the mist and darkness we started again, skirting the base of the rock walls in order not to lose the way, sinking at each step to the knees in the snow, fighting from habit but without strength against the elements. Soaked to such a degree that we should have to discard all our clothes, and hardly able to stand up, so overcome with fatigue were we, we made our entry at 10 pm into the Couvercle, where numerous loyal friends of the GHM welcomed us. But it may be guessed that we quickly sought forgetfulness of our trials in sleep and the rest which repairs all.

Even the most technically extreme of the French achievements in this period (e.g. P. Allain and R. Leininger on the north face of the Petit Dru in 1935) used little in the way of pitons, while others (e.g. Armand Charlet and C. Devouassoux on the Nant Blanc face of the Verte in 1928) used none.

Apart from Moore's route, there had been very little activity on the Brenva (east) face of Mont Blanc. When making the first descent of that route (the 'old' Brenva) in 1912, R. W. Lloyd had given thought to a way up the line of what later became Route Major. Mallory had also realised the possibilities and had asked Young to take a look at it. In 1919 Mallory, with H. E. L. Porter, had set out to examine at least the lower part of the route but had been turned back by high wind. Paul Preuss had it on his agenda when he was killed. E. G. Oliver, who had climbed the Innominata rib with S. L. Courtauld in 1919, projected a crossing of the col separating Mont Blanc from Mont Blanc de Courmayeur which would have used the line of Route Major. It was in 1927 that Graham Brown and Frank Smythe climbed their Sentinelle Route on the Brenva face. Their success had a curious origin; Graham Brown had designs on Route Major when he joined forces with Smythe fortuitously, and the latter was interested in a line by the Mummery rib nearer to the Old Brenva. In the event they compromised on a line between the two and made the most direct of the Brenva routes to Mont Blanc. Next year the same pair came back and climbed Route Major. In 1933 Graham Brown, this time with Alexander Graven, completed his triptych of climbs on the Brenva face by adding Via della Pera, up the 'pear' buttress between Route Major and the Peuterey ridge.

The Macugnaga face of Monte Rosa is in some ways similar to the Brenva face of Mont Blanc, but has received less notice in recent years. It extends from the Cresta Signal (or Topham Arête) to the frontier ridge from the Jägerjoch to the Nordend (this frontier ridge is also known as the Cresta di Santa Caterina). The first route went alongside the Marinelli couloir (1872, see Chapter 3); the Cresta Signal was climbed by H. W. Topham with Aloys Supersaxo and a porter in 1887 and the Cresta di Santa Caterina by Ryan and the Lochmatters in 1906. Luigi Brioschi, with Ferdinand and Abraham Imseng, had climbed up by the rocks to the north of the Marinelli couloir in 1876. In 1931, Jacques Lagarde and Lucien Devies made a route to the Signalkuppe over the ice of the Macugnaga face, 'one of the greatest and most difficult ice routes in the Alps', but unfortunately very exposed to falls of ice and stones in the lower part. In 1934, Ettore Zapparoli, solo, made an even more dangerous route direct to Colle Gnifetti. Zapparoli was a poet who specialised in wandering over this Macugnaga face by himself; he made several other perilous routes on it and finally disappeared somewhere on the face in 1951.

In the dog days of August 1931, the world's press was filled with excited descriptions of the ascent of the north face of the Matterhorn, one of the in-exhaustible 'last great problems of the Alps'. Not even the first ascent of that mountain, with the death of most of the party on the way down, had hit the headlines more dramatically. Two young brothers from Munich, Franz and Toni Schmid, had cycled all the way to Zermatt and climbed this crumbling and formidable face. The bally-hoo was no part of their doing; they had set about this sensational climb in a sober and sensible way.

At 2 am the young men called at the Hörnli hut to ask the *gardien* to warn parties to be careful of causing stonefall as there would be climbers on the north face. Going round by the Matterhorn glacier, they crossed the bergschrund at 4 am and climbed the 60° ice-slope above in crampons. A piton was wisely used for security on each pitch. Some 300 feet above the ice-slope they found a solitary stance where they took a short rest, then went on up very steep, iced and crumbling rocks. At about 8.30 they found a space some two feet square on which they lashed themselves for the night. Next morning, to their surprise, they came upon their greatest difficulty, a vertical slab covered with ice; they were eventually able to turn this by slabs even more thickly iced. After dangerous

The Brenva face of Mont Blanc, which Graham Brown climbed by three different routes between 1927 and 1933; the Sentinelle route and Route Major with Frank Smythe and the Via della Pera with Alexander Graven.

traverses between grooves, they struggled up by minute snow-filled cracks, reaching the summit at 2 pm. The weather now decisively broke and the snow storms were such that it took them two days to reach the Hörnli by the ordinary route!

The climb has been repeated many times in both summer and winter; indeed a face so loose is probably better climbed in winter when the rocks are cemented together by ice. Diether Marchart, who had already climbed the face with a companion in 1958, climbed it solo in six hours the following year.

The Schmids' climb stimulated an assault on unclimbed north faces which earlier generations had avoided because of their obvious danger. Soon afterwards the alpine atmosphere began to deteriorate as the lights began to go out over Europe once more. Nationalism and competition, never entirely absent, became sharper; there was in places incitement to death or glory, and the debate on artificial aids became exacerbated by the irrelevance that its chief practitioners were allied in the 'Rome-Berlin Axis'. The opponents forgot that pitons were primarily a safety device. The exploits of the German and Italian climbers were sometimes derided as an expression of their disastrous political régimes; it would perhaps be juster to assume that these young men went to the mountains to find that freedom which the dictators denied them in all other directions.

Unfortunately the north wall of the Eiger became the main arena; unfortunately, because it is as public a climbing ground as can be found in the Alps. Holiday-makers at Kleine Scheidegg can, weather permitting, watch every move through telescopes. The race for the north face of the Grandes Jorasses was equally competitive, and it was going on at the same time; but this face towers over the Glacier de Leschaux remote from public eye. As the death roll mounted on the Eiger, the crowd increased; the contest had become gladiatorial.

The climbing of notoriously dangerous places was not new. Sixty years earlier Oakley Maund and Middlemore were rebuked for their addiction to stone-swept couloirs (but in the arcane circles of the Alpine Club; the public knew nothing of their adventures). Nor was it altogether prudent to ascend the Col du Lion, as Mummery did with Burgener in 1880, an ascent which Güssfeld soon repeated. Guido Lammer had deliberately cultivated danger, principally by climbing alone; he lived, probably to his own disgust, to be 83. Today the general view among mountaineers is that danger for danger's sake is an aberration, but that in pursuit of other ends a party may calculate and choose to take its own risks. Nevertheless, it is wrong to expose professional employees to unjustifiable danger and some Himalayan expeditions have been criticised on this score. But there is no objective criterion for establishing what is justifiable, so no consensus is possible.

The Eigerwand is 5,000 feet from top to bottom, very steep, beset by bad weather and swept by falling stones. A first-class mountaineering route had been made in 1932 by a very strong Swiss party, Hans

The upper part of the Matterhorn. The north face (in shadow) was first climbed by the Schmid brothers in 1931. The ordinary, Hörnli, route follows the line dividing sun from shade.

Lauper and Alfred Zürcher with Joseph Knubel and Alexander Graven. This route is on the north face, skirting the eastern boundary of the wall; it is not on the Eigerwand itself.

In 1935 two young men, from Munich like the Schmids, Karl Mehringer and Max Sedlmayr, set out up the wall using a more direct start than is now usual. On the evening of the third day a terrible storm hid them from the valley. Next day the wall was still wrapped in cloud. On the fifth day they were glimpsed again, making yet another bivouac. The weather closed in. It was not until some days later that the body of one of them was seen, upright and frozen stiff.

Next year eight men camped under the foot of the wall. After one had been killed in a practice climb, his companions withdrew, leaving two Bavarians, Andreas Hinterstoisser and Toni Kurz, and two Austrians, Willy Angerer and Eduard Rainer, who combined forces. They started their ascent further to the west than the 1935 pair and had to traverse from under the Rotefluh to gain the First Icefield. The traverse was led by Hinterstoisser and has since borne his name. They made their first bivouac in storm at the upper edge of the Second Icefield. Next morning they were seen traversing leftwards to join the route of their predecessors, but were soon hidden and not seen again until the following day. Angerer was obviously injured, no doubt by a stone, and the party was retreating. At 5 pm they were still moving slowly down. The weather worsened. At 11 next morning they were seen again. They tried to reverse the Hinter-

The Eigerwand (opposite), the notorious wall beset by treacherous weather and cascading stones, and some of its challengers. Top right: the Austrians Edi Rainer and Willy Angerer, two of the four casualties of the dramatic attempt in 1936. Centre right: Andreas Heckmair, one of the quartet who reached the summit in 1938. Bottom left: Matthias Rebitsch on the key Hinterstoisser traverse, named after the German climber who fell to his death in 1936; this attempt (in 1937) was abandoned without casualties. Bottom right: Heinrich Harrer and Fritz Kasparek on a bivouac secured by a single piton during the first successful ascent with Heckmair and Vorg.

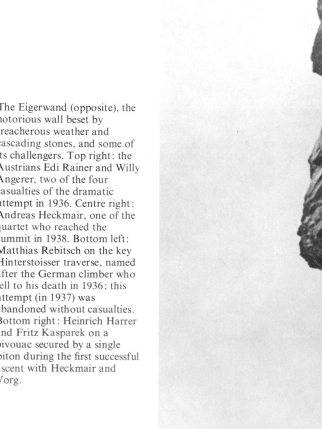

stoisser traverse; in the bad conditions and with a frozen rope, this proved impossible. (It has since become customary to leave a fixed rope across this traverse to prevent retreat being cut off.) They had to try to rope down the cliff below them. Their later manoeuvres had been watched by a workman from the hole cut as a rubbish-chute from the tunnel of the Jungfraujoch railway; when he heard cries for help, he hurried off to give the alarm.

It seems that, while collecting enough rope for the abseil (*abseil* is the process of roping down), Hinterstoisser fell, probably knocked over by a stone. Angerer was strangled by coils of falling rope and Rainer was dashed against a piton and soon died from his injuries and exposure. Kurz alone was left, hanging in a sling under torrents of falling water, ice and stones—one arm and hand frozen and useless, tied to two dead comrades.

81

Max Sedlmayr, one of the first to die on the Eigerwand in 1935.

Three of the best guides in Switzerland happened to be at the Eigergletscher station. The company put on a special train. The guides climbed out of the rubbish-chute and in only three-quarters of an hour reached the foot of the cliff where Kurz hung. They exchanged shouts with him, but nothing could be done in the darkness that night. At daybreak, having received reinforcement, Adolf and Christian Rubi, Hans Schlunegger and Arnold Glatthard raced across the wall. Kurz was still alive and lucid. It was impossible to climb up the vertical *verglas* (a thin layer of ice on rock). They told Kurz to cut loose from the dead man and thus free one rope. One-armed, he climbed down 40 feet, hacked through the rope near his friend's waist-loop, climbed back and fixed the rope thus gained to the peg from which he had hung during the night. The corpse, at first frozen to the cliff, soon came away, narrowly missing the guides in its 3,000-foot plunge. Kurz lowered the rope and the guides sent some pitons, karabiners and extra rope up on it. All this took four hours of terrible work for the injured and exhausted man, working with one hand and his teeth. At last he began to climb down. The guides noticed that he carefully removed loose stones that he might have knocked down on them. One guide climbed on the shoulders of another, himself held in place by a third; with the tip of his axe he could just reach Kurz's iced crampons. At this point a knot in the rope jammed in a karabiner; Kurz could move no further. He let go, swung out into space, and died.

Here was grim disaster, immense endurance and courage, but also high drama fixing public attention even more firmly on the Eigerwand.

In 1937 there were many parties camped at Alpiglen, among them Matthias Rebitsch and Ludwig Vorg. The weather was bad and most of the aspirants turned away, but these two stayed on. They had a gloomy interlude, bringing down the body of a Salzburg boy who had died of exhaustion and exposure near the top of the Lauper-Zürcher route and later finding and recovering Hinterstoisser's body. After several false starts, they succeeded in getting past Sedlmayr and Mehringer's 'Death Bivouac' but were assailed by torrents of rain and hail on the ice-slope beyond and had to bivouac where they were. The weather remained menacing and they wisely began their retreat next day. Soaked to the skin, they spent another night at their first bivouac, and climbed down safely next day with all their luggage. This safe and orderly retreat from the middle of the wall did much to lighten the shadow of mortality that hung about the cliffs.

Even so, 1938 started badly with the death of two young Italians on the wall. Undaunted, two Austrians, Fritz Kasparek and Heinrich Harrer, set out on July 21. On their way they equipped the 'Swallow's Nest' bivouac above the Hinterstoisser traverse as a strong-point in case of retreat. On their second day, near the top of the Second Icefield, they saw two men literally running up the ladder of steps which Kasparek had so carefully cut. These were Andreas Heckmair and Ludwig Vorg, who had started a day later. The two pairs united at the Death Bivouac and completed the first ascent of the wall on the afternoon of July 24. Both Heckmair and Harrer have described the climb but their accounts are too long for inclusion here.[4] It was a remarkable achievement by a remarkable team.

The war intervened and the wall was not climbed again until 1947, by two outstanding French guides, Lionel Terray and Louis Lachenal. The third ascent was by Hans Schlunegger (who had been present at Kurz's death eleven years earlier), his son Karl and Gottfried Jermann. The fourth successful party were two Austrians, Erich Waschak and Leo Forstenlecher, who completed the climb in one day. Twenty years after the first ascent the wall had been overcome fifteen times.[5]

Nowadays the Eigerwand is on the curriculum of ambitious young tigers of all nationalities and is climbed many times every summer. The ice seems to have receded since the 1930s, pitches that were ice for the pioneers being now polished rock. It remains a dangerous climb by reason of stonefall and avalanche, though the danger has been slightly mitigated by the use of crash-helmets, which did not appear on the wall till 1958. Here is Ian Clough's account of the Eigerwand, which he climbed with Christian Bonington in 1962:[6]

An ascent of the Eigerwand
from Ian Clough, *The Alpine Journal*, Vol. LXVIII
We arrived, panting and sweating, at a low, shallow cave with a sandy floor. It would be dark in an hour and we could both lie here comfortably so we settled ourselves in to bivouac below the Difficult Crack. The sudden decision, the rushing round trying to borrow money for the fare, the early morning train drawing out of Chamonix Station, all seemed a long way away now. The wall had looked black and dry as the train had rounded the last bend to Grindelwald and we had known that the journey had been worth while; conditions were very favourable. I remembered the girl in the bookshop, where we had copied the description from the back of Heinrich Harrer's book, trying to dissuade us with stories of the most recent fatalities, the look in the blacksmith's eyes as he had sharpened our claws, the bloodstains on the lower rocks where the fall of a solitary Austrian climber had been halted, the moments of doubt and indecision. But we were here now, on the Eiger's North Wall, happy and confident, with four days of fine weather ahead if the Zürich forecasters were correct.

Two small figures had been scurrying up the wall behind us. Like ourselves they wore crash helmets and carried bulging rucksacks on their backs. Now the first climbed the old fixed rope to the ledge near us. He introduced himself as an Austrian—Moderegger. Then his companion arrived: 'Hello'—we were surprised to hear English—'I'm Tom Carruthers.' We talked for a while. . . . We agreed that, should we all move at the same speed, it would be pleasant to have company, it would be a mutual morale booster against the frightening, cruel vastness of this notorious wall. The other pair went to bivouac round the corner. We cooked and ate a huge meal. Our sacks were too heavy, they must have weighed forty pounds but felt like eighty as we had staggered up the thousand feet of scree and broken walls that evening, but now they were much lighter. We dressed in our down clothing and were soon asleep on our little sandy ledge, reassured that we were well nailed on. It was already a long way down.

Chris was shaking me. He was impatient to get away for it was late – 5 am! A hasty breakfast, then away. Carruthers and the Austrian were just behind us as we scurried up the Difficult Crack but they didn't keep up with us. We moved quickly together, along a fault of ledges and easy pitches below a great yellow overhanging wall, to the Hinterstoisser. There were several ropes across this rubicon of the old days and we were soon over the traverse, past the overhang of the Swallow's Nest bivouac, and climbing up what should have been the First Ice-field. But the ice had receded and we were able to climb the rock beside it. We reached a steep step, the Ice Hose. Now we really began to appreciate just how good conditions were, for the Hose was a straightforward rock climb. Above us, bands of rock were showing bare beneath the Second Ice-field. Using these, connecting them by little verglassed ribs sticking up out of the ice, we trended leftwards until we were under the great, glassy, smooth sweep of the main part of the Second Ice-field. 'Whatever happens here, don't look up,' Chris called, drawing on the experience of his previous attempts on the wall with Don Whillans. Over a thousand feet above us, above a great vertical wall, was the mouth of the White Spider which usually belches forth debris from the upper part of the face. We were now entering the most dangerous area on the face; the zone of heaviest bombardment. I tried to make myself as small a target as possible, receding into my crash helmet as a frightened tortoise does into his shell. But the Ogre was frozen into stillness this morning. Not a stone fell.

There was no snow overlying the ice and crampons tended to scart off the tough surface. We decided to go directly up the ice-field to its upper lip. If we went diagonally across, as one normally does, we would have to cut countless steps in the hard blue ice. It would take hours and the mountain's artillery might have opened up before we were clear. By going straight up we could use our crampons to better advantage. We moved off; crampons crashing, pick and dagger thrashing, only a quarter of an inch into the ice; teetering in precarious balance until a great bucket was beaten out and a security spike hammered in. We kept pitches short because our straining calves tired quickly and also because it was safer. One couldn't hope to hold a long fall. Using ice-pegs and screws for belays, cutting small nicks to rest on between quick staccato crampon moves, leading alternately, we proceeded rapidly and in comparative safety. But security on ice is only make-believe, and nerves as well as muscles were taut as we stabbed our

way upwards. The angle wasn't that steep, about the same as a house roof, but the way the smooth giant of the slope plunged away beneath us to the meadows was awe-inspiring. It was a relief to be nearing the upper rim.

As I stood in the bucket step, protecting Chris's advance, I was able to look around me for the first time that day. From the foot of the wall a great dark pyramid, the shadow of the Eiger, reached out across the meadows to the tourist hotel of Kleine Scheidegg. The rubbernecks and pressmen would be enjoying their breakfasts. Later they would come to peer through the telescopes, to enjoy the free entertainment. Were we actors in some drama, gladiators in the arena? A long, low, plaintive note rang clear over the meadows and echoed across the wall. An alpenhorn. The old man whose daily task it was to play it for the benefit of the tourists was in position on his hillock. At first the sound was comforting, but as the day wore on, its repetitiveness became wearisome and irritating.

The upper rim went easily, sometimes providing a gangway to walk along, at other times giving a sharp edge for the hands. We tried to leave the ice-field too early but, quickly realising our error, abseiled back and continued the long traverse. A steep little rock buttress took us up onto the flank of the Flatiron, the ridge which separates the Second and Third Ice-fields. We were high on the face now, going well. It wouldn't be long before we were clear of stonefall danger, before we reached the safety of the Ramp. . . .

We reached the crest of the Flatiron and scrambled up to the overhang of the Death Bivouac. Glancing back over the Second Ice-field we saw two black dots, Tom Carruthers and Moderegger, hardly moving, at the foot of the ice-field and inching their way *diagonally* across it. We were worried by their mistake but they were too far away for us to shout advice and we had yet to get ourselves out of the danger zone.

The Third Ice-field is the steepest and has to be crossed more or less horizontally to the start of the Ramp, a steep gangway which provides the only break in a 500-foot leaning yellow wall. We slashed big steps and at one point saved time by making a long tension traverse from an ice-peg. The Ramp itself gave steep climbing reminiscent of the Dolomites. The rock was comparatively sound. We were glad, for this was technically the most difficult part of the climb. We enjoyed being on rock again. This didn't seem at all like the ferocious Eigerwand we had read about, it was just another great climb. But, on some of the stances were tattered remnants of polythene, occasionally a rusty can; some of our predecessors had had a hard time.

Wispy clouds, which had slowly been forming down at the base of the wall, drifted up over the face like a shroud, hiding us from the prying telescopes and baffling the sound of the alpenhorn.

We arrived at the Waterfall Pitch where the Ramp steepens to a shallow corner chimney. This is often, as its name implies, the most unpleasant pitch on the climb – icy water gushing down one's neck and sleeves

Crampons, which enable climbers to bite into snow and ice.

makes a poor prelude to a bivouac. Today there was no water pouring down the corner, but a thin veneer of verglas covered all the holds. It gave one of the hardest pitches on the climb; inch upwards, scratch the ice from the next tiny hold; inch, balance, scratch, reach carefully and clip into a rusty old peg. Once or twice a foot would skid off its slippery wrinkle giving a tense moment for the second man but the leader was too absorbed in the next move to worry. After another section of clean, dry rock we came to the Ice Bulge. It was a short chimney with verglas on one wall and thick, bulging, blue ice on the other. We climbed it back-and-foot. Now we were in a funnel of ice which led up to an amphitheatre of steep buttresses which lost themselves in the mist. It was cold. Another rope move from an ice-peg saved time and laborious step-cutting and landed us on a gentle rock rib beside the ice-funnel. We climbed upwards, wondering where the start of the Traverse of the Gods was. We must be near it now. Then we heard muffled voices. The mists thinned for an instant and we saw, on the precipitous skyline on our right, a horizontal step. On it we could distinguish two small figures. We cut steps across the upper edge of the amphitheatre, traversed a crumbling ledge and by a steep crack gained the ledge on the arête.

Sitting there were two grinning Swiss. They introduced themselves as Jenny and Hauser. Although it was now only five o'clock they were going to bivouac as one of them had been hit by a stone, but they didn't need any assistance. They were going slowly; they had spent the previous night, their second bivouac, in the Ramp. We decided to press on since we still felt quite fresh and there were a few hours of daylight remaining. With luck we might even make the summit that night.

The Traverse of the Gods, a series of broad but outward sloping scree-covered ledges, was almost clear of snow and we followed it easily towards the centre of the face, towards the White Spider. As we moved along, the veil of mists fell away from the face and the huge walls rearing up around us, plunging away below, glowed pink in the late afternoon sun. We looked out over the billowing clouds which still filled the valleys. We felt elated standing on that splendid belvedere, isolated from the world; it was truly a situation worthy of the Gods.

At the end of the ledge system we were confronted with a broad ice-gully leading up into another huge overhung rock amphitheatre. Chris had begun to cut the first steps towards the little ice-rib in the middle of the Spider when, suddenly, there was a tremendous crashing and roaring and an avalanche of rocks came thundering down the gully and screamed out into the void below. The sunshine which we were enjoying was loosening rocks from their icy clasps. Chris came back quickly and we looked at each other, shaken: 'It'll probably freeze tonight. Let's bivvy here.'

We sat on our ledge and watched the sun slowly sink below the cloud horizon. It was a cold night. We slept for a few hours, then sat talking and brewing hot beverages until it became light. Stiff and clumsy at first, but soon warming up with the strenuous work of cutting steps, we climbed the Spider. Jenny and Hauser, following up our steps, were just behind us as we reached the top of the ice-basin. The entrance to the Exit Cracks was a narrow gully of frozen rubble. The gully continued upwards until it became lost in a forest of overhangs. We consulted our description and decided that we had to climb a steep ice-filled chimney on the left. Chris climbed it slowly. It was vertical and fearfully loose, only the ice keeping the holds in place. It was by far the hardest pitch we had encountered. I followed with a struggle and we pulled the leading Swiss up to the stance to join us. I had run out half the rope again before I realised that we were directly above the Spider. Surely we should be going over to the left? There now seemed to be a way round the overhangs at the top of the gully line. We were annoyed at losing so much time as we abseiled back into the gully. It didn't help much when we had to teach one of the Swiss how to abseil and we weren't particularly sympathetic when he excused himself by saying he had only been climbing a year! But later, at Kleine Scheidegg, we were amused when we were told of the sensation we had created at the telescopes. Apparently there was tremendous excitement when it was announced by an 'authority' on the climb, that the British party were attempting a new Direct Finish!

The gully line, the Exit Cracks, became easier and easier as we climbed upwards. Soon there was no snow or ice. We marvelled that these were the same Cracks that had presented such great difficulties to men like Hermann Buhl. But, on the Eiger, conditions can mean everything. We were lucky to have it so easy. We took off the ropes and soloed up to the final ice-field. Hard ice again; on with the ropes. We were on the summit in the early afternoon and our happiness was so complete that we ran most of the way down the easy West flank. In less than two hours we were at Kleine Scheidegg. Jenny and Hauser reached the summit at about the same time as we entered the hotel.

In the hotel the joy of our success was taken from us. We were told that two bodies had been sighted near the foot of the wall that morning. Did we know who they were? It came like a vicious blow. We felt shattered, sick with pity. Tom Carruthers and his Austrian partner were dead.

The battle for the north face of the Grandes Jorasses started earlier, but only ended a month later, than the battle for the Eigerwand. Young and Knubel had made a start in 1907, and in 1928 the redoubtable Armand Charlet had made his first essay on the Walker spur; he was with the Italian guide Evariste Croux, two Italians, Zanetti and Gasparotto, and the American, Rand Herron. The Germans began their attack in 1931, this time on the central couloir which may look simpler but is impossibly dangerous as it is the general trough for the rubble of the mountain. After Heckmair and Kroner had been rebuffed, Brehm and Rittler were killed, no doubt by stones in the couloir. Toni Schmid, Bratschko and Welzenbach all tried their hands. In 1932 there were three Italian parties and Armand Charlet came back twice, but none of them was able to overcome the zone of slabs at the base of the buttress. Next year Chabod and Gervasutti turned their attention to the central spur leading up to Pointe Croz; they reached about 11,500 feet and had a terrible time with storm and avalanche on the descent. In 1934 Charlet, with the Swiss Robert Gréloz, followed the same route and got a little higher before being turned back by a wall which is probably unclimbable without artificial aid. On July 30 there were no less than four parties on the Central Buttress. The Germans, Peters and Haringer, had twenty-four hours' start, but Charlet, with his customary speed, climbing with Bellin, overtook them. The weather worsened; Charlet turned back; Chabod and Gervasutti and the fourth Austrian rope did likewise; the German pair delayed their retreat too long. Haringer fell to his death and Peters got back alone after five days on the mountain.

In 1935 conditions at the end of June were exceptionally good. Peters, back with a new partner, Maier, climbed the Croz spur, bivouacking on the summit at the end of the second day. Chabod and Gervasutti were just two days behind them. Here is Gervasutti's account:[7]

The ascent of the north face of the Grandes Jorasses
from G. Gervasutti, *Gervasutti's Climbs*

On the 28th we were in Courmayeur. It was still very hot, and the run of fine weather continued. We crossed the Col du Géant, taking the winter route by the Toule glacier, for there was still a great deal of snow on the rock spur where the normal summer path zigzags up. After spending the night at the Torino, on June 30 we went down to the Leschaux hut. At about 10 in the morning, when we reached the point on the glacier from which you can see the north face of the Grandes Jorasses, we could scarcely believe our eyes. The wall was in wonderful condition, dry and bare as we never remembered seeing it before.

'I bet the whole crowd are on the face today,' said Chabod, 'Germans, French, Swiss, and I shouldn't be surprised if there were some Japs as well!'

He was only too right. As soon as we reached the hut, we saw a climber with a funereal expression on his face, gazing upwards. It was the German Steinauer, the climbing companion of Franz Schmid, the conqueror of the north face of the Matterhorn, and he also had arrived late on the scene. He greeted us by name, then with outstretched arm he pointed to the wall: *Peters in der Wand.*

'Since when?' we asked. But he did not know. The guardian came out and told us that the two Germans, Martin Meier and Rudolf Peters, had gone past three days ago without even stopping at the hut. Since then nobody had heard of them. The Swiss climbers Roch and Gréloz had also attacked the face that morning, as well as two Frenchmen, Edouard Frendo and Chaix, from the Ecole de Haute Montagne.

So our hopes of three years were dashed to the ground. Chabod's reaction was to say that he didn't want to have anything more to do with this face, and

that the only thing was to pack our sacks and be off. But the news had made me furious; and I declared that now we were at the Leschaux we would get on to the wall, come what might. And anyway it was by no means impossible that we should find the Germans held up somewhere. After his outburst Chabod also came round to the view that we must make an attempt, and we decided to start at 1 o'clock next morning.

At midday we were surprised to see four men descending the glacier – the Swiss and French parties.

Gréloz had dislocated his shoulder and they had had to turn back. So there was nobody but the Germans ahead of us, and if they were not dead by now they must surely have succeeded. In the afternoon the guide Lambert and Mademoiselle Boulaz, who had already made an attempt the year before, arrived at the hut. When they learned of our intention to start out for the face, they came to tell us that they would be doing the same. Then we all went to bed.

First up and first to leave the hut were Lambert and Loulou Boulaz, but they stopped at the foot of the wall beneath the bergschrund, and waited for us; it was clear that they had hurried with this end in view. At 3.45 Renato [Chabod] crossed the bergschrund and began the work of cutting steps up the initial slope, which was bare ice. We gained height rapidly on these pitches, which were already familiar to us, and Chabod suggested a slight variation which made this first section easier. At 7.30 we came to the second tower, and at 8 o'clock we were back on the crest of the spur. Meanwhile the sun had begun to touch the upper slopes, loosing the first furious volley of stones as an ominous greeting from the wall above.

By 8.45 we had reached the beginning of the lower névé where we had stopped the year before. This lower part of the climb was made very much easier this year by the quite exceptional conditions of the mountain. We traversed slowly across the ice-slope to the right, taking it in turns to cut steps so as to husband our strength.

The upper part of the north face of the Grandes Jorasses. Point Croz tops the central sunlit buttress, first climbed in 1935 by Peters and Maier.

At 10.30 we were at the foot of the famous band of slabs which constitutes the crux of the face. A concealed slanting dièdre – or open groove – appeared to be the most vulnerable point. We thought the Germans had taken this way, and in fact, as soon as I started up the groove I found pitons at the back of it. The pitch was polished by water trickling down and looked extremely hard. I put on espadrilles and began to climb. When I came to the second piton, I could see quite clearly that it was very much easier on the right, where from the beginning Renato had wanted me to try. I traversed across, using the rope until I was clear of the groove, and here I found excellent holds which enabled me to climb straight up without using pitons. Then I came back to the left above the groove, thus by-passing the artificial pitch. A crack brought me out on to a ledge like the lid of a desk, where Peters and Haringer had probably bivouacked the year before. After this pitch the difficulties increased and so did the danger of falling stones. Below the barrier of slabs the steepness of the wall had protected us a little, whereas above it the stones ricocheted all over the place and some fell close beside us.

While we were busy with the crux of the climb, great clouds began to form on the summits, thunder rumbled in the distance, and one of those violent, shattering storms you get in the high mountains suddenly broke over us. At the same moment the Swiss couple appeared on the platform and finding themselves precariously placed they asked anxiously for a rope, which Chabod hurried to give them. So there we were, all four anchored to pitons, and there we remained for perhaps an hour while the hail beat down on us.

This storm was one of the most awe-inspiring spectacles I have ever seen in the high Alps. The upper part of the face acted as a gathering ground for all the hail that did not lodge on the rocks. Small avalanches formed, got up speed on the upper névé and then came pouring down on the slabs where we had stopped. With incredible violence the torrent struck us squarely, and if the pitons had not been well and truly driven in we should have been swept away like straws.

After the fury of the hurricane had abated the wall was a fearful sight. But now we were in full cry. We had already climbed more than half the face, and with the knowledge that others had gone before us we were determined not to give up. So the decision to continue was made and we remained roped together as a party of four. In the position in which the storm had stopped us – that is to say right in the middle of a pitch – it was impossible for me to change back into my boots, which anyway were in Chabod's sack, fifty feet below. So I was obliged to continue in espadrilles. Slowly, I started climbing again, clearing the hail from the holds, blowing on my hands to warm them and belaying myself frequently with pitons. I continued in this way for two rope-lengths, then I traversed over to the left towards the upper névé, where I was able to put on my boots.

We halted here in a sort of niche hollowed out in the ice beneath a big boulder. It was the most roomy spot that we found on the whole face, and gave us

shelter from the blast of an absolutely icy wind which now swept the face and froze our sodden clothes. We were completely enveloped in mist. Though the fury of the storm had abated, bad weather had set in, and huge clouds rolled along in a wild sky.

The main difficulties should, by rights, have been behind us, but we did not know whether we should be able to finish the climb in the conditions in which we now found it. Nevertheless, we decided without further ado to go on and bivouac as high up as possible. To speed matters up, we reverted to two ropes of two, put on our crampons, and Chabod began to cut steps on the upper névé. At first the two Swiss had wanted to bivouac where they were, but Renato yelled down a warning – and quite rightly too – that if they remained there they ran the risk of being caught like rats in a trap. This stirred them to action and they followed us up the ice-slope.

At the top of the névé I took over the lead again; we were once more on broken rock, which would have been easy if dry, but had become extremely dangerous in present conditions. Loose holds were cemented by ice and it was impossible to distinguish them from genuinely good ones. A few rope-lengths brought us to the foot of a chimney which ran up to a gap on the spur. We tried to bear over to the right to gain the great gully which lies to the right of the Pointe Croz, for we thought this was the way the Germans had taken. But in making an attempt to get round, I let slip a piton just as I was driving it in, and it flew out into space. In trying to save this valuable object, I made a sudden move which jerked the block on which I was standing; it gave way under the strain and I went with it. Fortunately the piton I had put in for a belay thirty feet lower down, and to which the rope was clipped, held firm and Chabod was easily able to take the strain.

'Are you hurt?' he cried anxiously.

'No. My hands are a bit grazed, that's all, and I've knocked my back, but it's nothing much.'

I traversed to the left and stopped on a ledge where Chabod joined me. As it was getting dark we decided to go up the chimney, where we ought to be able to find somewhere to bivouac. Renato wished to take the lead so that I could rest a bit, but I refused and went on, for I wanted to counteract the shock of the fall.

At 9 o'clock we stopped to bivouac, but it could hardly have been called a convenient spot. The two Swiss were able to settle themselves in more comfortably than we could, sitting on an overhanging ledge with their feet dangling in the air. But we had to stay on our feet, anchored to pitons, unable even to get inside the bivouac sack – one of us on a projecting spike of rock at the back of the chimney, the other hanging straddled across. Every half hour we changed places. Very soon the bitter cold began to penetrate and our clothes turned to suits of icy armour. From the overhang above a little stream trickled down, which we were in no position to dodge, and from time to time an avalanche of stones went humming past in the dark. Eight hours went by like this.

The Italian Giusto Gervasutti, who in 1935 also scaled Point Croz on the Grandes Jorasses, another challenging north face that was overcome in the 1930s.

We were on the move next morning at 5 o'clock. We climbed up to the gap; then, high up, we bore considerably to the right, traversing across a short ice-slope. But as soon as I had rounded the central rib which drops straight down from the Pointe Croz a fearsome sight came into view: the gully by which we hoped to reach safety was one immense unbroken sheet of ice with a few polished rocks sticking out here and there. Yesterday's hail, which had melted and then frozen during the night, was responsible for this pretty piece of work.

I brought Chabod up beside me so that we could make a joint decision; and we agreed that it was impossible to finish the climb that way.

'There are no two ways about it,' muttered Renato, 'we are properly beaten, and on our own ground. I suggest we try the rib on the left.'

We retraced our steps and called to Lambert, who was awaiting our decision on the other side of the rib, to begin climbing up so as not to waste time. And just then, as if to underline the dramatic character of the moment, the hail started. But it stopped again in a minute. If we could not force a way up the rib we were lost. Five hundred feet—perhaps only four hundred—separated us from the summit; yet there we were, caught in an icy trap. But the moment of despair had passed and as we traversed back across the ice-slope we gripped our axes as though we would crush them to splinters. Up we would go at all costs, for our lives depended on it.

'Is this the way?' the Swiss asked when we joined them.

'Maybe,' we answered briefly, for we did not want to scare them since they had blindly entrusted themselves to our leadership. We climbed up the rib over sound rock and glazed slabs to within a hundred feet of the summit, where further progress seemed to be barred by an overhang. It would be a joke in the worst of taste if we were not able to force this last pitch. I took off my sack, hooking it to a piton, and went to the attack. The rock was very friable and the pitons did not hold. I made my way up very slowly with extreme caution, for my fingers were damaged by frostbite and hurt like hell. Eventually I succeeded in wedging myself into the final crack, fifteen feet beneath the exit, and there I was able to put in a piton and rest on it for a bit before going on again. The top was easier, and a last effort brought me out on the summit. We had won, and we were saved.

The central buttress leading to Point Croz had been climbed, but the highest of the Jorasses is the Point Walker and the spur leading up to it is, to a purist, obviously the true route up the north face of the mountain. So the battle went on. Eventually, in August 1938, the Walker spur was overcome by a Lecco party, Riccardo Cassin, G. Esposito and U. Tizzoni. The height of this buttress, at nearly 4,000 feet, is 600 feet or so higher than the Croz buttress. The second ascent was made in 1945 by E. Frendo and Gaston Rébuffat; there is a good account of it in Frendo's book *La Face Nord des Grandes Jorasses.*[8]

The Walker Spur is, by reason of its continuous difficulty, its altitude, its steepness and the absence of stances for rest, one of the best climbs in the Alps. Robin Smith, who climbed it in 1952 with Gunn Clark, reported that its technical difficulties were never more than the 'mildest Glencoe Very Severe'. Although Glencoe Very Severes are not markedly mild, it must be remembered that Smith and Clark found the mountain in excellent condition, that the much greater altitude of the Jorasses compared to Ben Nevis adds to the exertion required and that the pitches of the Walker have an adamantine continuity.

The Walker spur, the highest point in the Jorasses, one of the finest climbs in the Alps. It was first ascended by Riccardo Cassin and others in 1938.

6 Further Afield

Above: Douglas William Freshfield, mountaineer, explorer and geographer.

Below: Dyktau, first climbed by Mummery in 1888, one of those who travelled to distant ranges to find challenge and adventure after the major alpine peaks had fallen.

Opposite: Elbruz, the highest point in the Caucasus.

All the tunes that he could play
Was Over the Hills and Far Away.
                              Nursery rhyme

As pointed out in Chapter 4, once all the main peaks of the Alps had been climbed there was a stimulus to find unclimbed peaks elsewhere. Even before the end of the Golden Age, W. C. Slingsby had been busy exploring the mountains of Norway and Freshfield, Moore, C. C. Tucker, Craufurd Grove, F. Gardiner and Horace Walker had travelled to the Caucasus, whose peaks were nearer than the great ranges of Asia, America and New Zealand. Climbing in the Caucasus, as in all these more distant ranges, involved much travel over passes and in wild valleys. There were no railways, few roads, only widely scattered valley settlements, rare inns and none near the mountains. Such areas, therefore, appealed particularly to the traveller-mountaineer such as Freshfield, Woolley, Rickmer Rickmers and Longstaff, or in our day, Shipton and Tilman.

Caucasus
It is generally the highest peak in a group that first attracts attack. As with Mont Blanc, so it was with Elbruz (18,480 feet). Freshfield's party climbed the lower peak in 1868 and Grove's the higher, the culminating peak of the Caucasus, in 1874.[1] Twelve years later Clinton Dent and W. F. Donkin climbed Gestola (15,945 feet). Mummery reached the top of Dyktau (17,074 feet) and J. G. Cockin collected Shkhara (17,036 feet), Jangitau (16,571 feet) and the north peak of Ushba (15,400 feet), all in 1888. The south peak of Ushba was not climbed until 1903 when Schulze and von Ficker of W. R. Rickmers' party succeeded. In the same season, Hans Pfann, one of the greatest climbers of the period, with G. Leuchs and L. Distel, traversed both peaks of Ushba, spending four nights on the mountain, six bivouacs in all.

In 1888, when Donkin and H. Fox were lost on Koshtantau, there were rumours of treachery by the inhabitants. A group went out next year to search for traces and found the last bivouac of the vanished pair. There was no doubt that they had perished from a climbing accident and there was no evidence of foul play. Herman Woolley, one of the search party, went on to climb Koshtantau (16,880 feet).

Dr T. G. Longstaff went out with L. W. Rolleston in 1903. They climbed Tiktingen (15,125 feet), at the time the highest unclimbed mountain in the Caucasus; then, after other first ascents, they ended their season by attacking the west peak (16,592 feet) of Shkhara. Here is Longstaff's account of the climb:[2]

The ascent of the west peak of Shkhara
from T. G. Longstaff, *This My Voyage*
We now lost a few days from bad weather, with new snow on the mountains, and it was time to be off to Shkara. It would take three full days to reach its foot and by then we hoped the new snow would have settled into good order. From Mestia we rode over the Uguir pass to Ipari. Amongst some grand old fir trees we heard a grating call which was new to me: then saw, in laboured flight from tree to tree, two black, satanic-looking birds with marked crests–the great black woodpecker *(Dryocopus martius)*–a bird I had not then met in the Alps. From Ipari we rode on to Ushkul, the last village group on the Ingur river, in a barren and treeless glen. Both the Russian priest and the Georgian schoolmaster offered us entertainment, but we had to push on, and we camped an hour above the village, in a convenient thicket, with the south face of Shkara in full view.

Shkara is the second highest peak of the Caucasus. Its south face has been likened to the great Macugnaga face of Monte Rosa. The summit ridge is well over a

mile long coming to a point at each end. The eastern one (17,036 feet) had already been climbed from the north by Cockin, with Ulrich Almer and Roth in 1888. The western peak (16,592 feet) which looked more impressive from our camp was unclimbed, and no one had yet set foot on the great southern wall facing us.

On August 23rd with Araman and his friend Simon, another bearded hunter, we struck up the right bank of the infant Ingur river mounting grassy slopes such as would have resounded to cowbells in the Alps. We followed the morainic ridge on the right bank of the Shkara glacier below the point marked 3,043 metres on Merzbacher's map. We pitched the Mummery tent on a natural platform at about 10,500 feet, which was not really high enough for our need, but was too tempting to pass by. Opposite was spread the whole lovely range of the Laila, its sweeping spurs forest-clad: away to the east we overlooked Imeretia and the hills of the Ossete clans, famed in war, and beyond lay the peak of Kasbek and the Dariel pass, through which goes the great road from Vladikavkaz to Tiflis, capital of Georgia. Vladikavkaz means Key of the Caucasus, just as Vladivostok means Key of the East. On modern maps the name has been unromantically changed to Ordzhonikidze, but as he has been recently liquidated the name will probably be changed again.

We had examined the western peak of Shkara from the west and also in face and had seen that a well-marked ridge led directly to the summit. There was a little wall of rock just below the top which might be difficult: and again, some distance below this, were slabby, snow-covered rocks which might check us. It was a fine direct route, but we had not yet seen the way to get on to the beginning of this great ridge. It was the more unwise that we allowed doubtful weather to delay our start next morning till five-twenty. There is no risk in *starting* early in doubtful weather; but the flesh is weak. We scrambled down to the Shkara glacier and traversed snow slopes under a gloomy cliff with a blind corner ahead. This revealed a deep rock-strewn ravine with a hanging glacier above it from which stones and ice must often fall: but on the far side we could get on to our ridge. As the weather improved we bolted across the danger zone in a few minutes, and on to our ridge which began with easy snow slopes broken by rather rotten rock. Then, of a sudden, we found ourselves looking down upon a knife-edge of snow, with excessively steep slopes falling away on either hand. At our feet the narrow crest led abruptly downwards: then it ran horizontal for about 200 feet, to rise steep again to the continuing rocky crest. This passage which we had to take astride was like the well-known Brenva ice-ridge on Mont Blanc, but longer: an unpleasant place to leave behind us because the snow would be pretty rotten late in the afternoon. Beyond it we encountered easy rocks alternating with snow crests, with only an occasional step to cut in ice. As we had feared, the ledges leading up to the upper section of our ridge were particularly vile, rather steep and with ice-covered slabs dripping with melting snow. Above this warm

Tom Longstaff, whose mountaineering career took in the Alps, the Caucasus, the Rockies, Greenland and the Himalaya.

dry rocks suggested a halt at one-forty-five. Here an eagle circled round: we could see its eyes: we remembered Prometheus. We were still fully three hours from the summit, and if we went on we would have to pass the night on the mountain. But the weather was now fine and we were both in very good form: we had only to go on and the peak was ours. So on we went, with Rolleston in the lead, along our narrowing ridge, with sheering slopes on either side, carefully noting several ledges where we could spend the night on the descent. The condition of the snow improved, but in one case steps had to be cut for a short distance into hard ice. Then we faced the final rock step below the summit. It had looked awkward through glasses, but there was a mantel-shelf on to which Rolleston boosted me, prodding my tail with his axe as I clawed at iced finger-holds. The passage seemed very exposed, but was fortunately short and we landed above it on easy snow. The actual summit (16,592 feet), which we reached at four-forty was a vast cornice and our small cairn had to be made on a rock outcrop just below it.

This was the highest climb we had made, yet we felt no effects from the altitude, unless it was the curious feeling of aloofness from the world below us that we both experienced. We only had time to gaze over to the north at the great peak of Dyktau rising so abruptly from the Bezingi glacier in the deep gulf below us. We had to hurry down, but as we moved one at a time, the heavyweights first, the last man could often spare an eye for the wonderful view over Georgia as the sun set and to Ararat, across the Turkish frontier, overlooking Persian lands. But the going was not easy for the last man, who had often to turn and come down backwards, which is hard to do quickly. Also the melting snow had now frozen on the rocks and a slip would have been very dangerous. In the very last of the light we reached the ledge at the foot of the steep final section of the ridge. We could not get down even to the highest of the sheltering rocks we had noted on the way up and had to spend the night on a narrow shelf with no hitch for the rope: we could sit with dangling legs, but there could be no dozing. Gingerly taking off wet boots and stockings we wrapped our feet in dry socks and putties and thrust them into our rucksacks. The height was about 14,500 feet and after midnight we felt the cold. We took it in turns to hold the lantern between our knees for warmth, and later Rolleston boldly lit our little snow melter: but 'who can hold a fire in his hand by thinking on the frosty Caucasus?' His clothes were sadly scorched.

Slow and stiff we started down at five o'clock next morning. The narrow snow ridge was well frozen and we managed it quickly, reaching our bivouac without incident just before noon. Faithful Araman had seen our lantern in the night and had tea and grilled mutton ready for us. Then welcome sleep till four, and so down to camp. As we passed the tent, for we could only cross the stream below the camp, we hailed Nestor to get a meal going. No answer. This was too much for Simon the Svan: 'the Georgian swine sleeps.' He unslung his rifle and loosed a shot, apparently at the tent, which brought Nestor scuttling out.

I count this as the finest climb I have ever had. The altitude is about the limit for alpine standards. There is no excessive difficulty on the great southern spur which we followed, though it is very long and demands constant attention, especially on the descent. The peak itself and every foot of the way was all new, and it was a good ending to a great season of seven peaks in twenty-nine days' climbing, five of them first ascents.

After the Russian Revolution fewer Westerners visited the Causacus. They usually had great difficulty over passports, but most of those with the persistence to overcome this hurdle were well received by the inhabitants. The Russians themselves only took to climbing in a rather humdrum way until after the Second World War.

German or Austrian parties got to the Caucasus most years. Count Ugo di Vallepiana was there in 1929 with three companions,[3] and climbed Giulchi (14,680 feet), the most important of the then unclimbed peaks. After Raeburn's trip in 1914 no British party went there until 1937, when the Oxford University Mountaineering Club initiated an excursion. Only two of the four young men[4] were actually from Oxford but they had a most successful holiday. They made first ascents of two new peaks (which they named Kupoltau and Trezubetz) and no less than six new routes on mountains previously climbed.

North America

A great chain of mountain ranges runs some 4,000 miles down the west side of North America from the giants of Alaska through the Rockies of Canada and the United States down to the high volcanoes of Mexico. West of the Rockies, and separated from them by the Rocky Mountain Trench, are the interior ranges of British Columbia, the Selkirks, the Purcells and the Cariboo range, and, further south, the Sierra Nevada of California; on the extreme west is the Coast Range. Conditions, of course, vary enormously from the bare Arctic wastes of Alaska, through the rain forest and devil's club thorn of the British Columbian Coast Range to the pleasant climate of California.

Perhaps the foremost of the early mountain explorers of the Canadian Rockies was Norman Collie, but he had been preceded by H. W. Topham, who left his name on the Topham ridge of Monte Rosa's Signalkuppe and on Mount Topham in the Selkirks, and by W. S. Green, who so nearly climbed Mount Cook in 1882. Even earlier James Eccles had been in the Rocky Mountains of the USA. It was not till the end of the century that the main peaks began to fall to British, Canadian and American climbers. Collie led the first British expedition in 1897, and ascended Mounts Lefroy and Gordon. In later years, variously with Woolley, H. E. M. Stutfield, Sydney Spencer and others, he explored much new ground and made many new climbs. His last visit to the Rockies was in 1911. The completion of the Canadian Pacific Railway did much to stimulate this acceleration; the company installed Swiss guides at their hotel, Glacier House, in

the Selkirks in 1899; these guides played an important part in opening up mountaineering in Canada.

In 1901 Sir James Outram climbed Mounts Columbia and Assiniboine. Mount Sir Sandford (11,590 feet), the highest peak of the Selkirks, is even today awkward to get to (except by helicopter); Howard Palmer journeyed there five times by canoe and on foot before he succeeded in climbing it in 1912; he was accompanied by Holway and two Swiss guides. Mount Robson (12,972 feet), the culminating point of the Rockies, fell in 1913 to A. H. MacCarthy and W. W. Foster, led by Conrad Kain, the famous Austrian guide who had settled in Canada. Here is Kain's account.[5]

The ascent of Mount Robson

from Conrad Kain, *Where the Clouds Can Go*
At 4.30 am, after an early but good breakfast, we left our bivouac. We followed the route of the previous day (ascent of Mt Resplendent), over the glacier. Before we came to the Pass, we swerved to the right. From this point began the real climb of Mt Robson. We climbed up an avalanche trough, then under some dangerous ice bridges to the right. The snow was in bad condition. We proceeded without any difficulties towards the steep snow-slope that descends from the Dome (10,000 feet) and reached it at 7 am. We took a rest and deliberated over the route ahead.

Two years ago I spent hours studying this route, and did not take the bergschrund very seriously. From the Dome, one had a nearer survey of the bergschrund. We approached it over the glacier, which is here not very steep. A rib of rock comes down almost to the schrund. Over this rock I planned to ascend, but after every possible attempt we were forced to give it up, for at this place the glacier breaks off sheer. For about two hundred feet we followed along the bergschrund

to the right. Here was the only possibility at hand of overcoming it. After long chopping at the ice, I stood on its 65-degree slope. Across the schrund I made more steps. Then I let both *Herren* follow.

A thin layer of snow lay on the ice, and, owing to the melting of the snow, the ice was in very bad condition for step-cutting. I made the steps in a zigzag. Mr Foster counted 105 steps to a ledge of rock. The rock, when seen from below, promised good climbing and a rapid advance. But it turned out otherwise. We climbed up an icy wall, and then to our disappointment had an ice-slope before us, fifty or sixty metres high. I kept as well as I could to the rocks that protruded here and there, which saved me a few steps. At the top of the slope we had another wall of rock, and above that an almost hopeless ice-slope. One could see the tracks of falling stones and avalanches. On this slope I made 110 steps. It was a relief to climb on rocks again, though they were glazed with ice. But unfortunately the satisfaction was short, and for several hundred metres we had to climb again upon a slope of ice and snow. The snow here was in danger of avalanching. For safety, I lengthened the rope on the dangerous slope.

At last we reached the shoulder at twelve o'clock noon. I do not know whether my *Herren* contemplated with a keen Alpine eye the dangers to which we were exposed from the bergschrund. In the year 1909 this route was attempted by Mr Mumm, Mr Amery·with the guide Inderbinen from Zermatt. The party were in danger of their lives from an avalanche. I spoke with Inderbinen: he said, 'I never before saw death so near.'

On the shoulder we took a mid-day rest. There came a snowy wind that wet us to the bone. We pulled out all the clothing stowed away in our rucksacks. We found the shoulder less broad than we expected. It was a snow ridge, on the north-east side of which were overhanging cornices fringed with long icicles glittering in the sun, a glorious picture.

For a few hundred metres we had to keep to the south-east side. The snow on this side was in good condition, so that we made rapid progress. There was on each side a splendid view into the depths below. The more beautiful view was that of the Robson Glacier, Smoky Valley and Mt Resplendent and the Lynx Range opposite.

From the shoulder to the peak, the route was no longer so dangerous, but complicated by the loose, powdery snow. It was as if we were on an entirely different climb on the south-east side. The complications arose from walls of snow. Never before on all my climbs have I seen such snow formations. The snow walls were terraced. The ledges between the walls were of different widths, and all were covered with loose snow. I often sank in to my hips. There were forms on the walls like ostrich feathers, a truly strange and beautiful winter scene. Unfortunately we had no camera with us. Some of the walls were fifteen to twenty metres high. It was difficult to find a way up from one terrace to another. At one place I worked for over half an hour without effect. We had to go

back. A very narrow and steep couloir offered the only possibility. I warned my *Herren* that the piece would take considerable time to negotiate. Both had a good stand and kept moving as much as possible in order to keep warm. The wind was so bad here that I often had to stop. The steepness alone, apart from wind, made step-cutting very hard work. For a number of steps I had first to make a handhold in the ice, and swing the axe with one hand. I do not think I need to describe this method any more fully, for everyone who has

ever bee:. on the ice, knows that cutting steps with one hand is a frightfully slow process. I know that in such places it is not pleasant either for those behind. As soon as I was convinced that I could make it, I called to my *Herren*: 'Just be patient, the bad place will soon be conquered, and the peak is ours.' Mr MacCarthy answered: 'We are all right here, we are only sorry for you. I don't understand how you can still keep on cutting steps.'

When we had the difficult place behind us, the reward was a fairly steep snow-slope, with the snow in good condition so that we could all three go abreast. At the top of the snow-slope was another wall, which, however, could be outflanked without difficulty.

The last stretch to the summit was a snow-ridge. I turned to my *Herren* with the words: 'Gentlemen, that's as far as I can take you.'

In a few seconds both stood beside me on the peak. We shook hands with one another. I added my usual Alpine greeting in German, *'Bergheil.'* Of course, I had to explain the word *Bergheil*, because both knew no German. There is no word in the English language which has the same meaning as *Bergheil*.

On the crest of the king of the Rockies, there was not much room to stand. We descended a few metres and stamped down a good space. It was half past five o'clock. Our barometer showed exactly 13,000 feet.

The view was glorious in all directions. One could compare the sea of glaciers and mountains with a stormy ocean. Mt Robson is about 2,000 feet higher than all the other mountains in the neighbourhood. Indescribably beautiful was the vertical view towards Berg Lake and the camp below. Unfortunately only fifteen minutes were allowed us on the summit, ten of pure pleasure and five of teeth chattering. The rope and our damp clothes were frozen as hard as bone.

Opposite: the north face of Mount Robson, the culminating point of the Rockies, first climbed in 1913 by the Austrian guide Conrad Kain and two others. Kain described the expedition as one of the most dangerous in his career.

Above: Kain, J. Monroe Thorington, James Simpson and W. S. Ladd during an expedition to Mount Columbia in the early 1920s.

And so we had to think of the long descent – 5.45 o'clock. . . .

Mt Robson is one of the most beautiful mountains in the Rockies and certainly the most difficult one. In all my mountaineering in various countries, I have climbed only a few mountains that were hemmed in with more difficulties. Mt Robson is one of the most dangerous expeditions I have made. The dangers consist in snow and ice, stone avalanches, and treacherous weather.

This route is exposed to danger and has seldom been used since. Kain was responsible for another breakthrough when he led Mr and Mrs A. H. MacCarthy and J. Vincent up Bugaboo Spire in 1916. The Bugaboos, a sub-division of the Selkirks, provide some of the best rock-climbing in America.

The exploration of the Coast Range of British Columbia was delayed by its impenetrable scrub and bad weather. Don Munday, who specialised in this range, with his wife and his brother reached the snowy north-west peak of Mount Waddington (13,260 feet) in 1928; the eastern peak, a little higher, was not climbed until 1936 by F. Weissner and W. P. House. The mountain, higher than any in the main range of the Rockies, is hard of access and a difficult climb. The whole massif with five glaciers more than ten miles long resembles Mont Blanc; although 2,500 feet lower, the zone of glaciation also extends much lower than in the Alps.

In the Yukon, Allen Carpé and Terris Moore, supported by Dr W. S. Ladd and A. M. Taylor, reached the summit of Mount Fairweather (15,318 feet) in 1931. Probably no mountain of its height rises so close to the sea; it has tide-water within twenty miles on either side; its ascent was the hardest yet achieved in Arctic regions.

The highest point in Canada, Mount Logan (19,850 feet), near the Alaskan border, was climbed in 1925 by an expedition set up by the joint efforts of the Canadian and American Alpine Clubs. The leader was A. H. MacCarthy. A preliminary journey with dog-teams was necessary to establish caches of supplies for the climbing party; this strenuous and difficult journey took 70 days. The climbers then took nine weeks to climb their mountain and return to base. Nowadays much of the delay and difficulty is removed by using aircraft.

Alaska boasts two giants: Mount St Elias (18,008 feet), which succumbed to the Duke of the Abruzzi in 1897 but not again until 1946, and Mount McKinley (20,320 feet), which is not only the highest point in North America but has a most fascinating history.

One Dr F. Cook, whose earlier career seems to have been highly creditable, claimed to have climbed Mount McKinley in 1906. The claim had always been suspect, but controversy continued until 1958 when it was finally quashed by a magisterial report by Bradford Washburn, summarised in the *American Alpine Journal*. Mr Washburn showed fine detective skill which, combined with his knowledge of the terrain, killed the Cook story as effectively as the

Balmat myth had been slain the year before.

The true story of the first ascent is better than any Dr Cook could invent. In 1910 six prospectors from Fairbanks set out to climb the mountain on $500 provided by the saloon-keeper. By the time they reached the foot of the climb, three of the party had gone home after a bout of fisticuffs. The remaining three, Peter Anderson, Billy Taylor, and Charley McGonagall, camped at the head of the Muldrow Glacier; though inured to hard living and hard travel, they had no experience of high mountains, no proper equipment and very little food. From the camp they climbed some 9,000 feet to the summit and back again in a single day. It is no diminution of their achievement that the peak they climbed, the northern peak, is some 300 feet lower than the highest point. Their story met with even less credence than Dr Cook's until 1913, when the Karstens-Stuck party[6] first climbed the higher summit; they then saw the flagstaff planted on the northern peak by the 'sourdoughs of Mount McKinley' three years earlier.

South America

The Andes stretch the whole length of South America. At the southern tip the mountains of Tierra del Fuego and Patagonia have one of the worst climates in the world and the whole range has a very high level of precipitation brought by the wet west winds off the Pacific. Apart from the windswept monoliths of Patagonia, the Cordillera Blanca and the Cordillera Huayhuash of Peru contain the finest mountains, although the highest point, Aconcagua (22,835 feet), is in the relatively dull central section. The Peruvian Andes are fantastically glaciated and snow clings to slopes that in other ranges would be too steep to retain it.

There is plenty of archaeological evidence that in the pre-Columbian period, Inca civilisation penetrated to great heights and to many of the more accessible summits, probably for religious reasons. Wilhelm Reiss, a geologist, and A. M. Escobar climbed Cotopaxi (19,350 feet) in 1872. Whymper took J. A. and Louis Carrel to the same area in 1880; they climbed Cotopaxi again and made the first ascent of Chimborazo (20,563 feet). Here is a press report of a lecture Whymper gave after his return to London.

A lecture by Whymper on Chimborazo and Cotopaxi

It is unfortunately impossible in a necessarily short report to give any idea of the charm of the narrative which Mr Whymper had to relate, brightened as it was by many quietly-given touches of humour. Personal matters, however, were only introduced when they served to illustrate some scientific observation. While purely athletic mountaineers had his sympathy in the practice of mountaineering as a sport, Mr Whymper confessed that his sympathies were much more with those who employed their brains as well as their muscles. His journey to the Andes was to be one of work, and all its arrangements were devised so as to economise time to the uttermost. In observations for

Above: the Duke of the Abruzzi in 1897, after the ascent of Mount Elias, the second highest peak in Alaska, a performance not repeated until 1946. The Duke not only pioneered winter climbing in the Alps but organised and led three major mountaineering expeditions to Alaska (1897), to Uganda (1906) and to the Karakorum (1909).

Opposite top: Mount McKinley, the highest point in North America, from Wonder Lake. Its lower, northern, peak was first climbed by a party of poorly equipped prospectors in bitter weather.

Opposite bottom: a group of sourdoughs (as prospectors and trappers were nicknamed) outside a saloon in Fairbanks. Third from the left in the front row is Billy McPhee, the saloon-keeper who financed the first successful ascent of Mount McKinley.

teams. About two tons weight of the most portable and most condensed provisions went out for their use, and, irrespective of the things which were bought already tinned, more than 2,000 tins were soldered down. When they reached the summit of Chimborazo, on the 3rd of January, after a most arduous climb, they found the wind blowing at the rate of 50 miles an hour from the north-east, and driving the snow before it. With extreme difficulty, a reading of the mercurial barometer was effected. The mercury fell to 14·1 inches with a temperature of 21 degrees Fahrenheit. This being worked out, in comparison with a nearly simultaneous observation at Guayaquil, gave 20,545 feet for the height of Chimborazo. They began the descent at twenty minutes past three, with scarcely an hour and a quarter of daylight, and reached their camp (about 17,400 feet above the sea-level) about 9 pm, having been out nearly sixteen hours, and on foot the whole time.

Passing from an extinct to an active volcano, Mr Whymper next gave an account of his journey to the crater of Cotopaxi. Observing with the telescope, during an enforced stay at Machachi, that much less smoke or vapour was given off at night than by day, he resolved, if possible, to pass a night on the summit. On the 18th of February the party got to the edge of the crater, having passed almost the whole way from their camp, at a height of 15,000 feet, to the foot of the final cone over snow, and then over ash mixed with ice. The final cone was the steepest part of the ascent, and on their side presented an angle of 36 degrees. When they reached the crater vast quantities of smoke and vapour were boiling up, and they could only see portions of the opposite side at intervals, and the bottom not at all. Their tent was pitched at 250 feet from the edge of the crater, and during a violent squall the india-rubber floor of the tent was found to be on the point of melting, a *maximum* thermometer showing a temperature of 110 degrees on one side of the tent and of but 50 degrees on the other; in the middle it was 72·5 degrees. Outside it was intensely cold and a thermometer on the tent cord showed a *minimum* of 13 degrees. At night they had a fine view of the crater, which has a diameter from north to south of 2,000 feet, and from east to west of about 1,500 feet. In the interior the walls descend to the bottom in a series of steps of precipice and slope a good thousand feet, and at the bottom there was a nearly circular spot of glowing fire, 200 feet in diameter. On the sides of the interior higher up, fissures, from which flickering flames were leaping, showed that the lava was red hot a very short distance below the surface. The height he found to be 19,600 feet. The party remained at the top for 26 consecutive hours, sleeping about 130 feet below the loftiest point. At first they had felt the effects of the low pressure of the atmosphere, and again, as at Chimborazo, took chlorate of potash with good effect. All signs of mountain sickness had passed away before they commenced the descent, and did not recur during the journey. . . .

The Prince of Wales in proposing a vote of thanks

Top: an engraving of Cotopaxi (1748), the world's highest live volcano. Though volcanoes fascinate geographers, they are not particularly challenging for mountaineers. Whymper's ascent in 1880 was the fifth.

Above: an English party on Popacatapetl in 1900. It was first climbed in 1521 by Spanish soldiers.

altitude and position, in studying the manners and customs of the country, in photography and sketching, in the collection of objects of interest, from beetles on the summits of mountains to antiquities buried in the ground, he found quite sufficient to occupy his time.

From Bodegas the party was composed of two Swiss mountaineers, the cousins Carrel, of Val Tournanche,[7] Mr Perring, some muleteers and their

to Mr Whymper, said the matter which he had laid before them that evening was such as must be of deep interest even to those who had not had any experience of the ascent of high mountains. . . .

Volcanoes have an interest of their own but their mountaineering interest tends to be minimal. Climbers' playgrounds are on older rocks that have been split by upheavals, weather and erosion, not on comparatively recent cones of lava.

In 1897, Matthias Zurbriggen, who had come to the Andes with Edward FitzGerald, reached the top of Aconcagua. This is the highest mountain outside Asia, a laborious ascent by the ordinary route. Next year, after repeating the climb of Aconcagua, Martin Conway went up Illimani (21,200 feet) in Bolivia.

The ice-clad Peruvian Andes were not attacked until later. The Cordillera Blanca was first crossed by C. R. Enoch in 1903 by a pass of over 17,000 feet. Miss Annie Peck (USA) reached the lower, northern, peak of Huascaran with R. Taugwalder and G. zum Taugwald in 1908 (Taugwalder chivalrously handed over his spare clothing, including his gloves, to Miss Peck and suffered damaging frostbite as a result), but the higher peak, which is the culminating point of the Cordillera Blanca (22,205 feet), was not climbed until 1932, when an Austro-German expedition led by Philip Borchers was successful. Here is Borchers' account. [8]

The ascent of Huascaran

from Philip Borchers, the *Alpine Journal*, Vol. XLV
On July 16, 1932, Bernard, Hein, Hoerlin, Schneider and I, with nine porters and two mule-grooms, set

out to attack Huascaran by its W. slope. We contrived to bring our mules up to thickly bush-covered moraine, some 3,750 m. high. On the following and very hot day we penetrated with swollen rucksacks through scrub and thorn, followed by great boulders and granite slabs, to some 4,750 m., where the 'dry' zone extends its utmost limits into the broad névé covering. On the third day the route led over easy névé to a height of about 5,500 m., where we bivouacked on a fairly roomy ice terrace still safe from any falling séracs. The fourth day brought serious ice work; in front, or rather right above us, lay the steep icefall, through and over which we had to hew our way to the *Garganta*, the saddle between the S. and N. peaks. Schneider and Hein led off, hacking such large ice steps that the porters, still in their novitiate, were able to mount easily. A proper staircase had to be cut, as we three others had three porters apiece roped to us and in our charge during the ascent. The icefall was extremely steep, and broken up into savage walls and séracs. It was not easy to find a way through. For instance, Schneider and Hein cut through one thin wall, but as soon as they had crawled through the tunnel, appearances became too ghastly and all the work was wasted. Still, we really had luck: not only did we find a way through this ice labyrinth, but of all the crumbling séracs, deep ice grottoes and rotten snow bridges not one

Above: the American schoolteacher Annie Peck with her guides Taugwalder and zum Taugwald. They reached the lower, northern, peak of Huascaran in the Peruvian Andes in 1908; the higher peak was climbed in 1932 by Philip Borchers. Left: Borchers' camp on Huascaran under the Garganta, the saddle between the north and south peaks.

ever collapsed, while two porters who had slipped out of their steps could be held on the rope. In the evening a camp of three tents was pitched on snow about 100 m. below the *Garganta*. On the fifth day, July 20, the issue was settled. The nine porters remained in camp, while we five Germans broke ground against the S. peak. The way led first over broad crevasses towards the *Garganta*, which provides comparatively high-reaching patches of névé; then to the right, over steep snow, wearing crampons, where many crevasses furrow the often *very* steep slope. Our times were good – with no cares about the porters, the ascent was a pleasure. This, however, soon changed for the worse. The summit cap with its endless and continuous slope was still 400 m. distant. The snow had not settled here, or perhaps the great height causes it to be always powdery; only a finger thickness of firm snow lay thereon – beneath this crust it was like flour. When a foot was placed on it the upper surface held for a bit, then one broke through to the thigh, while those behind sank still further in. It was terribly fatiguing and monotonous. Thin clouds drifted about us, concealing more and more the scenery below us. Where the surface formed into little hollows, the atmosphere was perfectly still, and there the tropical sun fairly blazed. The wind worried us much, for each time that a gust arrived the temperature became icy, not so much from cold (−10°C.) as from its all-penetrating blasts. At last, rather later than 4 pm, we reached the summit. We planted the 4-m. pole which we had carried up and hoisted the Peruvian flag as a mark of courtesy to our hosts. It was later on recognized by telescope from Yungay. Wind and cold, together with the approach of darkness, hurried us off. 'Go down as quickly as you can' were my orders to the first rope. The dark, tropical night overtook Bernard and me on the *Garganta*. After one quite harmless fall of mine into a crevasse, we waited, content but shivering, for four hours until the rising moon once more lit up the tracks. In the camp below the storm had also been fierce: the steel poles of the porters' tent had been smashed, as well as sundry cooking apparatus and a porter's sleeping-bag blown into the abyss. The descent into the valley took two more days.

This expedition subsequently climbed Chopicalqui (20,998 feet), Artisonraju (19,766 feet) and Huandoy (20,981 feet), the last proving 'quite remarkably difficult and dangerous'.

Throughout the Thirties the main explorations were by Austro-German parties.

New Zealand

The mountains of New Zealand are lower than the Alps, but the line of perpetual snow is also lower by about 3,000 feet. Thus, measured from the snowline, Mount Cook (12,349 feet) is much the same height as Mont Blanc. Heavy precipitation leads to impressive ice formation and the weather is poor; what are regarded as 'good' conditions in the Alps – fine weather and firm snow – are rare.

Two magazine illustrations of the attempt on Mount Cook in 1882. Below: W. S. Green with Kaufmann and Boss from Grindelwald fording the Hooker. They turned back 200 feet from the summit and were forced to spend an excruciatingly uncomfortable night out on a narrow ledge (below right).

Although surveyors had reached respectable heights, mountaineering proper only began in 1882 when W. S. Green with two men from Grindelwald, Ulrich Kaufmann and Emil Boss, arrived with the aim of climbing Mount Cook. To all intents and purposes they succeeded; after having passed all the difficulties they turned back about 200 feet short of the summit and suffered a painful night out on the descent.[9] The first completely successful climb of a major peak in the Southern Alps was made in 1883 when R. von Lendenfeld, with his wife and a porter, climbed Hochstetter Dome (9,258 feet).

The first complete ascent of Mount Cook was made by the New Zealanders T. C. Fyfe, George Graham and J. M. Clarke in 1894, after a long and determined siege by a handful of enthusiasts. Green's route being certainly dangerous (S. King with D. Thomson and J. Richmond were killed by an avalanche there in 1914), Fyfe went up on the opposite side by the Hooker Glacier and the north ridge, an exacting climb and also dangerous, with much loose rock. His route was not repeated for 61 years. Edward FitzGerald came out the next year with Matthias Zurbriggen. He was so disappointed at having been forestalled on Mount Cook that he did not attempt the mountain, but Zurbriggen reached the summit alone by the buttress bounding the Linda Glacier. FitzGerald, Zurbriggen and J. M. Clarke climbed Tasman (11,475 feet) and Haidinger.

The next major stimulus came in January and February 1907. H. E. Newton, E. Teichelmann and

Alex Graham pitched a camp on Pioneer Ridge in the centre of the névé of the Fox Glacier at about 7,000 feet. From there they traversed Mount Halcombe (8,743 feet) between the Fox and Franz Josef glaciers, up by the north face and down by the south; they climbed Glacier Peak (9,867 feet) by the west face, Douglas Peak (10,107 feet) in 16 hours going from their camp, and Torres Peak (10,376 feet), a long 17-hour rock climb. After Teichelmann left, Newton and Graham climbed Mount Haast (10,294 feet) from the saddle between Haast and Lendenfeld, then climbed Roberts (10,503 feet), descended to the saddle between Roberts and Tasman, returning to camp via the Heemskirk Glacier. On February 27 they climbed to the divide at the head of the north branch of Fox Glacier, traversed a peak of 9,508 feet, climbed Mount Conway (9,543 feet), descended to Frenchay Col, went a little way down the Franz Josef Glacier and over a pass back to their camp on Fox. All were first ascents and the weather was 'atrocious'.

The first traverse of the three peaks of Mount Cook was made in 1913 by the Australian Freda du Faur, with Peter Graham and David Thomson. They bivouacked on a patch of rocks at about 7,000 feet below the west ridge leading up to the lowest of the three peaks. Miss du Faur continues:[10]

The traverse of Mount Cook
from Freda du Faur, *The Conquest of Mount Cook*
One o'clock on the morning of the 3rd saw us sleepily consuming breakfast, hunched up in our sleeping-bags in a vain attempt to keep out the chill morning breeze. By two o'clock we stood outside in the clear starlight, roped together and ready for the start. Turning to the left, we followed the previous night's steps (by candle-light) to the base of the western arête, and then up a narrow and very steep slope, leading directly to the saddle between the third and second peaks of Mount Cook. At 3.30 am we came to the end of our steps, and as the dawn was breaking, we put out our useless candles. The slope was frozen hard, and soon the tuneful ring of ice-axes and the patter of falling crystals broke the morning stillness. Over the saddle a brilliant crescent moon sailed in a sky of velvet blue, while towards the west the sky flushed with the breaking dawn. The clear rounded headland of Bruce Bay rose from a silver sea, and the whole coast curved before us. The Cook River twisted and turned, stream intersecting stream in a waste of yellow tussock. Dominant on sea as well as land, Mount Cook threw its shadow over the shining waters, a phantom pyramid stretching up the horizon. The first rays of the rising sun caught the corniced east face of the highest peak, turning it to glittering gold in a wonderful contrast to the deep blue shadows of the still unlighted west.

After an hour's step-cutting we turned to the right, and gained the western arête. The rocks were heavily hung with icicles, and here and there coated with a thin film of green ice, which necessitated careful climbing. Slowly we crept up, the icy rocks chilling hands and feet. At last we emerged at the foot of the

Right: an aerial view of Mount Cook, which occupies the bottom half of the picture. The long summit ridge of the traverse by Freda du Faur and her companions is clearly shown.

Below: Edward FitzGerald, who came to New Zealand in 1895 intending to be the first to climb Mount Cook. He was forestalled, and instead went up Tasman and Haidinger for the first time.

final snow-cap. Here we paused for a second break-fast, gratefully clasping our cold fingers round the hot cups that held our Thermos tea. Much revived by our meal, we cut our way up the final snow slope, reaching the summit and the sunlight at seven o'clock. Strictly speaking, there is no summit, but only a narrow ridge falling away sheer to the Tasman Glacier. It was so narrow that the party preferred straddling it to standing upright. So with a leg on either side we contemplated the view. It was indeed our lucky day. Not a breath of wind stirred, the sun shone warmly from a cloudless sky. The whole of New Zealand lay spread beneath our feet, limited only by the vision of the human eye. We gazed in silence on rolling plains, deep green forests, and far-away seas. But longest and most earnestly our eyes dwelt on the cruel ridge on which we sat. It stretched away before us, onward and upward in zigzag curves. From the summit on which we rested it dropped sharply to a jagged saddle, then up again steeply to the mighty ice face of the second peak. Always to the east the ridge falls away sheer for thousands of feet, while on its west side it slopes steeply for a few yards to a big outward bulge, which overhangs the Hooker Glacier. After studying our perilous way for ten minutes, we started down the steep ridge to the saddle. The rocks were jagged and much covered with loose snow. We made our way with the utmost care, the guides considering this would probably be the worst part of the traverse. More than once my

knees shook under me as I followed Graham round the saw-like teeth of the arête, or let my eyes follow the flight of a dislodged stone, falling, falling, falling into the abyss beneath. It did not require much imagination to feel oneself sinking into those horrible depths. One little slip or false step and then – the end. At last we reached the saddle and started up the ridge leading to the middle peak.

We found to our joy it was frozen snow, and we chipped rapidly up, our spirits rising with every yard as we began to realize that if the weather held we might really accomplish this great traverse, which the most experienced mountaineers in New Zealand had declared impossible. Looking at the Mount Cook arête from below it seems one continuous ascent, with two well-defined drops between the third and second, and the second and high peak. In reality it is a series of ups and downs stretching away for a mile and a half, at an altitude varying from 11,800 feet to 12,349 feet. So narrow and exposed is this ridge, that to attempt to follow it, except under perfect conditions, would be madness. A still day is absolutely essential. If a party were caught on the middle of the arête in the bitter winds that so often rage above 10,000 feet, retreat would be impossible. Frozen stiff and helpless, in half an hour they would be powerless to fight against it, and would either slip from the narrow ridge into the abyss beneath, or die of exposure and inaction.

Our progress up the middle peak was better than

we had dared to hope for; but when we arrived at the foot of the final snow slope, we found it impossible to follow the arête, owing to a bad overhang at its steepest point. So we turned our attention to the south face and there the guides spent two hours' hard work cutting steps at an angle of 60 degrees. The ice was of the hardest variety, and the sun blazed down upon it. The brilliant surface reflected the rays back again, till our eyes smarted and our heads swam. At last a shout of triumph announced that the summit was in sight, and at half-past nine we stood upon the second peak.

The view from here was our most perfect of the day. To the west blue sea surged into blue sky, till it was impossible to tell where the one ended and the other began. Clouds soft as down hung motionless above the Sierras, or drifted slowly over the rolling golden tussock of the MacKenzie plains, out of which shone here and there the turquoise blue of a snow-fed lake. Directly in front of us towered the high peak of Mount Cook, and between it and Mount Tasman ran the curved coast line, till it lost itself behind the maze of northward mountains. Beside us the Tasman Glacier swept its fourteen miles in gracious curves, crowned on either hand with New Zealand's greatest peaks, their white summits shimmering in the sun, or contrasted boldly against some rocky giant, on whose precipitous side no snow might lodge. We spent half an hour on this summit drinking in beauty at every breath. Also, it must be confessed, since this is a practical world, we fed and took photographs. Then we were ready to start on the last and worst part of our long journey.

Ever since we had decided to attempt the traverse, the steep knife-edge ridge between the middle and high peak had been to me a haunting horror. From wherever you look upon it it appears impossible. Now, the moment I had dreaded had arrived, and the reality was all that imagination had pictured it. Steep, narrow, and horribly corniced, the ridge dropped sharply for a hundred feet. More than once as we descended it an icy shiver ran down my spine, as the ice-axe sank deeply into the overhanging cornice, and on withdrawal disclosed through the tiny hole the awful gap between us and the glacier thousands of feet beneath. Later, when we compared notes, we all confessed to wondering what would happen if a cornice broke away. Would the shock startle us into eternity? The mere noise and vibration of the falling mass would be enough to shake the strongest nerves, and we only stood about two feet from the junction of solid ice and cornice. At last we accomplished the many windings of the arête, and started up the highest peak. The relief of ascending with a wall in front to look at was tremendous, after the nerve-racking, downward ridge of the last hour. Fate was kind again, and we only had an hour's step-cutting on the final slope.

At half-past one we stood on the highest summit of Mount Cook, conquerors indeed. We were filled with mingled pride and thankfulness, as our eyes roved backwards over the great ridge we had spent the last six and a half hours in vanquishing. Very heartily we wrung one another's hands, and marvelled at our phenomenal luck in obtaining weather conditions which had enabled us to accomplish the greatest climb in New Zealand at the first attempt. Very happily we lay at ease on the summit, and putting all thoughts of the descent out of our minds, concerned ourselves only with the joy and triumph of the present.

The next wave was stimulated by the visit of H. E. L. Porter and Marcel Kurz in 1927. Lucky in their weather, they made the first traverse of Tasman, the second ascent of Haidinger, the third ascent of David's Dome (10,443 feet), the fourth traverse of Mount Cook, the first ascent of Le Receveur (9,562 feet). They traversed Haast and Lendenfeld, making a new route up Haast, and made the second ascent of Torres (10,376 feet). In between they also climbed Aiguille Rouge (9,731 feet) and Malte Brun (10,421 feet). This successful holiday, in particular their fast time on the traverse of Cook, was significant in that it converted New Zealanders to the use of crampons, which are of special value in the predominantly icy local conditions. Porter was out again next year (his fourth visit) but had more normal experience of the weather; out of fifty days at the Hermitage, the oldest and most famous hut in the New Zealand Alps (now a hotel), four were fine.

Africa

Mountainwise Africa is a disappointing continent. There is plenty of climbing but no great range such as each of the other continents can show.

In the north there are the Atlas and even in the Sahara there are mountains and rock outcrops. Ethiopia contains a great deal of high mountainous country, but it is little known. In the east are Mount Kenya and Kilimanjaro, which provides the highest point of the continent (19,334 feet); the ordinary route to the summit, Kibo, is arduous and dreary but good climbing can be found on the glaciers and on the lower peak, Mawenzi (16,890 feet). The Ruwenzori, the Mountains of the Moon, ought to be splendid and very occasionally are, but the weather is so bad that the mountains are seldom visible; they were first explored by the Duke of the Abruzzi in 1906. In southern Africa, from the Cape to the Chimanimani, on the borders of Rhodesia and Mozambique, there are plenty of mountains, plenty of fine climbs and an admirable climate. All this southern climbing is, of course, on rock only; the best of it is in the western Cape Province from Table Mountain to du Toit's Kloof.

In the intercontinental league Africa is really only redeemed by Mount Kenya (17,058 feet). It has steep, generally good rock, glaciers on the equator (which are, alas, shrinking fast and may even disappear) and a complexity of ridges, faces and subsidiary peaks that has been fairly compared to Mont Blanc. Its highest peak, Batian, was first climbed by Sir

Freda du Faur who, with Peter Graham and David Thomson, achieved the first traverse of the three peaks of Mount Cook in 1913.

The Drakensburg (South Africa): the north face of Monk's Cowl. Southern Africa offers plenty of excellent rock climbing—and fine weather.

sharp and clear, framing our own dark silhouettes. It was the Spectre of the Brocken – the only one I have ever seen. Mountains have many ways of rewarding us for our pilgrimage, and often bestow their richest treasures when least expected. For my part, all disappointment, all care for the future were drowned in the great joy of living that moment. We climbed slowly down the ridge and crossed the glacier back to camp.

In my experience, the lofty thoughts, the enthusiasms and good intentions of the night before seldom survive the early interruption of sleep, the hateful business of making and eating an early breakfast, the sullen struggle with frozen boots. The next morning was no exception. I could think of nothing but the futility of renewing our efforts to climb this confounded peak. But yet it had to be done, there was no way out. Anyway in a few hours I would be back again to resume my blessed slumbers.

Gustav had slept badly, and had a headache, so he stopped in bed. Wyn and I slouched across the glacier and sorted ourselves out on the other side. It was still very early and very cold. The peak was black and hard against a clear sky. Our only hope now was straight up the face of Nelion between the junction of the south and east ridges. I gazed up at it in dreamy bewilderment, without the faintest idea of how to start. But a fiery spark seemed to have kindled in Wyn during our short halt, and as soon as we had roped together he led off up the rocks with such energy and decision that he might have been an Alpine guide climbing a familiar peak. First up a gully to the left, then to the right along a broken terrace under a smooth wall – this was fine, I began to come to life. But it was too good to last. Our terrace ended abruptly against a vertical rib, and there was still no sign of a breach in the wall above us. Descending a little, Wyn disappeared round and below the obstructing rib, while I belayed the rope and prepared for the worst. The rope went out slowly, and I waited. Then came a wild cry from round the corner. I thought Wyn had fallen off, and braced myself to receive the jerk. But instead came an excited 'All right, come on!' When I joined him on a square platform I saw the cause of the excitement. A steep and narrow gully led up from the platform. It was crowned by an overhanging rock, and down it dangled a rope, white with age. It could only have been put there by Mackinder's party; no one since had succeeded in getting so far up the face. Though the rope was too frail to use, the discovery was a tremendous encouragement.

Wyn had found the way, and it was now my turn to take a hand. I led off up the gully and, after struggling for some time below the overhang, at last succeeded in reaching a firm handhold away to the right and swung myself, breathless, above the obstacle, where I pulled in the rope for Wyn to follow. The gully was certainly the key to the lower part of the face, and after some straightforward climbing we reached the place where the south ridge abuts against the upper wall of Nelion.

Halford Mackinder, with César Ollier and Joseph Brocherel, in 1899. It was not climbed again until 1929 when Wyn Harris and Eric Shipton reached it after crossing the slightly lower summit, Nelion. Here is Shipton's account:[11]

The ascent of Mount Kenya
from Eric Shipton, *Upon That Mountain*

It was now about six o'clock. The mists were clearing rapidly, as I had so often seen them from the farm more than forty miles away. I wondered if anyone were watching from there now. For us, in the midst of the scene, a part of it, it was profoundly impressive. First Point John appeared, we were nearly level with its summit, an island in a restless sea of soft pink and grey. Then, all about us were spires and wild buttresses, floating, moving; and above, infinitely high, the rocky dome of Batian. The level rays of the sun had broken through. We looked towards the east and saw there a great circle of rainbow colours,

Flushed with our success we sat down to reflect. It seemed amazing to find ourselves here after the hopelessness of the early morning. The day was still young and fortune appeared to be on our side. The sky was clear and the rocks were warming in the sun. We looked out over a vast sea of billowy white clouds, gently rising. They would envelop us before long. To the south, above the clouds, stood a great dome of shining ice. That was strange. We knew there was no peak of that shape and size in the Kenya massif. Yet there it was clear against the blue sky, and it seemed quite close to us. Then suddenly we realised it was Kilimanjaro, the highest mountain in Africa, 250 miles away. The atmosphere over East Africa is remarkably clear. I do not think I have seen mountains at that distance anywhere else.

But we could not spend long enjoying the view, and we had almost at once to turn our attention to the immediate prospect. This was far from encouraging, and our spirits soon clouded. It must have been from here that Mackinder's party had reached the Diamond glacier, and here too that they had been forced to bivouac after their successful but prolonged struggle with it. Above and to the left the great cliffs of Nelion bulged over steep white slabs that fell away to the Darwin glacier. Along the top of these slabs there was a possible line of traverse. But it was an ugly-looking place, and the rocks were plastered with ice. Even if it were possible to climb along the slabs in these conditions, which was very doubtful, we would then be faced with the Diamond glacier. We decided to try to climb the face of Nelion direct. It did not look very promising, but it was the only alternative to those ice-covered slabs.

We climbed to a little recess at the end of the ridge. Behind this was a smooth wall some 60 feet high. But in its lower part there were some tiny holds, and balancing on these I started climbing, hoping to find more holds higher up. But before I had got 15 feet up they petered out. I managed to make a little progress to the left, but without gaining height, and there I clung until my fingers and feet were aching painfully. Working my way back above the recess I tried to the right and here found a narrow sloping ledge that led round a corner out of sight. It was an airy place above a sheer drop whose depth I did not bother to estimate. But before I had got far round the corner I found a shallow crack which split the surface of the wall above me. It was obviously the only line of possibility and I took it, though I was not at all happy. The crack was not wide enough to wedge my foot in it, and the only holds were smooth and sloping outwards. My progress was painfully slow, but soon the prospect of beating a retreat was even more repugnant than climbing on up. At length I reached the top of the crack and found myself on a fairly wide platform above the wall. I felt rather ashamed of myself for wasting so much time on a fool's errand.

But Wyn, when he joined me on the platform, was jubilant, though what there was in our situation to be

pleased about I could not see. For the next hundred feet or so the ground was certainly easier, but above that the upper cliffs of Nelion frowned over us in a fearsome overhang, which, even in my somewhat desperate frame of mind, I could not imagine myself attempting.

We climbed on until we were directly under the overhang. From here a wide gully ran steeply down to the right and plunged out of sight. By climbing a little way down this it seemed that we could cross to the buttress on the other side, which formed our skyline in that direction. But if we could get round this it would only bring us out on to the terrific precipice of the eastern face of Nelion. However it was the only way, and Wyn led off down and across the gully. The full length of the rope was stretched taut across the gully before he found a suitable stand and I could join him. Then we climbed diagonally up the buttress. Before it disappeared round the corner, I looked back and saw that we were already

The Mitre Bastion, Chimanimani (Rhodesia) gives some idea of the quality of climbing to be found in Africa.

above the overhanging part of the southern face of Nelion. We crossed the crest of the buttress, expecting to be faced with a smooth perpendicular cliff. Instead, to our incredulous delight we found that easy broken rocks led on upwards. We could not see the summit, but it was clear that we were above the great wall of the east face and that there was nothing now to stop us. This sudden change from hopelessness to the certainty of success was among the most thrilling experiences I have known. There followed only a swift joyous

scramble and we were there, on the hitherto un-trodden summit of Nelion.

By now the cloud was all about us, though we could still see the Lewis glacier below. Gustav had been watching the summit through field glasses. He saw us now and let out a tremendous shout which came faintly to our ears. Across the gap, filled with swirling mist, we could see dimly the rocky dome of Batian.

After a short rest we started down the ridge towards the Gate of the Mist. Our first attempt to reach it failed, but by cutting steps down a hard snow slope on the northern side of the ridge we turned an over-hanging pinnacle and got down to the floor of the gap. Thence we reached the summit of Batian. . . .

I have since repeated the climb several times, and each time I was more amazed . . . that we should have regarded the ascent of Nelion as so very difficult. Each step became so engraved on my memory that it seemed commonplace and perfectly straightforward. Even the crack in the 60 foot wall, that had turned out to be the key to the upper part of the mountain, was no longer formidable. This experience of repeating a climb, the first ascent of which I had made myself showed me very clearly how it was that mountains in the Alps, which had resisted the attacks of the pioneers for so long and had appeared to them such

desperate ventures, should come to be regarded as quite easy.

A year later, Shipton and H. W. Tilman made a complete traverse of the twin peaks of the mountain from west to east. Since the last war, many new routes of high quality have been opened up by many fine climbers, among whom Arthur Firmin must be given pride of place.

Above: Eric Shipton in 1933, four years after he climbed Batian, the highest peak of Mount Kenya, with Wyn Harris. It was the mountain's second ascent.

Opposite: the twin peaks of Mount Kenya.

7 Himalaya to 1939

A hard time we had of it.
At the end we preferred to travel all night,
Sleeping in snatches,
With the voices singing in our ears, saying,
That this was all folly.

Then at dawn we came down to a temperate valley,
Wet, below the snow line, smelling of vegetation;
With a running stream and a water-mill beating the darkness,
And three trees on the low sky,
And an old white horse galloped away in the meadow.

                                                    T. S. Eliot

The Himalaya are the most massive feature of the earth's surface. They stretch 1,500 miles from the Indus to the Brahmaputra, cutting off the Indian sub-continent from Central Asia. There are very high passes which have been used for trade from time immemorial by local men. Apart from possible visits of Greek adventurers in the fourth century BC, of which there is no record beyond oral tradition, the first European contacts were made by Jesuits in the early seventeenth century. The first to cross the whole range were Father Antonio de Andrade and Brother Manuel Marques in 1624. Such crossings by Jesuits continued to be made from time to time for the next hundred years. Six small British missions penetrated into the Himalaya in the eighteenth century, but no systematic collection of geographical knowledge began until the nineteenth century.

Despite the understandable parsimony of the directors of the East India Company, Robert Colebrooke, as Surveyor-General of Bengal, was able to organise much exploration, largely by encouraging officers to map territory they were called upon to visit. The first maps of Nepal were produced in 1803 by Charles Crawford, who had commanded the Resident's Escort in Khatmandu. W. S. Webb was sent to investigate the sources of the Ganges in 1808, and two years later he calculated Dhaulagiri's height as 26,862 feet, only 33 feet out from the present official height; he was much derided at the time because of the deep-rooted belief that the Andes were the world's highest range. In 1812, William Moorcroft, who was veterinary surgeon to the Bengal government, set out with an adventurous character called Hyder Young Hearsey disguised as fakirs, crossed the Niti Pass and reached Manasarowar. On their return journey they were first detained by the Tibetans, then imprisoned by the Gurkhas. Undeterred by these irritations, Moorcroft continued to explore until his death in Afghanistan in 1825.

Perhaps most fascinating of all is the later era of the 'Pundit' explorers (1865-85). Surveys could not be pushed into territories where the British were unwelcome until local men, the pundits, had been trained. Most readers will have already met the Great Game that these men played in the pages of Kipling's *Kim*. They were, of course, explorers and surveyors rather than mountaineers, but in the course of their duties they did climb peaks as observation points; the altitude record was for long held by an unnamed Khalasi who climbed Shillah (23,050 feet).

All these men were mountain travellers; they kept on the whole to the valleys and passes, only climbing to set up their survey instruments. They were doing, on a far larger scale, the work done in the Alps by the botanists, such as the Thomases, and by men like Forbes and Ball.

The first accomplished climbers in the Himalaya were the three German geologist brothers Schlagintweit in the 1850s; but the purpose of their journeys in this part of the world was exploration, not the ascent of peaks. The first man to go to the Himalaya to climb was W. W. Graham, who visited Sikkim in 1883. He certainly climbed several peaks but his sense of topography was weak, and some of his claims, particularly his claim to have climbed Kabru (24,076 feet), are clearly mistaken. Harold Raeburn suggested that the mountain may have been Forked Peak (20,340 feet).

In 1892 the pacification of the Hunza-Nagir area enabled the Royal Society and the Royal Geographical Society to send the first major expedition out from England to explore and climb in the Karakorum, interest in which had been stimulated by Francis Younghusband's two great journeys across the range. The leader was Martin Conway and his party included Oscar Eckenstein,[1] young Charles Bruce (better known later as General Bruce) and Matthias Zurbriggen. They crossed the Nushik La (17,300 feet) and the Skoro La (16,644 feet), explored glaciers and climbed Crystal Peak (about 19,400 feet) and Pioneer Peak (22,600 feet).

In 1895 came the first, and no doubt premature, attack on a really high peak when Mummery, Collie and Hastings set out to climb Nanga Parbat (26,660 feet). Bruce joined them briefly but had to return to his regiment; he did bring reinforcement in two Gurkhas, one of them, Rhagobir Thapa, an experienced man. With Rhagobir, Mummery climbed a very hard rock rib in the middle of the Diamir face; they spent three days examining the ground above but had to come down when Rhagobir was taken ill.

Opposite: a climber on Yerupaja (Andes).

reached the summit had their Bhotia porters not refused to carry high.

As early as 1907 Mumm had suggested a reconnaissance of Everest, and this had been the original objective of Longstaff and himself when they went to the Himalaya that year. The then Secretary of State for India, the pacifist historian John Morley, refused permission. In 1920 Captain Farrar, the President of the AC, and Sir Francis Younghusband, President of the RGS, secured the goodwill of the Secretary of State, and Colonel Howard-Bury went to India to persuade the Viceroy while Sir Charles Bell won over the Dalai Lama. As General Bruce was prevented from doing so by his military duties, Howard-Bury was appointed to lead the resulting reconnaissance expedition.

The southern side of the mountain is in Nepal, which remained out-of-bounds until after the Second World War. The northern, Tibetan, side was quite unknown; it too had long been out-of-bounds and would probably have remained so but for the confidence established between Bell and the Dalai Lama.

The party contained four climbers; Harold Raeburn, who had been a brilliant climber but was now 56; Kellas, with great Himalayan experience but who had almost certainly strained his heart on Kamet the previous year; G. L. Mallory and G. H. Bullock. Finch had been chosen but the doctors turned him down. A. F. R. Wollaston went as naturalist and medical officer, Dr A. M. Heron as geologist, H. T. Morshead and E. O. Wheeler as surveyors. The two 'surveyors' were also notable climbers, Morshead having done much climbing in the Himalaya and Wheeler, a Canadian, in the Rockies. Kellas unfortunately died en route and Raeburn had to return to Sikkim, with a strained heart.

On inspecting the mountain, Mallory disliked the look of the slopes running up to the west ridge and although the North Col seemed to lead to a practicable route higher up, its westward aspect was uninviting. He went round to have a look at the Western Cwm (Mallory's name) but doubted whether the Khumbu icefall leading to it was passable; anyway it was in Nepal and out of bounds. The question thus became one of the practicability of the North Col from the east. Mallory and Bullock did not guess the existence of the East Rongbuk glacier, which gives easy access to the east side of the North Col, so they took a roundabout route up the Kharta valley and over the Lhapka La. (They saw traces of the abominable snowman near the Lhapka La.) They then climbed the North Col by its eastern slopes. That was the end; the party was overtired, the porters were done for and the weather was foul. But the reconnaissance had done its job; it had found a likely-looking route and rejected other possibilities as improbable. Writing of the prospects, Mallory said:[4]

Of all principles by which we hold the first is mutual help. What is to be done for a man who is sick or abnormally exhausted at these high altitudes? His companions must see to it that he is taken down at

the first opportunity and with an adequate escort: and the obligation is the same whether he be Sahib or coolie. . . . It may be taken for granted that such need will arise and will interfere very seriously with any organisation. . . .

In all it may be said that one factor above all others is required for success. Too many chances are against the climbers; too many contingencies may turn against them. Anything like a breakdown of the transport will be fatal: soft snow on the mountain will be an impregnable defence: a big wind will send back the strongest: even so small a matter as a boot fitting a shade too tight may endanger one man's foot and involve the whole party in retreat. The climbers must have above all things, if they are to win through, good fortune.

Opposite top: the junction of the Godwin-Austen and Boltoro Glaciers with K2 behind, one of Sella's unsurpassed photographs.

Opposite bottom: G. L. Mallory and A. F. R. Wollaston at 21,000 feet, below Lhapka La, on the first reconnaissance of Everest in 1921.

Top: the Lower Remo Glacier photographed by Filippo de Filippi on an expedition to investigate K2 in 1915.

Above: Mount Everest and (centre) the north peak: the North Col is between the two.

to persuade three of his four porters to carry Camp VI to 26,800 feet, whence the porters went down. In the morning Norton and Somervell went up and across the Yellow Band of rock which stretches across the north face leading to the big couloir below the summit pyramid. Somervell, whose throat was troubling him, had to give up but Norton reached and crossed the couloir. The fine powder snow made the climbing very dangerous and Norton was suffering from double-vision, which did not increase his security. He turned back at 28,126 feet and the pair of them regained Camp IV, guided in by Mallory and Odell. Norton, now snow-blind, felt that a fit and fresh party could reach the summit without oxygen. This party's fitness and freshness had been sapped by the early struggles with blizzards and porters.

Mallory and Irvine were up at Camp VI on June 7, with Odell in support at Camp V. Next day Odell, climbing up to VI, saw through a rift in the mist two figures on a snow slope under a rock step on the north-east ridge. They were about 600 yards away and it was 12.30. From what Odell saw, and from the position of the ice-axe found by Wyn Harris in 1933, and eventually identified as belonging to Andrew Irvine, it seems probable that the accident to Mallory and Irvine must have occurred while the climbers were descending after having been defeated by the first or second rock step. This is Mason's view, but it is not yet universally accepted; Ruttledge, for example, differed and some believe they may have reached the summit, though this seems impossible in view of their position as late as 12.30 pm. It cannot be taken as certain that the position of the axe marked the place of the accident; other parties have continued climbs after an axe has been dropped or mislaid.

Odell was perfectly acclimatised; he had enjoyed his first solitary night at Camp V and next day had gone out of his way to do a bit of unnecessary rock-climbing, a very unusual performance at over 26,000 feet. Mallory had asked him to be down at Camp IV in plenty of time to evacuate it, so after assuring himself that Mallory and Irvine were nowhere near Camp VI, Odell returned to IV. Next morning no movement could be seen, so Odell climbed to Camp V in the afternoon after arranging a code of signals with Hazard who had come up in support. After a bad night he went on up to VI and searched the slabs for two hours along Mallory's likely line. 'This upper part of Everest', Odell wrote, 'must be indeed the remotest and least hospitable spot on earth, but at no time more emphatically and impressively so than when a darkened atmosphere hides its features and a gale races over its cruel face.'

It was eight years before the Dalai Lama gave permission for another Everest attempt; meantime Kangchenjunga (28,208 feet), the world's third highest mountain, took the stage.

Paul Bauer took out a Bavarian party[5] in 1929. The Himalayan Club organised their journey to the Zemu Glacier to the east of the mountain. Bauer reconnoitred the whole avalanche-swept north-east quadrant and fixed on the north-east spur as the only possible route. After reaching the crest of this spur and being driven down by a blizzard, Camp VII on the crest at 19,128 feet was occupied ten days later. Three more camps were set up in ice-caves hacked out along the ridge. There were six Germans and four porters at the highest cave (22,700 feet), Allwein and Kraus had reconnoitred the way ahead, when, on October 3, their high hopes were wiped out by a three-day blizzard. The difficult retreat was carried out methodically.

Next year Professor Dyhrenfurth brought out a German-British-Swiss-Austrian party[6] to attack the mountain from the north-west. The long trip to base required more than 400 coolies. While they were preparing the route up an ice-wall, a great mass of ice broke away above, killing Chettan, one of the best of the Sherpas. The route was then abandoned as too dangerous and, a reconnaissance of the north-west ridge having revealed no alternative, the expedition withdrew to smaller mountains, of which they climbed several, including Jongsong (24,518 feet) and Nepal Peak (23,560 feet).

In 1931 Bauer returned to Kangchenjunga.[7] Shebbeare led them to the old base camp on the Zemu Glacier. They were six weeks earlier this time and the monsoon was in full force. Everything was more difficult and dangerous than in 1929. Hermann Schaller and Pasang fell to their death when the snow gave way. A fortnight later Camp VIII was re-occupied and Camp IX put at 24,150 feet. Hartmann and Wien reached the top of the spur at 25,260 feet, from which point the line dips a little before joining the north ridge of the mountain. Powder snow on ice made further progress impracticable and they withdrew. Next day another party examined the slope and all agreed it would be unsafe to go on. On the return trip, Allwein and Pircher crossed the Simvu Saddle and descended the untrodden and arduous Passanram valley. Kangchenjunga was unclimbed, but Bauer's leadership of these

Above: Paul Bauer, the outstanding leader of two German expeditions to Kangchenjunga in 1929 and 1931. Both were defeated by appalling weather and snow conditions.

Below: the north shoulder of Everest marked with the highest points known to have been reached.

Mallory & Irvine last seen about here 28,230 June 8.

Norton & Somervell about here 28,130 June 4.

Camp VI 26,700 about here

The Kangchenjunga group seen from near Darjeeling. Kangchenjunga, the world's third highest mountain, was the target of seven assaults before its first ascent in 1955.

two parties puts him high among Himalayan mountaineers.

In the same year Frank Smythe took a group[8] to Kamet (25,447 feet), which had already been attacked by Meade, Slingsby, Kellas and Morshead. Smythe's final assault was from Camp V, just below Meade's Col. This is his account:[9]

The ascent of Kamet

from Frank Smythe, *Kamet Conquered*

Shipton, Holdsworth and I took it in turns to lead. We did about a quarter of an hour each. Had there been only two of us to stamp out the steps the work would have been very exhausting, but the difference between taking a turn every half an hour and taking it every quarter of an hour at such an altitude is enormous.

In its lower portion the slope was between 30° and 40° in angle: it steepened gradually.

We sat down for a rest. As we sat, our thudding hearts and hard-pressed lungs gradually eased to a more normal rhythm. We had climbed the first 500 feet in an hour and had reason to congratulate ourselves. Immediately below us were Meade's Col and the camp – toylike tents and snow crumpled with footmarks. Only the Eastern Ibi Gamin overlooked us. To the right was the snowy edge of the eastern precipice. Fleecy clouds were beginning to twist up from the valleys. The plains of Tibet were opening out; their brown and yellow expanses melted into violet distances. Eastwards, Gurla Mandhata rose serenely.

We munched a little chocolate and sipped tea from a Thermos flask. It was gloriously hot in the sun, and as yet no wind had arisen to chill us. Lolling in the snow, I felt languid and sleepy. Further advance seemed unnecessary and even absurd. Why not continue to sit and drowse the day away in the warm sun? I forced myself to take some photographs and change a cinematograph film. It was simple and easy work, yet it involved expenditure of both physical and mental energy.

The few minutes we allowed ourselves soon passed. Shipton and Lewa rose to their feet and started up the slope. It was interesting to watch them. Shipton, a born mountaineer, has acquired to perfection the art of climbing a snow-slope with the minimum of effort. Lewa, on the other hand, is so constituted that he tends to expend more of his magnificent energy than is necessary. So much fire and dash is his to command that he cannot properly control its tumultuous outflow, and his eager jerky movements contrasted oddly with the almost leisurely rhythm of Shipton. As they toiled through the soft snow, I trained the cine-camera on them and 'shot' some film. I remember wishing as I did so that I had not burdened myself with the work of taking a film of the expedition, and I vowed that I would never do it again.

Holdsworth, Nima Dorje and I followed. One moment we had been sitting at ease, fully capable of

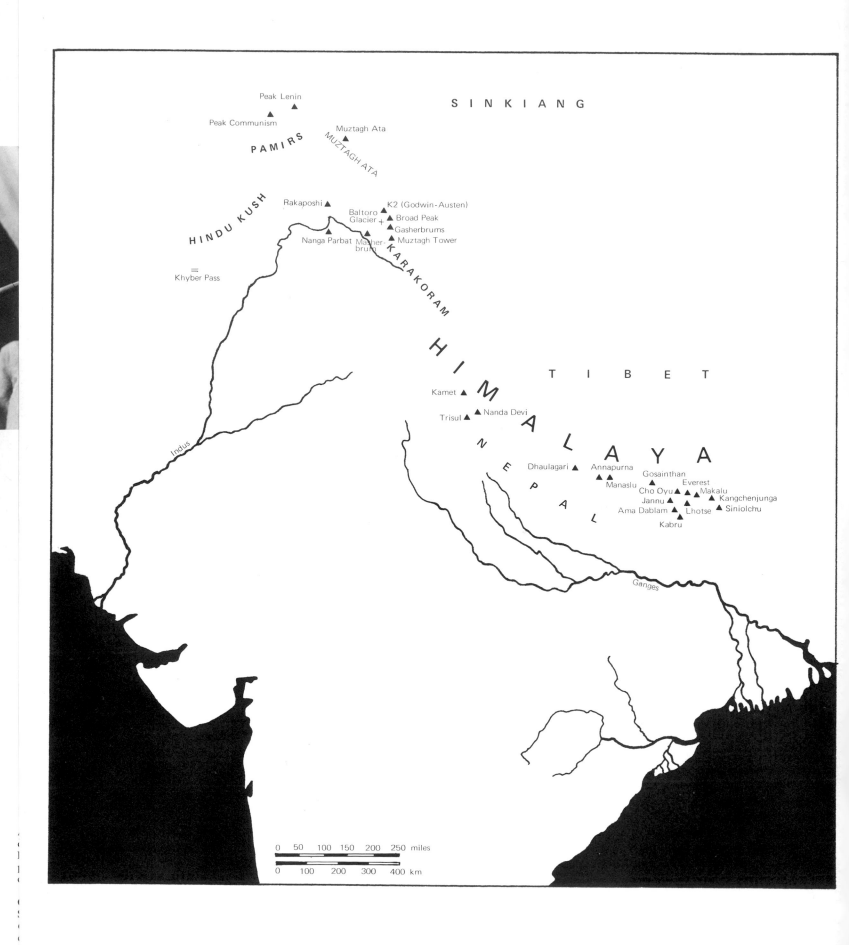

SINKIANG

Peak Lenin ▲

Peak Communism

PAMIRS

Muztagh Ata ▲

MUZTAGH ATA

HINDU KUSH

Rakaposhi ▲

K2 (Godwin-Austen) ▲

Baltoro ▲ Broad Peak
Glacier +   ▲ Gasherbrums
Nanga Parbat Masher- ▲   ▲ Muztagh Tower
brum

KARAKORAM

=
Khyber Pass

Indus

HIMALAYA

TIBET

Kamet ▲

Trisul ▲ ▲ Nanda Devi

N

Dhaulagari ▲ Annapurna
▲ ▲ Gosainthan
Manaslu ▲ Everest
E Cho Oyu ▲ ▲ ▲ Makalu
P Jannu ▲ ▲ ▲ ▲ Kangchenjunga
A Ama Dablam ▲ ▲ Lhotse ▲ Siniolchu
L Kabru ▲

Ganges

0   50   100 150 200 250 miles

0   100   200   300   400 km

minute I lay gasping like a stranded fish, then, pulling myself together, swung astride the sharp roof-like ridge and began taking in Holdsworth's rope round the ice-axe. Presently, we were all congregated on the ridge.

We had hoped to find ourselves on the summit, or within a few yards of it, but we saw immediately that we were separated from it by a knife-like crest of snow. As we gazed along the narrow path we must tread, we experienced a pang of apprehension. Some thirty yards distant the ridge rose up into a sharp point. Beyond this nothing was to be seen, but we realised instinctively that the point was not the summit. Slopes of rock and snow, which we could see sloping up beyond it, indicated something higher. Had Kamet a surprise in store for us? What if there was an impracticable cleft in the ridge between us and the summit? We would have given much for a rest, but to rest was impossible, until we had stood upon the point and seen what lay beyond.

We started to toil along the ridge. It was nearly horizontal and exceedingly sharp. On either hand the slopes fell away with great steepness; it seemed incredible that we could have ascended from those shadowy abysses to the right of us. I remember trampling and crushing the delicate snow edge with a careful yet savage deliberation. There must be no mistake now. On the slope below we had been mere automatons—toiling atoms incapable almost of reasoned and coherent thought–but now we were thinking men again, capable of realising our amazing position on this snowy edge of the world. Tiredness was replaced by a fierce exhilaration. The numbed brain leapt into renewed activity. The summit was almost within our grasp; surely it could not escape us now? We gained the point and gazed over and beyond it. At our feet the ridge sank down to a shallow gap. Beyond the gap it merged gently into a small cone of snow–the summit!

We seized hold of Lewa and shoved him on in front of us. As I clutched hold of him I could hear the breath jerking from him in wheezy gasps. I do not think that he quite understood what we were doing. And so he was first to tread the summit. It was the least compliment we could pay to those splendid men, our porters, to whom we owed the success of our expedition.

As we reached the summit we saw that there was another equally high summit a few yards away, so, to be quite sure, we trudged across to it. Nothing further disputed us and for the last time we sank down into the snow.

Greene, Birnie and Kesar Singh repeated the climb two days later.

In 1932 the Germans, led by W. Merkl,[10] opened up their siege of Nanga Parbat (26,660 feet). The Silver Saddle on Nanga Parbat, over which the route was planned, is much the same height as the North Col on Everest, with only a little less than 4,000 feet in height to go to the summit. On the other hand the whole north face, by which the Saddle has to be reached, is draped with broken glaciers and under constant avalanche threat. There was, to an outsider, something a little odd about the organisation of this expedition: none of Bauer's Kangchenjunga men was included; indeed there was nobody with Himalayan experience; neither Bauer nor the Himalayan Club was asked for advice or help; there was nobody who spoke any local language, and there was no transport officer. All were, of course, first class climbers, but in the Himalaya that is not enough. Captain Frier of the Gilgit garrison eventually helped them with porters, but these details should have been considered much earlier. When they reached their idyllic base at 'Märchenwiese', they found ten loads missing–warm clothes for forty porters. Merkl, Bechtold and Wiessner pushed their way as far as the col at 22,800 feet but were driven back by a snowstorm. They had carried out a useful reconnaissance and learned much of the complexity of high-altitude mountaineering.

In 1933 permission was again granted for an Everest expedition. The Dalai Lama insisted that all members must be British. Hugh Ruttledge was leader.[11] Radio weather reports were arranged; tents and windproof clothing had been improved; oxygen was in reserve.

They were driven back from Camp V by a gale, rising to a hurricane, but a few days later were able to set Camp VI at 27,400 feet, where Wyn Harris and Wager stayed while Longland took the porters down with great skill in appalling conditions. Wyn Harris and Wager were off at 5.40 next morning. They found Irvine's ice-axe some 250 yards from the First Step, which they were able to turn, but the Second Step proved impracticable. They accordingly abandoned Mallory's ridge route and reverted to Norton's route across the face to the couloir; they turned back at the same point as Norton. Smythe and Shipton, who followed, were shut up by storm at Camp VI and when they were able to set out the face was dangerous with new snow and Shipton much weakened by two sleepless nights. Shipton soon had to give up and Smythe went on alone. He reached the same point as Norton, Wager and Wyn Harris but earlier in the day; nevertheless the masses of fresh snow precluded further advance. They all returned to rest at base, the monsoon took over and no further approach to the North Col was feasible. The expedition had put their top camp some 600 feet higher than ever before, and they had established that Norton's traverse was definitely better than the ridge route, although Smythe had felt that the traverse should be made and the couloir crossed lower down.

Next year Merkl returned to Nanga Parbat after better preparation.[12] The Indian government lent Captains Frier and Sangster to help with transport and the Himalayan Club enlisted 35 porters. Unfortunately the expedition did not enjoy a repeat of the spell of fine weather of 1932, and was dogged by bad luck. Drexel was struck down with pneumonia and died. This loss and bad conditions imposed recurrent delays but eventually Camp VIII was

Opposite: a map of the Himalaya.

Above: Willi Merkl, leader of two German expeditions to Nanga Parbat in 1932 and 1934. The second was called the greatest mountaineering disaster of the time: Merkl perished with eight others in a desperate blizzard-torn descent from the Silver Saddle (24,560 feet).

down to VI which they failed to reach and spent another night in the snow. Next morning these four joined up with the three stragglers from the first group and continued down; three died of exposure and the others got to IV badly frost-bitten. Dakshi having died on the slopes of the Silver Saddle, Ang Tsering and Gaylay rejoined Merkl and Welzenbach at VII on July 12, and here Welzenbach died on the night of the 13th. The three survivors set out in the morning. Merkl collapsed, the two porters dug him an ice-cave where Gaylay stayed with him while Ang Tsering fought his way down to IV for help, but no help could avail in that flood of fresh snow. Kenneth Mason wrote.[13]

So ended this attempt – in the greatest mountain disaster of our time. It is easy to look back and criticise. But it must be realised how little was known at that time about the rapid deterioration of strength above 23,000 feet, especially under storm conditions. There was also no oxygen. As events turned out it would have been wiser to have had two assault parties as originally planned – one in Camp VI or VII, while the other set out for Camp VIII; the porters should have gone down on the afternoon of the 6th. There were too many eager men too high, and no one in support between Camps IV and VIII, a distance of over three miles and more than 4,000 feet in height. Had there been two fit climbers in Camp VI or VII to keep the route open the terrible nights spent in the intermediate bivouacs would have been avoided. But there was also great heroism. Climbers and porters alike freely gave of their lives for one another. Gaylay died with his master. Ang Tsering's achievement won for him the Medal of Honour of the German Red Cross, and he went to Everest two years later; Dawa Thondup and Pasang Nurbu received the same decoration, and went again to Nanga Parbat in 1937 and to Masherbrum in 1938. Pasang Kikuli, also decorated with the Medal of Honour, survived his terrible frostbite, and sacrificed himself on K2 in 1939.

Nanga Parbat, 1934. Above: the route through ice towers above Camp II. Right: Erwin Schneider on the north ridge of Rakhiot Peak. The summit is on the left, the Silver Saddle on the right.

pitched on the Silver Saddle at 24,560 feet and Aschenbrenner and Schneider prepared the track up to 25,280 feet. The wind then got up and rose to a hurricane, wiping out all chance of further assault. The retreat began on July 8, in appalling weather. Aschenbrenner and Schneider with three porters went ahead; near Camp VII they unroped to speed up the track making. They reached Camp IV in the evening, having lost sight of the porters in the storm; these three however had taken refuge in Camp VII. Merkl's rear party, including Welzenbach, Wieland and eight porters, were hard hit. They had to bivouac in the snow short of Camp VII, Merkl and Wieland both frost-bitten. One porter died in the night. Early next morning the climbers went on with four porters; Ang Tsering stayed behind in the snow bivouac with two others who were ill. Wieland succumbed during the day; Merkl and Welzenbach reached VII exhausted and sent the four porters on

might be the case in other parts of the Himalaya, monsoon conditions were clearly quite unfit for climbing Everest'.

In the same year, also intent on learning about post-monsoon conditions, C. R. Cooke went to Kabru in Sikkim with G. Schoberth and six Darjeeling porters. He made the climb of Kabru II (24,076 feet) success-

Permission to attack Everest again was given for 1935 and 1936, but too late to organise a full-scale expedition for the former year. Instead the Everest Committee invited Shipton to make a reconnaissance during the monsoon. Shipton took a small party: Tilman, E. Kempson, Charles Warren, E. Wigram and the New Zealander, L. V. Bryant. Michael Spender came to make a photogrammetric survey of the glaciers north of the mountain. Shipton budgeted for a total cost of £1,400.

Reaching the mountain, the party judged the snow slopes of the North Col to be safe and occupied the camp above it. They found the whole north face plastered with snow which the recent fine weather should, in the light of all experience, have consolidated but nobody knew whether snow ever did consolidate above 26,000 feet. Having plenty of time, they decided to wait for the weather to settle but were very disconcerted to find that the slopes of the col they had judged safe had, in fact, precipitated themselves in a vast avalanche. This established that nobody had the knowledge to judge snow conditions at that particular time and place. The party then turned 'with delicious abandon' to climbing peaks around the east and west Rongbuk Glaciers and round the Kharta valley. They climbed 26 peaks over 20,000 feet. Snow conditions were generally good up to 23,000 feet but there changed abruptly so that 'we found ourselves struggling in a bottomless morass of soft snow'.[14] It was obvious that 'whatever

fully in November and had fine weather throughout. It took him three weeks from base to summit. It cannot possibly have been this mountain which Graham climbed in 1883.

In 1936 Ruttledge was back at Everest.[15] At first all went well; Smythe and Shipton were soon encamped on the North Col with porters to carry the higher camps. However, deep snow prevented further progress and the camp was evacuated. Four days later the first monsoon snow fell, on May 24. By the next day the North Col slopes were already dangerous. On June 3 an attempt to reach the Col was frustrated by the snow. A full gale followed but Shipton and Wyn Harris got permission for one more shot. On their way up to the Col they were almost overwhelmed by a sinister windslab avalanche. There could no longer be a shred of doubt that the eastern slopes of the Col were barred once the monsoon had broken. Smythe and Wyn Harris went round to look at the western slopes. They found that this side was safer in monsoon conditions, but as the north face is then unclimbable the discovery was no great consolation. The route could be useful for a party caught above the North Col by the onset of the monsoon.

While Everest was washed out by the weather, an attack on Nanda Devi was much more fortunate. The original impetus came from America and the prime objective was Kangchenjunga, for which the expedition could not get permission so switched late

Above left: Sherpa Pasang Kikuli staggers into Camp IV, exhausted and frost-bitten after the terrible retreat on Nanga Parbat in 1934.

Above: members of the 1935 Everest Reconnaissance led by Shipton. Standing: L. V. Bryant, E. Wigram, Charles Warren, Michael Spender; seated: Tilman, Shipton and E. Kempson.

121

to Nanda Devi (25,645 feet). There were four Americans, Charles Houston, W. F. Loomis, Arthur Emmons and H. Adams Carter, and four British, Tilman, Odell, Graham Brown and Peter Lloyd. (Emmons had been badly frost-bitten when the American party had climbed Minya Konka (about 24,900 feet) in Western China in 1932.) There was no official leader but Tilman, by reason of his knowledge of language and people and, above all, by reason of the reconnaissance of the 'Sanctuary' which he had carried out with Shipton in 1934, was *de facto* leader and was indeed formally voted into the leadership for the final stages. The approach to base camp through the Rishi gorge is as complex and difficult as any, but Tilman had done it before. Above Camp II all carrying was done by the climbers. Houston and Odell made a bid for the summit from a bivouac at 23,500 feet, but the distance was too great. Tilman, Odell and Lloyd carried the bivouac up another 500 feet. Houston had fallen sick and had to go down; Tilman took his place at the bivouac. This is his record of his ascent with Odell:[16]

The ascent of Nanda Devi

from H. W. Tilman, *The Ascent of Nanda Devi*

By six o'clock we were ready, and shortly after we crawled outside, roped up, and started. It was bitterly cold, for the sun had not yet risen over the shoulder of East Nanda Devi and there was a thin wind from the west. What mugs we were to be fooling about on this infernal ridge at that hour of the morning! And what was the use of this ridiculous coil of rope, as stiff as a wire hawser, tying me for better or for worse to that dirty-looking ruffian in front! Such, in truth, were the reflections of at least one of us as we topped a snow boss behind the tent, and the tenuous nature of the ridge in front became glaringly obvious in the chill light of dawn. It was comforting to reflect that my companion in misery had already passed this way, and presently as the demands of the climbing became more insistent, grievances seemed less real, and that life was still worth living was a proposition that might conceivably be entertained.

This difficult ridge was about three hundred yards long, and though the general angle appeared slight it rose in a series of abrupt rock and snow steps. On the left was an almost vertical descent to a big ravine, bounded on the far side by terrific grey cliffs that supported the broad snow shelf for which we were making. The right side also fell away steeply, being part of the great rock cirque running round to East Nanda Devi. The narrow ridge we were on formed a sort of causeway between the lower south face and the upper snow shelf.

One very important factor which, more than anything, tended to promote a happier frame of mind was that the soft crumbly rock had at last yielded to a hard rough schistose-quartzite which was a joy to handle; a change which could not fail to please us as mountaineers and, no doubt, to interest my companion as a geologist. That vile rock, schist is, I believe, the technical term, had endangered our heads and failed to support our feet from the foot of the scree to the last bivouac. It was a wonder our burning anathemas had not caused it to undergo a geological change under our very eyes – metamorphosed it, say, into plutonic rocks. But, as has been said by others, there is good in everything, and, on reflection, this very sameness was not without some saving grace because it meant that we were spared an accumulation of rock samples at every camp. A bag of assorted stones had already been left at the Glacier Camp, and I tremble to think what burdens we might have had to carry down the mountain had the rock been as variegated as our geologist, and indeed any right-minded geologist, would naturally desire.

Thanks to the earlier reconnaissance by him and Houston, Odell led over this ridge at a good pace and in an hour and a half we had reached the snow mound which marked the farthest point they had reached. It was a ridge on which we moved one at a time.

In front was a snow slope set at an angle of about 30 degrees and running right up to the foot of the rock wall, perhaps 600 or 700 feet above us. To the west this wide snow terrace extended for nearly a quarter of a mile until it ended beneath that same skyline ridge, which below had formed the western boundary of the broad gully. On our right the shelf quickly steepened and merged into the steep rock face of the ridge between East Nanda Devi and our mountain. We were too close under the summit to see where it lay, but there was little doubt about the line we should take, because from a rapid survey there seemed to be only one place where a lodgement could be effected on the final wall. This was well to the west of our present position, where a snow rib crossed the terrace at right angles and, abutting against the wall, formed as it were a ramp.

We began the long snow trudge at eight o'clock and even at that early hour and after a cold night the snow was not good and soon became execrable. The sun was now well up. After it had been at work for a bit we were going in over our knees at every step, and in places where the slope was steeper it was not easy to make any upward progress at all. One foot would be lifted and driven hard into the snow and then, on attempting to rise on it, one simply sank down through the snow to the previous level. It was like trying to climb up cotton wool, and a good deal more exhausting, I imagine, than the treadmill. But, like the man on a walking tour in Ireland, who throughout a long day received the same reply of '20 miles' to his repeated inquiries as to the distance he was from his destination, we could at any rate say, 'Thank God, we were holding our own.'

The exertion was great and every step made good cost six to eight deep breaths. Our hopes of the summit grew faint, but there was no way but to plug on and see how far we could get. This we did, thinking only of the next step, taking our time, and resting frequently. It was at least some comfort that the track we were ploughing might assist a second party. On top of the hard work and the effect of altitude was

Opposite top: Two British explorers, William Moorcroft and Hyder Young Hersey, ride into Tibet disguised as fakirs (1812).

Opposite bottom: a British army camp in the Himalaya in the 1840s.

the languor induced by a sun which beat down relentlessly on the dazzling snow, searing our lips and sapping the energy of mind and body. As an example of how far this mind-sapping process had gone, I need only mention that it was seriously suggested that we should seek the shade of a convenient rock which we were then near, lie up there until evening, and finish the climb in the dark!

It is noteworthy that whilst we were enjoying, or more correctly enduring, this remarkable spell of sunshine, the foothills south and west of the Basin experienced disastrous floods. As related in the first chapter, it was on this day that the Pindar river overflowed sweeping away some houses in the village of Tharali, while on the same day nineteen inches of rain fell at the hill station of Mussoorie west of Ranikhet.

We derived some encouragement from seeing East Nanda Devi sink below us and at one o'clock, rather to our surprise, we found ourselves on top of the snow rib moving at a snail's pace towards the foot of the rocks. There we had a long rest and tried to force some chocolate down our parched throats by eating snow at the same time. Though neither of us said so, I think both felt that now it would take a lot to stop us. There was a difficult piece of rock to climb; Odell led this and appeared to find it stimulating, but it provoked me to exclaim loudly upon its 'thinness'. Once over that, we were landed fairly on the final slope with the summit ridge a bare 300 feet above us.

Presently we were confronted with the choice of a short but very steep snow gully and a longer but less drastic route to the left. We took the first and found the snow reasonably hard owing to the very steep angle at which it lay. After a severe struggle I drew myself out of it on to a long and gently sloping corridor, just below and parallel to the summit ridge. I sat down and drove the axe in deep to hold Odell as he finished the gully. He moved up to join me and I had just suggested the corridor as a promising line to take when there was a sudden hiss and, quicker than thought, a slab of snow, about forty yards long, slid off the corridor and disappeared down the gully, peeling off a foot of snow as it went. At the lower limit of the avalanche, which was where we were sitting, it actually broke away for a depth of a foot all round my axe to which I was holding. At its upper limit, forty yards up the corridor, it broke away to a depth of three or four feet.

The corridor route had somehow lost its attractiveness, so we finished the climb by the ridge without further adventure, reaching the top at three o'clock.

The summit is not the exiguous and precarious spot that usually graces the top of so many Himalayan peaks, but a solid snow ridge nearly two hundred yards long and twenty yards broad. It is seldom that conditions on top of a high peak allow the climber the time or the opportunity to savour the immediate fruits of victory. Too often, when having first care-

Top: Nanda Devi, in Indian legend the sanctuary of the goddess Nanda, photographed from the west by Eric Shipton, 1934.

Above: Shipton on a peak during his 1935 reconnaissance expedition.

Opposite top; the main base camp of the 1922 expedition to Everest, a photograph taken and coloured by Captain John Noel.

Opposite bottom: some members of the 1924 Everest expedition, also by Captain Noel.

fully probed the snow to make sure he is not standing on a cornice, the climber straightens up preparatory to savouring the situation to the full, he is met by a perishing wind and the interesting view of a cloud at close quarters, and with a muttered imprecation turns in his tracks and begins the descent. Far otherwise was it now. There were no cornices to worry about and room to unrope and walk about. The air was still, the sun shone, and the view was good if not so extensive as we had hoped.

Nanda Devi: loading up at Camp IV during the Anglo-American expedition to Nanda Devi in 1936. All carrying above Camp II was done by climbers.

Odell had brought a thermometer, and no doubt sighed for the hypsometer. From it we found that the air temperature was 20°F., but in the absence of wind we could bask gratefully in the friendly rays of our late enemy the sun. It was difficult to realise that we were actually standing on top of the same peak which we had viewed two months ago from Ranikhet, and which had then appeared incredibly remote and inaccessible, and it gave us a curious feeling of exaltation to know that we were above every peak within hundreds of miles on either hand. Dhaulagiri, 1,000 feet higher, and two hundred miles away in Nepal, was our nearest rival. I believe we so far forgot ourselves as to shake hands on it.

This was not only the highest peak yet attained but also, in the opinion of many, the finest climb. It is interesting that Tilman, to his great good fortune, had been excluded from the Everest party of that year as a slow acclimatiser (another casualty of the same medical board was a young officer called John Hunt). Accurate preselection of good goers at great height was, and is still, beyond the limits of science.

In October the neighbouring Nanda Kot (22,510 feet) was climbed by a small Japanese party, all five of whom reached the top. In the same year Bauer took a small German party to Sikkim. Bauer, Hepp, Wien and Göttner spent two nights without a tent on the ridge between Siniolchu (22,600 feet) and

Little Siniolchu. On the day between these two bivouacs Bauer and Hepp halted in support at about 21,200 feet while Wien and Göttner, now unladen, climbed Siniolchu.

In 1937 the Germans returned to Nanga Parbat, this time under Wien's leadership. The mountain had not relented. They had an early escape when an avalanche smashed their camp, but they excavated and stocked Camp IV at 20,280 feet; then there was heavy snow for three days. On June 14, Lieutenant Smart of the Gilgit Scouts, who was helping with transport, went down from this camp with porters, leaving Wien, Hartmann, Hepp, Göttner, Fänkhauser, Pfeffer and Müllnitter, the entire climbing team, with nine Sherpas in the camp. Four days later Luft, bringing porters and stores, reached the campsite to find everything buried under a gigantic avalanche. Only three rucksacks could be found. Bauer, Bechthold and Kraus immediately flew out from Germany. After great efforts most of the bodies were found, their diaries written up to June 15. In the same year Spencer Chapman put up a brilliant performance, climbing Chomolhari (23,997 feet) alone with Pasang Sherpa.

These successes on Kamet, Nanda Devi, Kabru II, Siniolchu and Chomolhari greatly strengthened the case of those who argued against large expeditions, but it must always be remembered that above 26,000 feet or so the problems of transport, acclimatisation/deterioration, oxygen and safety margins assume quite different dimensions.

In 1938 the last[17] attempt on Everest from the north was made under Tilman's leadership. Largely as a result of the Nanda Devi climb, this was a much smaller and cheaper expedition and much more to Tilman's taste. The other members were Smythe, Shipton, Odell, Warren, Lloyd and Oliver. They met the usual troubles of too much snow and a too early monsoon. Eventually, approaching the North Col by the western slopes this time, they established a camp at 27,200 feet. From here Smythe and Shipton set out before the sun and were driven back by the cold, making a second start when the sun arrived. To quote Shipton:[18]

Norton's route below the Yellow Band was quite out of the question for there was an enormous deposit of snow on the gently sloping ground. Also conditions in the couloir were obviously hopeless. Our plan was to try to make a diagonal traverse up to the ridge which we hoped to reach just before the First Step. . . . We started flogging our way up the steep ground through powder snow, into which we sank up to our hips. . . . We went on until, on the steeper ground, we were in obvious danger of being swept off the rocks by a snow avalanche. . . . It was bitterly disappointing, as we were both far fitter at these altitudes than we had been in 1933, and the glittering summit looking tauntingly near.

Coming down they met Tilman and Lloyd going up, who also tried to reach the north-east ridge. To

avoid snow-floundering they tried rocks, but without success and they, too, retired, leaving Everest undisturbed until after the war.

The Germans, under Bauer, were back on Nanga Parbat but met the same sort of weather as Tilman on Everest. At the site of the old Camp VI they found the bodies of Merkl and Gaylay. Attempts to reach the Silver Saddle were repulsed; the weather broke again, the porters were depleted, deterioration was setting

in, so Bauer withdrew after sending Luft and Zuck to study the Diamirai face.

In the same year Houston led a fine reconnaissance of K2, sponsored by the American Alpine Club.[19] After a look round he attacked the Abruzzi ridge. Camp VII was placed at 25,354 feet on the Shoulder and Petzoldt and Houston stayed there. After allowing adequate stores for a safe return, they had just one day to get as high as possible. They found a site for a future Camp VIII at about 26,100 feet but time had run out and they withdrew.

In 1939 the Americans came back, led this time by Fritz Wiessner, who had five other climbers with him.[20] Setting up their Camp VI at 23,400 feet was so exhausting that by July 11 only three climbers and two porters were fit; then Durrance fell sick and had to be helped down. The remaining force of Wiessner, Wolfe and five Sherpas was clearly in-sufficient to establish the higher camps, keep support lines open and attack the summit. Nevertheless they pitched their Camp VIII a little lower than Houston's Camp VII; Wiessner and Wolfe stayed there with Pasang Dawa Lama and the other Sherpas went down to VI and VII. They were then shut in by the weather for two days until July 17 when Wolfe fell ill. Wiessner's judgment must have been affected by the altitude, a not uncommon effect of lack of oxygen, for he left the sick man alone in Camp VIII for five days while he and Pasang explored the mountain above, making two forays for the summit and sleeping in a light tent.

Left: H. W. Tilman, leader of the 1938 Everest expedition, the last pre-war attempt from the north.

Above left: establishing Camp IV on Nanga Parbat in 1937. This camp was obliterated by an avalanche, killing all 16 occupants. The negative of the photograph was retrieved when the camp was dug out.

8 Europe since 1945

But to me the landscape is like a sea
The waves of the hills
And the bubbles of bush and flower
And the springtide breaking into white foam!

It is a slow sea,
Mare tranquillum,
And a thousand years of wind
Cannot raise a dwarf billow to the moonlight.
W. J. Turner

The most obvious development in the last quarter century has been the progressive overcrowding of the more popular mountains both in Britain and the Alps and relatively so even in the remoter ranges. Queues are now common on the fashionable routes, even on very arduous and difficult climbs on Clogwyn du'r Arddu or the Grandes Jorasses. It is welcome that more people should taste the mountain wine, but unwelcome in that it involves debasement of the vintage. To climb in a crowd may be jolly, but the fine bouquet is lost.

Governments and authorities spend money to lure, even to push, young people into the hills. While probably good for the young people, it is certainly bad for the hills. On Snowdon today there are areas fenced off because the trampling feet have caused damaging erosion of slopes long in natural, but precarious, balance. The feet of the hungry generations do literally tread the mountain down.

Another disturbing development was pinpointed by Charles Evans in 1970: '... mountaineering is more used than it was for ends not directly connected with mountains – education, the winning of prestige and the making of money. . . . interest seems to have moved towards prowess and technique and away from the setting, away from the mountains themselves.'[1] This, too, is a result of the mere number of climbers; the group is now large enough to be a recognisable consumer of goods and services. Consequently climbing has opened up as a career. While not new in principle, this is new in scope. From the beginning there have been professional guides, and men like Whymper and Smythe have derived a modest income from their lectures and books. Many years ago Eric Shipton decided to turn his back on the recognised professions and devote his life to mountains and exploration; he has certainly had, and still pursues, a most successfully adventurous and satisfying career. He has preferred the secret places of the earth to a secure pension. But now there are safe pensionable jobs in the climbing profession.

There are wardens and instructors, as well as glittering newspaper and film contracts. Television enables the public to watch dangles into space unconnected with any climb and the careful preparation of dizzy bivouacs by men about to retire for refreshment to a nearby hostelry.

Throughout this period there has also been a marked increase in the use of artificial aids, and an improvement in their design which has led to innovations in technique. The popularity of ironmongery has led to its use in places where competent climbers do not need it. Purist experts delight in removing unnecessary pitons, cleaning the climb and replenishing their own stock. It is definitely bad form to peg a climb that has been led free.

The vibram sole has virtually eliminated the nailed boot, and since vibram is less secure on ice than good nails its use has in turn, extended the use of crampons, for which new methods and designs have developed. During the 1960s 'front-pointing' came into vogue. This technique involves crampons with the front points projecting forwards at about 45°. The foot is placed in the ice with only the front points in contact; the weight is then moved up on the front points only. On very steep ice handhold is provided by a Chouinard ice-axe and hammer or something similar, the pick of which is hooked into the ice. In this way very steep, even vertical, ice can be walked up. The technique is very tiring because of the strain of keeping the boot horizontal, but can save much time by eliminating step-cutting.

Crash helmets, hideous though they are, have made a real contribution to safety. The waist-loop on the climbing rope has been very generally superseded by a multiple waistband of line connected to the climbing rope by a karabiner, or by a body-harness. The latter prevents discomfort, dislocation or even suffocation when hanging on the rope after a fall but has its disadvantages; it is less flexible as to point of attachment to the rope.

The prusik knot has been mechanised into a jumar. The prusik, long in use as a means of getting out of a crevasse, is a knot which, under tension, holds firmly on the climbing rope but which, when tension is released, can be slipped up or down that rope. Thus, with two slings attached to a fixed rope, the climber can walk upwards using the slings alternately. The jumar simplifies this; by using a hand-grip it can be made to seize or slide on the rope as required. Jumars are much used for climbing fixed ropes on expeditions.

Opposite: parties crossing the Bossons Glacier (top) and on a glacier trek (bottom). Since the war the once inaccessible Alps are crowded with climbers; the wild and lonely places are so no longer.

130

Synthetic materials, usually nylon, have generally displaced manila for ropes. Nylon, for example is much more elastic, therefore safer, and it retains less water; its chief defect is its fusibility when heated, for example, when a falling leader's rope runs round a projection, generating great heat by friction. For this reason, direct rock belays must be avoided when using nylon and the material has been generally abandoned for slings used as running belays. Each material has its own special advantages for particular uses. Similarly there are many designs of specialised axes and hammers; choice remains largely personal.

During the Second World War, mountaineering, except by the Swiss on their own mountains, was largely at a standstill. Hans Schlunnegger, Ernst Reiss and others were making new climbs on the north faces of mountains such as the Lauterbrunnen Breithorn, Wetterhörner, Gletscherhorn and Gspaltenhorn. The Italian, Gervasutti, too, was able to make two striking new climbs during these years: the north-east Pillar of Fresnay and the east face of the Grandes Jorasses. There was alpine warfare on the Franco-Italian front and in Norway, and many troops were trained in mountain-craft. There was the astonishing chapter of escapes by British prisoners-of-war over the main chain of the Pennine Alps into Switzerland; for many it was their first alpine expedition, and for too many, alas, their last.

The return to the Alps after the War was at first tentative. Rationing was still a restriction and transport variable, but within a year or two the alpine huts were crowded as never before. In the 1920s and 30s only Germans and Austrians used to bicycle to the western Alps on a shoe-string; now young people of all nations were doing it, the hitch-hike having replaced the bicycle.

The pre-war question 'Où sont les jeunes britanniques?' was no longer a worry. The Oxford and Cambridge clubs were soon on their feet with outstanding young climbers like Tom Bourdillon and Cym Smith. The less traditional clubs, like Rock and Ice and Creagh Dhu, cradled on their native hills, were invading the Alps with men like Joe Brown, Don Whillans and Hamish McInnes, instantly on serious climbs. Many of these new clubs resulted, paradoxically enough, from the unemployment of the 1930s. This had not only enabled but encouraged many young men in the northern half of the country to spend their time and energies among the hills and outcrops of Derbyshire, Yorkshire and Scotland; there they had become hill-walkers and rock-climbers.[2] These men were the fathers of the enormous post-war expansion of British climbing. Much of the strength of all these sections was united in the Alpine Climbing Group in 1953. This was inspired by the Groupe de Haute Montagne and provided much the same stimulus in Britain that its model had provided in France thirty years earlier. Though retaining its own individuality, the ACG was merged with the Alpine Club in 1967.

In 1952 L. Bérardini, G. Magnone, A. Dagory and M. Lainé climbed the west face of the Dru. After spending four days on the face, they came down and twelve days later traversed in to the point previously reached and completed the climb. The broken nature of the climb was a pity, but excusable on unexplored and very difficult rock. Two years later another French party repeated the route, taking three days. Within a week the third ascent was made by Brown and Whillans, taking two days. A few days earlier this same pair had put up a new route on the west face of the Blaitière. The *jeunes britanniques* were back.

Every season new climbs are made in the Alps. Almost all are difficult and almost all involve pitons, though in the western Alps pure piton climbs remain rare; most are a mixture of free and artificial climbing. New routes of any topographic importance are now hard to find, the natural lines have all been done. But there are still ribs of rocks, facets of ice, elegant variations straightening out time-honoured circumventions to be found, as well as lines which only the development of equipment and technique have brought into the realm of the possible. Alpine history nowadays is a filling in of unconsidered trifles, exploration is over. Overcrowding in summer has diverted attention to winter climbing, when the climber can still have the mountain to himself once he is above the zone of the ski-lifts.

By 1950 all the peaks had been climbed in winter and the winter attack began in earnest on the severe routes. In 1953 E. Amossi and O. Elli crossed the Silver Saddle from Macugnaga to Zermatt, making the first winter ascent of Monta Rosa's east face. Stärker, Marchart and Spiegler went up the south wall of the Dachstein in March 1959 and in March 1961, a German party led by Toni Hiebeler climbed the Eigerwand in eight days with six bivouacs. There was some controversy because, like the west face of the Dru, the climb was interrupted. On February 27, they climbed to near the Gallery Window where they bivouacked; bad weather set in and they retreated via the Gallery Window and the Railway. A week later they rejoined their bivouac site from the Gallery Window and from there completed their climb.

In August 1955, Walter Bonatti achieved a major tour de force when he climbed a very difficult new route and climbed it alone. He went up the southwest pillar (the Bonatti Pillar) of the Dru. He had made two earlier essays with strong companions and so had learned much about the lower part of the climb. (On one of these trips they had come upon a ledge with a heap of old wooden pegs: who had left them there or when remains a complete mystery.) The climb took Bonatti six days; here is his account of the last two:[3]

The ascent of the south-west pillar of the Aiguille du Dru
from Walter Bonatti, *On the Heights*
Usually the dawn which follows a night of anxiety and convulsive forebodings brings new energies and fresh hopes, but that morning the situation was changed and a fresh reason for preoccupation was added to the other and no less serious ones – my hands. They were so lacerated and swollen that I could not touch anything without a spasm of shooting pain. I especially felt the tip of my ring-finger throbbing as if the first stages of mortification had set in; it was the inactivity of the night which had reduced me to this state. To restore enough sensitivity to my hands to enable me to use them, I had to force myself to do exercises which made me clench my teeth in pain. When I managed to set out at last the sun was already high, and thirty feet farther up the whole difficulty of the problem confronting me made itself evident. All around me the face was smooth, concave in the centre and with a tremendous overhanging eave above me; it seemed like the apse of a cathedral. The obvious solution was undoubtedly to attack the great black roof above, where a succession of overhangs jutted out for at least fifteen feet, but the presence of a number of unstable slabs half-way up, in addition to the lack of security forced on me by my solitary climb, finally led me to reject such a route. A smooth chimney rose in front of me for several feet but I could not see where it led, and this induced me to try my luck to the left. Having mastered it, I was given fresh heart by the presence of some easy rocks which led to an enormous compact and vertical red slab at least a hundred and fifty feet high. It was a terrible sight but the thought that above it the face began to incline induced me to continue along this route. I attacked the slab decisively, filling a thin crack with pitons. At the start it seemed quite suitable, but after about seventy feet conditions changed, not so much because of the appearance of some small overhangs which seemed none too difficult, but because the crack unexpectedly became too wide to take pitons and at the same time too narrow for the wooden wedges. Furthermore it was slanting and overhanging for the remaining hundred feet. I know that with a drill and expansion bolts I should have been able to advance directly across the very compact granite slab, but I was bound by the rules of the game which at the moment seemed harsh and pitiless.

It was about midday when the throb of an aeroplane distracted me from this fresh problem, and a few minutes later, when a small, single-engined tourist plane appeared in the sky to my left, very close, I even managed to spare a thought for the intentions of the pilot. How unwise it was, I thought, to risk so much just to show tourists what is forbidden to them. But the aeroplane grew even larger, and came so near that I feared that it might crash on the Dru. A doubt assailed me, which was confirmed when the plane turned to pass a third time. It was looking for me and it was for my sake that it was flying so close to the rocks. With one foot in a stirrup and one hand grasping the piton which was holding me, I leaned out as far as I could, waving the other hand and the other foot and doing all I could to make myself more conspicuous, but unexpectedly a white cloud enveloped me and I soon heard the plane going

Opposite: climbers on the Eiger: top, on the summit; bottom left, the American mountaineer John Harlin; bottom right, Layton Kor and Dougal Haston on the First Band.

away. Who could tell if they had seen me, I thought, and I was overcome by the strange feeling that the plane was a living part of me which was now leaving me and tearing me apart. I became aware that I would have preferred absolute solitude. Everything that had happened in that short time seemed to me like a final effort to associate me with that life which no longer seemed to have any meaning for me. It had come unexpectedly and like a breeze had skimmed lightly over me several times and then vanished in the distance for ever, leaving me up here, out of the world, like a thing already dead. What terrible thoughts these were! When and how would I leave this mountain? I was filled with desperation. I had been deceived into thinking myself only a thousand feet from the solution to my problem, when suddenly it seemed insuperable. I would have to go back into the great apse, to the point of departure, and meanwhile a very precious half-day had been wasted.

From the time when I had completed that last unlucky rappel which had put me at the foot of the funnel, I had been using a single 120-foot nylon rope, keeping the other rope, the silk one, in the sack. Now the time had come to make use of both of them, since, after a careful examination, favoured by my position, I thought that I had found a solution. By a long swing I should be able to reach a long crack which furrowed the whole right side of the apse and was at least 120 feet long, perhaps even reaching the area of broken inclined rock which was unattainable from this side. After removing the pitons below me, leaving only the last one, the highest and most secure, I began a series of complicated swings to the right. The first of these was very long and brought me right back inside the apse under the great black roof, but when I tried to recover the rope I felt that it was not running freely because there was too much friction and was forced to retrace my passage in two swings. The third one was more like an almost horizontal rope traverse than a swing and enabled me to reach a long, thin ledge. I tried and tried again in vain to get up the smooth face above it to fix a piton sufficiently far up to allow me to make a final swing. I then tried to force a horizontal traverse to the right but after a few yards I had to stop in dismay: between me and the cleft there was an unsuspected immense concavity, flared and smooth as a monstrous shell. Wherever I looked, my gaze fell only on insuperable overhangs and vast smooth surfaces. The void was absolute and terrifying. Now I knew that I could not turn back. I could no longer either ascend or descend; I could not reach the beginning of the crack, now only an unattainable forty feet from me. I felt lost, drained of all physical and moral energy, glued to the only piton which still supported me and the sack in that total isolation. But faced with the certainty of death, human resources become greater than I could ever have imagined. Little by little I regained control of myself and finally, perhaps at the thought that I ought not to resign myself to wait for death without an effort when I had been struggling desperately for life for five days, a ray of hope was

rekindled in me and I again found the courage to confront that imponderable which I had already accepted when I left on an exploit of this nature. At the foot of the crack, which I would have to reach by diagonal rappels, there was an outcrop of rock shaped like a hand with the five fingers extended. I thought I might be able to lasso it and hoist myself up to it. I decided to try.

But the fingers looked treacherous and I soon realised that, even if I succeeded in lassoing them, they would not support me. I attached as many rings and hooks as I could to the knotted end of the rope, like a 'bolas', thinking that a sort of rope octopus thrown on to the outcrop must sooner or later catch on something or other. After a dozen tries the rope seemed to catch in the best possible way.

I gave a trial tug and shuddered; the rope broke loose and hung slackly. I tried again several times until the octopus held. This time it resisted when I tugged. Nevertheless I gave it several lateral tugs. Would the knots and the rings hold firm when I was hanging vertically under the outcrop? And would the outcrop itself, which looked so precarious, hold firm under my weight? Better not to think of that, since there was no other way out. I took the final precautions before launching out into space. At the other end of the thrown rope was the sack; in order to recover it from above, I untied it from the piton to which I too was anchored and balanced it carefully on the narrow ledge. I then passed the other rope up to half its length through the ring of the piton and tied the two ends to my waist, thus closing a noose of about a hundred feet in circumference. This would be the sole safety device possible for the unusual passage which awaited me. But woe to me if I should have to count on it, since it would mean a fall of more than seventy feet and it was almost too much to hope that the little piton would stand the strain. Every preparation was thus made. Nothing was left save to try my luck.

A last unnerving delay, a last inner prayer for safety, and then, as an uncontrollable tremor ran through me, before my forces grew less, I closed my eyes for a second, held my breath and let myself slip into space, holding the rope with both hands. For an instant I had the feeling of falling with the rope and then my flight slackened and in a second I felt that I was swinging back; the anchorage had held! In those moments my thoughts crowded headlong upon one another and yet they will remain in my mind with absolute clarity for the rest of my life. I let myself swing backwards and forwards for a few seconds more and then, before I began to spin round, I began climbing up the rope. With every foot the danger increased, because my oscillations on the rope became, despite all care, stronger and stronger and more direct in effect on the support, whose firmness I could only guess. It was a tremendous effort, very tense, which took toll of all my forces, now ruled only by instinct. When I had to let go of the rope in order to catch hold of the outcrop, I still had a moment of hesitation. I was afraid lest every-

Opposite: the Petit Dru from the west. The west face of the Dru was first climbed in 1952 and in August 1955 Walter Bonatti (above) achieved a very difficult new route alone up the south-west pillar. The climb took him six days.

thing collapse with me; but even as I was thinking this, I found myself clinging to its roughnesses and making myself as light as possible. Everything went well. I let my excitement subside and then began to recover the sack. Its gigantic pendulum in the abyss awed me. Then I took the rope from around my waist and when I was sure that it was running freely through the ring in the piton I felt a great relief. Now I could really feel that the *mauvais pas* had been passed.

I put the silk rope back in the sack, tied myself to the end of the nylon one to which the sack was attached and at once began to climb about thirty feet of loose rock until the crack became very difficult. Then I drove in a piton, attached the sack to it and, after adopting my 'System Z' for self-preservation, I tried and tried again to master an overhang on which I should have continued in free climbing. In the end I succeeded, supported more by the certainty of being able to belay myself with a piton just above than by anything else. But what I had thought to be a crack above me turned out in fact to be more like an open chimney with vertical walls, extremely hard and slippery. With an almost desperate effort I advanced another foot, and then a few more; but in the cracks I found only veins of hard quartz. However, a providential bottle-neck enabled me, *in extremis*, to drive in somehow or other a large wooden wedge on which, having looped the rope about it and attached a stirrup, I was able to recover without having to rely too heavily upon it. Once more I began to creep and wriggle upwards. I must go forward at all costs and as before I climbed on a foot at a time, always with the vain hope of being able to drive in a piton. Then I came to the end of the rope; to stop was impossible, so without hesitation I again made use of the 'Z System' to secure myself, tripling the amount of rope at my disposal and continued my way upward. Ten feet farther on, the rope got caught and stopped me suddenly. I was panting like a dying man so great was my effort and my desperation; but by good luck I was right under a small roof, in a zone of soft and crumbly rock like chalk which made it possible for me to drive in four or five pitons. In order that they should not all come out with the same ease as they went in, I bound them together with a short cord and thus obtained a fairly secure anchorage. I recalled that a similar operation had already solved a problem for me during a difficult passage on the east face of the Capucin. I unroped myself and holding gingerly with one hand to the rope attached to the bunch of pitons I descended as far as the sack which I had of necessity left behind attached to a piton.

After this experience, I finally discarded the idea of continuing in the crack and, as I was now higher than the roof of the apse, I decided to force a traverse to the left and try by this means to reach the broken and inclined slabs. This manoeuvre too succeeded, though after great difficulties, by a series of small diagonal rappels to the left which enabled me to cross several absolutely compact vertical slabs.

I had almost described a full circle since the morning and had at last come near to those blessed broken and easy rocks which seemed to continue for at least another hundred and fifty feet, but then . . . more roofs and overhangs, very fractured but also very marked. I braced myself to repeat the traverse in the opposite direction for the usual operations of recovering the sack and the pitons. At first the motion contrary to the direction of the swings I had just carried out disconcerted me but in the end, I don't know how, I managed to reach the famous bunch of pitons. A stirrup slipped unexpectedly out of my hands; my eyes refused to follow its fall and it was some seconds before I heard it bouncing down the face. Then for the third time I braced myself for those rappels. The rope and the rocks around me were spotted with blood. My poor hands were almost in ribbons, the pads of my fingers gripped the rock with open flesh, but the work they had to do was such that it made me insensible to pain. By the end of the third series of swings it was almost nightfall and I hastened upward in the hope of finding at least some narrow little ledge on which to pass my fifth night. I found one about fifty feet higher up. When I went down again to recover the pitons it was pitch dark.

At first the bivouac seemed even more dramatic than on the previous night, but suddenly I heard very distant shouts and I saw faint lights moving. They were my friends from the Charpoua hut, who were making signals and looking for me. I replied at once with what little breath I had left and in order that they might see me I lit a little torch made from a piece of paper. They saw me and it even seemed to me that I understood that they would come to meet me the next day (by an optical illusion they thought that I was already descending along the ridge of the normal route).

The mere presence of my friends, even though far away from me, was of no material use to me but it gave me a wonderful sense of power which made me feel that I was certain to reach the summit of the Dru and return to that life which during those days had little by little become so distant, so remote that it seemed as if it no longer had anything to do with me, but belonged to some imaginary person of whom I had only heard tell. As far as I was concerned nothing had changed materially from a few minutes before; the pain in my hands was still acute, I was burning with thirst and the dark shadow of the roofs above my head was just as repellent, yet within me the whole situation had changed and I was able to look at things in a very different way than I had been able to during the past few days. Only now did I feel that I had a true measure of comparison to help me to understand the intensity of all that I had lived through. The mountain, its rocks, the void, had become so alive as to make them seem, little by little, a part of myself, as if I formed a single body with them. Now, however, as if at an awakening, I was able to dissociate myself from these sensations and to reconcile them with reality. I even seemed able to toy with the idea of having always lived on this

Opposite: a view of the precipitous south-west (Bonatti) pillar of the Petit Dru.

Above: a bivouac slung from pitons on the Cima Piccola in the Dolomites.

141

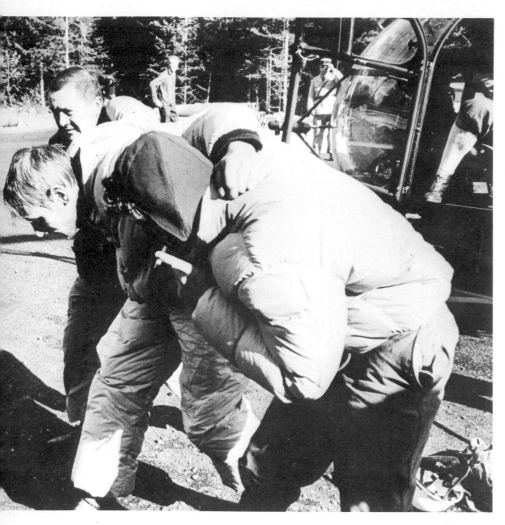

A rescued German climber being helped into an ambulance after five days stranded on the Dru. Mountains may have lost some of their mystery but none of their peril.

mountain, with the sole aim of suffering and of climbing ever upward towards an eternally unattainable summit.

For the first time I felt that victory over the south-west pillar of the Dru was in my hands, that I had surmounted the almost impossible barrier which had separated me from my true self and in the exaltation of the moment I felt a great longing to weep and to sing.

The sky began to grow light. I was about to begin the sixth day of struggle and all my energies were concentrated to overcome the last obstacle which still separated me from the summit, but my hands no longer seemed to want to respond to this last urgent appeal. During the night they had swollen, with intense pain, to such an extent that I could no longer close or open my fist and the exercises which I forced myself to do, as on the previous morning, to restore them to life brought on spasms of acute suffering. Not blood but a sort of plentiful clear matter oozed from every wound.

Voices reached me distinctly and then three men appeared on the gap along the normal route to the summit. I replied with deep emotion to their shouts and questions. I recognised only the voice of Professor Ceresa; the other two were speaking French. Though they continued to encourage me, I could sense from the snatches of their conversation which every so often reached me the anxiety they had felt for me; they thought me already victorious and on my way back.

To calm their apprehensions I began to climb, suffering the torments of the damned in my hands. A little later the voice of Professor Ceresa told me that they too were climbing to the summit of the Dru by the normal route and they would wait for me there with provisions.

An edge slanting upwards to the left led me almost directly towards the line of the south-west pillar. Soon the fifth and sixth grade difficulties gave way to those of the fourth and even the third or second grade, the edge began to slope, the rocks became easier and easier, and I advanced swiftly. By noon I was not more than three hundred feet from the summit and, in order to advance more swiftly. I decided to abandon everything no longer necessary and to carry the sack on my back. I was almost tempted to jettison the thirty or so pitons and the two stirrups I still had with me, but at the last moment I instinctively put them back in the sack, not knowing that by so doing I would be able to master the last deception of the Dru. In fact, just above me, a deep notch sharply divided the south-west pillar from the summit of the Dru and unexpectedly presented at least another hundred and fifty feet of overhang.

Up till yesterday this might have been my *coup de grâce*, but now I confronted the obstacle in an almost furious mood, face to face, as if I were now assured that nothing would be able to keep me from the summit. My hands began to hurt again. I drove in pitons and used stirrups in an almost brutal manner. A huge piece of stone weighing at least a hundredweight broke away unexpectedly when I was trying to fix a piton and struck me, numbing my left leg, but my hands were firmly in the chimney and did not slacken their grip. As if possessed of supernatural strength I continued to ascend, even mastering jutting overhangs in free climbing.

Little by little the rocks once more began to slope and below me on the normal route I could see my friends who, now sure of my victory, had stopped to watch me. At exactly 4.37 in the afternoon I was on the summit of the Dru. I glanced quickly around me and then, hurriedly, with my sack on my shoulders, I began to descend by the normal route.

The high standard of free climbing in the Dolomites was pushed even higher by Walter Philipp and D. Flamm. They made their famous climb on the north-west wall of the Civetta in 1957. In 1961 Whillans and Bonington climbed the Central Pillar of Fresnay. They had Ian Clough and Jan Djuglosz as second rope. Bonington prefaces his account of the climb by recalling the disastrous history of attempts earlier in the same season:[4]

The Central Pillar of Frêney
from C. J. S. Bonington, the *Alpine Journal*, Vol. LXVII

'It's too warm Don, we could always go up the Major.' I was afraid, standing there on the Col Moore. My mind, out of control, sought for an easy alternative. Water was trickling down the rocks in the shadows below us. The moon was full and the sky full of stars, but the mountains around us were not frozen into complete silence. Perhaps the weather was changing. The Col de Peuterey across the dark gulf of the Brenva glacier seemed very remote. The Pillars of Frêney were not even in sight. It would have been so easy to climb the long, easy snow-slopes of the Brenva face, and be on the top of Mont Blanc before dawn. Fear of the weather, fear of unknown changes, grew inside me.

'We've come this far, we'll go on.' Don spoke quietly and decisively. As we stepped down into the shadows, my fear left me. I revelled in the steepness of the hard snow, the feel of my crampons; biting home, and of my own movement and balance. We were now committed to our venture. After leaving the Col Moore, we never thought of retreat.

We were bound for the Central Pillar of Frêney. This granite tower, flanked by two buttresses, stands at the head of the Frêney glacier. Its base is at 3,900 metres, higher than the tops of nearly every major rock climb in the Alps. To reach it is an expedition in itself. As a result the Frêney cirque has been neglected. The two great ridges containing the cirque like the arms of a crouching sphinx were both climbed many years ago. The cirque itself was touched by Eustace Thomas and R. L. M. Underhill when they made a variant descent of the Innominata face in 1928. Graham Brown climbed up this route in the following year. The Pillars themselves were left untrodden until 1940 when Gervasutti, with Bollini, climbed the right-hand Pillar. This gave a magnificent climb of T. D. Sup.[5] It was climbed for a second time in 1953 by a French party which included the guide Julien.

He was tremendously attracted by the mass of rock on his left — the smooth tapering obelisk at the top, resting on a massive plinth of fissured granite. Other leading continental climbers were also interested and several attempts were made during the 'fifties. However, the remoteness of the climb made settled weather essential. As a result, all the attempts were abandoned at an early stage because of threatened changes.

On June 9, 1961, two parties arrived at the Col de la Fourche — Guillaume, Vieille, Kohlmann and Mazeaud from France, and Bonatti, Oggioni and their client, Gallieni, from Italy. That night they set out on the long approach to the foot of their climb, reaching the lower rocks on the morning of the 10th. They made good progress that day, getting two-thirds of the way up. On the following day they quickly reached the smooth tower near the top. The weather had been deteriorating all day, and as they slowly worked their way up the final tower a violent thunderstorm exploded around them. They retreated to two ledges, on semi-detached blocks at the foot of the tower.

They now had a difficult decision to make. Retreat back to the Col de la Fourche was impossible. The way down the Frêney glacier, to the safety of the Gamba hut, would be extremely dangerous, while

Above: Don Whillans, Ian Clough and Jan Djuglosz at the foot of the Central Pillar of Fresnay, which they climbed in 1961. Left: Whillans perched on a narrow ledge on the Central Pillar.

only two hundred feet of rock barred them from the comparative safety of the upper slopes of Mont Blanc, with the Vallot hut only just over the top.

They therefore decided to sit out the storm. After all, it was only a thunderstorm and it should have blown itself out after twenty-four hours or so. They sat there for two days and three nights. The conditions were appalling. The ledges were only wide enough to sit on and it was impossible to keep dry. On the third day they realised the inevitability of retreat, and started down the Pillar. Rappelling down the rocks presented few problems. Once down, however, it was a different story. The soft snow, rushing down in little avalanches, was thigh-deep. It was impossible to see more than a few feet, and finding a way across the *rimaye* [bergschrund] was a desperate business. That night they got back to the Col de Peuterey. Weakened, soaked to the skin, they spent the night in a crevasse.

On the morning of the 15th, on the top of the 'rochers Gruber', Vieille collapsed, and died from exhaustion. It took them most of that day to descend the rock spur. During a lull in the storm, a rescue party on the Innominata spur heard their shouts, but was powerless to do anything.

Once on the glacier, two ropes were formed — Bonatti, Gallieni and Kohlmann in one and Mazeaud, Oggioni and Guillaume in the other. As they fumbled their way through the drifting snow and round the crevasses on the glacier, Guillaume fell behind, exhausted. They reached the foot of the couloir leading to the Col de l'Innominata at nine o'clock that night. Mazeaud went back to find Guillaume but could see no trace of him. Oggioni was exhausted and could go no further.

The other three pressed on. The only hope of survival for any of them was to reach the Gamba hut and get help. Kohlmann collapsed only a few hundred yards from the hut; Bonatti and Gallieni staggered on, reaching the hut at three o'clock in the morning. The rescue party in the hut immediately went out to pick up the others. Kohlmann died before they could carry him back to the hut and Oggioni died during the night in Mazeaud's arms.

This was the end of a determined, well-planned and equipped attempt on the Frêney Pillar, by some of Europe's best climbers. It emphasised the great objective dangers in attempting this route. The rock was sound, there were no stone-falls, but in the event of bad weather retreat would be extremely difficult. Bonatti knew the area intimately. A party without the same knowledge would have little chance of getting back in similar conditions.

The technique of artificial climbing had been taken further and rigorously developed by a small band of Americans climbing in the Yosemite Valley. The European school had grown up on the mainly limestone rocks of the Eastern Alps. The Yosemite cliffs are of glacier-polished granite with few cracks or faults. For this different material John Salathé developed a hard piton in light alloy; European pitons are of soft iron and to some extent conform to the crack into which they are forced. The Yosemite piton does not so conform, is easier to extract from the rock and is not damaged by extraction. Nowadays these pitons are usually made of chrome-molybdenum steel, but the large 'bongs' are of aluminium alloy. The climber carries a stock of different shapes and sizes; many have knife-blades the size of a postage stamp and the 'rurp' (Realised Ultimate Reality Piton) is smaller still. These tiny pegs, or rather pins, go into minute shallow cracks and have opened up a new range of artificial climbing. The expansion bolt was an earlier Yosemite speciality, but rurps have diminished the need for them.

The hard Yosemite piton is not left in the rock, so successive climbs of a route are each as hard as the second climb; no ladder of pitons remains to help the late-comer. Nearly all Yosemite cracks are vertical, therefore the standard European double-rope technique alternating left and right is unhelpful. Nylon web slings are used instead of étriers.

Chamonix granite is by no means the same as Yosemite granite, but it differs even more from Dolomite limestone. It was only a matter of time before the Yosemite techniques appeared in Chamonix. The American John Harlin became intrigued with the possibility of making a *direttissima* on the west face of the Dru. With different companions he made two attempts in 1964. The next year he was joined by Royal Robbins, one of the grandmasters of Yosemite. After two weather-defeated tries, they succeeded on August 10-13.

In 1965 and 1967 long hard new routes were put up on Norwegian rock walls. The great Trollyggen buttress had been climbed by Arne Randers Heen and Ralph Hoibakk in 1958; now J. Amatt's party climbed its North Wall and two years later a French party contrived another route on the same wall, using fixed ropes and 700 to 800 pegs. A Norwegian-British team made a direct route on the east face of Kongen, while Amatt and Rusty Baillie (from Rhodesia) did the North Face Direct on Søndre Trolltind, involving very hard climbing, both free and artificial.

Winter climbing of increasing difficulty went on apace. Between 1953, when Couzy and Vialatte did the Old Brenva, and 1965, when the Olliers and Salluard did the Via della Pera, all four Brenva routes were accomplished. Bonatti and Zappelli did the Walker Spur of the Grandes Jorasses in 1963. In 1967 R. Desmaison and R. Flematty climbed the Central Pillar of Fresnay and next year made the first ascent of the Shroud on the Grandes Jorasses. This is the steep ice-field east of the Walker Spur and had been the objective of many climbers for years. Given a spell of fine weather, a few climbs are actually easier and safer in winter; the upper part of the mountain being frozen hard, it does not disintegrate into a fusillade of stones and ice. Such climbs include the North Face of the Matterhorn, the direct route on the Eigerwand (see below) and, probably, the Shroud.

Some equipment and techniques illustrated: above left: driving a piton into ice; above right; clipping a karabiner into a piton; far left: using jumars on an icefall. A jumar is a sophisticated prussik; it slides or seizes the rope as required and is much used for climbing fixed ropes on expeditions. Left: roping down an icefall. This is the controlled descent of a rope fixed above. The German term *abseil* or the French *rappel* are often used.

145

Some winter alpinists have used 'expedition' methods. Berger and Muller, for example, when doing the Davaille route on the north face of Les Droites, took a fortnight, descending fixed ropes to the Argentière hut each night. Also regrettably, expansion bolts have been fixed on the Walker; these had not been found necessary on earlier ascents, summer or winter. These are questions of etiquette, of manners rather than morals, and will be discussed in the final chapter.

John Harlin had nourished designs on a direct route straight up the Eigerwand for some time. It was clear that any attempt should be made in winter as the route would have to go straight up below the Spider which collects the falling stones from the upper wall and funnels them into a murderous stream in summer. Layton Kor, another Yosemite grandmaster, accompanied Harlin and Dougal Haston. The year is 1966. This is Peter Gillman's account.[6]

The Eiger direct

from Peter Gillman, the *Alpine Journal*, Vol. LXXI

. . . The team envisaged a ten-day climb. At this stage, there was no question of anything other than an alpine-style assault, with very heavy rucksacks and bivouacs on the face. The team rejected the Sedlmayer-Mehringer line in favour of one some 440 yards to the left, which had been considered by the four Germans who made the first winter ascent of the face in 1961. The new line, it was argued, covered almost entirely new ground, whereas the Sedlmayer-Mehringer route used the *voie normale* for part of the Second Ice-field; it followed a very definite line on the face; and, crucially, it was more direct.

The equipment was thoroughly planned. Key items were Le Phoque double boots; Mammoth perlon rope, known to resist freezing; and Chromolly hardware. Short-wave radios would be carried for weather forecasts. For bivouac rations they would take mineral and vitamin tablets and drinks, bacon and dried meat, dried fruit and candy bars. All three members conditioned themselves by ski-ing with no gloves all winter; Harlin carried snowballs *à la* Buhl.

On February 1 the team made a helicopter reconnaissance of the face. On February 4 they moved from Leysin to Kleine Scheidegg. On February 6 they were joined by Chris Bonington, who was to photograph the climb for the *Daily Telegraph* group, which was giving financial backing. Bonington was also helped by Don Whillans and Mick Burke. I reported the climb for the *Telegraph*. On February 14 Haston and Bonington took the train to the Eigerwand station with the team's three rucksacks, each weighing 50-55 pounds. Haston took them out onto the face so that they would be saved having to carry them up the theoretically easier, but extremely laborious, first third of the face.

On February 16 the eight-man German team arrived at Kleine Scheidegg. It became known that they intended to make a Himalayan siege of the route, fixing ropes for much of the way and bivouacking in snow-holes. Four of the team would act as an assault party, while the other four hauled supplies. They anticipated spending eighteen days on the climb. The two teams apparently planned to follow different lines from the foot of the First Band to the foot of the Flat-iron, but it was possible that they would converge there.

The German team started their attempt on February 16, the British–American team on February 18, but both retreated at the onset of one of the worst Oberland storms for many years, with gusts of 110 mph. The Germans started again on February 25, the British–American team on February 28. The teams used the same fixed ropes on the first third of the face — in theory easy, but taking two days to climb. The German co-leader, Jörg Lehne, said he thought it was harder than the North face of the Triolet.

The First Band was led by Kor, who classified all three pitches A3. The rock was smooth and compact and he used a number of pitons, some of them 'tied off'. A strenuous overhang on the third pitch, he said, was the most difficult artificial climbing on the route. The team used no bolts for direct aid on the whole route. The German team used eight.

Because no clear ten-day weather forecast had presented itself, the British–American team decided to modify its tactics. Fixed ropes were left on the First Band and a snow-hole was dug at its foot, quite close to one dug by the Germans. A pair of climbers would lead for a section of the route, while another hauled supplies and sometimes returned to Kleine Scheidegg. Chris Bonington became for a time as much a full climbing member of the team as a photographer.

On March 3 Kor and Harlin reached the top of the First Band and started on the iced-up gully system leading to the Second Band, a second cliff penetrated by gullies and chimneys. At this stage the two teams were almost at the same level. The Germans were following a line as much on rock as possible, whereas the British–American team had attacked the First Band at its narrowest point: they felt that although the ice above it would be difficult, it would go quickly. Lehne said he thought the ice-climbing envisaged by the British–American team was impossible.

On March 5 Harlin and Haston had to spend their first complete day in a snow-hole. The main problem lay in keeping out the clouds of spindrift that burst into the hole whenever a powder-snow avalanche came down the face. On March 6 they were able to climb again. Haston led one particularly difficult pitch consisting of crackless slabs plated over with ice, with very poor protection. They reached the foot of the Second Band that night, bivouacked where they were, and set off up a gully system cutting through the Second Band the next morning. The German climber Karl Golikow took a fall of thirty feet or more into snow on that day, and this appeared to lead the Germans to change their mind about following rock, for they traversed left to the British–American line. For a time Harlin and Lehne led separate ropes almost level up the same gully. Harlin reached the top of the Second Band ten minutes ahead of Lehne! Again he and Haston bivouacked at their high point.

On March 7 the British–American team decided to organise its supplies and restock rucksacks. Peter Haag and Günther Strobel traversed below the Flat-iron and climbed up the extreme left-hand end of the Second Ice-field. They attempted a new way up the rock band at the top of the Second Ice-field, but eventually traversed right to the pitch of V on the *voie normale*, bivouacking below it. The next day Harlin, Haston, Bonington and Kor climbed the whole way from the top of the Second Band to the Death Bivouac, taking with them five full rucksacks. In darkness and a storm they dug themselves a precarious snow-hole in a cornice at the very top of the Flat-iron. The Germans made themselves two snow-holes at the same level.

On March 9 the two teams diverged again. Haag and Strobel moved right and started up a crack system.

The Eigerwand marked with the original 1938 route (dotted line) and the 1966 direct route (broken line).
1 First Band. 2 First Icefield.
3 Second Icefield. 4 Death Bivouac. 5 Central Pillar.
6 White Spider.

Haston and Kor traversed left on to the Third Ice-field, and climbed two long, steep pitches to its top. A mixed pitch led to the foot of a high, smooth pillar that became known as the Central Pillar. There they met Haag and Strobel again, and then roped back down to the Death Bivouac.

It snowed that night, and more snow was forecast in the morning. It was decided that Kor should go back to Kleine Scheidegg (Bonington had gone down the morning before), while Haston and Harlin sat out the bad weather in the snow-hole. The Germans started to climb that day and had a desperate retreat when the storm hit the face, losing a rucksack full of supplies. Haston and Harlin spent five days in the snow-hole. For the first two they were plagued by spindrift, but eventually the entrance was blocked by snow. The cold, estimated at $-20°$ to $-25°$C., was tolerable. They avoided rheumatic pains by having foam rubber mattresses to lie on. On the third day Harlin reported to Kleine Scheidegg that he was not feeling well — he had fever, a fast pulse and weak breathing. *Five* doctors — all in the same party from Paris — were found, and they held consultations by walkie-talkie. On the fourth day food ran out.

On the fifth, Bonington, Whillans and Kor struggled to the foot of the face with food; Golikow and Lehne continued to the foot of the First Band, returning to Kleine Scheidegg at 10 pm.

On the sixth day — March 16 — Harlin and Haston decided to come down. There had been severe storms for four days; the weather was improving, but powder-snow avalanches were pouring down. On March 17 Bonington and Kor returned to the Death Bivouac. Harlin went to Interlaken hospital, where he was told he was recovering from bronchitis. On the way, he and I went to the funeral of Hilti von Allmen in Lauterbrunnen. In the evening Kor and Bonington radioed to Kleine Scheidegg that the Germans had reached the top of the Central Pillar, but this turned out to be a misunderstanding. The next day Bonington and Kor could see that the Germans were attempting a chimney to the right of the Central Pillar near the top of which was a large, bulging snow overhang. Kor had already decided that he would attempt to traverse the foot of the Central Pillar. He did so on March 19. It was a full rope-length, mostly artificial on poor and brittle rock, classified by Kor as A3. This was one of the most important leads on the whole climb, as it opened up the route to the Spider. Bonington then led up steep ice to within a rope-length of the top of the Pillar. That evening Lehne told Bonington that they had decided their chimney was too dangerous, and he asked if Bonington and Kor would drop a rope when they reached the top of the Central Pillar. Bonington naturally agreed. The next morning — March 20 — Lehne asked if Bonington would agree to join ropes instead, so Kor and Golikow climbed together up the gully to the left of the Central Pillar to its top. In his account of the climb in *Alpinismus*, May, 1966, Lehne ignores this episode. Diagrams in *Alpinismus* and *La Mon-*

149

Top: Miss Michiko Imai, one of six Japanese who made a new route up the Eigerwand in 1969. Above: three members of the party on the summit.

Spider and into the ice-field of the Spider proper. The British–American team's intention was to push for the summit on March 22. But on the evening of March 21 bad weather was forecast, so Harlin and Haston, joined later by Kor when he came down from the Spider, decided to postpone the push until good weather was again forecast.

On March 22 they confirmed the decision. Kor came back down to Kleine Scheidegg. But at lunch time the weather forecasts said the onset of the storm would be delayed by a day. When base camp radioed that a German climber had reached the Fly, the smaller ice-field above and to the right of the Spider, Haston and Harlin decided to bivouac in the Fly themselves that night and go hard for the summit the next day. Kor would follow and join the German summit party.

Haston and Harlin started prusiking up the fixed ropes from the Death Bivouac to the Spider, Haston ahead. At 3.15 pm Harlin was on the penultimate fixed rope below the Spider, when it broke at the point where it ran over the edge of a slab. Harlin fell 4,000 feet.

The immediate reaction in both teams was that the climb should stop. But that evening the climbers decided to continue. The clinching argument was that if the climb were called off, the weeks of effort and John Harlin's death would have been for nothing. Success would be John Harlin's memorial. The teams would form an international rope, and the route would be known as the John Harlin *Gedächtnisweg*, or the John Harlin route.

On March 23 the climbers decided to put all their efforts into getting one summit party to the top, particularly as the ropes below the Spider were seen to be worn in places. That afternoon Bonington and Mick Burke were dropped by helicopter on the glacier between the Eiger and the Mönch, making their way to the West face ready to meet the climbers. That night the storm came.

On March 24 the five made slow progress in the face of a hammering wind and bitter cold. From the West face, Bonington radioed that conditions were the worst he had ever known. A party of four Germans prepared to go up the West face as a precaution, in case the climbers on the face needed help — radio contact had been virtually lost. One of the few audible messages came at 9 pm; Lehne said that he had no idea where he was and that he was looking for somewhere to bivouac.

On March 25 the West face party set off. On the North face Haston led the second rope of himself, Siggi Hupfauer and Roland Votteler. The Zurich weather bureau later reported that the wind had been gusting at 95 mph with a temperature of −26°C. The summit ice-field, thought to be straightforward, presented severe technical difficulties. Lehne and Strobel reached the summit at about 4 pm, followed an hour or so later by Haston, Hupfauer and Votteler. Haston and Bonington both suffered from frost-bite, but made complete recoveries after hyperbaric treatment in the London Hospital under Dr Ward.

tagne, April, 1966, show the direct route as following the German false line to the right of the Pillar, with Kor's key traverse not marked.

Kor now led an artificial pitch of 110 feet, negotiating an 8 feet overhang near the top. On March 21 Bonington returned to Kleine Scheidegg, and Haston and Harlin returned to the face. Kor climbed with Lehne; Lehne led from the previous day's high point, and Kor led the next pitch up the right leg of the

Votteler and Strobel both lost all their toes, and Lehne lost one big toe.

The laconic 'followed an hour or so later by Haston, Hupfauer and Votteler' hardly does justice to this final lead of Haston's: the first party had left fixed rope but there was a gap of 150 feet. The later party, no doubt on the assumption that they could rely on fixed rope over any difficulty, had no ice-axe, no hammer and only one piton. Up this steep blank ice, in these appalling conditions of storm and cold, Haston had to make his way equipped only with a piton as a tool to scratch the ice.

In the summer of 1969 the Japanese made a new route to the Eigerwand, well to the right (west) of the previous routes. This seems to have advantages and may develop into the standard route. It was repeated by a Swiss party the following January. It is interesting to note that, with all this concentration on the Eigerwand for a generation, the very steep Kalli (south-east) face of the Eiger, first climbed by O. Eidenschink and E. Moeller in 1937, had to wait nearly thirty years for a second ascent. As Ernst Reiss remarked, 'there are no spectators on the south side.'[7]

Also in 1969, the Poles did a new route on the Grand Pilier de l'Angle (between the Brenva face and the Peuterey ridge of Mont Blanc) to the left of the Bonatti-Gobbi route. The next year a Czech party climbed the spur leading up to Pointe Hélène on the north face of the Grandes Jorasses. This completed the spurs of this face; Walker and Croz had been done before the war, as already related, Punta Margarita by Couzy and Desmaison in 1958 and Point Whymper by Bonatti and Vaucher in 1964.

The summer of 1971 produced excellent conditions in the Alps and a consequent burst of activity. Unfortunately the splendid weather exaggerated the problem of overcrowding. Incredible as it may seem, there were at one time more than two dozen parties on the Walker Spur. How are the mighty fallen! Not yet quite an easy day for a lady, but very far from the 'last great problem' that baffled so many superlative climbers for so long. The other two terrors of the 1930s, the Eigerwand and the North Face of the Matterhorn, both became well-worn routes this exceptional year.

For a century now, men have talked of the exhaustion of the Alps. A hundred years ago there were no big peaks, except the Meije, still to be climbed. New and progressively harder routes have been made ever since and will continue to be made. The pressure for achievement brings increasing numbers into the search. Those immune from, or who have outgrown, this pressure, can explore the wealth of valleys, peaks and ridges for an alpine lifetime. If you have not done a climb before, it is a new route to you and some old friends grow dearer with repetition. While the mountain aura is weakened by the presence of contemporaries, it is not spoiled, rather enriched, by the ghosts of predecessors.

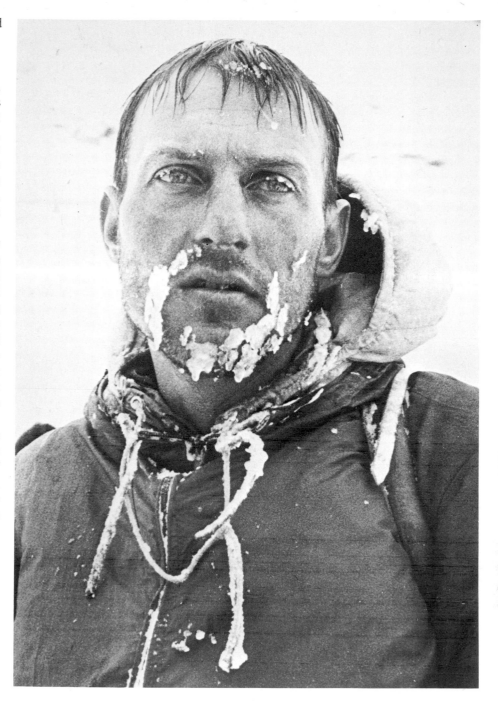

Jörg Lehne, one of the first to reach the summit on the 1966 direct attack on the Eiger.

9 Since the War, mostly America

And everyone said, 'How tall they've grown!
For they've been to the Lakes, and the Terrible Zone,
And the hills of the Chankly Bore.'

Edward Lear

The Andes

The last twenty-five years have seen a great expansion of activity in the Andes as everywhere else. The crowding of the Alps has sent more and more climbers from Europe; easy flights bring many from the USA and Canada; the Andes are particularly popular with groups like University clubs whose purses or holidays are too short for a Himalayan expedition.

In the Peruvian Andes, it was two young men from Harvard, Harrah and Maxwell, who climbed Yerupaja (21,765 feet) in 1950, a fine effort only achieved at the cost of several fingers and toes; the climb was not repeated for 16 years. Next year a Franco-Belgian party reached the North, and lower, summit of Alpamayo. In 1953 no less than three expeditions set out for Salcantay (20,574 feet), which had already been attempted in 1950 by Piero Ghiglione. In June, two Swiss, M. Broennimann and F. Marx, reached the plateau some 300 feet below the top, and in August G. I. Bell, F. D. Ayres, D. Michael, W. V. G. Matthews, Claude Kogan and Bernard Pierre of the Franco-American party reached the summit. Ghiglione's international party arrived on the scene too late.

The diorite needle of FitzRoy (11,072 feet) in Patagonia is one of the most striking mountains in the world. It is protected by its extreme steepness, by very bad weather and, above all, by a murderous west wind from the Pacific. In 1937 Count Aldo Bonacossa had been to investigate; he saw no means of getting up the final spire except by artificial methods. After the war Hans Zechner, an Austrian settled in the Argentine, made several attempts but all were beaten back. The challenge was taken up in 1952 by a French party led by M. A. Azéma. At first they had bad luck and Jacques Poincenot was drowned in a torrent. The final assault was by Lionel Terray and Guido Magnone. They pegged and roped the first section, returning to their companions in an ice-grotto for the night. On February 1 they bivouacked with the last of the light, having overcome many of the difficulties. The weather showed some signs of breaking next morning, but they pushed on as soon as the sun had restored some warmth to their limbs and to the rock. Azéma takes up the story at one o'clock on that day.[1]

The ascent of Fitzroy

from M. A. Azéma, *The Conquest of FitzRoy*

The start, a twenty-foot ice-filled crack, was difficult. The initial step had to be made on a wooden wedge and continued with the help of minute pitons with heart-shaped blades, the only ones that would fit in the thin cracks. Clenched fists were jammed between ice stalagmites, feet found what support they could. Fifty feet of easier going on loose ice-glazed rocks gave Magnone an opportunity to get his breath if not to collect his wits. But before he could contrive a stance in the bed of the ice-filled chimney he was obliged to master another long pitch of artificial climbing.

The chimney steepened into an overhanging runnel. The only means of getting up was with stirrups. It was no use looking for hand or footholds on the viscous ice coating the granite. Cracks seen through the ice were cleared with the *marteau-piolet* [combined hammer and axe], pitons driven in until they jammed convincingly. Once again the exit was most hazardous, requiring a pure gymnastic effort from weary limbs.

The next pitch, a hundred feet on snow-covered blocks, was fairly easy, but as usual the top steepened into a little vertical wall. Then at last came the final rope's length before the exit. Lionel and Magnone scrutinised these rocks eagerly for they were, no doubt, the ultimate defences of the fortress. The two men were now beneath the battlements of the keep, in the neighbourhood of the gap opening on to the final platform over which floated long cloud streamers. They were impatient to reach the platform and make certain of their victory.

The pitch was thick with snow and Lionel took over the lead. In crampons he would gain time on the glazed holds on which Magnone's rubber soles slipped. He climbed up a long slab without much difficulty and then lost time again negotiating a steep wall without artificial aid. The chimney became increasingly encased. It ran up, cutting deep in between the lateral walls, turning first into an alcove and finally into a deep cave between two storeys of blocks one on top of the other. The floor was formed of jammed boulders covered with snow, the ceiling of one colossal heart-shaped boulder sticking right out of the chimney. A portcullis of heavy ice stalactites hung from the point of the heart while inside the cave the ceiling was coated with a thick layer of powder snow plastered on by ascending air currents.

The two men were puzzled.

'We might have expected this, considering the way the wall faces,' said Lionel. 'We're lucky not to have to go right out on to the wall itself, which would be all in artificial, and our five stirrups left hanging from the gutter of this damned roofing.'

Guido took over the lead. The obstacle would certainly succumb only to artificial technique.

Straight up was obviously impossible. They would have to try the side walls. On the left the wall was smooth and compact. On the right a broken crack offered a fairly reasonable start, but later turned at an angle and was lost to view. Guido succeeded in driving in a small wooden wedge over six feet up. Once again the manoeuvre was repeated; karabiner, rope, stirrup.

'Pull away!'

Guido was standing up with one foot in the top rung, his waist on a level with the karabiner; the other foot swung free while he explored the rock with his hands. Three feet above the crack reappeared and would take a second wedge. At full stretch Magnone tried with the tips of his fingers to clip a karabiner to the loop of line attached to the wedge. But it was twisted and kept escaping his grasp. Once, twice he swung his body to gain height as he stretched his arm out desperately to the uttermost limit. At last he got it, the karabiner hung ready. The second rope and a stirrup were clipped in. The proud rock was harnessed.

At this point Magnone was about ten feet from Lionel. He stretched his left leg right across behind him and found a hold on an icicle which kept him in balance. The crack continued above but it was very narrow.

'If we can get a piton in, FitzRoy's in the bag! To make a bad pun — hanging by a thread!'

Magnone looked at his belt. There were two pitons left, scored and twisted by the rock and by hammer blows. No matter, they would be sufficient. He unclipped one from the karabiner at his waist, held it against the rock and tapped it with the hammer to straighten it out as well as he could, particularly near the point.

'It should do.'

He tried the piton up and down in the crack searching for the best place, the widest and above all the deepest.

'Ah, it's in.'

He took the hammer in his left hand, aimed carefully and tapped gently. Ping! The piton slipped sideways, jumped out of the crack, described a circle beyond the reach of the hand which shot out to grab it, hit a block, bounced off and plunged into space. 'Hell! Must try the other one.'

With beating heart Magnone began all over again. It was the last piton, and he had no string to belay it with. Lionel kept watch, no longer for a fall on the part of the leader but for the piton!

This time the hammer hit true on the iron head. The point went in a quarter of an inch; a second blow, it gave out a dull sound and would go in no deeper. A third and harder blow; the piton twisted and bent

and Magnone pulled it out easily with one hand. He straightened it and sought a fresh spot. He tried in vain up and down the length of the crack; it was too narrow, the edges split away beneath his redoubled blows, but the piton would not go in. What they needed was an 'ace of hearts'. Magnone broke out into a cold sweat of apprehension.

The last heart-shaped pitons had been left three hundred feet below in the iced corner which had cost more than an hour's work. Even supposing they

FitzRoy in Patagonia, remarkable for its extreme steepness and atrocious weather. Its summit was first reached by Lionel Terray and Guido Mangnone in 1952.

▲ Ixtacihuatl
▲ Popacatapetl

▲ Mt Roraima

▲ Cotopaxi
▲ Chimborazo

CORDILLERA
BLANCA

Chacraraju ▲
Huandoy ▲ ▲ Huascaran
▲ Jirishanca
▲ Yerupaja
▲ Huaguruncho

CORDILLERA
HUAYHUASH

▲ Pumasillo
▲ Salcantay

▲ Illimani

▲ Aconcagua

▲ San Valentin

Patagonia

▲ FitzRoy
Cerro Torre ▲ ▲ Poincenot
▲ St Exupery
▲ Towers of Paine

Tierra del Fuego
▲ Mt Darwin

0   200   400   600 miles

0   200 400 600 800 1000 km

went down to fetch them, it wasn't certain they would be able to get them out of the crack into which they were twisted and bent. And would it be possible to climb back up that desperate icy pitch without pitons, even though held from above? And above all, in such conditions, would they ever find the courage to climb up again to their present level?

Magnone was almost crying with anger and despair. 'It's no good, Lionel. We're beaten.'

Magnone was lowered down on the rope which ran through the karabiner attached to the last wedge. He sat sideways in the snow, worn out and beaten, and waited awhile before untying to pull down the ropes— before taking the irrevocable decision to turn back.

FitzRoy would remain unconquered.

'It's under a curse — bewitched mountain. Up to now we've alternated between hope and fear. Each time things have turned out all right. But now, only six feet from the top of the final pitch, the way is barred! It's almost four o'clock. Only five more hours of daylight. We'll have to retreat quickly. If we don't we'll lose the lot, FitzRoy and our own skins.'

It had been like a game of Patience: fifty-two cards to turn up and so far the right one every time. At each card a tightening of the heart and one thinks — this time it will be all up! But no, the game goes on. Only ten cards left! Again, the right one! Only three! Again the luck holds. Only two! With a trembling hand one turns the card — and it is the wrong one . . .

Lionel went back into the cave where he began to bite his nails and scratch his head. He, too, was

miserable, but, but oddly it was he now who would not accept the turn of events and still believed in victory. Suddenly he said:

'Guido, the sardine tin!'

Guido looked up. Had Lionel gone mad? That sort of thing happened at 23,000 feet, but at 10,000?

Lionel fumbled hastily in his sack, explaining the while:

'You remember that tin of sardines, yesterday on the triangular snow-patch? I opened it with an "ace of hearts" which I think I put back in my sack, in the inner pocket. It must be there.'

Lionel pulled his things out, plunged his hand in and felt around. Then he gave a yell of triumph: 'Here it is!'

He held up the tiny piton, a jewel without price, between the tips of his swollen fingers. The grain of sand that changed the face of the world.

The ace of hearts was driven in. The thin steel blade just fitted into the crevice and was twisted and hammered in up to the hilt. At the last blow of the hammer the sound rang sharp and clear. Magnone knew he could trust his whole weight to it and even take the risk of a fall. He stood straight up in the stirrup, holding on to the karabiner with his left hand, then he reached up to the ridge above his head, let go with his other hand, grabbing a projecting hold and with a violent heave, the last effort of all, pulled himself to the top of the east face.

'Lionel, we've made it!' yelled Magnone beyond himself with joy.

FitzRoy was virtually conquered.

A fairly strong westerly wind sent clouds heavy with moisture and sleet scudding by. A long bank of snow at an angle of forty degrees ran up to the right and soon disappeared in the mist. The summit was 600 feet further.

In his turn, Lionel hove up out of the depths and at a glance took in the situation. Providentially, the weather had not deteriorated dangerously. It was almost unbelievable. It was a contradiction of all they had learned, of every prediction. This was bad weather such as one meets with often enough in the mountains, but not a storm as it is understood in the Patagonian Andes. There was no saying whether it would hold, but neither need they suppose that it would worsen. Anyway, they would go to the summit now, even at the risk of a second bivouac.

'Come on, Guido!'

Lionel took the lead, this time for good. His crampons bit into the frozen snow and he climbed quickly up the slope. But Magnone's rubber soles slipped on the sloping surface. He had to cling to his hammer which served as an ice-axe as he kicked his toes in at every step. Though Lionel fretted as he felt the rope drag behind him, holding him up, he could not but wait for so valiant a companion. He urged him on and encouraged him with persuasive tugs of the rope. He chose out places where the snow was deeper, or the neighbourhood of protruding rocks which rose like reefs out of a solid foam. In the mist a mountain scene is anonymous. Lower down

Opposite: a map of South America.

Left: Kempe rounding an icy corner on Huagaruncho during the British expedition in 1956. After difficulties with deep snow and honeycombed ice, Streetly and Westmacott reached the summit.

Above: Huagaruncho, the south face. The route taken in 1956 followed the shelves, top right.

Opposite: Chacraraju, climbed from the north by a French party also in 1956. Terray described the ice-pitches as almost unequalled anywhere else in the world.

it had been FitzRoy, but here?

The slope led to a broad safe ridge which ran up to the right into a vertical wall.

Surely not another obstacle! Their cup was full. They could do no more. Ah, thank God! It was an illusion, an optical illusion in the mist. They kept a steady pace. The rocky outcrops increased, the snow had been swept away and they knew that here the wind was sole master. The slope eased and led up to a long almost horizontal slab pocked all over by wind erosion. Beyond, the mists rose up as from a well: a sudden gust tore the veil apart, there was void all round and nothing above Lionel's head:

'Guido, we're there! It's the summit!'

The two men linked arms and gave tongue to their victory.

Though they were able to descend fast by means of the ropes fixed on the ascent, night had fallen when they rejoined their companions at Camp III.

Mount San Valentin (12,717 feet), on the Patagonian ice-cap, which had been under attack for 23 years, was climbed in 1952 by three ropes from the Club Andino Bariloche.

The Munich Academic Club made a successful foray into the Cordillera Vilcanota the next year. They made several first ascents, including that of Ausangate (20,945 feet). A number of subsidiary peaks of this mountain had already been climbed the year before by Ghiglione's party consisting of himself, the Austrian Rebitsch and the Swede Bolinder.

In 1954 René Ferlet led another French expedition to the Argentine to attack the formidable south face of Aconcagua (22,835 feet). After some very hard climbing (on one day it took 14 hours of effort to make some 800 feet of height), the assault team bivouacked at about 19,700 feet suffering very much from the cold. Here is Guy Poulet's account of the next three days.[2]

The south face of Aconcagua
from Guy Poulet, the *Alpine Journal*, Vol. LX
23rd February: At five we wake to a dim light. Pushed by the wind off the Pacific, a layer of cloud veiled the sky, racing by at 25,000 feet. The snow whirled round the summit ridge, above us a livid green cloud wheeled slowly.

In spite of these sure signs of bad weather, we thought we could reach the top and decided to go on. The upper glacier's brow of séracs had a vertical section more than three-hundred feet high. We succeeded in making height up a trench; this enormous crevasse ended in a slightly overhanging wall of living ice sixty feet high. To overcome this obstacle Lucien Berardini, then Robert Paragot, had to use every resource of artificial technique.

When at last we got out onto the upper glacier, we thought we had victory within our grasp. However, to get up it took six hours of exhausting work, ploughing a trench through the new snow.

We set up our third bivouac at 21,000 feet, on a snow bridge in the bergschrund cutting off access to a slope of ice.

It was a hard night. Temperature had fallen as the height had increased, −30°, −35°. . . . We struggled against the cold as we tried to get some rest.
24th February: Snow torn off by the squalls had covered us with a thick layer. We left our perch at 8 am to attack the bergschrund. Lucien, in the lead, had to take his gloves off to overcome an up-thrust of rock covered with verglas. In the cold, intensified by wind-squalls, this passage was at the limit of possibility.

By the time we were all together on the ice-slope, it was one o'clock; five hours to get up a hundred feet.

Tormented by thirst, we slowly mounted the slope. It ended on the roof-ridge of the spur we had been using since morning.

Six o'clock: no question of getting to the top this evening. Yet again we prepared to bivouac. Four

Top: Terray triumphant on the summit of Chacraraju and, above, members of the French team and their Peruvian porters.

Opposite top: Taulliraju, which Terray's party went on to climb in 1956. Though lower than Chacraraju, the route included a huge granite slab which Terray held to be the hardest rock pitch then achieved at that altitude.

Opposite bottom: members of Eric Shipton's party on the Patagonian ice-cap. In 1962 the expedition crossed the ice-cap, a journey of 52 days in almost continuous blizzard.

fingers of Lucien's left hand were frozen, our feet had lost all feeling. We had had nothing to eat or drink all day. Crushed by fatigue, we cut out a narrow shelf in the ice on which we sat as well as we could, our legs dangling down the slope.

The fierce effort sustained over several days made itself felt. We used up the rest of the fuel to make a half mess-tin of tea. It was passed from mouth to mouth: by the time it reached the last of us, it was already covered by a layer of ice.

This last night was particularly painful. We fought with all our strength against the encroaching cold. In the intervals of this struggle we dozed into brief, nightmare-haunted naps.

25th February: We harnessed ourselves up. It was very difficult to pull on boots, stiff with frost and covered by a thick coat of rime.

It was absolutely necessary to get to the top by the evening, or else. . . .

The start was eased by the ropes which Lucien and I had fixed in two chimney-cracks the night before. Adrien Dagory and Pierre Lesueur were the leading rope. Our way continued as a series of difficult rock buttresses, covered with snow and verglas.

The hours slipped by inexorably as we neared the north ridge.

The wall played us one last trick. The spur we had been following since yesterday did not run out onto the ridge; it ran out into an unclimbable wall.

To reach the ridge we had to climb yet another slope of very steep ice. Happily the consolidated snow took our crampons well; even so it took us another three hours to get up this exposed slope.

At last at six o'clock we set foot on the summit ridge, and we could see the gentler contours of the northern slopes and, far, away, a bar of deep blue: the Pacific Ocean.

Staggering with fatigue, we followed the rounded shelves leading to the summit platform.

Stimulated by John Oberlin's article, 'Invitation to the Andes'[3] a British party set out to attack Huaguruncho (18,799 feet) in 1956. After Kempe, Band and Tucker had been turned back by the lateness of the hour, it fell to John Streetly and Michael Westmacott to try again. After considerable difficulties with deep snow and honey-combed ice, they duly reached the summit.

Chacraraju (20,055 feet), a peak whose ferocious aspect had deterred any previous attempt, was the objective of a French group in the same year. After making a tour of the mountain, they decided to attack from the north. Here is Terray's report of the final climb:[4]

The ascent of Chacraraju

from Lionel Terray, *La Montagne et Alpinisme*

The first camp was established at about 5,100 m., some 100 m. below the start of the difficulties. It took five days of hard work to put a second camp on the wall, at about 5,500 m. We had to fix ropes over most of this section to facilitate load carrying, as there were many difficult pitches, including 40 m. of smooth rock. It was necessary to climb pitches of V, and to resort to artificial means on a long and very steep ice-traverse threatened by ice-fall from cornices and séracs; the whole route was exposed to serious objective danger.

A first sally from Camp II, over slopes of snow and ice, sometimes at an angle steeper than 60°, led us to the main ridge, less than 300 m. from the summit. Ropes were fixed throughout this section. On July 31 we left Camp II at 5 and, thanks to the fixed ropes, reached our previous highest point at 7.30.

Here the real battle began. After three rope-lengths of mixed climbing diagonally below the crest of the ridge and an exposed rock traverse, we had to climb an icy gully between two 'organ pipes' of ice.

This pitch was almost vertical for 20 m. and, to complicate things had a little overhang in the middle. It took me more than an hour of hard, delicate and exposed work, for the ice was very fissile and I was only able to put in one ice-piton. While I was struggling with this pitch, Sennelier lost his balance trying to take a photograph; he slid down the gully taking Souriac with him. Happily Souriac fell down a parallel gully so that their rope buried itself and stuck on the organ pipe between them, holding them both.

The next two pitches, partly rocky, were less difficult but very delicate and took a long time. It was only about 1 that we reached the prominent shoulder on the right of the summit. This is, perhaps, 100 m. below the top; there only remained a narrow, corniced ridge of alarming appearance.

Because it faced east, and because of the altitude, now over 6,000 m., this ridge was all of very soft snow, in spite of the steepness of the slopes; progress was only possible by digging a trench, at times waist-deep, through it. Only after hours of exhausting work and the climbing of a vertical wall, were we able to destroy the myth of Chacraraju's inviolability, at about 5 pm.

Night overtook us as we began to descend. In order to avoid an icy bivouac, we decided to go on down by the poor light of our head-torches. We came down almost entirely by rappels, but with every precaution; nevertheless I shall not forget one exposed traverse when my torch battery was almost exhausted. . . .

We only got back to Camp II at 7 in the morning on August 1, after 26 hours of continuous effort.

The ascent of Chacraraju, 6,100 m., is certainly the hardest climb yet made at that altitude; the ice-pitches we had overcome have few equals on any routes anywhere in the world. Success was only achieved by more than fifteen days methodical work, by the systematic use of fixed ropes, and by the resolute enthusiasm of the team.

The East peak of Chacraraju, a little lower but certainly even more difficult, seemed too heroic an objective for our remaining three weeks, so we decided to turn to Taulliraju (5,830 m.).

They duly went on to climb Taulliraju (18,940 feet), a much shorter but equally difficult course. There was nothing so hard as the ice-gully on Chacraraju, but there was a huge granite slab which Terray thought the hardest rock pitch then achieved at that altitude. Chacraraju East, rejected as too heroic an objective in 1956, was climbed by Terray and four other Frenchmen[5] in 1962. It was by then the last unclimbed 6,000 m. peak in the Andes; it proved extremely difficult and had to be equipped with fixed rope almost throughout.

Jirishanca (20,100 feet), one of the most striking peaks of the Peruvian Andes, was climbed by Toni Egger and S. Jungmaier in 1957. In the same season, Pumasillo (19,915 feet), 'claiming some notoriety as probably the highest virgin peak outside Asia', was climbed by a Cambridge University party[6] and Alpamayo's higher, south, summit (19,600 feet) fell to four members of the Schwaben section of the DAV led by Gunter Häuser.

In 1959, Cerro Torre (9,908 feet), on the edge of the Patagonian ice-cap, was climbed by Cesare Maestri and Toni Egger. Although only a few miles from FitzRoy, Torre enjoys even worse weather, taking the first brunt of the storms. There had been two Italian parties there the year before. Bruno Detassis, leader of the first to arrive, pronounced the mountain to be impossible. Bonatti and Carlo Mauri, finding Detassis' party already on the east (lee) side of the mountain moved round to the west (weather) side; they reached the col, but soon after turned back in face of extreme difficulty and danger. Maestri, who had been with Detassis, returned next year with Egger, a small expedition on a shoe-string, at their own expense. After battling with storms for six weeks, they fixed ropes up the first 600 feet. The weather cleared and they went on up ice which had to be cut away to insert expansion bolts in the rock behind. After three bivouacs they reached the summit but the weather had broken again; the ice began to melt and to slide off. In two more days they had got to within 200 feet of the top of their fixed ropes when a vast mass of ice swept Egger to his death. Maestri struggled down and several days later was rescued from a snow-hole in a state of collapse. Terray considered this climb 'the greatest mountaineering feat of all time'.[7]

Piero Ghiglione, who was by now a vigorous 76, recorded seven new mountains in southern Peru in this year; he was accompanied by his Indian porter, Mautino. The highest of these was Chicchiccapac (16,800 feet). Godfrey Francis's party, who arrived on the summit a few days later, were a little disappointed to find Ghiglione's footprints there.

Meantime Shipton was exploring the Patagonian ice-cap, which Tilman had crossed with E. H. Marriott and J. Quinteros in 1955. He solved the mystery of the ice-bound volcano, whose existence had long been doubted; this proved to be the rift near the summit of 'Lautaro' (11,089 feet), the highest point of the Cordon Pio XI, in the middle of the ice-cap. In 1962 he crossed the ice-cap more or less lengthwise, from north-east to south-west, with Jack Ewer, Eduardo Garcia and Cedomir Maragunic; it was a journey of 52 days in almost unbroken blizzard. Next year the same party (except that Ewer was unable to get away and his place was taken by Francisco Vivanco) went to Tierra del Fuego, crossed the Darwin range from north coast to south coast and climbed the culminating point, Mount Darwin[8] (about 8,100 feet). Next season, again with Garcia and Maragunic, plus a young Spaniard, Miguel Gomez, Shipton crossed the northern ice-cap, making the first ascent of Cerro Arco (9,843 feet) and the second of Arenales (11,277 feet).

Six New Zealanders selected Nevado Cayesh (18,770 feet) as the outstanding Andean problem and set out to climb this 'almost impossible pinnacle of ice' in 1961. They suffered a number of injuries and one case of pulmonary oedema; smart work and local help procured oxygen in the nick of time, and the patient recovered so completely that he was one of the trio that eventually completed this difficult climb.

Towards the end of the year a group of young men from Irish universities went out with Don Whillans to attack the Aiguille Poincenot, the fierce but smaller neighbour of Fitzroy. This is from Whillans' account:[9]

The ascent of the Aiguille Poincenot
from Don Whillans, the *Alpine Journal*, Vol. LXVII

We had been on the mountain about a month, and Ruffino was due to arrive any day with his horses to evacuate us. As we staggered into Base Camp, the sun appeared and a spell of fine weather began. The idea of a last attempt to climb to the summit began to formulate itself. It would have to be in the Alpine style, a fast party of two installed at the ice-cave of Camp II with food for three days. With an early start, they might make the Shoulder by midday. If great technical difficulty were found, they could place the pitons during the afternoon, then retreat back to the Shoulder for a bivouac. Next day should see them on the top. If it was not too difficult, they might reach the top and get back to the Shoulder the same day.

While Frank and I strolled comfortably up in the perfect weather, the others sweated and puffed beneath our loads. We brewed some tea for them;

then they wished us luck and stamped off down the slope to Base.

It was clear and starry when I looked out at 3 am next morning, but some cloud in the west made me wonder if we might have another desperate descent before the day was through. As we trudged up the frozen Piedras Blancas glacier, the moon shone brightly, and the huge 5,000 feet East face of FitzRoy was bathed in light. Steadily we approached the big bergschrund and the first fixed rope. But the monumental storm of a few days before had completely filled it, and likewise buried our fixed ropes higher up. At the top of the third fixed rope the sun warmed us, and very soon we were sweating as we hauled on endless ropes.

Frank had been very impressed on the Ramp and was greatly relieved when we stood on the Shoulder. The ridge ahead looked hopeful, but the weather did not; great clouds were banking up on the west side. Frank was doubtful about going on, but we both wanted to press on to see the problem at close quarters; and without stopping even for a drink we crouched behind the ridge and quickly sorted out the equipment. The wind blowing on the west side was a continuous roar, and the slap of wind on the rock sounded like a giant slapping the rock with a wet towel. Not at all eager to be exposed to the full force of nature, we made towards the foot of a long, wide crack on the east side.

After a tentative attempt, and deciding it was much too difficult to begin with, we felt we should have to brave the wind and see what lay round the other side. Following a zone of ascending ledges, we gained height and were soon clinging to the rock for fear of being blown over. Cloud moved past at fantastic speed, and snowflakes shot by like bullets. I glimpsed the Cerro Torre across the valley before the clouds closed in, and an unforgettable sight it was. I can best describe it by quoting Azéma in the FitzRoy book: 'I seemed to be looking at supernatural monsters, a fantastic ride of the Valkyries; nightmare aiguilles stared across at us, hurled defiance and then vanished. From a bubbling devil's cauldron, where clouds heavy as pitch boiled up from the depths, and eddies of snow chased each other in the gale, there emerged at intervals the summits of the Cerro Torre and its satellites. Like immovable reefs in a raging sea, the black slabs reared up towards the sky, to be smothered by the stupendous ice-caps, sparkling with fresh snow, which overhung on all sides – glittering lighthouses, whose foundations were submerged in foam.'

It is a perfect description of my glimpse of the Torre, which was missed by Frank round the corner. An amphitheatre seamed with cracks ran a long way up the wide ridge. Quickly we made our choice. The snow was being blown straight up the rock, and if the climbing stayed reasonable we might get up. Clinging to the rough rock even on stances, to avoid being blown away, we climbed quickly up grade IV rock, rejoicing that we were making such good progress. At length we were stopped, and a semi-pendule

had to be made to gain another break on the right. The odd pitch of V was ruthlessly dealt with by banging in a peg whenever slight difficulty showed itself.

Our estimated 800 feet of climb on the ridge had been away off the mark; it was nearer 1,000 feet already, with the top still not in sight. I was relieved to see that there was no chance of Frank wanting to give up in face of the uncertain weather, as he was waiting impatiently for me to get up the pitches. I wriggled up a small chimney through which the wind howled at fearful force, and looked along a wedge-shaped ridge which was the summit. I quickly looked round to see that there was nothing higher, then brought Frank up; and we took turns in sitting on the top for photographs. I banged in a French piton as a memorial to Jacques Poincenot, and Frank dropped an Argentine *pesa* into a small crack. It was 3.15 pm on January 31. It had taken us eleven hours to reach the summit; could we possibly reach Camp II before darkness? Quickly we began the descent, climbing wherever possible – it was impossible to throw the abseil rope down because of the wind. When the rope was pulled down, it refused to drop and stood vertical, lashing like a mad thing in the air.

Abandoning surplus equipment at the Shoulder, we slid quickly down the rope onto the sheltered side of the mountain. But the rope jammed behind a flake, and I had to lead the icy chimney again to free it. Quickly we slid down the fixed ropes, walking down the steep ice with the rope across our backs, and arrived at the steep couloir at the bottom of the Ramp as darkness fell. Frank was very tired, and slowly we plodded back down the Piedras Blancas glacier to the little haven of ice that seemed to offer everything a man could wish for after almost twenty hours' gruelling effort: a drink, food and a bed.

Opposite: Cerro Torre in Patagonia.

Left: Whillans, descending the Central Tower of Paine in 1961, meets Azziazi of the Italian party on the way up. The Italians made the ascent the day after the British, using the same pegs.

163

Later in the year Whillans was back in Patagonia with a rather similar objective, the Central Tower of Paine, a fierce rock spike beset by the same or even worse weather. The others in the party were Bonington, Clough, V. Bray, B. Page and John Streetly. They were slightly disconcerted when an Italian party arrived in the field a few weeks later with the same objective. After weeks of wind and struggle, the weather improved. Whillans and Bonington made the ascent, which the Italian party repeated on the following day, using their predecessors' pegs.

Peter Bebbington led a London School of Economics expedition to the Cordillera de Raura and later visited Cordillera Huayhuash, where he was much impressed by Rondoy (19,300 feet), which had defeated the redoubtable Bonatti. In 1963 he came back with another LSE party, reinforced by Vic Walsh and Pete Farrell, two of the New Zealand group who had climbed Cayesh. Their first attempt was washed out by snow, the second established the route. On the third attack seven of them reached their ice-cave below the north (lower) summit, not without contretemps. The weather turned foul and it was agreed that three ropes of two should go for the summit, leaving David Wall in the cave. Farrell and Walsh reached the summit, followed the next day by the others, but Bebbington and Sadler disappeared on the descent. The rest of the party found their bodies a few days later.

The Colorado Mountain Club had a meet in the

Cordillera Blanca, making first ascents of Copa-pamparaju (17,815 feet) and several other peaks. Many new mountains were also climbed by a Spanish party from a camp near Huascaicocha Lake, and by some Swiss in the Huayhuash.

In 1964, Lautaro (11,089 feet), the volcano in the Patagonian ice-cap, was climbed by P. Skvarca and L. Pera from Argentine. L. Ortenburger with a very strong US party made a new route on the north ridge of Chacraraju's west peak, and another North American party led by Leif Patterson made the first ascent of the very hard north peak of Jirischanca. Next year G. Frigerio's Italian team climbed Aguja Nevada (19,308 feet), the somewhat lower east peak of which had been climbed by the Swiss in 1959. South African, Japanese, Swiss, American–Brazilian, Catalan, Argentine, Brazilian and Chilean teams were all active.

By this time most of the highest peaks of the Andes had been climbed and ambitious mountaineers had already been devoting much effort to new routes on 'old' mountains, many of them of great difficulty. There remain unclimbed giants in the volcanoes of the Atacama desert, shared by Argentine, Bolivia, Chile and Peru. As climbing problems they are probably minor, but they are not readily accessible. In describing them as unclimbed we mean only that there are no recorded ascents; on those that have been ascended this century unmistakable traces have been discovered of earlier climbs by Inca and Atacameñan Indians centuries ago, and they are probably also to be found on the 'unclimbed' summits.

Andean mountaineering was now at the stage reached in the Alps a hundred years ago. The more accessible areas were a holiday playground and the less accessible a field for exploration. Nevertheless, away from the spectacular giants of Peru, there were plenty of big mountains that were still little known. In 1966, for example, a group from Bangor University was able to make 15 first ascents of peaks over 18,000 feet in the Cordillera Real. In this year Peru listed no less than 31 climbing expeditions, among them a British party that set out to climb Alpamayo by the north ridge. It had been on this ridge that a slice of cornice had come away in 1948 and carried three Swiss down 650 feet, miraculously unhurt; and it was by this ridge that the Franco–Belgian party had reached the northern summit in 1951. The southern and higher summit had been reached by Gunter Hauser's German party in 1957, but the intimidating ridge connecting the two summits was as yet untraversed. Bathgate and Smith of the British party succeeded in reaching the higher summit over this ridge.

Domingos Giobbi and Carlo Mauri of an Italian–Brazilian team climbed Uruashraju (18,815 feet) and Robert Paragot's French party overcame the north face of the north peak of Huascaran (21,834 feet), while Peterek and Patterson of a Canadian–Argentine party traversed Yerupaja (21,759 feet) after making a direct route up the west face; they needed 13 bivouacs. Perhaps the most notable

success of the next year, 1967, was achieved by the Japanese who at last climbed Santa Cruz Norte (19,160 feet). H. Adams Carter and Jack Miller got up Cashan Oeste (18,704 feet), a fine ice spire.

Next year Patagonia again held the stage. After great struggles and weeks of weather-bound waiting, a British attempt on the south-east ridge of Cerro Torre had to bow to the storm, but in the Cordillera del Paine a party, mainly of Peak District climbers, got up the aptly named Fortress (about 10,000 feet). After this success the weather washed out further plans. There was one fair day, seized by a Chilean party led by Eduardo Garcia to complete their climb of the Principal Cuernos and by a Bergamesque team to finish their climb of the Shield, the Fortress's neighbouring castellation.

In Peru, the New Zealanders did a different traverse of Yerupaja, up by the south-west and down by the north ridge. At the same time an Anglo–American foursome attacked the north-east face. This is Chris Jones's report:[10]

Opposite top: the fierce rock spires of the Towers of Paine.

Opposite bottom: John Streetly, a member of a British expedition, climbing on the Central Tower in 1961.

Above: the New Zealander Pete Farrell approaching the north summit of Rondoy during the British expedition led by Pete Bebbington, who was killed on the descent.

The formidable spike of the Aiguille (Aguja) St Exupéry in Patagonia, climbed by five Italians in 1968.

The north-east face of Yerupaja

from Chris Jones, the *Alpine Journal*, Vol. LXXIV

Notwithstanding our supposed ethics, we had brought 1,200 feet of thin line, everyone seems to take the stuff. As we got nearer the mountain, the truth of Patterson's remark, that the main problem lies in getting to the face, became only too apparent. The Yerupaja glacier was an ice-fall, and our way was through it. Malcolm Slesser had led two Scottish parties attempting the East ridge, and one of his party recommended we follow their approach. José Fonrouge, on a reconnaissance, had taken the other side and suggested it was much quicker. Would-be believers in the quick dash, we thought this would save time; it didn't.

The scheme involved skirting the glacier by rock climbing on Yerupaja Chico, before starting on the ice-fall. In the next few days we were involved in some improbable manoeuvres as we tried to force a route across glacier-polished walls. The only way was into the ice-fall, and it was an unholy place. The weather remained cool and cloudy, the ice-fall relatively quiet, as we wound through the worst mess of séracs any of us had seen. Next day an ice-bridge had collapsed, but I was able to persuade Paul [Dix] he could jump over at another spot. We put an intermediate camp by the glacier, so that we could start on the ice before sunrise, and hopefully find the route intact. But now the skies were clear, the heat terrible, and the glacier dissolving. A few days later we got up in the dark,

yet as soon as the sun arrived the melt began. An improbable ice-fin crossed a vast crevasse, and today, as we were on it, it was splitting apart. Twenty minutes later we heard a thunder behind us; the fin had died. Going on or going down both looked equally bad, so we had some food where we stood, trying not to think about the creaks and groans from under our feet. It really hotted up when a sérac 50 feet away keeled over, crashing through our route, as we ran nowhere looking for shelter. All this spoiled our breakfast and enthusiasm; our world was a shambles, our existence in doubt, and our quick way a slow, unpleasant one. We turned back and began to patch up our route. Near where the fin had been, I again got Paul – 'You're a specialist' – to slide and leap over, then crawl across an ice-boulder jammed in a crevasse. Down was what interested us, but most crevasses required working on – someday we had to get back up. The collapsed fin had supported an ice-wall, now we ran over the debris, beneath the wall. Next time up, it too had gone. In two more places ice-bridges had disappeared; it was becoming absurd. Off at last we grinned at each other and the Gods – it had been a bad day. . . . We made three more dawn starts, but knew better when the sun came up. Finally, the clouds we needed, and we had our camp under the face.

The climb looked good, a two- or three-day push; our other problem was how to get off. Yerupaja has no *voie normale*, and climbing back down a mile of steep ice wasn't attractive. We would have to rappel, and, as we could only carry a certain number of pickets and pitons, they would have to be long rappels. Being of the Yosemite mould we had rather strangely brought sixty rock pitons and ten pickets. The thin line was our white hope, and to try it out we had a rapid look-see. The bergschrund was under constant stonefall, very unpleasant. Rock climbing to one side got us onto the face itself. We fixed a rope over the schrund, and the following day were on our way.

The dihedral in the face receives all the rockfall from the summit and East ridge, and as the sun got up the stones began to come down. 'That missed me, too,' I shouted, as Paul, having avoided a quick one, looked around for some sign of encouragement. Generally moving together, except on the harder pitches, we tried to keep two pitons between us, joining when the leader ran out of hardware. We turned back at midday, hoping to be down for tea.

I had had my doubts about the effectiveness of a 1,000 feet rappel line. I did expect however, that some sort of progress would be possible. It wasn't. We wrestled and coaxed, and after two hours were nowhere. The master plan was beginning to crack, had cracked, so we cut the rope in half and tried again. It began to snow, supper was long gone, it got dark, we cursed and fought. Sometime before midnight we dribbled into our tents – up had been faster than down. . . .

With bivouac equipment I usually end up bivouacking, and if we'd carried ten days food

walked over them. Had a long way to go. One of those humps had to be it, can't all be false summits. Paul's there, a tricky summit, can see through it. The Scots' East ridge seems a place to avoid. Look around in clouds, only Huascaran greets us.

Later that year Jones was in Patagonia with Y. Chouinard, Dick Dorworth, Lito Tejado-Flores and Doug Tomkins. They looked at Cerro Torre, 'the hardest mountain any of us had ever seen or heard of', and went across the FitzRoy where they did a new route by the south-west buttress. 'It had taken eight weeks, during which there had been about eight possible climbing days. Patagonia cannot be denied or explained. The atrocious weather, the weeks spent waiting and some of the world's greatest climbs remain untouched.' Also in Patagonia, five men from Trieste got up the difficult Aguja Saint-Exupéry (9,711 feet) and J. L. Fonrouge and A. Rosaco did a new route on the Aiguille Poincenot.

In 1969 Riccardo Cassin and his Lecco friends, who had had designs on the north-east face of Yerupaja, switched their attention to the east ridge when they found the former had been climbed by the British–American party. On reaching Peru they found Austrians already in action on their chosen objective. The Austrians, Peter Habeler and Reinhold Messner, duly climbed this ridge, while the Italians went up the west face of nearby Jirishanca (20,100 feet).

Left: Jirishanca seen from Rondoy North. The west face was climbed by a party of Italians led by the veteran Riccardo Cassin in 1969 and described by him as the most compelling problem of the Cordillera Huayhuash.

Below: an ice-storm on the Patagonian ice-cap. The bitter cold and ferocious wind add considerably to the difficulties of climbing in the Andes.

I've no doubt it would have taken ten days to ferry it up and down. Theoretically, then, we had a light load, but prusiking over the schrund it didn't seem like that. There was a long way to take it, and by midday the climbing was harder, the day hotter, the air getting thinner and the lads tired. We hoped the séracs would be our home, but as time passed the dismal possibility of a bivouac *in der Wand* increased. More time, more front points, finally the séracs, delusion, a head wall – no more. Too tired to cut a platform, as a last chance I went up; our crevasse was waiting for us. Sleep was a problem, too. Paul had convinced me his *pied d'éléphant* was shot, so we left them and took a sleeping bag. Worked great at base, not now. It was a one-man bag. A fiasco. Hardly slept, shivering or cooking most of the night.

The great red morning sun watched us doing nothing, the golden midday sun saw us turn back. We had tried a few pitches, but it was hopeless, our legs disjointed, our throats as the desert sand. The bivouac sack doubled as a sunshade, while we watched and waited. The day before, Dean [Caldwell] and Roger [Hart] had bivouacked lower, at the top of the rock spur, now with evening came voices. Cloud obscured the schrund, so they were carving a hole in the middle of nothing. Shouts; they joined us; tomorrow we would try again.

It was tomorrow, 1,200 feet, an ice gully, the summit ridge. Cornices and sad memories of Rondoy. We began by passing the cornices on the face, later

New routes were also made in 1967 on Chopicalqui, Huascaran, Alpamayo and Ausangate by British–Australian, North American and German parties. An Australian expedition was very active in the Pumasillo area, doing a dozen new climbs. A Spanish expedition was similarly successful in the Cordillera Apolobamba and then went south to Illimani, where they succeeded in climbing the north ridge of the North Peak (21,200 feet), fog being for once helpful in enabling them to survive a fusillade from Bolivian gendarmerie. In the Cordillera Real, Germans and Italians also mopped up many new peaks. In Patagonia, New Zealanders climbed round the northern rim of the ice-cap, while Japanese crossed the southern ice-cap, climbing a peak of the Cordon Risopatron en route. J. and P. Skvarca of a Club Andino Bariloche party climbed Cerro Norte (9,679 feet) north of Lake Argentino, and the northernmost and last summit of Paine Grande fell to the Japanese.

An earthquake in May 1970 limited climbing in the Cordillera Blanca and, indeed, destroyed an unlucky Czechoslovak expedition camped near Huascaran. New Zealanders put up some new climbs in the Alpamayo and Pucahirca groups; Bavarians climbed seven new *fünftausenders* (5,000 m., 16,405 feet), another New Zealand party (plus a Rhodesian) made new climbs in the Cordillera Urubamba and a French party were active in the Cordillera Vilcanota. The highest peak of Nevada Solimana (20,730 feet) was climbed by M. Bignami, Julian Blanco and Paul Gotz.

The rush continued in 1971; among the American, Austrian, British, Canadian, French, Italian, New Zealand and Peruvian parties was one of five British ladies in the Cordillera Carabaya, all working mountaineering instructors.

In 1972, a South African expedition climbed the Sword (8,200 feet) and Cuernos Norte (8,530 feet) in Patagonia. Imperial College were climbing in the Cordillera Real of Bolivia and the Royal Military College of Science in the Sierra Nevada de Santa Maria (north-east Colombia). In the Cordillera Blanca, Adam Carter's American party climbed Tumarinaraju (18,603 feet) and a Polish–Chilean expedition ascended several summits of Ojos del Salado (about 22,600 feet) and Cerro El Solo (20,300 feet).

There are still plenty of virgin peaks, but they are relatively minor and have little defence except their remoteness from the assaults of modern equipment and technique. Future interest is likely to centre on excessively difficult routes on unclimbed ridges and faces; the scope for such pioneering remains immense.

North America

The mountains of the far north, in Alaska and the Canadian north-west, have seen much notable climbing since the end of the last war.

In the Alaska Coast Range, Fred Beckey, Robert Craig and Clifford Schmidtke climbed Kate's Needle (10,002 feet) and the Devil's Thumb (9,077 feet) in 1946. In 1949, in the course of a scientific expedition led by Walter Wood, an Anglo–American–Canadian foursome (Odell, W. Hainsworth, R. McCarter and Bruce Robertson) climbed Mount Vancouver (15,700 feet) in the St Elias range. This mountain had been attempted as early as 1886 by an American party led by a British naval officer, Lieutenant Seton-Kerr, and again, in 1888, by the Tophams. Mount McKinley, hitherto only climbed from the east and west, was climbed from the north and south in 1954. Both parties used aircraft, which has become standard

practice in this area to minimise the difficulties of approach and supplies. Elton Thayer, George Angus, Morton Wood and Leslie Viereck climbed the mountain via the Ruth Glacier and the south buttress, using a route plotted in advance by Bradford Washburn. Descending by the usual route, the party suffered a bad fall, which killed Thayer and injured Angus, who spent a week alone on the glacier while Wood and Viereck struggled down to get help. Helicopter and aircraft were involved in this rescue. Meanwhile Fred Beckey, Donald McLean, Charles Wilson, Henry Meybohm and Captain William Hackett were forcing their way up the long north-west buttress. Beckey and Meybohm, joined by Heinrich Harrer, went on to climb Mount Deborah (12,540 feet) and Mount Hunter (14,570 feet).

Nineteen sixty-one was a busy year, with several ascents of McKinley, including the south peak by the south ridge and a strong assault on the Wickersham Wall, and the first ascents of Mount McArthur (14,000 feet) and Mount Queen Mary (13,000 feet) in the Logan massif. Here is Fosco Maraini's description, based on Cassin's personal account to him, of the climb of McKinley's south face:[11]

The south face of Mount McKinley

from Fosco Maraini, the *Alpine Journal*, Vol. LXVIII
One must not forget that Cassin was fifty-three at the time of the McKinley's South face expedition. There is something indestructible about this man; something palaeolithic and Neandertalish. He certainly would have been a legend had he lived before fire and wheel were invented. Climbing together with him you sense an inner force utterly alien to our complicated, mechanised, intellectualised world. And, hidden inside that compact, leathery, tough lump of a body, you feel the presence of a soul both elementary and dignified, while his small eyes reveal the shrewdness of a peasant, the humour of a Chinese sage.

Riccardo is entirely a self-made man. He has been successful in life and now owns a sports-goods business in Lecco, near Milan; yet he is really only himself when pitted against nature in some formidable or utterly desperate enterprise. May I here mention the names of two other famous Italian climbers whom I have seen in action? First of all, Emilio Comici. Emilio considered mountaineering as a sort of music; climbing for him was a sort of ballet, an art similar to that of an oriental painter jotting down a poem in intricate and elegant ideograms with the point of his brush. Then Bonatti. Bonatti is an engineer, a magician; each of his great climbs seems to be complete in his brain long before it takes shape on rock and ice. Riccardo, compared to the other two, though he employs all the refinements of modern technique, is totally instinctive and primeval. His attitude to nature is fundamentally poetic and, one might say (though he would be furious if he heard me), religious.

Climbing with Emilio Comici was like listening to Bach or to Vivaldi. The mountain somehow vanished,

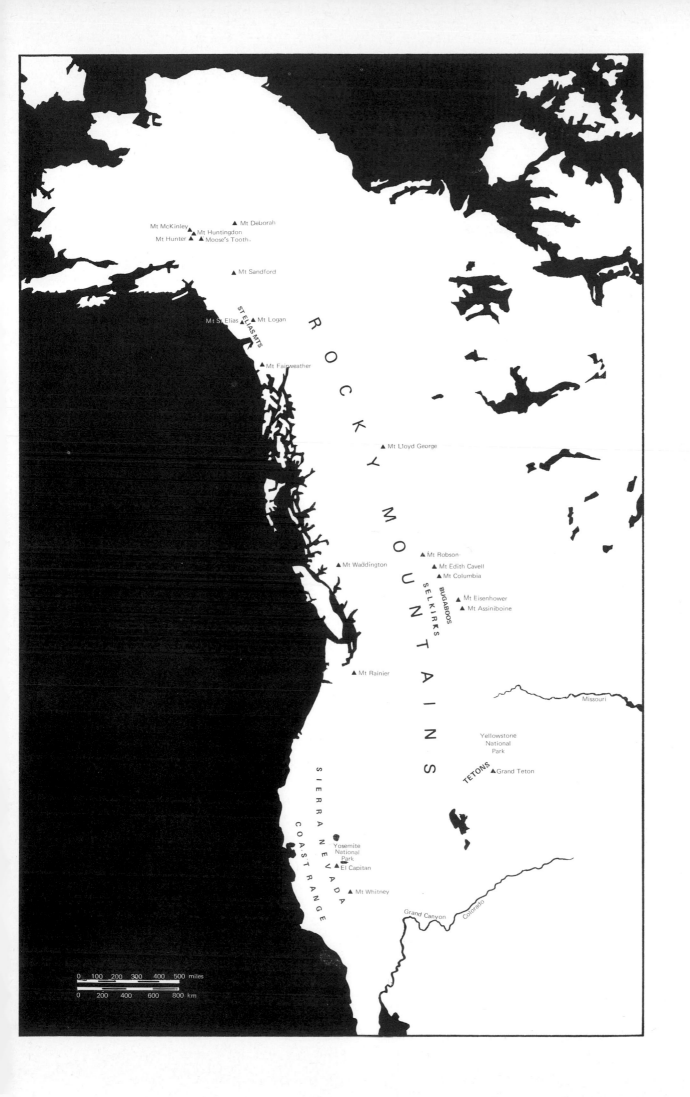

Mt McKinley ▲ ▲ Mt Deborah
▲ Mt Huntingdon
Mt Hunter ▲ ▲ Moose's Tooth.

▲ Mt Sandford

ST ELIAS MTS
Mt St Elias ▲ ▲ Mt Logan

▲ Mt Fairweather

R O C K Y

▲ Mt Lloyd George

M O U N T A I N S

▲ Mt Robson·
Mt Waddington ▲ ▲ Mt Edith Cavell
▲ Mt Columbia

SELKIRKS
BUGABOOS
▲ Mt Eisenhower
▲ Mt Assiniboine

▲ Mt Rainier

Missouri

Yellowstone
National
Park

TETONS ▲ Grand Teton

S
I
E
R
R
A
Yosemite
National
Park
N
E
V
A ▲ El Capitan
D
A
C
O
A
S
T
R ▲ Mt Whitney
A
N Grand Canyon Colorado
G
E

0 100 200 300 400 500 miles

0 200 400 600 800 km

Mount Deborah, Alaska, climbed by Fred Beckey, Henry Meybohm and Heinrich Harrer in 1954.

it was transformed into rhythm and counterpoint. Bonatti, on the other hand, is a man of our century, he personifies the power of science over nature; all human values, even courage, are transformed into factors of a formula out of which come inevitable results. Climbing with Riccardo is fascinating for reasons which are quite opposite. It means achieving a supreme and subtle contact with rocks and sky, with ice and wind. Any Zen master would claim him

as one of his own. Mountains are never matter, time, danger (factors, known and unknown, in some sort of vast differential equation), but living, mysterious and powerful essences with whom one deals on a purely personal, on a totemic, basis. I can just see Riccardo snuffing his way up the crags and ice of McKinley in the horrid subarctic gales, like an old bear who plays a difficult and long-drawn game with the gods of darkness and cold, of loneliness and

170

ahead by sea. On June 6 Cassin met Bradford Washburn at Boston, and the two men had a long conversation poring over Washburn's splendid aerial photographs of McKinley. Cassin was very much impressed by Washburn's kindness and by American hospitality in general.

Anchorage gave the climbers a great reception. The local folk dined and wined their guests with dances and ceremonies. The mayor gave Cassin a key of the city and each man received a small, golden nugget as a symbolic gift. Cassin, among many other things, noted that out of a population of some 45,000 people at least 500 owned private aeroplanes; probably a world record!

Now in fact aeroplanes take the place of Sherpas, Bhutias, Baltis or other Asian men in expeditions to the mountains out East. Don Sheldon became the expedition's pilot and transport officer. A first step was to take men and goods over from Anchorage to Talkeetna, a village of five hundred souls (dogs included) much nearer to the mountain. Unfortunately some precious days of good weather were lost because of a serious mishap in the transportation connections. About seventy small containers of liquid gas had to be bought on the spot, this operation taking place in the very last minutes before shops closed down for the long American weekend.

On June 18 Don Sheldon flew his plane for the first time up the Kahiltna glacier and managed to find a suitable place for a landing. Next day the plane went to and fro between the glacier and Talkeetna, carrying a substantial part of the expedition's goods. Airoldi and Alippi remained on the glacier, pitching a tent there. Unfortunately the weather broke on the 20th and remained very bad till the 24th. For a brief period, the party was divided into two groups.

At Talkeetna, Cassin and Sheldon examined carefully the maps of the district. They came to the conclusion that, somehow, a mistake had been made, and that the goods of the expedition had been dropped on the North-east branch of the Kahiltna glacier instead of the East one; some four miles from the spot which should have been chosen. This meant a lot of extra work, not only for the plane, but for the climbers' shoulders, as some of the material had been dumped in a spot where no aircraft could land. It was only on June 27 that men and material managed to be united in the right place; the expedition could then consider its first phase over. The spot – which will henceforth be called the Landing Camp – was not suitable as a Base Camp because it was both too low (8,500 feet) and too far from the mountain. A suitable place for the real Base Camp was discovered some 2,000 feet higher. The hard work of carrying all the material up there, along some very tiring snow-slopes, started in earnest and lasted four or five days. . . .

Weather on McKinley was nearly always bad, and often horrible. July started with a series of stormy days: mists hung over the mountain, or were blown along by ghastly winds, and it snowed all the time. Climbers had to keep to their tents and wait. On

hunger, knowing quite well that they may be very powerful, but that he is tougher, shrewder, keener than all of them put together.

The expedition started by air from Milan on June 5, 1961. The original members of the party were as follows: Riccardo Cassin, Luigi Airoldi, Luigi Alippi, Giancarlo Canali, Romano Perego and Annibale Zucchi. They had with them most of their material, though some of the heavier items had been sent

171

July 5 the sun appeared briefly, and the climbers started to explore a long couloir above the Base Camp. It proved to be very steep, and a number of ropes were fixed to the ice as an aid for progress later on. Soon the weather deteriorated again and the parties were obliged to return to Base Camp.

The next seven days were entirely taken up by the extremely tough proposition of opening a way up the first couloir, up a succeeding one and up some very difficult (grade IV) slabs of steep, granite rock. A few hours of good weather, for instance on July 10, seemed quite miraculous; then clouds would close in again upon the climbers and it would either start snowing or a gale would make work excessively difficult: sometimes wind and snow combined together. The cold was also getting worse as height was slowly gained. Ropes were fixed at all critical points so that loads could be carried higher. On July 12 Camp I was established by Perego, Alippi and Canali on a diminutive col at about 13,100 feet.

Above the site of Camp I there rose a very long, and often quite steep, snow ridge that led straight to the centre of McKinley's southern face. The ridge was excessively thin in places, and required a lot of delicate work to enable loaded men to tackle it successfuly. July 13 was one of those rare days when the sun shone nearly all the time. Movements were active all along the route. Canali, Perego and Alippi completed the exploration of the snow ridge and planted a small 'Nepal' tent just below the berg-

The south face of Mount McKinley, first climbed in 1954 and in 1961 by the south ridge by an Italian party led by Riccardo Cassin.

schrund limiting a small hanging glacier. Two other teams carried loads up from the Base Camp.

The weather seemed to have settled for a while. This meant hard work for all. July 14 and 15 saw teams moving up and down, from Landing Camp to well above Camp II. Here there was a comparatively easy stretch of steep snow on a hanging glacier. Then came some really touch obstacles: a fearsome gully full of ice and, worse yet, a frozen gully 120 feet high, of good grade V standard. This stretch was first opened by Zucchi and Perego. Above this very hard section, which might be said to represent the key to the whole ascent, a suitable place was noticed for an eventual Camp III, but for the moment the advance party had to return to Camp II.

On July 16 the weather broke again. The magic spell of three sunny days had run its course. Grey clouds closed upon the mountain, and soon it started to snow. The cold was so intense that the snow was like dust, or sand. It seemed to settle nowhere and managed to get through the smallest crannies of clothes and tents. No new ground was explored, but loads were lifted from the Base Camp to Camp I and from Camp I to Camp II. A stronger and larger tent of the 'Pamir' type was substituted for the small 'Nepal' tent of Camp II. The following day, it snowed so heavily that all parties had to keep to their tents in Camp I. At five in the afternoon, suddenly, the wind abated and the sky partially cleared. One of the few advantages of climbing at very high latitudes is that days last for nearly twenty hours. Cassin realised that there were still at least five hours of light and decided to start off at once. The whole expedition, in two parties, all men heavily loaded, climbed from Camp I to Camp II, which was reached at 10 pm as the sun was setting.

The morning of July 18 was glorious. Hopes were high. Only one more camp was required, and a suitable place had already been noticed above the long, frozen gully. If Camp III could be set up and equipped that very day, then a dash for the summit could be attempted in the next twenty-four hours. The route had been explored and partially furnished with fixed ropes by Zucchi and Perego, but difficulties were very great, and everybody was heavily loaded. The small level spot which had been considered suitable for a tent (Camp III) was 17,400 feet or higher. The parties left at 7 am and slowly started climbing up the hanging glacier. Soon the drone of an aeroplane was heard. It must be Sheldon! Post was probably being dropped at the Landing Camp and Goodwin was definitely leaving. Goodwin had been very helpful and everyone liked his company, but he had to be back on his job by the 19th. Now the six men were utterly alone on the great face of McKinley. The sun continued to shine for a while; some of the toughest parts of the climb were dealt with in fairly good conditions. The hardest stretches – as already mentioned – came above the hanging glacier where the mountain face is girt by a solid wall of granite. Some steep and slippery couloirs led to a frozen gully which taxed everybody's energies to the extreme. Camp III was finally set up at 5 pm – after ten hours of very hard work – just as the weather started again to deteriorate.

Six men crowded into two small Nepal tents. It was very cold. Everything got frozen. Prospects seemed, however, very good. Nearly everything now depended on the weather. Conditions were not definitely bad, but heavy clouds continued to move slowly along the face of the mountain. Would they completely cover the sky, as had happened so many times?

July 19 seemed to hold good promise. Everything was now ready for the dash to the summit. Waking up in the morning and getting things ready took longer than usual because of the height and the cold. The six men left camp at about 7 am in two parties: Zucchi, Perego and Airoldi went ahead, followed by Cassin, Canali and Alippi. From now on there would be no fixed ropes. Fortunately the face seemed easier in its second half; most of the really hard obstacles were concentrated in the lower part, up to Camp III.

This, however, was only broadly true. In detail, the parties had to reckon with a number of tricky spots. Two rope-lengths above Camp III, for instance, there was another frozen gully which required some very delicate work. Then came some fairly easy slopes which permitted the two parties to gain height. It was hard work, for many reasons: all were tired after so many days on the mountain, the packs – though everything had been reduced to essentials – were heavy, the altitude was considerable, the snow

was very bad; sometimes it was as hard as ice and crampons barely managed to scratch its surface, sometimes it had a light crust which broke under the weight of the body, and sometimes there were patches of deep, utterly incoherent dust, like sugar. On top of it all the wind was growing stronger and stronger, an icy gale that blew snow into sore eyes and through layers of clothes. Hours slowly passed as the two teams gained ground towards the summit. Midday passed, the afternoon slipped away. At a certain moment a small plane flew over the mountain; it was pleasant to detect a human sign!

The climb was not yet finished, however. The snow-slopes ended against some steep rocks below the summit. More difficult passages had to be tackled. Finally a slope of the hardest snow led to a point where everything seemed to fall away; it really was the summit! Cassin looked at his watch: it was 11 pm. It had taken the two teams sixteen hours from Camp III. Everyone was tired. The cold was extreme. Most of the men felt great cold in their feet. Canali seemed to suffer most.

After a few minutes' rest, and the usual ritual of flag-waving and photographs, all started back towards Camp III. While descending the rock belt below the summit Canali felt sick and started vomiting. Since leaving Camp III nobody had taken any food, except a small can of fruit salad: unfortunately this only bit of nourishment had disagreed with him. Further down Canali slipped. Luckily it was on an easy slope and Cassin managed to hold him on his ice-axe thrust into the snow. Clearly Canali was in very poor condition and everyone had to look after him. The wind had stopped, but it started snowing. Also it grew quite dark. As the two parties descended, Canali seemed to get better, but he went on complaining that his feet were cold.

Barrie Biven aboard the raft he and Tony Smythe hoped would help out after reaching Mount Dan Beard (Alaska) in 1961. The raft soon ran aground, but the occupants were rescued.

173

Some time during the night, when the arctic dawn was well on its way, the teams reached the difficult gullies above Camp III. Cassin decided here to send Canali and Zucchi ahead to Camp III, so that Canali's feet could be examined to see if there was any serious damage. When Cassin and the others finally reached Camp III, it was exactly 6 am (July 20). The whole climb had taken twenty-three hours; sixteen up and seven down. All were utterly exhausted,

though from time to time the thought of success was deeply rewarding.

In the same year Barrie Biven and A. G. Smythe climbed Mount Dan Beard (10,260 feet). To save money they decided to walk and raft it out to Talkeetna; they were fortunate to be spotted and rescued.

In 1962 the summit of McKinley was reached by the south-east spur and next year the Wickersham Wall was climbed, first by a Canadian party led by Hans Gmoser and, a little later, by a Harvard party led by H. L. Abrons using a route nearer its centre. The first winter ascent of McKinley was made in February 1967 by a team of four Americans, a Frenchman, a German, a Japanese, a New Zealander and a Swiss. During their forty days on the mountain temperatures ran from $-35°F.$ to $-40°F.$; on the summit it was $-62°F.$ Sadly, Jacques Batkin was killed falling into a crevasse. Next summer Boyd Everett organised a triple assault on the south face; he led a party up the Cassin ridge, another prong made a new direct route, while a third repeated the Japanese route of 1965 on the south buttress. Though much higher, colder and lonelier, the climbing geography of McKinley began to resemble Mont Blanc's, and its visitors were becoming almost as international.

In 1964 a Munich party joined three Americans and at last succeeded in climbing the Moose's Tooth (10,335 feet), reaching the top during an exhausting forty-four-hour day. (In this northern region, as in the Andes and New Zealand, it is quite normal to climb by night when the snow is hard.) A French group led by Terray climbed Mount Huntingdon (12,240 feet); Mount St Elias resisted several attacks but a Japanese party climbed its long north ridge. Five men from Denver did a new route on Mount Logan (19,850 feet), which was also climbed by no less than three Japanese expeditions. Mount Huntingdon was climbed again the next year by a Harvard party, using the west face where Terray had used the west ridge. This is from Dave Roberts's account:[12]

The ascent of Mount Huntingdon
from Dave Roberts, the *Alpine Journal*, Vol. LXXI
But for all the fun the climbing was, for all the pleasure of clean rough granite, we were not getting anywhere. We had so far always climbed in pairs; after July 16 we also camped in pairs. Matt [Hale] and Ed [Bernd], with four days' food, got established in the tent, which they had pitoned to a protecting rock wall, just before a storm hit; Don [Jensen] and I stayed below in the cave. For three days none of us could budge. At last Don and I forced our way up to the others, scraping the ice off the fixed ropes, and Don stayed with Ed while Matt went down with me. On July 20 Don led our twenty-fifth pitch, the first of the real face, a fierce pitch about which he said to me later, 'When we saw it I was sure it'd require aid. But I got up there, and there were these beautiful holds. . . .' Ed led the long exposed pitch above, his crampons scraping steep slabs and knocking ice

chunks down on Don. This was the most difficult climbing we had met, evidently a preview of things to come.

Two days later Don and Ed had just repaired their defective stove when Matt and I showed up. They were not very glad to see us, since it meant switching, going out supperless into the cold. But they gallantly left us their warming chicken stew.

At this point Matt and I were pretty pessimistic. Two new pitches did not seem much gain for four days, and when it took Matt and me six hours to get light loads to the top of them on our first effort, we saw nothing to justify the enthusiasm Don and Ed had expressed at their progress. We only sensed that our chances were shrinking.

But the next day, the second clear one in a row, we got quickly past the old pitches and put in seven new ones. The first was a steep ice-filled chimney that required aid past a chockstone; the last was a fifty-foot ceiling in which Matt found a series of cracks he could nail nicely up. Suddenly we were at 11,000 feet, and the summit seemed within reach. Descending late in the night, we passed Ed and Don, who were coming up in the gloom. 'Tremendous, guys, we saw you way up there!'

They pitched our other tent that night, then carried it up to just below the ceiling the next day, following Matt and me as we carried food and equipment for them. We left them that night knowing we might not see them until after they had reached the summit. Matt and I thought it quite possible that they had our only chance of reaching the top. But any success would be enough; we had done our part.

For Ed's third time, they laboriously chopped out a platform in the ice. Again, they secured the tent to rock pitons above. It was a beautiful site; the door opened on the distant hulks of Foraker and Hunter above the door-mat of the Tokositna. They had to pitch the tent narrow, or it would have overhung the edge of the platform.

The next day they only had time to put a fixed line of stirrup-loops over the ceiling. But on July 29, our thirty-first day, they got an early start. The weather was still perfect; none of us could believe it, and I often looked uneasily south for the sign of a storm. With only a minimum of hardware Don and Ed led pitch after steep pitch. Don solved the last rock problem, twice using aid from small, shaky pitons far above any protection.

Ed led up a short steep fluting, and emerged on the summit ice-field. Soaring, sweeping in the afternoon light at an angle of 50° toward the summit, it seemed as featureless and open as a desert. They alternated leads on the slope, but the sun had warmed it dangerously. Around 5 pm they stopped on a rock ledge, the highest on the mountain, to wait for night and better snow. They pitched Don's tiny bivouac tent and crowded inside.

Matt and I meanwhile were bringing up the last of the hardware from the lower camp. We got to the higher one quickly and found Don and Ed had left it. We knew they were short on pitons, so we climbed the ceiling and followed their steps and fixed lines. We could help safeguard their descent by improving the protection, and if we felt strong, perhaps. . . .

We were amazed at their pitches. With so few pitons on such steep snow, ice, and rock, they had climbed marvellously. It was getting late, but there was not the slightest breath of wind, and we continued.

Late that evening we popped onto the summit ice-field and caught up with Don and Ed. As the sun faded behind McKinley, we ate some candy bars and hooked up as a rope of four. Don led in the growing darkness. The snow was still not good, and ice lay a few inches beneath. Once he had to belay from a rock piton driven in ice. A little after midnight, in the eerie starlight, we reached the summit ridge. We were almost there; yet it had taken the French four and a half hours on this last stretch, the only part our route had in common with theirs.

As the first light sprang from the tundra beyond McKinley, I took the lead. We faced two short, vertical, fluted walls. Attacking them very high, almost on the cornice, I found they were made of airy, soft snow. After a lot of excavation and some delicate pull-ups on an axe and a picket, I was over them. Carefully we belayed each other up the fluted steps. Extremely tired, for we had been going seventeen hours straight, we climbed the last few pitches. The world seemed to hang in a held breath, perfect, still, a world of glacial snow and soaring rock and, out to the limitless horizon, the hazy blue of the vast tundra; ours, ours only for that hour as we stood together on the summit.

Unfortunately Bernd was killed while roping down on the descent.

A mainly Harvard party climbed St Elias by the north-west ridge and six from the Sierra Club made a new route on Mount Logan via the Hummingbird (central south) ridge, also making the first traverse of the mountain. The following year, 1966, Boyd Everett's party climbed Logan's west ridge while in 1967 the east-south-east ridge was climbed and two parties made routes by different ridges from the north. Next year two men and a girl spent a month in the South Logans. They climbed Mount Savage (9,004 feet) but were surprised to find a cairn on top; it had been left by John Milton on his solitary ascent in 1961. Nevertheless they got in some fine first ascents.

In 1969 Raymond, Fitschen and Robbins made three new ascents of mountains over 8,000 feet in the Cathedral Spires at the western end of the Alaskan range, in spite of rain or snow on 25 out of 26 days. Further north, five new ascents among the Arrigetch Towers were made by Ripley, the Robertses and Waldrop. Alone and with others, Grace Hoeman climbed two new mountains, Bard Peak and Bounty Peak in the Chugachs. In the St Elias range, one Japanese party climbed Mount Craig (13,250 feet) and Avalanche Peak (13,818 feet) while another traversed Mounts Lucania (17,147 feet) and Steele (16,644 feet).

Opposite: still in Alaska. Top: the Moose's Tooth, climbed in 1964 by an American-German party. As is common in the far north, the party continued to climb during the night when the snow is hard. Above: Mount Huntingdon from the north-west slopes of Mount Dan Beard. It was climbed, also in 1964, by the west ridge by a French party led by Terray, and again the following year by a Harvard party using the west face.

175

In the Rockies, exploration of the less accessible areas continued while enthusiasts worked out new routes on unclimbed faces and ridges of the better known peaks.

There are 25,000 square miles of country north of the Peace River and between it and the Liard River. By 1947 no mountain in this area had been climbed. In the recesses of this untravelled sector lie the Lloyd George Mountains, so named by Paul Haworth who made two considerable journeys, mostly by canoe, to reach them. On his second trip, in 1919, he reached the lake called after him which lies at the foot of the range. Frank Smythe and Rex Gibson (Canada) planned an expedition to explore and climb here. Together with Henry Hall, John Ross, David Wessel (Americans), Odell and Mrs Smythe, they flew in to Lake Haworth in 1947. From there they climbed the main peaks, Glendower (9,400 feet), Lloyd George (9,450 feet), and Criccieth (9,050 feet). Some of the perils of Alaska and Canada are non-alpine. Smythe wrote:[13]

Among the peaks ascended towards the end of the month was a fine twin-headed mountain opposite to the base-camp which we had named the Cloudmaker on account of its tendency to manufacture clouds and storms. In order to reach the other side of the lake and avoid a traverse of its shores through well-nigh impenetrable bush, Wessel and I utilised a raft we had made, a heavy construction of four dead trees and a couple of cross-pieces to hold them together.

We set out early one morning with three days' provisions and were poling and paddling along the shores of the lake when on turning a corner we suddenly came on a bear a few yards away seated on the bank. The bear was far larger than a grizzly and a light brown in colour. It transpired that it was an Alaskan brown bear and there is a fine specimen in the New York Natural History Museum which weighs 1,550 pounds and stands about 8 feet high.

As soon as he saw us the bear jumped into the water and commenced to swim for the raft making for the end on which I was balanced astride the logs. I had to turn round to face him and, in doing so, nearly upset the raft and tipped my companion and myself into the water. Then I yelled at the bear and beat at the water with my paddle. This was without effect and as he was only a yard or two from the raft I raised my paddle intending to hit him on the nose as a last resort. But suddenly he turned, swam to the bank and crashed off into the bush.

Later that day we had two narrows escapes from lightning when sheltering from a thunderstorm near the summit of the Cloudmaker. We were driven down, cold and soaked to the skin, but returned and managed to reach the summit. We descended to timberline in the last light and sat all night by a great fire

In more accessible areas it was a question of even harder routes on often-climbed peaks. Take, for example, the small group of the Bugaboos. Here Snowpatch Spire, first climbed in 1940, had a route

An aerial view of the Bugaboos, a sub-division of the Selkirks, which provide some of the best rock-climbing in America. In the centre is Snowpatch Spire, on its right, Bugaboo Spire. Behind is Howser Spire, the South Tower to its left.

Howser Spires was made in 1969. On the other side of the Rocky Mountain trench, Mount Robson's Emperor ridge was climbed in 1961 and the north face in 1963, Mount Edith Cavell (11,033 feet) had new routes in 1961 and 1967. It was while returning from this last achievement that Yvon Chouinard remarked that the trouble with reaching a summit was all the unclimbed routes you could see. In this section of Canada it is the unclimbed routes, not peaks, that set the problems, but over in the Coast Range there were still plenty of new mountains, long defended by implacable bush; a party of British Columbian Mountaineers collected thirteen in 1966.

The accessibility of the Rockies improved greatly during the 1960s; the motor car on the tarmac road can now largely replace the mule-trains and bush-whacking of the pioneers. The weekend climber has far greater opportunities. The Calgary Mountain Club has a hut on the ledge between two tiers of cliff on Mount Eisenhower; the upper cliff now has many routes on it and bids to become a standard playground like Lliwedd or Clogwyn du'r Arddu. There are, of course, thousands of similar but remoter cliffs which will keep climbers busy for generations. There are also plenty of big challenges like the 2000 feet of near-vertical cliff on the north-east face of Mount Babel, climbed in 1969 by Bryan Greenwood and another. In 1970 the shapely Mount Columbia was climbed by its north-east face and north ridge, and the route on the north face of Mount Temple was completed. In 1972 another 'last problem' was solved twice with two new routes on the huge north face of Mount Alberta.

The Tetons of Wyoming are probably the most popular climbing ground in the USA, with routes of all grades and new ones added all the time, mostly by established artists such as Beckey, Ortenburger, Chouinard and Robbins. The area is sometimes, like Zermatt, foolishly disparaged for its classic popularity, but few would not be impressed by the north or west faces of the Grand Teton, or its Black Ice Couloir.

The Yosemite valley, part of the Sierra Nevada of California, has no great peaks but its smooth walls, up to 3,000 feet of exfoliated granite, vie with the Dolomites and Norway's Romsdal for steepness. Its importance lies in the fact that a small number of Yosemite addicts have evolved a new school of climbing whose artificial technique increasingly supersedes the earlier methods developed in the eastern Alps. (Yosemite climbers do not use a double rope, do not clip into a piton above themselves and use no direct upward tension.) They are rock specialists, but many have already distinguished themselves in mixed climbing on great peaks elsewhere. Apart from the basic climbing problem, the chief difficulty in Yosemite is the absence of water on the faces and the great heat in summer. In earlier days this led to the Yosemite school making great use of fixed ropes so that they could descend to water and comfort after having made a few pitches each day. This method is now much less popular and they prefer to do their routes straight through, carrying supplies of water

Above: Mount Edith Cavell— a neighbour of Mount Robson—on which new routes were made in 1961 and 1967.

Opposite: Mount Assiniboine in the Canadian Rockies.

on its west face in 1956, on its north-west ridge in 1958, on its east face in 1959, on its south face in 1966 and a direct west face route in 1967. Bugaboo Spire, first climbed by Conrad Kain in 1916, had its east ridge ascended in 1958 and its east face in 1960. The west face of the south tower of Howser Spire was climbed in 1961, the north face of the south tower in 1965, the west face of the north tower in 1968, its south-west face in 1970 and the first traverse of the

and bivouacking on the cliff, often hanging in slings. Although originally pioneers of an artificial technique, they are now very strict about climbing free where this is within the limits of human possibility and have thus established a standard of free climbing unsurpassed elsewhere.

Until a dozen years ago Yosemite climbers seldom left their own valley and few outsiders visited it, so the school solved its special problems in remarkable isolation. The climbing is up vertical cracks, often with very difficult pendulum movements from one crack to another when one crack peters out; holds, where present, are vertical; stances hardly occur, so that any tolerable foothold is christened a stance. Natural belays being rare, protection by pitons is standard, but pitons are always removed. There is very little objective danger from storm or rock fall. While more routes will doubtless continue to be made, nearly all the natural lines have been climbed; new routes may well be harder but probably less satisfying. Thus Yvon Chouinard could write, in 1966, that the future of Yosemite climbing lay in the use of its technique on the high mountains of the world. He added:[14]

A certain number of great ascents have already been done in other areas as a direct result of Yosemite climbers and techniques; notably the two new routes on the West face of the Petit Dru, the South face of the Fou, the Humming-bird arête on Mount Logan, a new six-bivouac route on Chacraraju in the Andes, and numerous big walls in the Bugaboos and other ranges in Canada and Alaska. Although these ascents are as fine and difficult as any in their respective areas, they are merely the beginning of a totally new school of American climbing, that is to say technical climbing under alpine conditions. All of the climbs just mentioned are characterised by directness, technical difficulty and by the climbers living on them rather than using siege tactics.

From experiences gained on the El Capitan walls, I believe that it is possible for a four-man party to be self-contained, carrying all their necessary gear, leaving no fixed ropes to the ground, and to live on a wall for a period of twenty days. Two men would be climbing and two hauling up the gear. Theoretically, a climb equal to two El Capitans could be done in a one-push effort – that is, a wall 6,000 feet high and extremely difficult all the way.

I have personally seen in Canada untouched walls that are as difficult and as beautiful as any ever done in the history of alpinism. The western faces of the Howser Spires, in the Bugaboos, are from 3,000 feet to 5,000 feet high. The Coast Range of British Columbia, the Logan Mountains, the Katchatna group, and the other innumerable ranges of Alaska, the Andes, the Baltoro Himalaya, the Patagonian Alps – all have walls which defy the imagination.

Who will make the first ascents of these breathtaking rock faces? From the Americas, the climbers can only come from Yosemite. These extraordinary climbs will be done by dedicated climbers who are in

superb mental and physical condition from climbing all the year round; who are used to climbing on granite, doing much artificial climbing and putting in and taking out their own pitons; who are familiar with the problems of living for a long time on these walls, hauling up great loads, standing in slings, sleeping in hammocks for days at a time; and who have the desire and perseverance needed to withstand the intense suffering which is a prerequisite for the creation of any great work of art. Yosemite Valley

Above: Cathedral Spire in the Yosemite Valley, one of the breathtaking rock faces that has inspired a new school, originally using artificial techniques but now unsurpassed exponents of free climbing.

Opposite: El Capitan in the Yosemite Valley.

older type of Yosemite climb; it took six weeks, the route being pushed up in stages with descent and re-ascent on fixed ropes. Even so 25 nights were spent on the wall. The other was the newer type, the Salathé Wall. Although Tom Frost, Chuck Pratt and Royal Robbins set ropes up the lower part of the climb, less than a third of it, they then climbed on continuously for six days. This is thought by many good judges to be the best (not necessarily the hardest) rock climb in the world. Although the early history of Yosemite is almost wholly contained in oral tradition, Salathé Wall earned four sentences in the *American Alpine Journal* and Yosemite was on the way to recognition. Year by year new routes were made, the longer climbs usually taking about a week.

By the late 1960s, the Valley had been discovered by British climbers, who were very hospitably received so long as they showed due respect to the great rock walls around them. This is Chris Jones's account of the Salathé Wall:[15]

The Salathé Wall

from Chris Jones, the *Alpine Journal*, Vol. LXXV

By the summer of 1969, although I had made a number of the Valley climbs, I had yet to climb El Capitan – but not for lack of attempts. The first had been pretty much inspired by the appearance of Mick Burke in the Valley in the previous year. It seemed humiliating to have Mick gain the distinction (if indeed there *is* any!) of being the first British climber up El Cap, when I was now living in California. At any rate, stirred into action, we waited for the film crew that was working on the face and got away with Mick and partner a few pitches behind us, in amiable competition; but at about midday a sharp thunderstorm washed this attempt off the wall, though Mick in fact did it later.

During the early spring of 1969 I had been press-ganged into an attempt on El Cap's unclimbed Wall of the Morning Light, but this too had faded when we ran into blank dihedrals requiring more bolts than we possessed or even cared to use. For my third effort I was on the Nose again, yet my partner suffered one of those proverbial 'mind inversions' and down we came again.

This was becoming absurd, so when Gary Colliver mentioned the Salathé, although secretly appalled at the idea I quickly agreed. At that time, although it had had six ascents, they had all been by legendary hard men – whereas we were neither legendary nor hard.

As with all great routes, the Salathé has its key pitches and the stories that surround them; but what makes it unique is the variety and continuity of the climbing.

One of the peculiar Yosemite customs is to prepare the first pitch or two of a climb the evening before the real start. At least it ensures that you have to go up the next day, if only, as is sometimes the case, to get your gear back again. Not wanting to break with tradition, and, more to the point, needing the time it would gain us anyway, we struggled with our

Yvon Chouinard leading the difficult pendulum pitch on Mount Watkins in the Yosemite Valley.

will in the near future be merely the training ground for a new generation of alpinists who will venture forth to the high mountains of the world to do the most aesthetic and difficult walls wherever they may be found.

In 1958 the nose of El Capitan was climbed by Warren Harding; this was a breakthrough. In 1962 two new routes were added on El Cap. One was the five gallons of water, food, bivouac gear, seventy karabiners and sixty pitons to the foot of the wall.

Nowadays no one leaves the ground on these routes without an extensive 'topo' (a pitch-by-pitch route map) and I had studied ours minutely, almost obsessively. For with each pitch known, one could, theoretically at least, 'weight' the pitches, and so discover if the odd or even ones were less terrifying. So, when we came to the apparently sporting decision of who was to lead the first pitch, I knew it had to be Gary. For it was of the fifth pitch, originally graded 5.10, that Robbins had said to Chouinard and Roper, who were about to attempt the second ascent, 'Roper's too chicken and Chouinard's too short'. When Roper succeeded it was downgraded to 'hard 5.9', but that was bad enough.

It had been raining slightly that evening, and when we approached the wall the next day it looked no better – but perhaps we would be spared the oppressive heat. Gary led the fifth pitch with great coolness, and I managed to use a sky hook, probably illegal here, on the tricky traverse on the one above. Things were moving well on this magnificent lower section of predominantly free-climbing, as we rappelled on to Heart Ledge. By now it was late afternoon as Gary led up, and eventually came to an embarrassing halt; he couldn't make the reach from his last piton to the only possible next placement. Flakes, sky hooks, trickery were all tried, and all failed. This was distinctly discouraging, as I regarded him as our strongest aid man (I later learned he thought the same of me!). Back on the ledge we discussed the key to the situation – if we can't nail it, should we place a bolt? If some flake had broken off, then that was OK, but if not . . .? 'Damned if we do, and damned if we don't.' I even remembered hearing a piton being placed in North Wales some years before, and cursing out the unfortunate leader – now *I* was on the spot.

In my turn I couldn't make the reach, but by this time I was determined that a failure of will was worse than a failure of morals, and placed the dreaded bolt. At least we were moving on. Next morning Gary made the pendulum into Hollow Flake Crack, began to layback, fell off, jammed it instead, and had me sweating as he went up this totally unprotected, awe-inspiring 150 feet crack. By the late afternoon I joined Gary beneath the Ear, a horizontal 5.8 chimney that is one of the crux pitches. It was here that Galen Rowell had found the sides covered in water, and almost slipped out. I am convinced that chimneying is my worst technique, and the Ear looked damp, so obviously I urged Gary to the attack. Unfortunately it seemed to him that chimneys were also his weak point, so I was soon clutching the smooth, dark sides of the beast and chanting to Gary, 'Watch me, this is awful . . . oh hell, watch it.' Somehow I placed a 4 inch bong for protection and at last emerged. By now it was late, so we rigged up a bivouac in our belay seats, and swung gently above a lot of space, waiting for the sun.

Our third day we passed El Cap Spire, where we should have spent the previous night, and climbed the only unpleasant pitch on the climb, a wet and devious affair, that led to our next bivouac, the Block. All day it had been cool; we weren't parched from lack of water and we even left a bag of food on the ledge.

The fourth day we had to climb the key artificial pitches, and climb them quickly enough to avoid spending the night on the overhanging head wall. Layton Kor had discovered his own way from the Block to Sous Le Toit ledge, a typically intricate piece of aid climbing, but it avoided the even worse manoeuvres used by the earlier parties. Gary found Kor's variant; I persuaded him his sky hook would hold, and after my short pitch he led the hardest aid pitch on the route up to beneath the Roof. By the way he pounded in four anchor pins I could tell the traverse under the Roof looked pretty grim, and he didn't want me pulling him off. After much gallantry I reached the tip of the Roof, to discover I needed a rurp to exit; and I had none with me. I did have an aluminium block, a 'bashie', which you place in a crease in the rock, hit the correct number of times to mould to the rock and stand up. This works pretty well on the boulders in Camp 4, but here it came flying out, and I plunged down. Finally I brought up a rurp and continued to an incredible sling belay on the head wall. Gary carried on past, his haul line tailing far out beyond the vertical – one of the most exposed pitches in Yosemite, where Roper, Steck and Long had been forced to bivouac in slings, much to Roper's amusement and Steck's concern.

With the fading light we reached the first ledge in 500 feet, and made our fourth and last bivouac. With just three pitches to the top it was almost over, and as the following day arrived we lay in our sleeping gear and looked down over this fabulous wall, and now we had no doubt, the world's best rock climb. A few hours later we joined our friends on top, who had hiked up to meet us with food, water and a bottle of champagne. Yosemite's beautiful trails never looked so good as we wandered back down to the valley, and the bolt business was cheerfully dismissed by Chuck Pratt: 'So you placed a bolt, why worry, we placed eleven.'

The Wall of Morning Light, mentioned above by Jones, was climbed the next year by Harding and Caldwell.

Russia and China

Because of the closed nature of these two societies, their mountaineering has grown up largely free from capitalist contamination from the less captive world. Russian isolation in this respect has diminished in the last twenty years; even now little is known, though much reported, about Chinese activities. One characteristic remains common to both; as Tilman has pointed out, it has long been the habit of these peoples to go about in hordes and the habit persists among the hills.

In 1956 the Soviet and Chinese Trade Unions

from the cone of the summit'. (In 1932 the Americans had found no rock within 1,000 feet of the summit.) On the descent the second rope of three slipped and were lost.

Three years later, in 1960, the Chinese claimed to have climbed Everest from the north. The expedition consisted of 214 men and women, a third of them Tibetans. On May 3 four men 'reached the foot of a 3 m. high vertical slab at the top of the Second Step, 28,200 feet', where they bivouacked. Next morning the weather was perfect; there were camps at 27,900 and 27,600 feet and a party in support. Nevertheless, at this apparently favourable moment, all returned to Base Camp at the snout of the Rongbuk glacier. On the 14th they started the task of equipping and provisioning all camps up to 27,900 feet. On the 24th the assault party left the top camp. It took them three hours to climb the 3 m. slab at the top of the Second Step, where they found that their oxygen reserves were running low. Shih Chan-Chun's account continues:[16]

The Chinese ascent of Everest
from Shih Chan-Chun, the *Alpine Journal*, Vol. LXVI
The three Communist Party members, Wang Fu-chou, Chu Yin-hua and Liu Lien-man, and Konbu, then held a brief Party group meeting. It was decided that the assault group should advance to the summit as quickly as possible and Liu Lien-man should remain where he was.

After the three others left, Liu Lien-man, at the risk of his life, switched off his oxygen in a heroic, self-sacrificing spirit to save the last few dozen litres of oxygen for his comrades assaulting the summit.

It was getting darker and darker. Since they had expected to return to the assault camp before dusk, they had brought no lighting apparatus. In order to reach the summit before bad weather set in, they boldly decided to continue their march, taking advantage of the experience of night climbing gained in scaling Minya Konka in 1957. They had to pick out their way with the help of the twinkling stars and the reflection of the snow, and due to over-exhaustion they could only advance at a snail's pace, sometimes crawling on all fours.

When they came to about 8,830 m. their oxygen reserves ran out completely. They glanced at each other. It was Wang Fu-chou who spoke first: 'We are shouldering the glorious task of storming the summit. Can we turn back?'

'Press ahead!' was the determined answer from Chu Yin-hua and Konbu.

They discarded their oxygen apparatus and started on what must have been the most arduous and dangerous trek in mankind's history.

Excessive panting, troubled vision, feebleness and other reactions to oxygen deficiency further slowed down their advance. It took them more than half an hour to tackle a one-metre-high rock. Despite all this, they encouraged one another and persistently pressed on.

After crossing a snow-covered slope in the east,

A crevasse gapes on the Inycheck glacier in the Pamirs.

organised a joint attempt on Muztagh Ata (24,758 feet) in the Pamirs. The Chinese contingent had five months training in their own hills and then further training with their Russian colleagues in the Caucasus; in due course 31 men marched onto the summit. This, according to Shih Chan-Chun, marked the start of China's excursion into mountaineering.

Next year the All-China Federation of Trade Unions sent a 29-man expedition to make the second ascent of Minya Konka (about 24,900 feet). One man was lost in an avalanche on the way to Camp III. The final assault party of 17 was reduced to 13 when four 'tumbled down a slope and lost their equipment', and later to six when several were overcome by the altitude. These six eventually 'cut a piece of granite

they wound around to a rock slope in the north and continued their climb. At long last, the trio reached an oval-shaped crest between snow and rock – the summit of Mount Everest.

Looking around in the dim pre-dawn light, they saw all the other peaks in the Everest massif lying far below and there was no higher peak to be climbed. To the south of the summit, there was white snow and to the north mainly grey and brown rock. It was 04.20 hours Peking time, May 25. The final assault on the summit of the world's highest peak had taken them a total of 19 hours, during which they had not a mouthful of food or water except a piece of dried mutton and some ginseng soup which they ate as breakfast before leaving the assault camp.

With great excitement Konbu drew from his rucksack the five-star national flag and a small plaster bust of Chairman Mao Tse-tung, placed them on a

Chinese mountaineers on Gosainthan (Shisha Pangma) in 1965. An assault party of 13 is claimed to have reached the summit—the last 8,000 metre peak to fall.

A Soviet climber in action, apparently crossing a crevasse; with one foot in an étrier, he has lodged the other on the far side and is clipping a karabiner into an ice piton. Soviet climbers are awarded Masterships of Sport by successfully completing a series of graded trials.

boulder and secured them with small stones. Wang Fou-chou produced his diary and pencilled the following words:

'Wang Fu-chou etc. three men, conquered Mt. Jolmo Lungma 04.20 May 25, 1960.'

It was bitterly cold up there, and it took him several minutes to scribble these few words. Then Konbu tore the page from the diary and put it in a white woollen glove and buried it in a heap of small stones. They had a small cine-camera with them, but it was too dark to take any shots.

As a souvenir, they picked up nine rock specimens to present to Chairman Mao Tse-tung. At 04.35 hours Peking time they began the descent. When they came back to 8,700 m. it was light enough so Chu Yin-hua turned back and took a few shots.

When the three returned to where Liu Lien-man was, Liu offered them the oxygen he had saved for them. All of them were moved to tears.

At 13.30 hours Peking time, May 30, they returned safe and sound to the Base Camp, together with all other members of the climbing party.

Summing up our conquest of Everest, we must in the first place attribute our victory to the leadership of the Communist Party and the unrivalled superiority of the socialist system of our country. Without all this, we, the ordinary workers, peasants and soldiers

could never have succeeded in climbing the world's highest peak.

The published accounts were unsatisfactory and the claim was generally doubted. There were no photographs of the uppermost part of the climb because the summit was reached at approximately 2 am (Indian time). B. R. Goodfellow calculated that the crucial picture was taken on or near the ridge about 600 feet below the summit; Hugh Merrick computed that it was taken some 600 feet lower, at about the height of the First Step. After seeing the Chinese film of the climb, Professor Dyhrenfurth accepted Mr Merrick's conclusion, but L. R. Wager, working from his own photograph taken from the First Step in 1933 and Hillary's photograph taken from the summit in 1953, concurred with Goodfellow's view. The story remains totally lacking in topographical detail on the higher part of the mountain and has a number of large and puzzling lacunae.

In 1964 another large party, 195 of them, of Han, Tibetan, Manchurian or Hui nationality, set out to climb Gosainthan (Shisha Pangma, 26,398 feet) on the borders of Tibet and Nepal. After a 'stirring, drum-beating ceremony', the assault party of 13 set out from Base Camp on April 25 and reached the summit on May 2. This was the last unclimbed 8,000 m. peak.[17]

As regards Russian climbing a good deal more is now known. The ice was broken when Hunt visited Moscow in 1954 and he has constantly striven to keep open contacts between Western and Russian climbers. Charles Evans made a lecture tour in Russia in 1955; British parties were in the Caucasus in 1958 and 1961; Austrian, French, German, Italian and Japanese groups have also been there. In 1961 Hunt and Malcolm Slesser applied for permission to take, respectively, British and Scottish expeditions; the Soviet reply was to accept a joint group of 12 to spend 65 days climbing there the next year.

E. Beletsky, who was soon to lead the Sino–Soviet ascent of Muztagh Ata, read a paper to the Alpine Club in 1956. He dated the origin of Soviet climbing to the ascent of Kazbeck by two large parties in 1923. The Caucasus, of course, had already been explored and climbed extensively by British, German and Austrian parties, and the first ascent of any of the 7,000 m. peaks of the Pamirs had been that of Peak Lenin (23,383 feet) by Allwein, Schneider and Wien in 1928.

The modern Russian mountaineer cannot avoid the direction and organisation he meets in other aspects of life. Russian mountains are officially graded from 1a to 5b. Mountaineers are similarly graded; having grasped the bare essentials of technique and climbed a mountain of 1b, the recruit is awarded the badge of 'Mountaineer of the USSR'; he can then ascend through Third and Second to First Class Climber. The highest ranks are Master of Sport and Honoured Master of Sport. The Russians make tremendous efforts to qualify as Masters for the rank carries privileges, including the priceless one of being allowed to choose one's own climbs. Very minute classification is a feature of the classless society. The All-Union Physical Culture and Sport Committee awards Bronze, Silver and Gold Medals to the prize winners in the annual mountaineering competitions. There are some twenty camps provided for training, mostly in the Caucasus.

Apart from mass-assaults (in 1935, 500 collective farmers climbed Elbruz and 502 persons celebrated the 30th anniversary of Soviet climbing by ascending Kazbeck), the Russians specialise in long traverses involving several bivouacs. Beletsky led the first Russian traverse of the Bezinghi Horse-shoe, taking 18 days in bad weather; the traverse had been done some years earlier by Austrians in six days. I. Galustov's party made a 31-day traverse of 15 summits from Koshtantau to Shkara, Aylama and Tsurungal; this made them All-Union Champions in the Traverse Competition, and each received a gold medal. In 1960 a team of Georgians traversed 30 km. over five peaks in the Pamirs. It must be added that the climbers on these marathons do not carry food and fuel for a month; it is usual for dumps to be delivered to points on the route.

In 1962 Hunt led the party referred to above, Slesser, with his slightly mutinous Scottish contingent, being Deputy-Leader. There were vexatious delays and changes of plan due to inscrutable official obstruction, but they reached the Pamirs and split into three groups, each comprising four Britons and two Russians. Hunt's group made the first ascent of a peak of 18,500 feet, since named Peak Co-operation (variously translated, sometimes as Peak Concord); the Russians of Slesser's party climbed Peak Patriot (20,013 feet) by the west ridge; for various reasons, including intense dislike of the rotten and dangerous nature of the ground, the British members turned back. Noyce's group climbed Peak Garmo (21,637 feet) also by its west ridge, but Noyce and Robin Smith were lost on the descent. Hunt and half the British contingent then returned home, but six stayed, as the Russians were very keen to carry on, particularly those busy completing their qualifications for Masterships. The remaining dozen set out to climb Peak Communism (erstwhile Peak Stalin, 24,590 feet). 'Anatole Ovchinnikov produced a scheme which would, in theory, get us to the top, thirty miles away and 16,000 feet above our Base Camp, in ten days with five days to get down again. There would be no rest days, no fixed camps, no room for weakness, accident or sickness.' Sickness had already struck Joe Brown and now struck Slesser, Nicol and Bryan. The last had to be escorted back to base and Ralph Jones volunteered to do this. The others pressed on; the British, less dominated by the 'sports plan', were at one stage a day behind the Russians. This is how I. G. McNaught-Davis described the last stage of the climb.[18]

The ascent of Peak Communism
from I. G. McNaught-Davis, the *Alpine Journal*, Vol. LXVIII

At last we were on the final pyramid, the summit out of sight. My altimeter showed 24,000 feet; I tapped it, hoping to gain a few feet without effort, then slipped it back in my pocket vowing not to look at it again until I had counted a hundred steps. A muttered phrase between a gargle and a cough broke into my oxygen-starved brain; with some effort I came to attention, and switched off my motor and slumped into the snow. Eugene, the irrepressible climbing commissar, was calling us to attention. 'We are going to have a union meeting.' I took out the heavy ciné camera and wafted it about, trying to look professional. I looked at the other five, the four Russians and Joe, buried deep in their windproofs; below, Slesser and Nicol were labouring in the deep, soft snow, occasionally flopping over like stringless puppets.

Anatole was standing as if he had energy to spare. He spoke sparingly in English. The time is late, the snow is bad and we are far from the summit of the highest peak in the Soviet Union. To give us the best chance, the strong will climb with the strong, the weak with the weak . . . It sounded like a prepared speech and my concentration lapsed. I tried to decide if I were weak or strong. I flexed a few muscles surreptitiously and put on a 'hard man' expression, then crammed in a few boiled sweets to make up for the food we hadn't eaten over the past three days. Anatole droned on, the Russians listening with rapt attention. Joe seemed to be asleep.

The result of the meeting was for both Joe and myself to rope up with a Russian for the final section. We moved on, myself at the rear taking what film I could, quite sure as a result of Anatole's talk that despite the altimeter we were miles from the summit. Eugene and myself as the slower movers watched the other four draw away, and as the last one disappeared over a bulge some 50 feet above I felt sure I should never see the summit. Anatole was right, I was weak. The ground became easier and we synchronised our movements, kicking in the claws with renewed vigour. Then quite suddenly the others came into view sprawled on a large, rocky platform. 'They've cracked; the weak shall be strong and the meek shall inherit the earth', I muttered at Eugene. He didn't hear and, looking at his face, it was evident why not. His plans over the past years had come to fruition and at least some of the party had reached the final objective. We caught our breath, then thumped each other, produced Buckingham Palace type flags for filming, took the note from the previous summit party to prove our ascent and left one of our own and generally went through a typical continental summit ceremony.

As we lay back flushed with whatever it is that makes people climb mountains, to our delight the two Scots rolled into view. We repeated the summit procedure for their benefit, and with our minds on food, comfort and England made our way back to the cave.

A Russian medallion commemorating the British-Soviet Pamirs Expedition in 1962. During this expedition a British and Russian group climbed Peak Communism (once Peak Stalin). It was a high-speed ascent in the Russian manner, with all members aiming for the summit and all carrying equipment.

The descent during the following days was a mixture of agony and anticipation, enlivened by Joe Brown falling into a crevasse and myself doing some alarming antics on the fixed rope on the ice-face.

In retrospect, the climbing of Peak Communism was a classical high speed ascent by the Russian method. With no porters or Sherpas to assist in carrying the amount of equipment necessary for a chain of camps, theirs seems to be a reasonable if somewhat dangerous solution. In the Russian eyes a successful expedition is one where all the members reach the summit. In this I agree with them, but how this would work out on new routes of a high standard of difficulty or in areas with less stable climatic conditions remains an open question. Throughout the whole ascent we relied heavily on our Russian comrades; without them and the complete confidence they had in their 'sports plan', I feel sure we would never have attempted to climb a 24,600 feet peak in fifteen days up and down from a Base Camp at 9,000 feet and over twenty miles away. We have the strength and confidence of the Russian party to thank for the successful outcome of the expedition, particularly the skill and forceful leadership of Anatole Ovchinnikov, and although the climb was rarely pleasurable it was nevertheless unforgettable.

Taking into account the differences of tradition and attitude, relations between British and Russian climbers were very good, as were personal relations with individual Russians all along the line. The unexplained tergiversation and obstruction of the authorities proved very costly to the visitors. The behaviour of the security arm, including confiscation and theft, hardly encouraged prospective climbing ventures in this part of the world.[19]

New Zealand

As in America and Asia, there was still plenty left in New Zealand to explore in the post-war period. The pattern has been the same; exploration of the remoter and generally smaller ranges plus new routes of ever increasing difficulty on the better-known mountains. In addition New Zealanders have played a notable part in the Himalaya and the Andes, where their native icemanship has stood them in good stead.

Snow caves bid fair to supersede tents for higher bivouacs; they don't have to be carried and are sturdier in storms. Winter climbing in the Southern Alps came of age in 1949 when E. P. Hillary's parties made a number of swift and successful climbs. That much was still undone, indeed unknown, is witnessed by an expedition by four members of the Tararua Tramping Club of Wellington; they set out in 1950 to complete a piece of exploration begun by A. P. Harper half a century earlier. They moved from the headwaters of the Makawhio River over a new pass into the Troyte valley, which they descended to the Karangarua River and the coast, discovering en route a lake, three new glaciers and four new peaks.

New routes multiplied annually. The great south ridge of Mount Cook, the north-east ridge of Dampier,

the north-east ridge of Aspiring, the south-west ridge of Nazomi, north-east ridge of Cook, south ridge of Mount Green, north buttress of Aspiring, south face of Cook, and so on. In 1970 P. Gough and J. Glasgow succeeded in climbing the Caroline face of Cook, and their achievement of this long-standing objective triggered off a whole spate of new climbs. Max Dorflinger climbed the Caroline face solo two years later. By 1973 this face was reported as 'rapidly becoming a trade route' and the number of climbers able to lead the really hard climbs multiplies fast, here as elsewhere.

Other places

There is not space in this survey to review the climbing history of many mountain areas such as Greenland, the Pyrenees, Tatra, Atlas, Ruwenzori, the Antarctic or the Karstenz range in New Guinea. We have also had to omit most of the mountains of smaller stature, although for those who do not live near big mountains much of their climbing is on this lower rock and, in winter, ice. These areas, such as Scotland, the Lake District, North Wales, Fontainebleau and the Saussois, have a very high place in the affections of many mountaineers. Many great climbers, Archer Thomson, Colin Kirkus, Menlove Edwards, for example, did nearly all their climbing on such humble hills and there made major contributions to the development of rock-climbing technique. There are sea cliffs from Australia to Cornwall and Anglesey which provide splendid climbing. Ski-mountaineering is a specialist art with a literature of its own.

Opposite: an avalanche rolls down the slopes on the Inycheck Glacier.

Top: Mounts Torres and Tasman from the west, two of the highest peaks in the Southern Alps of New Zealand. The difficult ice and weather conditions of New Zealand have schooled some of the world's finest mountaineers. Above: a climber in crampons on the Fox Glacier.

10 Himalaya, Post-War

Long ago Tilman remarked that, if you liked climbing, the Himalaya were the last mountains to visit. The time spent climbing on a venture to these hills is tiny compared to the time spent in other active or passive ancillary pursuits. First you must get your permit to climb the desired mountain, and pay for it; you may get a permit to climb some quite different mountain and have to do all your homework again. Then you must collect your party, acquire your equipment and stores, arrange for their shipment to Karachi or Bombay (having previously organised their packing), and book passages by sea or air, unless you go by Landrover which involves even more deskwork. Later you find that the ship with your stores is late and you kick your heels waiting to tackle the big hurdle of Indian, Pakistani, Nepal customs. The stuff still has to be got across a considerable distance to a rail-head. You have probably invoked the assistance of the Himalaya Club, but they cannot solve all your problems in this tricky field. The

march in probably goes happily enough in spite of rain, the attacks of leeches, larceny by ingenious locals and threatened strikes by porters. You reach your base camp, thankfully pay off all except your high-altitude porters after a dispute about wages in a wholly unknown tongue so that you haven't a chance. Now, you feel, climbing will begin. Not at all; for a further purgatory you become a porter humping loads over moraine and glacier until Advance Base is established. From then on, a pair of you may be climbing while the rest ferry loads, over and over the same ground. That is in good weather; in bad weather you may be tent-bound for days on end, supine in a sleeping bag except when you have to go out into the storm to shovel away snow or for other essential purposes. And, as Shipton said, there is something inevitably squalid about a high camp in the Himalaya. He added that the occupational disease of Himalayan climbers was bed-sores. (Indeed, in the argot of the 1953 party, the 'Everest position' was supine in a sleeping bag.) In the end the weather improves but your laboriously uplifted stores have been consumed, and you are several moves back, re-provisioning all the higher camps.

Perhaps the trouble and toil makes the prize the more valuable. Certainly the number of Himalayan venturers has increased at least in proportion to the explosion in numbers elsewhere. The greatest mountains in the world obviously have an immense attraction in themselves, but another factor has been the much greater ease with which the aspirant Himalayan climber can obtain financial assistance to aid his ambitions. This applies not only to sponsors such as newspapers and television concerns willing to buy a story or a film, but also to public or semi-public trusts such as the Mount Everest Foundation in Britain.

The list in Appendix II strikingly reflects the growth in Himalayan activity. The list is restricted to first ascents of mountains over 24,000 feet merely for convenience of handling. Since the first 24,000-er was not climbed until 1930, the Appendix also records the five earlier ascents of mountains over 23,000 feet. All the peaks on the list are in the Himalaya except Peaks Lenin and Communism, and Muztagh Ata, which are in the Pamirs, Peak Pobeda in the Tien Shan and Minya Konka in the Chinese province of Sikang. The Appendix shows that only nine mountains of 24,000 feet were climbed in the millenia up to 1950, while 57 fell in the next twenty years. The rate is now falling off owing to the shortage of mountains

Porters carrying supplies across a bridge in Nepal. Transporting large quantities of equipment and supplies over long distances is only one of many formidable tasks facing organisers of Himalayan expeditions.

of this size, though there is still an almost unlimited supply of smaller mountains

Striking as these figures are, they greatly under-state the post-war rush to the Himalaya, for most parties with limited resources go for smaller peaks and there have been very many such parties from most European countries, from New Zealand, North America and, above all, Japan. (In 1965, for example, there were 53 Japanese expeditions to overseas mountains.)

The post-war harvest began when André Roch's Swiss party climbed Satopanth (23,213 feet) in 1947, but the rush only started in 1950 when the French climbed Annapurna (26,545 feet), the first peak over 8,000 m. to be climbed. The French expedition, led by Maurice Herzog, had a look at Dhaulagiri then switched to Annapurna. After reconnaissance they had little time left before the normal monsoon date of June 5 and so mounted their attack swiftly. The first rope was Herzog with Lachenal; Couzy, Rébuffat, Schatz and Terray were in support. Here is Herzog's account of the final stages.[1]

The ascent of Annapurna
from Maurice Herzog, the *Alpine Journal*, Vol. LVIII
We left at 6 o'clock, Louis Lachenal and I, to launch the final attack on the summit. We decided not to rope up for it would have been useless on the vast Sickle glacier, which, albeit steep, had no crevasses. It was fine but cold. Our very light crampons bit well into the patches of hard snow. Occasionally we broke through the crust and sank deep into very soft powder snow. After several hundred metres I stopped to look at the mountains round us, while Lachenal took off one sock that was making his boot too tight. We were higher than them all, save the gigantic Dhaulagiri. Below us stretched out the land of our reconnaissances which was so well imprinted on our minds. It all seemed strangely unreal and I felt I was living in a private world, although my thoughts were perfectly clear.

We took it in turns to lead, for kicking steps at this altitude was very tiring. We could by now see the summit ridge and could make out a corridor to the extreme right which, although steep, seemed to lead to the top. We made for it. Hours passed, but we were not conscious of the passing of time. We seemed to be making good progress as compared to a man climbing Mont Blanc and my heart was full, for I felt nothing could keep victory from us. Then the last slope neared, as in a dream. It was steep and I was grateful for our crampons, which helped us to march fairly easily over the dangerous terrain towards our couloir – the snow was fairly hard. Lachenal and I, close together, panting and making frequent halts, kept looking up to know how much more of this purgatory had to be endured. The memory of the last hours is blurred and only certain incidents stand out in my mind. I well remember reaching the ridge and, after a traverse to the left, attaining the peak.

It seemed incredible that we were at last treading this snow after all our efforts to get there. Lachenal,

in spite of the inner elation he felt but did not show, wanted to descend immediately as he could feel his feet beginning to freeze. We looked quickly down the precipitous southern slopes; I could not see the bottom, for a few clouds were floating several kilo-metres below us; I hardly knew if I were in heaven or on earth and my mind kept turning to all those men who had died on high mountains and to friends in France. Our moments up there were quite indes-cribable, with the realisation before us that we were actually standing on the highest peak in the world to be conquered by man. The green valley of Chamonix where I had spent my youth, at the foot of the lovely Mont Blanc massif, seemed far away. In those days the 4,800 metres had impressed me greatly and I revered those who had climbed them as heroes – and now, 8,000 metres! It seemed incredible and yet there I was!

We descended to the highest rocks on the summit, 2 metres below the actual peak ridge, to take photo-graphs of the flags and pennants which we had brought with us. At that time these actions were a tremendous effort – the fixing of the flags was difficult – we could not find stones to make a cairn with – everything was frozen in – the setting of the camera required a great deal of concentration; I hurried on to get it all finished and return to the land of men. Lachenal had already left when I took a little condensed milk and repacked my rucksack. One last look at the summit which represented our joy, our glory, and our consolation, and I hurried to the couloir where Lachenal was – from there it was to be a veritable rush back to Camp V, which we had left that morning. As I left I pulled on my gloves, but suddenly one of them dropped and fell gently but unhesitatingly to the bottom; I watched it helplessly, knowing the catastrophe it meant – unfortunately it never occurred to me that I had a pair of socks in my rucksack. Ice-axe in hand, I lengthened my stride and hurried across the long traverse to try to catch up with Lachenal. The weather had deteriorated and the wind blew hard. Ugly clouds were surrounding us. The monsoon had arrived and our race against death had begun. In the distance in a gap in the clouds I saw Camp V, but the mists soon covered it again. Lachenal, still ahead, could be seen 50 metres in front of me through the mist till he reached the ice-slope just before the tent; and there I lost sight of him. Snow was now falling and it was bitterly cold. I reached camp and was thrilled to see – not one, but *two* tents. Rebuffat and Terray were there waiting for us. I shouted and asked where Lachenal was, but Lachenal had not arrived. . . . Terray shook me by the hand and noticed it was white and hard as wood. I had not even noticed it on the way down. He looked after me like a brother and rubbed it while I told him how sorry I was he had not been with us on the summit, he who had done so much to help the whole expedition; his reply warmed me: 'You got to the top, Maurice, so we all got to the top.'

There was a shout outside and Terray jumped up and rushed out. It was Lachenal. A quarter of an hour later he brought him in. He had fallen about a hundred yards down the slope and had been very lucky in stopping his fall with his crampons.

So began our second night at 7,500 metres. Terray and Lachenal were in the tent we had had the night before, Rebuffat and myself in the other. Another horrible night, though the presence and devotion of our friends was a tremendous comfort. Snow fell again and piled up between the tent and the slope. Half-way through the night I was again buried, my hands over my lungs to give them breathing-room. The weather went from bad to worse, clouds covered us, and snow fell relentlessly. We could not delay. We must get down as quickly as possible to lose height and find our fresher companions, who would look after us. When day came we started the descent. It was of course impossible to find our tracks, and we could only see 10 metres ahead of us. We tried to identify ice-walls and went on down, knowing that soon we should have to turn left to commence the traverse down to Camp IV. It was still early then, but we searched desperately for the tents for the rest of the day, ploughing our way through snow, waist-deep. Terray, who was the freshest, led most of the way, and in order to see the dangers that lay ahead of us the better, took off his glasses. He paid for it next day by complete snow-blindness.

Night came and we still could not find Camp IV. We seemed to have visited every serac in the region, for it could have been hidden behind any of them. The mist was opaque and snow falling ceaselessly, the ground was always treacherous. Eventually we had to resign ourselves to bivouacking, although all four of us knew full well what a night spent in those conditions would mean. The best we could do was to find a crevasse in which we could shelter. Lachenal went several metres ahead to the end of the rope to search for one, and then suddenly disappeared before our eyes. Worried and alarmed, we approached the hole, when to our relief a sepulchral voice came from below and told us that the *bottom* of the crevasse, all in all, would be as good as we could find. So in turn we descended into a sort of underground room, several feet square, which was to be our sleeping apartment that night. I felt it might also very probably be our tomb!

It was impossible to eat and we had nothing to drink as we got ready for a terrible night. Lachenal could feel his feet hardening and my four limbs were freezing. Terray rubbed us both hard. Rebuffat made himself as comfortable as possible although his feet were worrying him too. Terray had brought a sleeping-bag which he generously shared with us – six feet fighting for a place in this cramped nest! Rebuffat put his feet on us to try to protect them a little; perched on the little camera I waited for the hours to pass. I did not even shiver. My senses seemed to be clear. I resented the hellish situation we were in, and I thought it very likely that night would be our last.

Dawn glimmered at last through the hole over our heads, to be followed immediately by an avalanche of powder snow which completely enshrouded us. A sinister portent. But it hardly worried us; we were already in pretty dire straits. It was essential we should escape from our prison, and Rebuffat climbed painfully up the gully we had descended the night before, and fixed a rope by which Terray clambered out, followed by the bare-footed Lachenal. I stayed below, for everything had been deeply buried in the snow, and above all we had to find Lachenal's boots and mine, that had been taken off when our feet were rubbed. Without them this would indeed be our last resting-place. Some of the photographic equipment turned up though the little camera was never found. After a feverish search in the snow, with bare feet and bare hands, for over an hour, I unearthed and sent them up. Then I too climbed out, digging my toe-nails in the walls of fresh snow. Outside it was marvellously fine – our last day was to be fine – the mountain had taken on the strangest, most mysterious colouring – darker than usual and ominously calm. Lachenal wanted to leave at once in his bare feet; he had become feverish and was rambling a little. Terray was blind. Rebuffat was blind. Lachenal's feet, and my hands and feet, were frost-bitten. I looked around and realised Camp IV was on our left, not on our right, but we could not grope our way there. To start with we had to get our boots on. Lachenal succeeded, but even with everybody's help my wooden and swollen feet could not be pushed into mine. Our last moments seemed to have come and I told Terray to take the others down. He would not leave me. We all shouted loudly, hoping to attract the attention of Schatz and Couzy in Camp IV, but got no reply. With a terrific effort, Terray got my boots on and we were ready to go, although more dead than alive. Annapurna was avenging its defeat. Mists were covering the top of the Sickle glacier. Suddenly, only 200 metres from us – I could hardly believe my eyes – a miracle appeared. Schatz was there, saw us, and came towards us as quickly as he could in the waist-deep snow. Our troubles seemed ended with his arrival. He came to us, and without a word embraced me. I told him we were not up to much but that we had reached the top. His presence and friendship warmed us, and gave us back the will to live which we seemed to have lost. The mountain cleared and became lighter – once again I noticed the sun and the blue sky. Life had begun again. It was wonderful just to be near Schatz, who symbolised for me at that moment the need of man for man, the joy that wipes out misery, the miracle that saves distress. We are too blind to realise what true charity and humanity mean. I learnt it that day.

Saved though we were we still had to be got down. I had to be towed behind Schatz back to Camp IV, where Couzy was. He tried to make me eat, but I had only one desire, to get to Oudot at Camp II and see what he could do to save my hands and feet. On a tight rope I descended the difficult ice-wall between Camp IV *bis* and Camp IV. At that hour of the day the snow was soft, and as my feet were of little use I let my body scrape through the snow, braking as much as possible. At Camp IV were our Sherpas, our good Sherpas that we thought we would never see again. They gave me a hot drink, but all I wanted was to hurry down. I explained to Sarki and Aila that I was to go down between them on the rope, that I could not stand properly and that we must get to the Doctor-Sahib at Camp II. The descent began. We passed the large crevasse which blocked the whole glacier. The Sherpas went slowly and I asked them to hurry. We passed the ice-walls and I had to choose the way down, the way that could be taken with least risk.

It was midday. The sun was at its height and shone down on all the snow that had accumulated during the bad weather the day before. It was truly glorious and the colours were magnificent – but I could feel that the mountain was ready to crumble under the tremendous weight of top snow – I seemed to be able to feel it vibrating, shuddering and alive. Climbers often have this sixth sense that warns of impending danger, and it increased every minute until I could feel it in every pore. And then what I feared happened. The two Sherpas were ahead of me (and Rebuffat behind) when suddenly an entire slab fell away under their feet. I could see them being carried away and my instinct was to climb up quickly, quicker than the slab was falling. But it was inevitable, and I got carried away too. I shouted, hit the ice, wheeled round in the air, pirouetted, hit the ice again, shouted once more . . . the rope pulled and dragged me, I supposed to my death. But suddenly, like a condemned man when the platform is taken from under his feet and he finds himself hanging from the end of the rope, I found myself swinging over a vertical shaft of ice, at the bottom of which I could see a dizzy corridor running to the base. Hanging as I was with the rope round my head, arm, and leg, and of course face downwards, I was not exactly comfortable! I tried to improve my position by holding on to the ice where I could reach it. It was nice to be alive, but my left arm was hurt and I had no feeling in my hands; they might even be broken. I was afraid for my friends and shouted to warn them – then I felt something give on my rope apart from the naturally elastic nylon. I lay flat against the wall and looked up, and suddenly the head of Sarki appeared against the skyline. Three minutes later I was on the surface, looking at the mountains again. This time with a different eye. They did not seem to me as beautiful as before!

What ill fortune we had encountered in so short a time; the goddess of Annapurna – 'goddess of the harvest' – she doesn't merit her name. She should have been called 'Kali, the beautiful but cruel'.

Rebuffat was unhurt; he only fell about 50 metres.

The descent continued: we reached the ice-walls. I could not stand at all and the question was, how was I to get down without using hands, feet, or crampons? Nevertheless it had to be done. The skin flaked off my hands and stuck to the ropes – my hands were so terrible to look at that I hid them in a scarf. The descent seemed interminable; the Sherpas had

not secured me properly and I kept slipping around, for I could no longer grip the ground. Below in the distance I could see men at Camp II and wondered if I could get there. The Sherpas seemed to understand and kept me very close to them. The last ice-slope was reached, and how my companions got down it without being pulled off by me, I just don't know. Two more Sherpas came up to meet us, Ichac and Oudot had sent them from Camp II. They were the good Phu Tharkay and a friend. They gave me a comforting drink and Phu Tharkay looked despairingly at me. I put my arm round his neck and rested my entire weight on him. It was good to know confidently that he had strength to support me. Angtharkay steadied us behind, and so we crossed the last long plateau to Camp II where Oudot, Ichac, and Noyelle were anxiously awaiting us, and I handed myself over thankfully to their care. I was already lying in my tent with my eyes bandaged when the others arrived – Terray, Lachenal, Rebuffat, and the Sherpas. Annapurna was evacuated. No one remained on the mountain. We had beaten it, and I could lie back and think: the job has been finished; the struggle is over.

Louis Lachenal is supported to safety after the harrowing descent from Annapurna in 1950. With Herzog he reached the summit – the first to ascend a peak over 26,000 feet.

It had been a terrible descent; Herzog lost fingers and toes and Lachenal all his toes. The mishaps that marked the descent have been variously attributed to the altitude and the speed of the assault; these no doubt played their part, but it has been plausibly suggested by Dr Raymond Green that drugs used to protect against the effects of altitude and exposure were counter-effective and diminished dexterity and judgment.

In 1951 the New Zealanders climbed Mukut Parbat (23,760 feet) and in 1952 the Swiss made the first assault on Everest via the Western Cwm and the South Col. After negotiating the Khumbu icefall, they found the Lhotse face too icy and used the Geneva Spur to reach the South Col, of which blasted spot they were the first to enjoy the miseries. Lambert and Tenzing got to 27,560 feet, after climbing 650 feet from their highest camp, before having to turn back. The Swiss had another shot after the monsoon and, in spite of prohibitive wind and cold, reached 26,575 feet in November.

Next year John Hunt's expedition climbed Everest. More difficult mountains have been climbed but nobody will ever climb higher, and the problems of sheer altitude are themselves a technical difficulty. It was a fine achievement; no lives were lost and there were no damaging accidents. The news broke in London as the Queen was crowned and inspired hopes of a new Elizabethan age of achievement.

For most of the way they followed the trail blazed by the Swiss. The always dangerous Khumbu icefall was successfully negotiated; there was a twelve-day struggle with the Lhotse face, mostly led by George Lowe, and when Wilfred Noyce and Annullu broke through to the South Col, 'the most crucial problem of the whole climb', in Hunt's words, had been overcome and the push for the summit was on. The first pair, Charles Evans and Tom Bourdillon, using the closed-circuit oxygen apparatus, were to attempt the summit from the South Col without an intermediate camp. This decision has been criticised on the reasonable ground that the task was impossible; no experience suggested that climbers could make over 3,000 feet of altitude, starting at 26,000 feet, and return in one day.[2] It is true that they were given the South Summit as primary objective and were only to go further if all conditions were favourable, which is perhaps another puzzling feature about the plan. Evans and Bourdillon were delayed in starting by trouble with the closed-circuit apparatus; the defective part had to be replaced by a less suitable component from an open-circuit set. By the time they were able to start John Hunt and Da Namgyal had already set out with 45 lb each of gear for the highest camp. In spite of further trouble with the oxygen apparatus, Evans and Bourdillon reached the South Summit at one o'clock. Quite apart from considerations of time, they had not enough oxygen to get them to the summit and back; they wisely descended and after a troublesome journey were back on the col at 4.30. Meantime Hunt and Da Namgyal had dumped a tent, food, kerosene, their own oxygen bottles,

matches and a candle at 27,350 feet.

After a terrible night on the col, the next day proved unfit for a further attempt but the wind eased off on the following morning. Lowe, Gregory and Ang Nyima set out carrying stores and oxygen. Hillary and Tenzing followed in their track carrying 50 lb each. They picked up the stores dumped by Hunt. Heavily burdened, they toiled up another 450 feet and at 2.30 decided to camp. Left alone Hillary and Tenzing made their preparations; after checking their stores, Hillary decided that they would have to reduce their oxygen flow from 4 to 3 litres a minute for the climb, plus four hours sleep at one litre a minute. This is Hillary's account of the next day:[3]

The summit of Everest
from John Hunt, *The Ascent of Everest*
At 6.30 am we crawled out of our tent into the snow, hoisted our 30 lb of oxygen gear on to our backs, connected up our masks and turned on the valves to bring life-giving oxygen into our lungs. A few good deep breaths and we were ready to go. Still a little worried about my cold feet, I asked Tenzing to move off and he kicked a deep line of steps away from the rock bluff which protected our tent out on to the steep powder snow slope to the left of the main ridge. The ridge was now all bathed in sunlight and we could see our first objective, the South summit, far above us. Tenzing, moving purposefully, kicked steps in a long traverse back towards the ridge and we reached its crest just where it forms a great distinctive snow bump at about 28,000 feet. From here the ridge narrowed to a knife-edge and as my feet were now warm I took over the lead.

We were moving slowly but steadily and had no need to stop in order to regain our breath, and I felt that we had plenty in reserve. The soft unstable snow made a route on top of the ridge both difficult and dangerous, so I moved a little down on the steep left side where the wind had produced a thin crust which sometimes held my weight but more often than not gave way with a sudden knock that was disastrous to both balance and morale. After several hundred feet of this rather trying ridge, we came to a tiny hollow and found there the two oxygen bottles left on the earlier attempt by Evans and Bourdillon. I scraped the ice off the gauges and was greatly relieved to find that they still contained several hundred litres of oxygen – sufficient to get us down to the South Col if used very sparingly. With the comforting thought of these oxygen bottles behind us, I continued making the trail on up the ridge, which soon steepened and broadened into the very formidable snow face leading up for the last 400 feet to the southern summit. The snow conditions on this face were, we felt, distinctly dangerous, but as no alternative route seemed available, we persisted in our strenuous and uncomfortable efforts to beat a trail up it. We made frequent changes of lead on this very trying section and on one occasion as I was stamping a trail in the deep snow a section around me gave way and I slipped back through three or four of my steps. I discussed with Tenzing the advisability of going on and he, although admitting that he felt very unhappy about the snow conditions, finished with his familiar phrase 'Just as you wish'. I decided to go on.

It was with some relief that we finally reached some firmer snow higher up and then chipped steps up the last steep slopes and cramponed on to the South Peak. It was now 9 am. We looked with some interest at the virgin ridge ahead. Both Bourdillon and Evans had been depressingly definite about its problems and difficulties and we realized that it could form an almost insuperable barrier. At first glance it was certainly impressive and even rather frightening. On the right, great contorted cornices, overhanging masses of snow and ice, stuck out like twisted fingers over the 10,000-foot drop of the Kangshung Face. Any move on to these cornices could only bring disaster. From the cornices the ridge dropped steeply to the left until the snow merged with the great rock face sweeping up from the Western Cwm. Only one encouraging feature was apparent. The steep snow slope between the cornices and the rock precipices seemed to be composed of firm, hard snow. If the snow proved soft and unstable, our chances of getting along the ridge were few indeed. If we could cut a trail of steps along this slope, we could make some progress at least.

We cut a seat for ourselves just below the southern summit and removed our oxygen. Once again I worked out the mental arithmetic that was one of my main preoccupations on the way up and down the mountain. As our first partly full bottle of oxygen was now exhausted, we had only one full bottle left. Eight hundred litres of oxygen at three litres per minute? How long could we last? I estimated that this should give us $4\frac{1}{4}$ hours of going. Our apparatus was now much lighter, weighing just over 20 lb, and as I cut steps down off the southern summit I felt a distinct sense of freedom and well-being quite contrary to what I had expected at this great altitude.

As my ice-axe bit into the first steep slope of the ridge, my highest hopes were realized. The snow was crystalline and firm. Two or three rhythmical blows of the ice-axe produced a step large enough even for our oversized High Altitude boots and, the most encouraging feature of all, a firm thrust of the ice-axe would sink it half-way up the shaft, giving a solid and comfortable belay. We moved one at a time. I realized that our margin of safety at this altitude was not great and that we must take every care and precaution. I would cut a forty-foot line of steps, Tenzing belaying me while I worked. Then in turn I would sink my shaft and put a few loops of the rope around it and Tenzing, protected against a breaking step, would move up to me. Then once again as he belayed me I would go on cutting. In a number of places the overhanging ice cornices were very large indeed and in order to escape them I cut a line of steps down to where the snow met the rocks on the west. It was a great thrill to look straight down this enormous rock face and to see, 8,000 feet below us,

the tiny tents of Camp IV in the Western Cwm. Scrambling on the rocks and cutting handholds in the snow, we were able to shuffle past these difficult portions.

On one of these occasions I noted that Tenzing, who had been going quite well, had suddenly slowed up considerably and seemed to be breathing with difficulty. The Sherpas had little idea of the workings of an oxygen set and from past experience I immediately suspected his oxygen supply. I noticed that hanging from the exhaust tube of his oxygen mask were icicles, and on closer examination found that this tube, some two inches in diameter, was completely blocked with ice. I was able to clear it out and gave him much-needed relief. On checking my own set I found that the same thing was occurring, though it had not reached the stage to have caused me any discomfort. From then on I kept a much closer check on this problem.

The weather for Everest seemed practically perfect. Insulated as we were in all our down clothing and windproofs, we suffered no discomfort from cold or wind. However, on one occasion I removed my sunglasses to examine more closely a difficult section of the ridge but was very soon blinded by the fine snow driven by the bitter wind and hastily replaced them. I went on cutting steps. To my surprise I was enjoying the climb as much as I had ever enjoyed a fine ridge in my own New Zealand Alps.

After an hour's steady going we reached the foot of the most formidable-looking problem on the ridge – a rock step some forty feet high. We had known of the existence of this step from aerial photographs and had also seen it through our binoculars from Thyangboche. We realized that at this altitude it might well spell the difference between success and failure. The rock itself, smooth and almost holdless, might have been an interesting Sunday afternoon problem to a group of expert rock climbers in the Lake District, but here it was a barrier beyond our feeble strength to overcome. I could see no way of turning it on the steep rock bluff on the west, but fortunately another possibility of tackling it still remained. On its east side was another great cornice, and running up the full forty feet of the step was a narrow crack between the cornice and the rock. Leaving Tenzing to belay me as best he could, I jammed my way into this crack, then kicking backwards with my crampons I sank their spikes deep into the frozen snow behind me and levered myself off the ground. Taking advantage of every little rock hold and all the force of knee, shoulder and arms I could muster, I literally cramponed backwards up the crack, with a fervent prayer that the cornice would remain attached to the rock. Despite the considerable effort involved, my progress although slow was steady, and as Tenzing paid out the rope I inched my way upwards until I could finally reach over the top of the rock and drag myself out of the crack on to a wide ledge. For a few moments I lay regaining my breath and for the first time really felt the fierce determination that nothing now could stop us

reaching the top. I took a firm stance on the ledge and signalled to Tenzing to come on up. As I heaved hard on the rope Tenzing wriggled his way up the crack and finally collapsed exhausted at the top like a giant fish when it has just been hauled from the sea after a terrible struggle.

I checked both our oxygen sets and roughly calculated our flow rates. Everything seemed to be going well. Probably owing to the strain imposed on him by the trouble with his oxygen set, Tenzing had been moving rather slowly but he was climbing safely, and this was the major consideration. His only comment on my enquiring of his condition was to smile and wave along the ridge. We were going so well at three litres per minute that I was determined now if necessary to cut down our flow rate to two litres per minute if the extra endurance was required.

The ridge continued as before. Giant cornices on the right, steep rock slopes on the left. I went on cutting steps on the narrow strip of snow. The ridge curved away to the right and we had no idea where the top was. As I cut around the back of one hump, another higher one would swing into view. Time was passing and the ridge seemed never-ending. In one place, where the angle of the ridge had eased off, I tried cramponing without cutting steps, hoping this would save time, but I quickly realized that our margin of safety on these steep slopes at this altitude was too small, so I went on step-cutting. I was beginning to tire a little now. I had been cutting steps continuously for two hours, and Tenzing, too, was moving very slowly. As I chipped steps around still another corner, I wondered rather dully just how long we could keep it up. Our original zest had now quite gone and it was turning more into a grim struggle. I then realized that the ridge ahead, instead of still monotonously rising, now dropped sharply away, and far below I could see the North Col and the Rongbuk glacier. I looked upwards to see a narrow snow ridge running up to a snowy summit. A few more whacks of the ice-axe in the firm snow and we stood on top.

My initial feelings were of relief – relief that there were no more steps to cut – no more ridges to traverse and no more humps to tantalize us with hopes of success. I looked at Tenzing and in spite of the bala-clava, goggles and oxygen mask all encrusted with long icicles that concealed his face, there was no dis-guising his infectious grin of pure delight as he looked all around him. We shook hands and then Tenzing threw his arm around my shoulders and we thumped each other on the back until we were almost breathless. It was 11.30 am. The ridge had taken us two and a half hours, but it seemed like a lifetime. I turned off the oxygen and removed my set. I had carried my camera, loaded with colour film, inside my shirt to keep it warm, so I now produced it and got Tenzing to pose on top for me, waving his axe on which was a string of flags – United Nations, British, Nepalese and Indian. Then I turned my attention to the great stretch of country lying below us in every direction.

To the east was our giant neighbour Makalu, unexplored and unclimbed, and even on top of Everest the mountaineering instinct was sufficiently strong to cause me to spend some moments con-jecturing as to whether a route up that mountain might not exist. Far away across the clouds the great bulk of Kangchenjunga loomed on the horizon. To the west, Cho Oyu, our old adversary from 1952, dominated the scene and we could see the great un-explored ranges of Nepal stretching off into the distance. The most important photograph, I felt, was a shot down the North ridge, showing the North Col and the old route which had been made famous by the struggles of those great climbers of the 1920's and 1930's. I had little hope of the results being particularly successful, as I had a lot of difficulty in holding the camera steady in my clumsy gloves, but I felt that they would at least serve as a record. After some ten minutes of this, I realized that I was becoming rather clumsy-fingered and slow-moving, so I quickly replaced my oxygen set and experienced once more the stimulating effect of even a few litres of oxygen. Meanwhile, Tenzing had made a little hole in the snow and in it he placed various small articles of food – a bar of chocolate, a packet of biscuits and a handful of lollies. Small offerings, indeed, but at least a token gift to the Gods that all devout Buddhists believe have their home on this lofty summit. While we were together on the South Col two days before, Hunt had given me a small

crucifix which he had asked me to take to the top. I, too, made a hole in the snow and placed the crucifix beside Tenzing's gifts.

Nanga Parbat (26,660 feet) had a sinister reputation; Mummery had disappeared on the mountain in 1895, the German expeditions in the 1930s had lost 26 men and in 1950 two more British climbers had perished there. In 1953 an Austro-German party mounted another attack; although an unhappy and confused expedition, the mountain was at last climbed, by Hermann Buhl alone. He reached the summit, on all

fours, at 7 pm. On his descent he chose to tackle an ice-slope rather than go over the rock ridge which had caused difficulty on the way up. While on this slope one of his crampons came away and the strap was lost. He had ski-sticks but no axe, as these would have been more useful on the snowfields. It was an awkward moment; he managed to traverse the rocks across a series of snow ribs. Darkness fell and he found a stance with room for both feet, but no room to sit. He put on every garment he had, took five tablets of Padutin (a supposed protection against frostbite), clutched his ski-sticks, grasped his solitary hold and fell asleep; his account continues:[4]

The descent of Nanga Parbat
from Hermann Buhl, *Nanga Parbat Pilgrimage*
I woke with a start, and straightened my head up. Where was I? I realised with a pang of fright that I was on a steep rock slope, high up on Nanga Parbat, exposed to the cold and the night, with a black abyss yawning below me. Yet I did not feel in the least as if I were 26,000 feet up and I had no difficulty with my breathing. I tried hard to keep awake, but sleep kept on defeating me. I kept on dozing off, and it was a miracle that I didn't lose my balance.

Oh God, where are my sticks? Keep calm! You've got hold of them. I clutched them in a grip of steel. Cold shivers ran down my spine, but I didn't care; I knew it would have to be a tough night. I wondered whether my mind was by now in such control of my

The Everest expedition, 1953. Opposite, top left: a crevasse below Camp IV in the Western Cwm. Opposite, top right: the summit ridge. Opposite bottom: Tenzing and Edmund Hillary, the first men to reach the summit of the world's highest mountain. Above: John Hunt, the leader of the expedition, and Alfred Gregory.

body that I could no longer feel bodily discomfort. I longed for the moon to come; if it came out, as I hoped, at midnight, I could start on down, and the night would not seem so long. Next time I tore my eyelids apart, the plateau below was agleam with silver; everything down there, the Subsidiary Summit, the North Summit, shone in a ghostly light, edged by dark shadows. Where I stood, it was still dark; why didn't the moonlight come? It looked as though I should after all have to spend the whole, long night till the dawn came, on this minute spot. By now that seemed to be bordering on the impossible.

I kept on looking across at the dark shadow of the block over there, thinking how nice it would to be sitting down. An occasional breath of wind moved gently over the slope, then everything was still again, in the wide hush of eternity. . . .

I discovered that my body had after all not achieved insensibility. The cold grew more and more unbearable; I felt it on my face and, in spite of my thick gloves, on my hands, which were nearly numb, and worst of all in my feet. It crept further and further up my body; my toes had long ago gone dead, though at first I had tried to keep them moving by trampling on my little stance, but I had to be careful, because it was loose. Never mind, I thought: I had often had cold, dead feet before without suffering serious frostbite as a result.

I was caught up again in the immensity of the night . . . in the glory of the starlit sky stretched overhead. I gazed up at it for a long time, seeking out the Great Bear and the Pole Star over there on the horizon. A light flared down in the Indus Valley – a car probably. Then it was dark again.

My body began to take charge again. Hunger and thirst asserted their needs, but I had nothing to give them. Time passed incredibly slowly, so slowly that I thought the night could never come to an end. Then, behind a toothy mountain range in the far distance, a streak of light broadened and rose gradually higher – the new-born day. For me, its light was the light of salvation.

There were still stars in the sky, and the morning never seemed to come. I looked longingly across to that strip of sky, till my eyes grew almost fixed; for that was where the sun must be coming up. Eventually the last stars grew dim – day was dawning at last.

I leaned against my rock, motionless, my right hand still clinging to the hold, my left still gripping the sticks like a vice. My feet were like blocks of wood, my boots frozen stiff, my rubber soles clogged with rime. The sun's first rays fell on me with their blessed comfort, resolving my stiffness and immobility. I began to move again and got back into the gully. But now I really had to watch my step; everything was twice as dangerous under the smooth glaze of ice. I went down in the gully for ages, still wearing a crampon on one boot, while the other reposed in my Anorak pocket.

During those hours of extreme tension I had an extraordinary feeling that I was not alone. I had a partner with me, looking after me, taking care of me,

belaying me. I knew it was imagination; but the feeling persisted. . . .

There was a steep pitch interrupting the gully; its rocks were splintery and friable. I had to take my gloves off and pocket them, while I tried to regain the bed of the gully; but everything I touched came away. It seemed too great a risk, for one small slide or fall would be the finish of me, and I should certainly drag with me my companion and friend, non-existent though he be. . . . I had to exert extreme care every foot of the way down.

In the mountains at home I should just have jumped down into the gully. Here I climbed back again and wanted to put my gloves on once more. I couldn't find them. Horrified, I asked my mysterious companion: 'Have you seen my gloves?'

I heard the answer quite clearly: 'You've lost them.' I turned round and there was nobody there. Had I gone crazy?

Was I being mocked by some phantom? I recognised a familiar voice, but did not know to which of my friends it belonged. All I knew was that I knew it. . . . I looked for my gloves, but couldn't find them anywhere. They must be lying about somewhere, or could they have fallen down the slope? I hunted through all my pockets again, and as I did so I remembered the terrifying tragedy of Herzog's hands on Annapurna – till I discovered my reserve pair of gloves and felt better again.

I went on down, succeeded in getting into the snow gully and out of it again on to the rocks beyond. There on my right, almost level with me, was the Bazhin Gap; but I had to go still further down, to the bottom of the rocks. The whole of this time my companion was with me, that staunch companion whom I never saw, and whose presence was more definite at danger spots. The feeling calmed me, lulled me into security: I knew that if I slipped or fell, this 'other man' would hold me on the rope. But there was no rope; there was no other man. A moment or two later I would know that I was quite alone and dared not risk one moment's heedlessness.

There was one more steep pitch, an almost vertical crack, which took all the breath out of me; then at last I was on the snow. I had escaped from the clutches of the Face, which now lay behind me. Steep snow slopes, hard as iron, led down to the rocks which plunged from the subsidiary summit. Here crampons were indispensable, and I tried to fasten the second one to my foot; I used the cord of my overall-trousers to tie it to my boot, but after a few steps it was at right-angles to the sole. Patiently I fastened it on again, only to find the spikes standing away from the sides of my boot very soon afterwards, so that I had to repeat the dangerous game every ten or twenty yards. Bending down was a fearful exertion, which got me completely bemused. I raged at my partner behind me for giving me such a wretched crampon. (He was still following close behind me!)

Then I sat down on the snow again, with my head in my hands, resting and panting. My ankles ached from being flexed so much and I found the going fearfully exhausting, but I eventually reached the rocks below the Diamir Gap, where I dived under a huge snow-mushroom for shade. The way the time went was fantastic; it was noon already. I was racked by a terrible thirst, but had nothing left to drink. The sun burnt viciously down, but there was no water anywhere, though the rocks were plastered with ice; not a drop trickled from them.

Now I had to face the rise to the Subsidiary Summit, which had worried me on my way up. I wanted to recover a bit before tackling it and sat down in the snow again. My reasoning processes were suddenly blotted out, though it was quite a pleasant feeling.

I opened my eyes and looked about me. I must have fallen asleep, for another hour had gone by. Where was I, anyway? I saw tracks and cairns everywhere. Was I on a ski-ing trip? Gradually consciousness returned: I was nearly 26,000 feet up on Nanga Parbat, and all alone. The ski-tracks were nothing but wind channels and the cairns over there – rock towers. Up among the rocks of the Subsidiary Summit I heard voices, or was it only the wind? Perhaps my friends were waiting for me up there. I staggered to my feet again with a great effort and circumvented a steep crag, from which a rubbish shoot went up. I worked my way up it from stone to stone, hanging on to my ski-sticks for support. After every step my weary body sank down on the debris, and this time I really thought my strength had given out for good. How often have I said it? But I had to go on, for I knew there was no other way of getting back to living people; so I had to get up that slope. It took me an hour to cover a hundred feet, and as I felt then, the long ascent I had made yesterday seemed more and more improbable. Some flat snow-patches followed, apparently without end; but I had reached the Diamir Gap at the lowest point between the Subsidiary and North Summits.

Before me there now lay once again that enormous wavy snow plateau, scored and furrowed – far away behind it, the Silbersattel. My eyes sought the horizon, working inwards over the sill of the Silbersattel, across and along the plateau's snow up towards where I stood. I hoped to see someone coming up to meet me, but could distinguish nobody. If only I had a drop of tea – one single drop – that might see me safely across the next few hours. I could think of nothing but drinkable liquid; my thirst had become a torture of hell, driving me literally mad. I had swallowed my last drop yesterday, and now there was this murderous heat, this positive dehydration. My gums were like straw, my blood must be thick and viscous. . . .

As I went slowly on I kept my eyes fixed on the Saddle. At last I saw some dots, or were my eyes deceiving me? No, those must be my friends. I wanted to shout and cheer, but could not produce a sound. Anyway, they were coming. Should I wait for them? No, it was too far for them to come, I would go on and meet them. I went on, step by step, mechanically, stumbling, weary. Next time I looked across the waves of the plateau the dots had vanished.

The disappointment was shattering, till I caught sight of them again; then – no – the vast expanse of snow was empty! I was definitely alone in that endless, hopeless waste of ice.

Hunger became as unbearable as thirst. I knew there was a packet of Ovosport in my rucksack, somewhere over there. Somewhere . . . where? I crossed slopes without end, going a long way off the direct line, just to get a bite of something, in the hope of renewing my strength. All the time I had to take great care not to hurt my ankles, which were giving out on me, with my crampons. A slight sprain would be enough to put paid to me. I looked at the Saddle again; the dots were in a different place and I realised that they were rocks on some mountains thrusting up from behind it.

But this time I heard voices, most distinctly. I heard them calling me by name: 'Hermann – Hermann!' I even heard people talking to each other; but there was nobody in sight. These must be hallucinations. Could this be the beginning of the end, or was it the end itself? Where was that rucksack of mine, which was so difficult to find?

Perhaps I could find my old track, by climbing down and across to the right. It went on interminably, back and forth, up and down. I knew I couldn't keep it up much longer. The only thing that kept me going was the thought of having some food inside me. I had almost decided to give up the search, when I saw the clear imprint of a boot – I was back on my trail. Which way, though, to my rucksack – up or down? I went on down, but was soon racked by maddening doubts. I ought to be able to see a ruck-sack. . . .

I found it at last. I fell down and rummaged in it as I lay there, but couldn't locate any Ovosport; instead I found a package of Dextro-energen. When I tried to swallow a tablet it stuck like flour in my mouth, so I did the only thing left and grabbed some snow. I wasn't keen about it, as I knew it might have disastrous results, but there was no other way out. I crushed the tablets, mixed them with the snow and ate the remaining mess. It tasted wonderful and revived me beyond expectation; I found I could swallow again, there was spittle in my mouth once more and I tried to move on again. Very soon, however, my thirst was more searing than ever, my tongue stuck to my gums, my throat was as raw as a rasp and I foamed at the mouth a good deal. So I took another dose of the same brew, but the relief was very short, and my thirst came back even more unendurably than before. The snow robbed me of my last vestige of strength and my progress across the plateau became a veritable torture.

I moved on at a snail's pace, finding it necessary to take twenty breaths to a single stride. Every yard or two I fell down on the snow. My ski-sticks were my last succour; Samaritan-fashion they supported me and saved my life.

I suppose I fell down again and slept. When I woke my eyelids were like lead, and when I tried to get up I collapsed again, utterly exhausted. This was it,

Hermann Buhl, suffering from exhaustion and frost-bite on his return from his ordeal on Nanga Parbat in 1953. After reaching the summit alone, he spent a night out on the descent in sub-zero temperatures.

I thought – journey's end. . . . But the will to live still flickered in me. I looked for my sticks; only one of them was there. Fear gripped me, but it acted like a whip-lash, revitalising my body. I saw now that the other stick had rolled down a little way, and crawled after it on all fours. Once I had them both firmly in my grip, I was able to get up again, to stand, to move on. . . .

I could see across to Rakhiot Peak now, and there was a dot – the tent. Over by the slope I saw what must be rocks or friends. I tried to shout, though the distance was far too great, but I had no voice. Perhaps they would see me if I waved the ski-sticks. . . .

Evening was drawing on; once again the sun was going down and long shadows moved slowly across the snow. I knew I could not survive a second night in the open and fought my way onward, using my last reserves. I stumbled on, pursued, hunted and confused by my own shadow. I was no longer myself; I was only a shadow – a shadow behind a shadow. I cursed the wind-whorls which made my way so fearfully difficult. At length I was at the plateau's lowest dip, with only a few hundred yards separating me from the broad sweep of the Silbersattel, opening like a gateway before me; how the tempests must have raged to produce the upheavals on these flat expanses! There were no means of avoiding the snow-structures, many feet high, however much I tried to skirt them. I was staggering like a drunkard, falling, crawling, standing, walking, falling again . . . then I remembered the Pervitin again. It was the only chance; its brief renewal of my strength might last long enough for me to get down to the tent. That is, if I hadn't already used the last reserve of strength left in me, for I felt absolutely finished. Blood and spittle were coming out of my mouth, which was completely gummed up; and I had to force the three tablets down as if they were wooden wedges. I began counting the yards, as the rim of snow drew nearer.

At half past five I was on the further rim of the Silbersattel, and at last I could see down to the Rakhiot Glacier and the Camps on it once again. The whole route of the climb lay spread before me, and I could see the tents clinging, half buried, to the slopes. It was an indescribably comforting sight; I felt just as if I were coming home. Yet I could see nobody moving about down there. Surely they could not have evacuated the camps? Peace unbroken reigned over everything, not a soul stirred, not a sound marred the silence. I looked across to Rakhiot Peak and again I noticed the dark spot, the little hurricane tent – and then, two smaller dots. Those were definitely people, on the Rakhiot Traverse, porters perhaps. This time there could be no mistake, they really were people!

Then at last I knew I was safe. The knowledge that I was near my team-mates gave me new-born confidence. My old tracks were still in good condition and I traversed slowly along them to the ridge. For the moment I felt fresher again, either because of the Pervitin or because of the blessed feeling of relief; breathing became easier, too, but I still had to use

extreme care. The crampon came loose again and I took it off in a rage and threw it out over the South Face, without further ado. I made relatively rapid progress down the exposed ridge, moving forward through crust past the 'Whipped Cream Roll', till at seven pm – forty-one hours after leaving the spot – I approached the tent.

Hans now came to meet me. He did not know how to hide his emotion and buried himself behind his camera. We embraced, speechless. I was so parched that I could not utter a sound, and Hans was satisfied to see me back safe and sound.

After climbing Broad Peak four years later, Buhl's party went on to attempt Chogolisa, where he fell to his death through a cornice.

Yet a third of the pre-war battles for the greatest peaks was resumed in 1953 when the Americans led by Charles Houston returned to K2, the world's second highest peak. They pushed their way up the Abruzzi ridge; by August 1 all eight climbers, seven Americans and H. R. A. Streather, who had been invited to join as Transport Officer, were at Camp VIII at about 25,500 feet. Colonel Ata Ullah was in charge of six Hunza porters at Base. There was a well-stocked line of camps below the climbers, who hoped to establish one more camp from which to reach the summit. Let Streather continue the story:[5]

The descent of K2, 1953
from H. R. A. Streather, the *Alpine Journal*, Vol. LIX
In spite of the efforts of the last few days we were all in extremely good condition and had acclimatised well. Our gear was in good shape and morale was high. Most of the difficult climbing was over and we were less than 3,000 feet from the summit. All we needed now was a break in the weather, just three days might be enough, so that we could put the last part of our plan into action. Our basic plan was simple. On the first clear day we would all carry loads to Camp IX, which we hoped to establish at about 27,000 feet. The strongest two climbers would go ahead with light loads and reconnoitre the route. These two would remain at Camp IX, with supplies for several days, and would make a bid for the summit on the next clear day. If they failed, a second pair would try, and there would still be time and food for a third or even a fourth pair if necessary.

We had not planned to use oxygen, and we had none. The problem of carrying the extra loads up the steep ridge, without the help of a large number of porters, was too great and we did not consider oxygen essential to reach a height of 28,250 feet. We had already spent nearly a month above 20,500 feet, and far from deteriorating, we had been getting fitter from day to day. There were none of the usual signs of mountain sickness and we attributed this to the length of time we had been acclimatising with strenuous exercise, as we worked our way slowly forward from camp to camp. We had made six or more carries each, between most of the camps.

Such was the position when Bates and I reached Camp VIII on August 2.

That night the storm continued with unrelenting ferocity and the wind seemed to have some personal malice against us, as though it was determined to blow us from the mountain. It continued through the following day. We were confined to our bags and unable even to talk to each other without shouting at the top of our voices. The stoves would not stay alight in the flapping tents, so we were not able to get more than a cup or two of liquid to drink; not nearly enough at that altitude.

On the morning of the 4th, we heard a pathetic cry from outside, 'Help, our tent has gone.' Houston crawled in to join Bates and me while Bell joined two of the others. We were now eight of us in three small mountain tents.

Every evening we spoke to the Colonel on our wireless and always he had received the same weather forecast from Radio Pakistan; 'Snow and storm'.

So it continued until the morning of the 7th. I would be wrong to say that on that day we awoke to a bright morning, for there had been little sleep during the previous nights; but the clouds were clearing and the sun was shining although the wind was still blowing strongly.

For the first time since our arrival at Camp VIII we were able to think of further movement. Bell and Molenaar had been slightly frost-bitten during the storm so they would go down. Bates and I would go down with them to VII and bring up more food and fuel. The other four would kick steps up the snow slope and start working the route towards IX. We would have to be more certain of the weather before we could think of establishing IX, but we could start preparing the way.

When we crawled from our tents, intent on continuing with this plan, Gilkey complained of pain in one of his legs. He tried to stand with his full weight on it but collapsed in a faint. Houston looked at it and soon diagnosed thrombo-phlebitis. If Art was to have any chance of recovery we must get him down at once, there was nothing else for it. All our plans of going higher were abandoned and we set about preparing to carry Art down. We bundled him in sleeping bags, wrapped him in the torn tent and set off dragging him through the snow. We soon realised that we were in grave danger of starting an avalanche and we were forced to return and re-establish Camp VIII. Craig and Schoening set out to find an alternative route and reported a steep rock and ice ridge some hundred yards to the south of the snow slope. By this time the weather had again reverted to storm and further movement became impossible that day.

The days passed but still the storm showed no signs of relenting. Each evening the forecast was bad. On August 10 we realised just how serious the situation had become. We were suffering particularly from de-hydration, for we had not been able to melt much snow and we were suffering too from the effect of having spent ten very worrying days, cowering from the storm. I'm sure that our deterioration was due more to these factors than simply to altitude. Art was in a bad state. We must get him down as soon as possible. Both his legs were now affected and clots of blood had moved to his lungs.

We wrapped him again in a sleeping bag and tent and set out, in the raging storm, to get him down by the new route. This was a desperate attempt but we had no alternative. First we dragged him a short way through the deep snow and then we lowered him

Broad Peak and K2. Broad Peak was climbed by Buhl in 1957 (he was killed later that year) and in 1953 the Americans led by Charles Houston returned to K2. They abandoned their attempt in order to bring down an injured man, and nearly lost their lives during the perilous descent.

down the steep ridge and ice slope below. After many hours of exhausting work, feeling extremely tired and cold, we had descended little more than 400 feet. Somehow we would all have to spend the night on the small ledge at Camp VII for there was no chance now of reaching Camp VI as we had hoped.

We had just lowered Art over a steep rock cliff, when one of the climbers slipped. We were climbing, for the most part, in pairs and in some miraculous way our ropes crossed and became entangled. Five of us were pulled off the steep ice slope. Pete Schoening, who was at the time holding the rope on which we were lowering Art, had the only strong belay and somehow he held us all. Bell had fallen more than 200 feet and the rest of us a little less. Again, by some miracle, none of us was badly hurt although Houston was unconscious for a time and Bell had badly frozen hands, through having lost his gloves in the fall.

Those of us who were able, made our way to Camp VII and managed to erect a tent on the tiny platform there. We then helped the casualties to the shelter of this tent. During the rescue, Art had been left securely anchored on the snow slope by two ice axes.

While we were getting the others into shelter we were able to shout back and forth at Art, only about 200 feet away over a small rise; but we could not hear what he was saying, above the noise of the wind. He was very heavily drugged so that he would not know too much of the awful discomfort of the descent.

The rescue operation took about half an hour and then the only three of us who could still move went back to try and do something for Art. We realised that we could not move him but we hoped to be able to cut a small ledge in the slope, feed him and help to make him comfortable for the night. When we got back he had gone. At first we could not believe our eyes but slowly we realised that a small avalanche had come down and taken him away. The surface of the slope was soft and broken. There was no trace of Art or of the axes which had anchored him.

Once over the shock of having lost Art, we realised that his passing was a miraculous deliverance from a situation which might well have meant disaster for all of us. If we had continued the attempt to carry him down over the increasingly difficult climbing below, it is most improbable that we could have avoided further and perhaps even more serious accidents.

That night at Camp VII is the longest I can ever remember and certainly the worst I ever wish to spend. Four of us were squatting in one small mountain tent, on an even smaller ledge, and the other three of us in a tiny bivouac tent, with just a pole at one end. Charlie was delirious and would not keep still for a second except when he collapsed unconscious. He had cracked some ribs and his chest was paining him terribly and making it even harder for him to gasp the rarefied air. George Bell had frozen hands and feet and all of us had some degree of frostbite. Pete Schoening was exhausted from the effort of having held us all for some considerable time while we sorted ourselves out after the fall.

I had some tea and sugar in the pocket of my parka and Bob Craig had a stove with him. We spent the night making tea and passing it round for all to sip. We were able to make pathetically little but it helped. We huddled in our tents, trying to warm our bare feet against the belly of the man next to us, and wondering what the morning would bring. The wind had ceased and the night was calm. This was almost the only kind thought that the mountain spared us until we were well below Base Camp many days later.

Next morning we took stock and found seven very tired and battered climbers. We were determined to keep our heads and climb carefully down through the line of camps we had taken so long to build on the ridge. How Charlie and George climbed that day I shall never know. Charlie was still very dazed from his concussion and George's feet were in a bad state. But there were no slips and late that afternoon we reached Camp VI.

It was four days before we eventually reached Camp II. The descent had been slow and painful but now at least we were safe.

Next year, 1954, K2 was climbed by Dr Ardito Desio's Italian expedition. Dr Desio had been on the Duke of Spoleto's expedition of 1929 which had explored the Baltoro area around the mountain. With the usual delays from weather, and suffering a check when Puchoz was struck down by pneumonia, camps were methodically advanced up the Abruzzi ridge. A light windlass was used to move stores up and ropes were fixed up the route to Camp VI, not only to speed up movement but to keep open an escape route. The final assault was mounted by Compagnoni and Lacedelli; while struggling with final difficulties their oxygen ran out but they reached the top at 6 pm. After an awkward descent they were back in Camp VIII by 11 pm. Both had fingers frostbitten.

In the autumn of same year the French carried out a reconnaissance of Makalu (27,825 feet), near neighbour of Everest and fifth highest of the world's mountains. At that time of year it is too cold to assault so high a summit (primarily because snow never consolidates if it remains too cold), but they settled on a route which looked hopeful, and, as a by-product, they climbed Makalu II (now called Kang-chungste) and Chomo Lönzo. As a result of their report, an expedition, also led by Jean Franco, set out next spring to climb the mountain. Not only the first pair, Jean Couzy and Lionel Terray, but, on the following days, all the French climbers[6] and Gyalzen reached the summit. This was the first time this desirable end had been achieved on one of the really big mountains, a very successful and well-organised expedition. As Lucien Devies wrote, the mountain was climbed *'avec la rigueur d'une démonstration'*.

Meantime a British party under Charles Evans was at grips with Kangchenjunga, at 28,208 feet, the third highest mountain. Of this peak John Hunt had reported that it 'combined in its defences not only the severe handicaps of wind, weather and very high altitude, but technical problems and objective dangers

Opposite: Dr Ardito Desio at Base Camp on K2 in 1954. Two of his party, Lacedelli and Compagnoni, reached the summit in spite of running out of oxygen. Above: oxygen cylinders stacked ready for use by the expedition.

Above: Chomo Lönzo and Makalu, both climbed by French mountaineers in 1954 and 1955. The first pair on Makalu were Jean Couzy and Lionel Terray, followed by the rest of the party on the next two days.

Opposite, New Zealand: top, Mount Cook; bottom left, an artist's impression of Mount Cook; bottom right, the Fox Glacier.

Overleaf: the Annapurna range.

of an order even higher than those we encountered on Everest'. Officially, Evans' task was to reach the great shelf on the Yalung face at about 24,000 feet and to examine the upper part of the mountain. They early met difficulties on the proposed route by Kempe's rock buttress and moved their attack further west to a buttress leading to the slopes on which an avalanche had swept away Pache and three porters fifty years earlier. By this route they reached the great shelf from which a gangway appeared to lead to the west ridge and so towards the summit. The first assault pair were George Band and Joe Brown; here is part of Band's account.[7]

The ascent of Kangchenjunga

from George Band, the *Alpine Journal*, Vol. LX

The God of Kangchenjunga was kind to us, for May 25 dawned fine. We woke automatically when the oxygen was exhausted at five o'clock. We breakfasted on a couple of pints of tea and a biscuit or two and made off up the Gangway at 8.15, swerving out left to meet the sunshine. Near the top of the Gangway we had planned to turn off right at a string of snow patches and climb across the face, because we had seen earlier through binoculars that the West ridge itself was extremely broken and difficult.

Unfortunately, we had very little idea as to how far up the Gangway we really were and we turned off too early at the wrong snow patch. By the time

we had realised our mistake and turned back, an hour and a half of precious time was lost. So we hurried on up the Gangway as fast as possible to try and make up time. Apart from the snow of the Gangway, most of the climbing would be on rock, so we had left our canvas overboots behind, and now, when we reached the first rocks, we took our crampons off.

We were aiming for a little subsidiary snow-ridge which would lead us back to the main West ridge beyond its worst difficulties. The approach to this snow-ridge was steep and we had to climb pitch by pitch for about three hundred feet. There was one tricky section where you had to swing round a corner on your hands. It might have ranked as 'difficult' at sea-level, and Joe safeguarded it with a piton since I had a poor belay. Just above was an impressive ice-slope, sixty degrees in places, which required two pitches. There was a sensational rocky eyrie half-way; one seemed to be poised in mid-air thousands of feet above the Shelf and the glacier below.

Because of the time we were taking, every breath of oxygen was vital, so we cut down our supply to the minimum rate of two litres per minute, only increasing the flow when wrestling with some difficulty. This low rate seemed hardly sufficient for a person of my size and weight, and may have accounted partly for the fact that Joe was now definitely going better than I was. I had led at first, then we had a period leading through, and now Joe was in front.

He offered to stay in the lead, and I was happy to agree.

We came out on to the crest of the snow-ridge and the summit pyramid was at last visible, culminating about 400 feet above. We had been climbing for over five hours without a rest, such was our feeling of urgency, so after cutting up the snow-ridge, we joined the west ridge and sank down in a little hollow behind and above the cluster of pinnacles. My throat was parched. We took off our oxygen masks and had a quick snack of lemonade, toffee and mint cake.

A strong breeze was blowing up the North-west face, carrying flurries of snow over our heads. I looked over at the North ridge and then photographed our route ahead. The ridge was easier at first, and by keeping a little down on the right we would avoid the wind. But at the last a nose of rock reared up, sheer and smooth. We could have no idea what it held in store for us. It was 2 pm. We only had a couple of hours' oxygen left.

'We ought to turn back by three o'clock, Joe,' I said, 'or we may have to spend the night out.'

'We've just got to reach the top before then,' he replied.

We carried on. The West and South peaks of Kangchenjunga were now well below us. We skirted below the rock nose, round a corner, and up a little gully. There above us the wall was broken by several vertical cracks about twenty feet high, with a slight overhang to finish. Joe was keen to try one. As he said later: 'I knew that at sea-level I could climb it quite easily, but at that height you don't know just how long your strength's going to last you if you hang by your arms for any length of time. You might just fall off in sheer exhaustion.' Turning his oxygen to the full six litres a minute and safeguarding his lead with a couple of running belays, he struggled and forced his way up. It was the hardest part of the whole climb; perhaps 'very difficult' had it been at normal altitudes. From the top, I remember him shouting, 'George, we're there!'

The next day Norman Hardie (New Zealand) and H. R. A. Streather repeated the ascent; this had been another smoothly organised and successful expedition.

In 1956 the Japanese climbed Manaslu (26,760 feet), the Swiss made the first ascent of Lhotse (27,923 feet) and the second of Everest, and the Austrians climbed Gasherbrum II (26,360 feet). Many of the highest giants had now been climbed and, as in the Alps eighty years earlier, men's thoughts began to turn to the challenges of difficulty and elegance; the glamour of sheer size was less compelling.

For forty years Vittorio Sella's famous photograph of the Muztagh Tower (23,860 feet) had fascinated and appalled mountaineers; it shows a peak apparently totally inaccessible. This, of course, is partly due to the angle from which the picture was taken; the mountain did not so appear to its discoverer, Conway, who recorded that it was 'the peak we ought to have climbed'. Conway was wrong too; the mountain was well beyond the resources of his

Opposite top: a yak train moves through the Khumbu valley.

Opposite bottom: Camp II on the International Himalayan Expedition, 1971.

Below: Manaslu, first climbed by a Japanese expedition in 1956, one of the three ascents of peaks over 26,000 feet made that year. By now many of the highest Himalayan peaks had fallen and expeditions began to seek more difficult and elegant routes on the fallen giants.

Kangchenjunga, south-west face. The main icefall is in the centre. Charles Evans' party in 1965 reached the central shelf from the left, from there continuing to the west ridge and summit. The final pair, George Band and Joe Brown, reached the summit but left it untrodden in deference to the religious feelings of the people of Sikkim.

expedition and altogether too ambitious an objective for that date. In 1956 the time seemed ripe to two parties of young men, one in France and one in England. Planning was quite independent and neither party was particularly pleased to meet the other at the foot of the mountain. The British were on the Chagaran glacier first, so Guido Magnone led his men round to the Younghusband glacier. Relations soon became cordial and Hartog records that (just as in Chamonix) the French 'were neatly dressed and clean-shaven; we, of course, were very scruffy'.

The British party consisted of John Hartog, Joe Brown, Ian McNaught-Davis and Tom Patey. Hartog has recorded the later stages of the climb.[8]

The Climbing of the Muztagh Tower
from John Hartog, the *Alpine Journal*, Vol. LXI

From Camp IV to the summit the trail was broken by Mac and Joe, who both described it as the hardest day's work they had ever done in their lives. They got to the West summit at 6.30 pm, and after visiting the col between the summits they went back down the ridge 300 feet to bivouac for the night.

Next day, July 7, Tom and I followed up the footsteps of the first rope. After a start on mixed rock and ice we embarked on a long snow-and-ice section leading up with increasing steepness to the first of two rocky bands coming in from the South face and extending half-way across the ridge. The first of these 'slopes' Joe had tried to 'peg' up, as it turned out to be overhanging. As the pegs would not hold, it was necessary to traverse underneath and up a couloir at the side, thus turning the excessively steep rocks. The couloir was filled with loose snow, about three feet deep, lying non-adherently on ice. Above it, forming the opposite wall to the rocks, were ice-cliffs and séracs. Below there was no obstacle to a rapid descent to the Moni Glacier, 6,000 feet below.

The labour of getting up this was extreme, and the avalanche danger was always there. The second day the steps had consolidated somewhat, and though

care was necessary the danger was much lessened.

But for Mac and Joe it was hair-raising, a breast-high treadmill arrangement of exhausting character, on which the steps were made in zigzag pattern looking for the soundest snow. The snow couloir was about 250 feet in vertical height before it opened out into a wide slope of bare ice for about 200 feet, leading to the base of some rocks. Two rope-lengths (Grade III) took one to the start of an easier section from which one climbed continuously up snow at an easier angle, until there was a steep rise of 90 feet. Breasting it, the ground dropped sharply at one's feet. It was the West summit – a narrow ridge, perhaps 350 yards long, with the highest point towards the south. The East summit appears from the west to be a little pinnacle of snow, very dainty, with a 10-foot rock step near the base. In reality it is a knife-edge ridge of snow, the narrowest that I have ever been on, and across this ran a vertical wall of rock, mentioned just above. Although the East summit looked to be the higher one, Mac and Joe just couldn't summon up the energy to tackle it. Of course, it was getting late and they would have to bivouac out as it was. So they descended about 300 feet below the West summit to a hollow between the rocky top of the South face and the snows of the North face. Mac had always had the idea that a bivouac might be necessary on this section and the two of them were fairly well prepared for it, except that they were short of food and, of course, drink. (They had no stove.) For this top section there was a great question of how much weight it was necessary to carry.

Anyhow, they didn't have too bad a night, and actually slept a little. Joe didn't take his boots off. Early next morning they started down, hungry and thirsty, and we met them at 9.30 on the snow/ice slopes of the North face. We compared notes with them and learnt all about their doings. They offered us some of the special extra down clothing that we had for bivouacs, but as from their timetable of the previous day we discovered that we had already made up three hours we decided that we ought to be able to get back to Camp IV without a bivouac. They were frankly sceptical, but Tom and I felt that if we could manage without carrying any further loads we should go all the faster. So after a quarter of an hour's halt we separated, they to go down to Camp III, and we up to the top. We arrived on the West summit at 2.30 pm (four hours earlier than the first pair, entirely due to being able to use Mac's and Joe's steps). Tom got up ten minutes before I did, and was shouting down to the French when I arrived.

The French camp (it was their IV) was in the middle of the hanging glacier, 2,000 feet below. We could see one little dot just by their tent, and two more above the bergschrund, on a snow/ice slope leading up to a gap in the South-east ridge. Vague shouts, quite unintelligible, were coming up from below, and Tom was yelling back. We saw the two figures on the slope descend rapidly and return to their camp. The previous night Joe and Mac had seen their camp, too, and called down to them, but, as we learnt later,

210

the French were all in their tent, playing bridge.

At the West peak Tom and I roped up again and set off for the East summit. Mac and Joe thought this looked higher and had taken on a bet about how much higher it was.

I have told of the appearance of the East summit as seen from the West top, and now Tom and I went up to the foot of the rock step, Tom leading, and I belayed only to an ice axe buried to the top in the snow of the arête. On either side this fell away in the great slopes of the North and South faces. To the south the exposure was only 2,000 feet, but to the north, the side Tom might fall down, it was about 8,000 feet to the glacier. My safeguarding move in the event of emergency would be to move down the opposite side of the snow arête to that of the falling man. We had all this carefully worked out before Tom started up, wearing crampons.

Although only 10 feet in height, the rock was a smooth slab, and an apparent crack which slanted across about 8 feet up was very shallow and filled with debris. At the third attempt Tom was able to balance up on a scrape hold for two crampons' points, and then levering himself up on the inadequate lip of the crack, albeit now excavated, reach over the top for what the French call the *prise d'arrivée*. At the top Tom put in a piton, as a belay for himself, and also to fix a bight of rope as a fixed rope to give me additional handhold. On the descent we abseiled down this pitch.

I would certainly have demanded a shoulder in leading such a place. Part of the trouble was that the take-off was very poor, being just the soft snow forming the crest of the arête. However, it was brilliantly achieved, and the standard was V, i.e. Grade Five. Here Tom invited me to lead the final 150-foot section on the ridge to the East summit. It was a knife-edge such as I have never been on before: the snow had a thin softish crust on it, and underneath was small-granular and sand-like. We were climbing on the North side, which was less steep but more exposed, and, as before, the only safeguard against a slip was to nip quickly on to the opposite side of the arête. The whole proceeding was such that we only moved one at a time. Eventually we got to the East summit. According to my aneroid it was just three metres higher than the West summit. The top was a gracefully fine knife-edge of snow, soft and feathery to the touch, easily disturbed and trodden down. But no trace of our ascent will remain apart from the piton in the rocks 150 feet down towards the col. This piton is a French one! When the French expedition came up the South-east ridge they reached the East summit from the opposite side to us, in a snowstorm, and they did not go on to the col nor to the West summit. Indeed, they did not realize how nearly the tops are the same height.

The descent was a struggle; both climbers were in poor shape, perhaps as a result of an anti-frostbite

Muztagh Tower, which attracted two expeditions in 1956, one French, one British; both reached the top within a week by different routes. Here the British route is not visible: the French route is up the facing ridge—the line dividing sun from shade, which is much foreshortened.

211

drug, and Hartog's feet were frostbitten. He was taken off the mountain by the French. He concluded his account: 'The kindness, gentleness and care of the whole French expedition were beyond words. They all individually helped to carry me. They mothered and befriended me, nursed me, and gave me medical treatment until I reached Karachi.'

The very image of inaccessibility had been climbed twice within a week by two different routes. While not offering the special hazards of more extreme height, this was, for climbing technique, the hardest Himalayan peak yet climbed.

From inspection of the list in Appendix II, it might be thought that the three years following 1953 were years of unbroken Himalayan success, but of course there were failures and set-backs. To correct any too glittering impression, we add an example of the threats never absent from climbing on big mountains. In 1957 some members of the Oxford University Mountaineering Club invited Tony Streather to lead their reconnaissance of Haramosh (24,270 feet). Bernard Jillott and John Emery were climbing up the north-east ridge of Haramosh above their Camp IV, which was at about 20,000 feet. A slab of snow slid off, carrying the climbers far down over cliffs to the snow below. Cushioned by the mass of falling snow they were not injured, but they could not climb out of the basin without the axes they had lost in the fall. Tony Streather and Rae Culbert saw the accident and the figures moving below. They went back to camp, had a meal and picked up food and warm clothing. They were back on the ridge at 10 pm; using torches and fitful moonlight they descended. As dawn lighted they could see Jillott and Emery again, but they had to make a steep ice traverse to avoid the cliffs. On the long slow descent Culbert lost a crampon, a very serious mishap. The light was already failing when they joined the two below. It was twilight as they started to climb out of the basin. Before long Culbert's cramponless foot slipped; in falling he knocked Streather off and they were all dragged down back over the bergschrund; nobody was hurt but Streather lost his axe. With only one axe left, they tried again but at about the same point Jillott, going to sleep in his steps, fell and dragged the whole party down again. This time the last axe was lost and they took shelter in the crevasse. Next morning, with infinite care, punching and kicking the steps, they went up again. After a while, Emery spotted one of the axes and Streather was able to cut up to the platform they had so nearly reached twice before. He brought Emery up on the rope; leaving the latter to hold the others, he remade the steps of the traverse. He got Emery and Jillott across and went back to belay Culbert across a descending section of the traverse, an almost impossible task on ice with only one crampon. Culbert came off and dragged Streather from his axe belay. They lay stunned back once more beyond the bergschrund. In time Streather heard a voice saying 'We'll go back to camp, get some food and come to help you as soon as we can'. It was now two and a half days since the original accident.

So far we have abridged Wilfred Noyce's account which he based on personal reports from Streather and Emery; we continue in Noyce's own words:[9]

The descent of Haramosh
from Wilfred Noyce, *They Survived*

The voice from above had been Jillott's. There was nothing else he could do. He crossed the last part of the traverse himself and climbed on, shouting up to Emery, who stopped, astonished to be joined by Jillott and not by the other two. The bitterness of the situation came home to them. Now the rescuers were below, the rescued free to climb out. And there was nothing that they could do except climb on and vow to return for the two below.

They struck the ridge, finally in the dark, at the point of the avalanche. Emery led off towards the break in the cornice through which they had first climbed, but he could see nothing and almost immediately fell heavily through the cornice himself. This new fall of some thirty feet shook him badly and dislocated his hip again. Again he managed to turn so that the joint slipped back into position. He called up, 'Keep going along the ridge. I'll meet you at the cut in the cornice.'

Here, where Streather had flogged a way through on the 15th, they met and started searching for the rucksacks left behind. In one of them was a water-bottle, and each in turn had to tear at it before he could convince himself that the contents were frozen solid. In their haste and confusion they searched only one rucksack thoroughly and failed to find the glucose tablets.

They started down. Soon they were jumping the big crevasse fifty feet below the cornice. It was so dark that Jillott, jumping second, landed on top of Emery and knocked him over. Troubled again by dysentery, Emery was forced to relieve himself; then they went on. After a few steps Emery said that they should wait for the moon to come up, since they could see nothing, but Jillott had no thought but to push on down, and on occasions like this the man who makes the move has the whip hand. He went on, unroped, and Emery knew that he must keep with him. Jillott seemed to be finding the way very skilfully, but instead of detouring round the crevasse area, as they had done before, he started to go straight through it. Emery, following, shouted, but there was no answer. He remembered the crevasse at the bottom, where the angle of the slope changed, and hoped that he would catch Jillott up before they had to negotiate it. Going on, he came suddenly to bare ice, where Jillott must have kicked off the surface snow, and once again he was slipping, falling, down towards the crevasse.

His next memory is of a dream that he had fallen into a crevasse and could not get out. In his dream he seemed to be asleep in his tent at Base Camp, dreaming that he was in a crevasse, and that, if he made an effort, he would wake up. But however hard he tried he could not stop this dream.

Wilfred Noyce, mountaineer and writer, who here tells the story of the nightmare descent from Haramosh in 1957. Two of the four-man summit party were lost. Noyce himself was killed in the Pamirs in 1962.

At last he did wake up. It was daylight, but the light had a cool, filtered quality from the ice-walls around. He was jammed in the crevasse where its walls narrowed like an hour-glass, pinioned at the pelvis. One leg hung below, but he felt no emotion at the situation, as if he was detached from it, his mind 'agreeably insulated'. After some time he kicked out with the free leg but made contact with nothing. He drew the leg up, jammed it and levered himself until he could free the other leg. Then, with crampons against the wall opposite, he started to 'chimney' sideways in the crevasse.

Of his state of mind while he did this he has written:

'These movements, though slow and deliberate, were logical; the curious thing was that I seemed to be rather separate from them. I considered and performed them almost automatically, for only part of me seemed to be concerned with them; a large part of my consciousness was hardly interested in them at all. It was rather as if I had two minds or as if I was two people. One mind, or person, was occupied with the drudgery of movement; the other was completely detached, simply an observer. At times the observer was the only one in possession, and I would do nothing at all: at other moments the odd conflict would begin again, the impulse to action would assert itself, and I would move on a bit farther between the walls, while that other half of me just watched and watched.'

At last he came to a place where the crevasse opened out into a depression. He climbed the short distance to the surface on frozen snow-patches, and fell asleep. When he awoke, the sun was shining from a blue sky. Jillott's footsteps were near him. 'My dichotomy of the mind had gone; I could think clearly, seeing the next steps ahead. I moved on again.'

Going on through the crevasse area, he came to a point where, on a steep slope, Jillott had slipped to the bottom, then got up and gone off to the right, in the direction of the old tracks. Emery cut straight across the slope to reach the tracks above the point where Jillott would have joined them. When he reached them, he turned left. When Jillott's tracks came in from the crevasse area he expected to see them turn left also, towards the tents, but they went straight on, to the ridge five or six feet beyond. On the other side the ground fell sheer into the great crevasse, which at this point bit into the ridge, six hundred feet on, down towards the Stak Valley in the distance. Jillott must have walked straight over.

He could not believe it and called down hopelessly. Then dazed, conscious only of the next thing he must do, he went on down to the tents. He needed drink more than anything: for three days, apart from a few mouthfuls of soup, he had taken nothing but snow melted in the mouth, and of this one cannot take much. He tried to open a tin of grapefruit juice, but his hands were numb, lifeless, and as he pressed he noticed, as if they belonged to somebody else, strips of skin peeling from the fingers, leaving a red jelly underneath. His hands did not hurt; they were not his hands. He took about half the tin and felt better. He decided to get the primus going, but fell asleep

and slept, fully clothed, until late afternoon. When he came round he started work on the primus, but his hands would not obey him, the matches were damp and it took over an hour to light it. He made a drink, then started water for soup. The tent was growing dark when he heard a voice outside. It was Streather, alone.

Streather and Culbert recovered consciousness when it grew light on the 18th. They moved very slowly across to the beginning of the climb-out, but the morning was cold and windy, and they sheltered again until the sun came up. Streather's eyes were playing tricks; he had lost his snow-goggles and was partially blind. He saw two dots above, to the right, which he thought must be Jillott and Emery. While he shouted, a small avalanche obliterated them, but they were still there after the avalanche, for they were only holes in the snow or jutting rocks.

They started to climb out again. Uncovering the old steps, Streather saw them red from the blood of his knuckles, where he punched them. On his left hand he still had a woollen glove and overmitt. With his teeth he pulled the sleeve of his jersey down over his right hand. Soon Culbert's left foot slipped, he came off again and slid back to the bottom.

'Are you all right, Rae?'

'Yes, I'm all right. I'll try again.'

This time Streather had almost reached the platform and Culbert was coming up well, when again there was a slither behind and again Culbert was sitting at the bottom. This time he was all in.

Streather balanced in the steps, his half-blind eyes searching for the others. Short of taking off his own crampons – and this Culbert would not allow, even if they fitted – there was nothing he could do. He was aware dimly that it was after midday; they had made no progress at all, had not even started the traverse. Somebody must go on up. He shouted down, 'Hang on where you are for a bit. I'll go on making the steps. The others are sure to be down soon, then we'll be able to help you.'

He went on. He knew little now, having passed beyond conscious thought, but that he must go on. As he worked, he kept looking vainly for the others.

He began to traverse. Loose snow had been blown over and obscured the steps, and he used his frozen overmitt as a tool with which to clear them. He dreaded the last, downward-slanting hundred feet, where Culbert had come off, because there, with his overmitt, he could reach only the beginning of each step; but miraculously he got across, and in the better snow beyond he found the ice-axe with which he had tried to belay Culbert the day before. He was, however, beyond feeling pleasure or relief.

He moved up painfully, slowly using elbows to help clear the steps. As he climbed he gradually began to sense something, somebody above, helping to pull him out, as if from a black pit. . . . With this somebody or something he must co-operate by doing his own part. If he climbed, he would be helped. . . .

Towards evening he reached the ridge and moved

left towards the break in the cornice. He found the glucose packets but could not open them with his hands, and they spilled in the snow. He scooped them up and crunched them with snow, which tortured his cracked lips, and went on down. Where the new track bent leftwards he followed it; like Emery he slipped and fell, above the crevasse, but managed to push himself clear and landed heavily on the other side. Then he followed Emery's track beyond. It was almost dark, on the evening of the 18th, when he reached Camp IV.

Once these two were together again, in the comparative comfort of a tent, surrounded by food and drink, there was a reasonable chance that, whatever the discomforts, even amputations, they might have to suffer, they would survive. But they still clung to the myth that they were going back for Culbert. Streather even returned unsteadily up the slope to shout down at the point where Jillott might have been, for the mind will not accept facts if it does not want to, and they could not allow, having been so close to them for so long, that the other two had died. At any moment, it seemed, Culbert's grin might appear in the doorway.

Emery's feet were very badly frostbitten, he could barely walk. He had to be got down and his survival now depended on Streather. The descent was a nightmare, but they managed it safely.

Haramosh was climbed the next year by members of the Austrian Himalayan Club.

Ama Dablam (22,494 feet) has not sufficient altitude to qualify for Appendix II, but it is an extraordinarily beautiful peak with an air of inaccessibility rivalling the Muztagh Tower. It was attempted by Emlyn Jones's party from the north-east in 1959, when Mike Harris and George Fraser were lost high on the mountain and may, conceivably, have climbed it. It was climbed in 1961 as a by-product or afterthought of the Himalayan Scientific Expedition led by Sir Edmund Hillary, so much of an after-thought that they were fined for climbing it without official permission. Part of the scientific programme was investigation of the longer-term effects of altitide on man; with this in view a hut had been placed at 19,000 feet on the Rakpa glacier and continuously occupied from the beginning of December until the end of April. Among the physiologists and medical men were Michael Ward and Mike Gill; there was a glaciologist, Barry Bishop, and an electrical wizard, Wally Romanes. Gill and Romanes were from New Zealand. About the middle of February, the hut became overcrowded, so a public-spirited decision was made to relieve the congestion by going to look at the south ridge of Ama Dablam. This is Michael Ward's relation of subsequent events:[10]

The ascent of Ama Dablam
from Michael Ward, the *Alpine Journal*, Vol. LXVI
On March 6th, Wally, Barry and myself rejoined Mike Gill for a final look at the mountain. In our absence Mike and the Sherpas had moved about 100 pounds of

food and equipment to the north. We also decided, on Mike's suggestion, to move our present camp on to the top of the Red Tower just before the notch. His reasoning was that by the time we had climbed the second rope ladder we were tired and hopes of getting to the ice shelf, a considerable way, were much diminished. Our route was very exposed throughout and, despite the two rope ladders, difficult; in addition, our two Sherpas did not like the mountain at all and found climbing rope ladders very frightening. We wanted, therefore, to carry the top camp ourselves. That night about two to three inches of snow fell, making progress on the rocks extremely slow and rather dangerous. We waited until it had melted a little and then we all moved camp – hauling loads up the first tower. It took six of us all day to move our camp up 200 feet and a quarter of a mile along the ridge.

Next day Mike and Wally set off again to try and get through to the ice shelf, whilst Barry and I fixed more ropes and took loads up to the ledge below the second step. On their return Mike and Wally were rather depressed. Beyond the Second Step a ridge led towards the ice shelf. About 100 yards before this, extraordinary mushroom towers of ice – overhanging on both sides – blocked the crest of the ridge. Below the mushrooms the ridge sides were too steep and too dangerous to climb along. In addition, the ice shelf was guarded by a small but steep ice wall about 20 feet high which would have to be climbed by artificial means. Their opinion was that although this section would go, it would take some time. One encouraging fact, however. was that they thought that we could dig an ice cave on the shelf and use that as our last camp rather than take up tents – this would, of course, lighten our loads considerably.

On March 9th, Barry and I set off for the ice shelf whilst Mike and Wally ferried more loads. The gully by which the second step was traversed was very loose and nasty. However, we made quick progress to the top of the step and along the horizontal ridge. The mushroom area looked rather formidable. Closer inspection showed that the ridge proper on which they balanced appeared firm enough so we set off. Luckily, although portions were rotten, we could always belay in a convenient crevasse or crack and then safeguard each other over the unstable bits. We came eventually to the edge of the ice shelf. This was climbed by means of a few pitons, an *étrier* and a tight rope. The ice shelf was a beautiful site for a camp. About an acre in extent, it was gently sloping and, although overlooked by a hanging glacier higher up on the face, a convenient ridge directed all the falling ice to one face or the other of the mountain. The best find of all was that the snow was perfect for making a cave.

As we came down, the weather, which during most of our time on the mountain had been good except for a cold and blustery wind, showed signs of breaking up. Great black cumulus clouds were boiling up and the wind grew colder. At the ledge we met Mike and Wally who had come up to get some kerosene

Opposite: Ama Dablam from the Imja Khola, a peak remarkable for its beauty and air of remoteness. It was climbed by members of the Himalayan Scientific Expedition in 1961.

215

as we were running out at Camp II.

On March 10th whilst Barry and I took some more loads up to the ledge and fixed ropes on the gully skirting the second step, Mike and Wally managed to take two full loads up to the ice shelf. We had originally bargained for them to take loads to the top of the second step and this unexpected bonus was extremely useful for the next day, when we all four carried up to our last camp on the ice shelf. We arrived here at 4.0 pm and immediately set to work hacking an ice cave under Wally's instructions. This was really hard work at what must have been 21,000 feet. To start with, only one person can work at the entrance until it is widened out – then a small hall is made with its floor a little below the entrance. Finally a shelf was made about three feet from the floor on which all of us could sleep. This cave took until 9.30 pm to make – we managed to get to sleep at midnight after a somewhat sparse meal. We were compensated by a gorgeous sunset.

On the 12th Mike and Barry stayed to make the cave more habitable – whilst Wally and I set off to reconnoitre the upper slopes of the mountain. We had first to cross a small avalanche runnel, the only dangerous place on the whole mountain. This was clear ice and, after some fancy crampon work by Wally, needed some steps. We roped this and made for a small rock buttress – which turned out to be rather rotten. Above, a 300-foot snow slope led to the right-hand edge of the hanging glacier that guards the final upper flutings of Ama Dablam. At convenient points on this slope we put ice pitons to save time next day. The slope ended on a small horizontal ridge and then we crossed another ice runnel and were on some rocks beyond the hanging glacier. A further two pitches and we landed on the slope above the glacier. We went up there for some way and could see no definite obstacle between us and the summit. It all depended on the snow conditions. If good we should get up and down in fair time, if bad we had little hope.

Next day we started at 8.30 after a good breakfast cooked by Mike Gill. The first part we climbed easily thanks to our steps of the day before. At the flutings we were agreeably surprised to find a small ridged fluting that led from the bottom right of the face to the top without interruption. We cut the whole way up this. Wally and I who had led from the camp were getting tired by the end of the first two pitches of the flutings, so Mike and Barry took over and led to the top. The general angle was between 40° and 50°. The snow was in almost perfect condition and we got to the top at 2.30 pm. This was a small snow cap about 100 yards long by 30 yards wide. A crevasse ran lengthwise along it. We looked down on the Silver Hut easily and wondered if they had seen us. We also looked down the North Ridge, the upper part of which appeared very hard. We found no trace of Mike Harris or George Fraser. The high peaks, Makalu, Everest, Lhotse, and Cho Oyu, were veiled by grey cumuli so after about three-quarters of an hour we returned to our ice cave. Barry took a con-

trolled series of photos to tie in with his map of Mingbo Valley.

Next day we packed up our kit and descended to Camp II where Pemba Tensing and Gumen Dorje were relieved to see us. We removed as many pitons and ropes as we could. In all we must have used over 1,500 feet of fixed rope.

On the 15th, the Ides of March, Mike and Wally set off early with a lot of rope to make an aerial ropeway from the top of the Yellow Tower to the small hanging glacier. This was soon fixed up whilst the rest of us struck camp. We then sent loads down the ropeway – Mike at the bottom and the rest of us at the top. Gumen Dorje and Pemba Tensing went down early, roped up and set off down the ridge. About an hour later we followed with light loads. We left some loads for more Sherpas who had come up from the Green Hut. About ten minutes from the Yellow Tower I came across a small group of Sherpas looking rather frightened. A piece of rock had broken under Gumen Dorje. With his heavy load he had been unable to save himself and his right leg was broken just below the knee. I gave him some morphia and antibiotic tablets, reduced his fracture and fixed his leg using cardboard as a splint. We now had to get him down. The Sherpas were too small to carry him so Mike and I set about doing this. First of all Wally went off with Penuri to take a note up to Griff Pugh at the Silver Hut. Barry with our Sherpas started belaying the loads down and also flashing the Silver Hut with a mirror. Luckily, our walkie-talkie set was in good condition so that communication should be good. Mike set off, Gumen on his back, and myself belaying him. He took him over a nasty toe traverse and then prepared to do the small knife-edged ridge. It was obvious by this time that one person carrying a 120-140 pound load with a projecting leg and one person belaying him was too dangerous, so we waited until Wally came back. The system then evolved was of either Mike or I carrying Gumen with Wally belaying. The non-carrying Sahib and one Sherpa would generally steady and hold in position the feet, hands and other portions of the carrying Sahib's anatomy. He would also protect Gumen's projecting leg. In this fashion we went along the ridge. We could do about 5-10 minutes at a time without changing over. Wally's ropework was superb, protecting and helping us all the time. As the afternoon wore on the weather began to break up and it was obvious we could not get off the ridge on to easier ground that night. We had to find, if we could, a camp site. The only possible site was just before we descended the tower down which Cunningham had put a fixed rope. Here we left Gumen tied to a rock whilst we made two rudimentary tent sites. Soon snow began to fall.

Barry came in with some of the loads, whilst Mike and I put up tents and made Gumen comfortable. Wally went down to Camp I to meet a Sherpa sent up by Griff Pugh (we had made radio contact by now) with some kerosene and food – and a Kramer wire splint. We were pretty well out of fuel and food as we expected to be down at the Green Hut that night.

Wally appeared with these, having rescued a somewhat reluctant Sherpa who had been overcome by darkness some way from Camp I. He then returned looking more like a snowman than ever. All night the snow fell and next morning about six to eight inches lay on the rocks. It would have been suicidal to move so we waited until midday until the rocks were dry. As the rocks became clearer so the weather got worse, and we resigned ourselves to another fall of snow and wondered if we could abseil down the ridge anywhere. However, at 11 o'clock we set off again. The crest of the tower was still covered in snow, but the east side was freer. We decided that the only way to solve the problem was to pendulum in an arc around the east face with the rope fixed at the top. This Mike did with Wally at the top, myself holding Mike's feet on. This manoeuvre was observed through the telescope from the Silver Hut and looked fearsome. After another few hours of snail-like progress over the snow-covered rocks we got on to easier ground. Here one of the Sherpas, Da Tensing II, took over. As we had reached easier ground the pace speeded up and we quickly passed Camp I. However, the weather now broke in earnest. If it had done so an hour or two earlier we should have had tremendous difficulty in getting off. Beyond Camp I we got into a sea of great boulders, which being now snow-covered were incredibly slippery and dangerous. Da Tensing II did a magnificent carrying feat, redeeming his almost 'shock-like state' of the day before. As darkness began to fall we got to a further camp hurriedly pitched amongst the boulders. A little later, Barry came in having got everything off the mountain.

This climb was probably at a higher technical standard than any preceding it in the Himalaya.

In 1962, the most distinguished, but by no means the only, feat was the ascent of Jannu (25,296 feet) by a French party[11] They had tried before, in 1959, and had wisely turned back in adverse circumstances. It was the climax of a great achievement when three Frenchmen and a Sherpa reached the summit of this very difficult mountain; better still, all the other Frenchmen and another Sherpa repeated the climb next day. As Terray remarked, the systematic use of fixed ropes opened up a new field of mountaineering, and this has been proved by many subsequent expeditions.

The great achievement of 1963 was the first traverse of Everest. The Americans, Willi Unsoeld and Tom Hornbein, went up the west ridge and came down by the now standard south ridge and South Col. It was a big and expensive expedition with powerful sponsors, and that was nearly its undoing. It was not, as Norman Dyhrenfurth, the leader, noted in his diary, until they had got rid of their camp-followers that they were able to talk frankly about what had been in the minds of all the climbers, namely the West Ridge. Some, particularly Hornbein, wanted to go all out for the West Ridge. Dyhrenfurth, with his 300 sponsors looking over his shoulder,

couldn't go as far as that but agreed to a serious attempt to climb the West Ridge and make a traverse. Unsoeld was put in charge of the West Ridge effort with a team of six climbers; unfortunately Breitenbach was killed by a falling sérac in the Khumbu icefall and later two others asked to be reassigned to the South Col, leading to postponement of the western attack.

Jim Whittaker and Gombu reached the summit from the South Col in bad weather; Dyhrenfurth and

Top: Terray and Wongdi on the summit of Jannu in 1962, two of the the French party that reached the summit of this very difficult mountain in 1962, greatly helped by the systematic use of fixed ropes. Above: below Camp III on Jannu.

217

Ang Dawa had followed them but, burdened by heavy camera equipment, were unable to reach the South Summit. In the prevailing visibility the film equipment merely wasted effort, a vain sacrifice to dubious gods. Whittaker and Gombu ran out of oxygen on the summit and had to descend without oxygen until they reached bottles dumped on the way up.

After a spell of bad weather came four fine days with the second South Col assault party champing at the bit; they had to wait to synchronise, as support, with the pair hoping to make the traverse from the West Ridge. Let Dyhrenfurth carry on the story:[12]

The traverse of Everest

from Norman Dyhrenfurth, the *Alpine Journal*, Vol. LXIX

Originally, plans called for two further camps on the West Ridge, but now, with the serious losses in tentage, oxygen and butane, it was decided to carry up one camp as high as possible, and to make a two-man assault from there. It was a long shot, but the men knew it was now or never. May 22 was set as the final target date.

This was the signal for the South Col team to start its long-postponed move up the mountain. Lute Jerstad, Barry Bishop and three Sherpas left Advance Base on May 18, while Dave Dingman, Girmi Dorje and two other Sherpas followed a day later. Camp III had been partly buried by an avalanche, but efforts to dig out the tents and reoccupy them were successful. The weather held good, and on the afternoon of May 21 Barry and Lute established themselves at Camp VI, after Pemba Tensing and Nima Tensing had made an amazing carry before returning to the Col.

On the other side of the mountain, Camp 4-W was reoccupied on May 20. All India Radio announced that the monsoon was expected to reach Everest any day now. Time was running out fast. On the morning of May 21, Barry Corbet and Al Auten set off from Camp 4-W to lead the way and prepare the route toward 5-W. Five Sherpas followed an hour and a half later, with Willi Unsoeld, Tom Hornbein and Dick Emerson bringing up the rear. Above camp they first followed what they called the Diagonal Ditch, a long gully slanting upward across the North face. In the ditch itself the climbing was mostly on packed snow, but now and then the men had to negotiate rocky slabs covered with a thin layer of snow, with the well-known rock strata of the North face slanting downward at an unpleasant angle.

During a previous reconnaissance, Willi and Tom had reached an altitude of 26,200 feet, at the base of a snow-filled gully several hundred yards west of the famous Great Couloir. Willi had named it the Hornbein Couloir, and here was the route they proposed to follow as far as possible. At the entrance to the couloir, Dick Emerson reached the end of the line. Plagued by altitude sickness during most of the time above Base Camp, Dick's achievement in reaching such heights is truly admirable.

Jim Whitaker and Nawan Gombu on Everest in 1963. They reached the summit in bad weather and then ran out of oxygen. Members of the same American party made the first traverse of Everest three weeks later.

218

With Barry Corbet leading and cutting steps up the steep couloir, the others followed. Hours went by, and the men began to tire. Toward mid-afternoon, right at the base of the Yellow Band, they reached a tiny ledge. It couldn't have been more than eighteen inches wide and eight feet long. Here, at 27,250 feet, Camp 5-W became a reality. Their job done, the support team immediately began the descent to 4-W, some 2,100 feet below. Willi and Tom spent the next hour and a half chopping out a platform that would hold their tiny tent, working without oxygen to conserve it for the next day. They set up the tent, secured it with pitons and axes, and crawled inside. Just before leaving, Barry Corbet had made a reconniassance of one of two possible routes up ahead. He decided that the one which moved out towards the crest of the ridge would not go and suggested that Willi and Tom try the other one first. After the evening meal of freeze-dried shrimps and tomato paste, prepared by the indefatigable Tom Hornbein, they turned on their sleeping-oxygen and managed to sleep until 4 am. On the other side of the mountain, some 200 feet higher, the South Col team too was getting ready for the big push. Everything was still going according to plan.

Around 5 am on May 22, Lute and Barry lit their stove to prepare breakfast. There was a sudden burst of flame. It singed Lute's beard and burned Barry's plastic sleeping mask. The tent was instantly filled with smoke, but the men managed somehow to dive out before suffocating. It was a miracle that they were alive, but the near-disaster greatly weakened them and caused serious delay. It was not until eight o'clock that they were able to get started.

Willi and Tom left an hour earlier, but Tom's oxygen regulator developed a leak which caused them serious concern. Willi was in the lead, and the route turned out to be more difficult than anticipated. They continued up the steep couloir, cutting steps most of the way. At first Tom wasn't going well at all. Each time upon reaching Willi's belaying position, he would gasp for breath and ask Willi to continue in the lead. (It was not until much later that he discovered that due to his faulty regulator he was actually climbing on less than one litre per minute!) The couloir altered in character, at one point narrowing down so much that a man's body could barely squeeze through. Above this they emerged onto a broad shelf which moved up towards the crest of the West Ridge. So far the terrain had been so steep that there had been no place to sit down, and they were getting tired. Above them the couloir degenerated into a very steep, narrow crack. Willi discovered a possible route to the right, another crack which provided a broader break in the vertical wall above. It was with great surprise that they found themselves still moving one at a time on the shelf itself. The angle was still such that there was not a moment's relaxation and no place to sit. By now they were getting close to the top of the Yellow Band.

Tom took over the next lead which turned out to be a very difficult one. Willi drove in a safety piton, and Tom moved up the smooth rock wall. When he reached snow again he thought he'd be able to walk up, but it turned out to be of such floury consistency that he had to clear each step. The snow cascaded down like a waterfall, and Willi, who was also on unconsolidated snow, became increasingly unhappy. Tom did not like the looks of this pitch, but somehow he kept going. When he drove in another piton, the crumbly rock did little to reassure him. By this time some forty minutes had gone by, and Willi yelled up to him: 'For goodness sakes, come on down! We'll find another route.' So Tom used the doubtful piton as a pulley and rejoined Willi who then attempted another lead further to the right. After one rope length he realised that the vertical wall directly above offered little hope. There might have been a possibility to traverse over to the crest of the ridge at this point, but that too looked forbidding. The wall itself was about 100 feet high, broken only by a series of vertical cracks which looked rather frightening at this altitude. As Willi looked back it became apparent that the best route was the one Tom had just tried. So back they went to its beginning and Tom, who was not feeling well, asked Willi to try it. With Tom belaying, Willi moved up to the piton and snapped into it. He then had to take off his mittens and climb bare-handed for the next stretch. By using cross-pressure, chimney techniques and jam-holes, he was able to worm his way up for the next 20 feet. It was at this point that he suddenly ran out of oxygen. With rapidly ebbing strength he clawed his way up another 15 feet to a tiny nubbin of rock where for the first time he was able to bring up Tom with a sitting belay. And here, at 3 pm, at about 28,200 feet, Willi said: 'Well, Tom, it looks like we have a decision to make.' The decision was whether to go on or turn back. Tom acknowledged the necessity for making it and then ignored it. In complete silence they made it, in fact weeks later upon looking back on it they were convinced that the decision had been made several days before! To descend the way they had come, over technically difficult and dangerous terrain, without adequate piton cracks and without a rappel rope, would have been hazardous in the extreme. They had passed the point of no return and so informed Base Camp via walkie-talkie. Most of us were up on Pumori's South-east spur that day to scan the upper reaches of Everest with binoculars and telephoto lenses, but Big Jim Whittaker had stayed behind to maintain radio contact. Upon being told by Willi that they were going on, he became greatly concerned. He begged them to reconsider and not cut off their only escape route. But Willi and Tom knew that retreat was impossible, and on they went.

Meanwhile Lute and Barry had moved up the South-east Ridge to the South Summit. Barry, after a very bad night at Camp VI and the almost disastrous explosion, felt extremely weak and close to exhaustion during the entire ascent. This made it necessary for Lute to do all the leading and cutting of hundreds of steps. After a much-needed rest on the South

Opposite: the north face of Nuptse, neighbour to Everest, towers above climbers in the Western Cwm during the International Himalayan Expedition of 1971.

The débris-choked upper crevasse of the Khumbu Icefall. Climbers are using a ladder to cross it near the lip of the Western Cwm. On the left is the vast south-west shoulder of Everest.

Summit during which they took stock of their dwindling oxygen supply, they continued along the final ridge on reduced ration.

And then, shortly before 3.30, they saw the American flag flying from the summit of the world. Placed there three weeks before by Big Jim, the aluminium pole still stood straight and tall, only the ends of the flag were slightly tattered. Tears of emotion and relief came to their eyes, and together they stepped up to the summit. For the next forty-five minutes they took pictures of the world around and beneath them – with Lute taking the highest motion pictures ever – and they looked down the West Ridge for signs of the others. They waited, and they shouted, but finally, with the shadows lengthening, they began the descent.

For a while Willi and Tom weren't certain of their exact location on the mountain. Again they contacted Big Jim at Base, but nothing he could tell them about the configuration of the summit seemed to fit their immediate surroundings. At last they were able to orient themselves: they had come out of the couloir to the east of it, in the direction of the North-east Ridge. At one time they had planned to follow a route marked in Hugh Ruttledge's book which would have taken them on to the crest of the North-east Ridge and the base of the final snow-slope leading to the summit. But now they couldn't find a previously selected gully, and everything looked unfamiliar. They then traversed back to the west

across long, wide, open slabs and reached the crest of the ridge. At this point the wind hit them with full force. The climbing became increasingly difficult, and finally the ridge narrowed to a near-vertical knife-edge. There they took off crampons and over-boots and soon became involved in the most enjoyable and exhilarating four rope-lengths of exposed rock-climbing of the entire venture. Tiny ledges, relatively good rock, and just enough handholds to be able to use them with their mittens on. To their right they could see across the top of the South Summit. And then, moving up slowly across the final snow-slope, Willi raised his eyes and about forty feet ahead was the American flag, shining in the slanting rays of the sun and flapping wildly in the breeze. He turned around, raised his fist, and waited for Tom to catch up. They threw their arms around each other and together moved up to the summit. They were quite beyond words.

It was 6.15, and the last light of day was fading fast. They left some memento, took a few pictures, and hurried down the ridge toward the South Summit. They were grateful for Lute and Barry's footprints to show them the way. At one point Willi stopped long enough to contact Advance Base and inform Maynard Miller of their whereabouts. To the latter's amazement the next words coming over the airwaves were from Robert Frost:
'. . . I have promises to keep,
and miles to go before I sleep. . . .'

The sun had set as they descended Hillary's chimney, and twilight set in before they reached the South Summit. There was a momentary scare when Tom, who by now was in better condition than Willi, heard the loud hiss of escaping oxygen. His fear of having broken his regulator when it banged against a rock was unfounded, and soon he was able to remedy the situation. They traversed the South Summit and started down the steep ridge as fast as they could. By now it had become too dark to follow the footprints of their predecessors, and their rapidly fading flashlight was of little help. They shouted, and to their joy shouts came back from below. Lute and Barry, who were close to total exhaustion, had been descending very slowly and with extreme care. By eight o'clock they were still on the steep portion of the ridge, at about 28,300 feet, and it was here that they first saw the occasional pinpoint of light above, and then they heard voices. They waited for two hours until the West Ridge team, guided through the darkness by recurrent shouts, caught up with them. The moment of rejoicing at the reunion soon turned into sharp disappointment for Willi and Tom, for they had assumed that they had reached the shelter of Camp VI. Together the four men resumed their descent in total darkness, but after several tumbles down both sides of the ridge they realised that they would never reach camp at the rate they were moving. They were out of oxygen, and shortly after midnight, still at 28,000 feet, they called a halt and decided to bivouac on a tiny ledge of rock below the crest of the ridge. But the gods were smiling, and although the temperature dropped to 18° below zero, the wind died down. Had there been the usual Everest weather, none of the four would have survived the highest night out ever spent on a mountain.

This ascent of the West Ridge and traverse of Everest was a fine performance, the more so as it is plain that the ridge party were starved of support and porters. This is not to blame the leader who loyally fulfilled his obligations to those many who had financed the expedition.

With the very highest mountains climbed, with the successes on the Muztagh Tower, Ama Dablam and Jannu, with Everest traversed, the psychological barrier in the Himalaya had worn thin. The problem of acclimatisation, the treatment of frost-bite, the use of oxygen were all better understood. The advantages of the systematic use of fixed ropes was appreciated. Just as 'expedition' technique had been adopted, not very appropriately, in the Alps, so sophisticated alpine or Yosemite techniques came to be adopted in the Himalaya. As in the Alps long before, men began to seek out hard lines on mountains already climbed. It was this change that marked the end of the Golden Age in the Alps and the same could be said of the Himalaya around 1970, though there were still plenty of virgin peaks in the latter.

In 1970 Bonington took a party[13] to attempt the south face of Annapurna, which had been climbed from the north by Herzog's party in 1950. (It so happened that the second ascent from the north by the Army Mountaineering Association was proceeding simultaneously with the south face assault.) After nearly two months' climbing up a very difficult ice ridge followed by mixed ice and rock, the party put Whillans and Haston in position to make the summit successfully. This was a fine team achievement of technical climbing at high altitude; it was unfortunately clouded in the last days of clearing the mountain when an ice-wall collapsed and killed Ian Clough.

Another remarkable achievement this year was the ascent of the Rupal face of Nanga Parbat by Reinhold and Günther Messner. Reinhold set out at 2.30 am on a solo rush for the summit; later he saw his brother following and they made the ascent together, but having set out alone neither had brought a rope. Günther did not feel well enough to make the Rupal descent unroped, so they went down the Diamir face, thus making the first traverse of the mountain. Near the base of the mountain, Günther was killed by an avalanche. P. Scholtz and F. Kuen also ascended the Rupal face on the following day. The expedition was followed by considerable controversy in Germany; whatever may be thought on certain aspects, it was undoubtedly a climbing *tour-de-force*.

New routes on old mountains continued in full swing in 1971; the French put up one on Makalu and the Japanese on both Manaslu and Ganga Purna. A very large international expedition set out for Everest under the leadership of Norman Dyhrenfurth and J. O. M. Roberts; their objective was to climb the south-west face, the so-called *direttissima*, which had been attempted twice by Japanese parties. A further aim was to climb the west ridge direct without the deviation onto the north face which Unsoeld and Hornbein had used in 1963. There were twenty-one climbers, a BBC television team of seven, an American oxygen expert, a Nepalese geologist and an Australian reporter.

The climbers were a constellation of skill and experience but little was achieved, partly through bad weather but mainly because of the sad practical difficulties besetting any international organisation. Discipline was lax; the stars carried loads or not as they chose, apt to accept the authority of some nation-state rather than of the appointed leaders. One prima donna declared that, as a member of the French National Assembly, he could not carry loads behind Anglo-Saxon and Japanese leaders.

The Khumbu ice-fall is a variable place; the Indians took five days to get through in 1965, the Japanese eight days in 1970, but in 1971 it took three weeks. Douglas Haston records:[14]

Staying in Dump Camp was never a restful experience. There was always cracking and rumblings all night long. Immediately above was one of the most dangerous parts of the ice-fall, a 150-foot detached overhanging sérac under which we had to pass. Every conceivable way of avoiding this was tried, but in the end we were forced to admit it was the

A Sherpa examines a Yeti scalp, carefully preserved at Tyangboche monastery near the base of Everest.

only way through. The Sherpas called it the Mane Wall, after the Tibetan prayer chant *Om mane padme hum*. When crossing it they would throw rice as an appeasement to the gods, or chant prayers. I preferred to run.

I had one terrible day with Uemara, trying to find a way out to the right of the Mane Wall and going in the Nuptse direction as the exit ice cliffs looked lower there. If Hieronymus Bosch had been given the opportunity to paint a nightmare climbing situation this would have been it. Everything was falling around us. Eventually we became so committed that upward progress seemed the only way out. This was close to the climbing impossible; that is, if one was still interested in living, as we were. Collapsing bridges, falling towers, rumblings, crackings beneath one's feet. Incredible tension in the mind, knowing that one little block is enough. We were blocked completely in the upward passage, but somehow forced out onto some of the fixed ropes on our original route. Completely wiped out mentally, we had eliminated just another variation.

Then came the death of Harsh Bahaguna, a most popular member of the expedition. He had been working on the ridge with a companion, moving Camp III up. They were tired and the weather was worsening. They came down unroped, a quite usual procedure on relatively easy ground with fixed ropes; unfortunately they lost touch, a mistake. When Bahaguna did not arrive a strong rescue team set out, usefully accompanied by two BBC men with camera and sound gear! By now a blizzard was blowing full force and Bahaguna was far gone, unable to help himself. Vaucher and Eliassen tried to push him along the fixed rope, but the wind made this impossible. They decided to lower him and try to swing him across to easier ground. After a few feet Bahaguna turned upside down. Whillans lowered himself, righted Bahaguna and tried to swing him to the shelter of a crevasse. This, too, proved impossible. By now the rescuers' hands were frozen, they could barely tie knots or open karabiners. There was nothing to do but to continue lowering in the hope of reaching another crevasse below; the rope was too short and they had to leave Bahaguna hanging on the ice.

Days of storm followed; sickness was rife and morale threadbare. Indeed the expedition was now so weakened that the ridge attempt was called off and the resources earmarked for it were switched to the by now well-worn South Col route. But as the effects of the storm and the weakness of the force became more apparent, it became obvious that a two-pronged attack of any sort was beyond the powers of this all-star cast. A vote was taken as to which route should be abandoned. Everybody voted to continue the attack on the south-west face, except the two Vauchers, Mazeaud and Mauri. Unable to accept this decision these four went off to nurse their dignity (and stoke the press) in Khatmandu.

Whillans and Haston, Uemara and Ito, continued to flog up the face, establishing camps and fixing rope. Uemara (the man who had climbed McKinley alone and had been on both Japanese Everest expeditions) needed to interrupt his work to send pictures and story back to Japan. Ito stayed up, giving consistent support to the other two. Schlommer then threw a tantrum; not getting a Sherpa to carry his personal gear up the face, he also retired to Khatmandu to tell the press of his ill-usage.

Whillans and Haston turned back at about 27,500 feet. They had another 1,500 feet or so to go and would need another camp. The only climbers in support were the two Japanese; the trickle of supplies coming up from below was dwindling to vanishing point. They were 'out of rope, oxygen and food'.

There was a feeling among the dissidents that Whillans, Haston and the Japanese had tried to hog the glory. It is true that Whillans does not lightly play second fiddle on a climb (except in early days to Joe Brown), but the decisive factor was that those out in front on this kind of endeavour have to be willing to carry as well as to climb and some who fancied themselves in the forward positions were unwilling or unable to accept this chore. In any case the question of who does what on an expedition is a matter for the leader, not for the led.

We have dealt at some length with this expedition, not because its achievement was significant but because its failure illustrates some important points. First of all, the necessity for homogeneity, or the need for a team rather than a collection of stars; second, the undesirability of split or multiple objectives; and, third, the limitations of grandiose internationalism in anything so intimate as the squalor of a high-altitude tent.

The idea of the *cordée internationale* commands universal support; a great many such *cordées* have proved most happy and successful. Every year there are ropes of mixed nationality climbing together because they are friends and have similar attitudes. This is true international brotherhood, a shared outlook on a venture enjoyed together. But an international expedition, collecting stars from each country, in the full glare of press and television sponsorship, is folly. Each member is apt to look on himself as a national representative, as at the Olympic Games and similar well-intentioned disasters which exacerbate nationalism in the name of international friendship. Mountaineers recognise each other as brothers, as, no doubt, do yachtsmen, fishermen, or chess players. Organised inter-nationalism is bound to fail because it is based on the outworn notion of the nation state. The nation was a tenable abstraction in the days of Queen Elizabeth I when there were only four or five units to which it could apply; now, when the wide world has shrunk to the size of the village square, when population multiplies as space shrinks, the number of 'nation states' runs well into three figures and the dictator of Mumbo-Jumbo assumes all the airs of the *roi-soleil*. No real unity can be fabricated out of an assembly of these imaginary entities. The realist must seek, not for an inter-play of nationalisms, but for the eradication

225

of nationalism. As things stand, an international expedition, with stars, sponsors and publicity, courts the appearance of competition within the party, which is far worse than competition between parties.

The attack on the south-west face of Everest was resumed the next year by the 'European Everest Expedition'. This was organised by the controversial Dr Herrligkoffer, who was nominally in charge when Buhl climbed Nanga Parbat alone and when the Messner brothers traversed that mountain in 1970 and who was still involved in litigation with the surviving Messner. Herrligkoffer's party was basically Austro-German but he needed more money which, he thought, could best be raised from the media in Britain; thus it came about that Don Whillans, Hamish MacInnes and Douglas Scott joined his party. It was unhappy from the start; a rush approach with insufficient acclimatisation, trouble with the Sherpas, trouble between the Austrians and the British, trouble with sickness and injury. The upshot was that the British trio walked out, just as the 'Latin' group had walked out of the earlier International Expedition. There were eventually four Austrians, Kuen, Huber, Schneider and Sager, at Camp VI when the weather broke and their slender resources forced a retreat. They had reached approximately the same point as Whillans and Haston the year before, but had apparently intended to deviate from the face onto the south ridge by the escape route Whillans had discovered.

Four months later Chris Bonington was leading another party[15] on the approach march to Everest for a post-monsoon attack on the south-west face. They met a heavy hammering from extreme cold and murderous wind, which took a lot out of them. As he moved up to Camp VI for the summit attempt Haston noted that he felt fit but 'the wind, always the wind, was viciously asserting its authority'. The sky, when he could see it through the spindrift, was blue, but that hardly helped when, at every gust, he had to crouch hanging on to his axe. He reached the place where the equipment was dumped for Camp VI. 'Thinking was difficult. I had to turn away and crouch. Two things were blatantly self-evident. There was no way we could attempt to climb on the Rock Band and no way a tent could be pitched. I looked up at the couloir that we had followed before. Another disillusioning surprise. Whillans and I had climbed a hundred metres of it, mainly on snow and easy rock, with the potential continuation also on snow. Now it was bare rock.' He moved round the corner to look at the escape route to the south ridge, but here the wind hit even harder and it would have been impossible to have clung to the slabby ground. 'Turning back to try to find some kind of shelter, I saw Doug at the top of the ropes. We just muttered a few obvious things. He took some pictures. Hands were turning white, even with double gloves. There was nothing to do but turn around. I jerked my head downwards. He nodded.'[16] There was no question of another assault; resources, human and material were strained, and at this time of year the cold is steadily intensifying.

The accounts of these three Everest expeditions do not give a representative picture of modern Himalayan mountaineering. The big, expensive expedition is no longer typical. Many parties are on the lesser, but still very considerable, Himalayan mountains each season; the Hindu Kush, in particular, has developed as a playground with plenty of worthy objectives. The virtues of the large, highly organised expedition have been under attack for a long time. All through the 1930s Shipton and Tilman urged the advantages of small parties; today the voices are more numerous and almost unanimous. Mountaineering is a pleasure of refined subtlety and, as such, can only be enjoyed in a select company of friends. Beyond this ultimate argument is the subsidiary practical one (a particular instance of Parkinson's Law) that every extra man requires extra equipment and stores, and therefore extra porterage; every extra porter requires extra stores, therefore more porters, and so on, to the miserable end that you travel in a crowd and are short of everything. The huge International Expedition of 1971 petered out because the advance unit could not be supplied. Even Hunt's 1953 expedition ran out of porters; Hunt's high dump and the highest camp were both lower than planned because the porters were not there.

The small expedition has an impressive record of success in the Himalaya from Trisul onwards. Both parties on the Muztagh Tower were of four, so was the Ama Dablam party; Kamet took six and Nanda Devi seven. Nevertheless a small party has not yet sufficed for the very biggest mountains; there are long and precarious lines of communication; a whole line of camps has to be carried and stocked and men must be in support along this line, as is well shown by the 1939 catastrophe on K2. The preceding pages will have shown that mere numbers do not ensure communications and support, but without numbers they cannot be provided at all. Now that all the highest peaks have been climbed, it is to be hoped that the large national or international expedition is out of date.

A large expedition needs financial sponsors, sponsors want pictures, story, film. There is a very proper desire to give the sponsor his money's worth and this may lead to putting too much stress on achievement. A lot has to be done (and carried) that is irrelevant to the mountaineering objective. We have seen Norman Dyhrenfurth struggling on the south ridge of Everest with film equipment in nil visibility. We have seen sound and film equipment rushed out to get pictures of the doom-struck Bahaguna. Bonington had to make a 'difficult' choice among the many things needed for the front pair on Annapurna; he took a ciné camera. Apart from governments (the most dangerous of all) and charitable foundations, the big sponsors are the mass-media and they, naturally, want exciting journalism and programmes; they, too, have to compete in a popularity contest. The art and joy of mountaineering are essentially private; turned into a circus it is destroyed.

11 The One and the Many

O the mind, mind has mountains; cliffs of fall
Frightful, sheer, no-man-fathomed. Hold them cheap
May who ne'er hung there.

Gerard Manley Hopkins

We have surveyed the history of mountaineering and seen changes in technique and achievement develop over two hundred years. Certain general questions press to be answered. Apart from being limited to some kind of steepish place, is there any principle to classify and unite the variety of practice? What sort of men are mountaineers? Why do they court discomfort in a pursuit both arduous and unsafe?

It is vain to seek enlightenment from pseudo-science. Behavioural psychologists have sought to classify the characteristics which make a mountaineer. The Americans, who have even keener an appetite for this sort of jargon than the British, took psychologists and sociologists with them on their 1963 Everest expedition, which is probably why their great achievement of the West Buttress became a barely tolerated aberration from their main, sociologically approved, aim. In spite of the temptation to do precise logical butchery of a few examples of this mixture of cliché and clap-trap, it is better to quote Kevin FitzGerald's urbane criticism.[1] He writes:

Some time ago, an attempt was made to fit members of 'the climbing fraternity' as it was odiously called, into a set of tables. Questions were set, types were selected, other interests were sought, views on marriage, fast motoring, women on expeditions, cooking in Alpine huts, the possibility of the world being flat; all the absurdities which men produce when it is their profession to think up absurdities. The results were surprising. It emerged that a man doing the very hardest rock routes should be fit, tough and used to heights. That a man finding himself on a great mountain, and expected to carry loads, should already have been found capable of doing that, nay, had done that sort of thing before. It was even discovered after profound analysis that a man engaged in teaching the elements of rock-climbing should have some facility for imparting those mysteries, and should in addition be patient and tolerant of early failure. It was revealed that the hard core of hard men seldom went out on the Anglesey cliffs with young gentlemen who had not as yet set foot on rock. It was, in fact, surprisingly found that top climbers were remarkably like top men anywhere, top sailors and soldiers, top explorers, writers, painters, musicians, poets, critics; they were men with minds of their own who sought the company of their peers rather than that of inferiors. Rabbits were displayed in one of the tables. Climbing and mountaineering rabbits it was shown were not quite as good at their chosen pastime as they would wish to be. Certain mountains, many rock routes, were beyond their powers; they lacked the strength to ascend Flying Buttress without using their feet, or the grace and balance to run down the Ordinary route of Idwal Slabs hands in pockets. They would be out of place, the table implied, cleaning an abandoned eagle's nest from a ledge on some fearsome pinnacle. They were rabbits.

The mountaineer resists pigeon-holing. Indeed, climbers vary so much, not only in their characters but in their practice and style, that it might at first be thought that there was no underlying discipline. There are no rules laid down by authority as in cricket or contract bridge; there is no authority. There are no referees, the climber is his own umpire. The guiding conventions vary from time to time, from place to place, and from climber to climber. In the 1920s pitons were bad form in England, eccentric in the Western Alps, conventional in the Eastern Alps. Walter Bonatti, a virtuoso of pegging, is fiercely opposed to expansion bolts. The same apparent inconsistencies have arisen over the whole field; ladders, grapnels, axes, boots, crampons, ropes, oxygen, porters, guides, helicopters, explosives. Obviously climbers play different games with different sets of rules. This discovery was made by Lito Tejada-Flores. We quote his classic article:[2]

From Lito Tejada-Flores, 'Games Climbers Play', *Ascent*, May 1967

Climbing is not a homogeneous sport but rather a collection of differing (though related) activities, each with its own adepts, distinctive terrain, problems and satisfactions, and perhaps most important, its own rules. Therefore, I propose to consider climbing in general as a hierarchy of *climbing games*, each defined by a set of rules and an appropriate field of play.

The word *game* seems to imply a sort of artificiality which is foreign to what we actually feel on a climb. The attraction of the great walls, above all, is surely that when one is climbing them one is playing 'for keeps'. Unlike the player in a bridge game, the climber cannot simply lay down his cards and go home. But this does not mean that climbing is any less a game. Although the player's actions have real and lasting consequences, the decision to start playing is just as gratuitous and unnecessary as the decision to start a game of chess. In fact, it is precisely because there is no necessity to climb that we can describe climbing as a *game* activity.

The obstacles one must surmount to gain the summit of Indian Rock in Berkeley or the Hand at Pinnacles National Monument are scarcely of the same order as those defending the West face of Sentinel Rock in Yosemite or the North face of the Eiger. And the personal satisfaction of the climber upon having solved each of these problems could hardly be the same. As a result, a handicap system has evolved to equalise the inherent challenge and maintain the climber's feeling of achievement at a high level in each of these differing situations. This handicap system is expressed through the rules of the various *climbing-games*.

It is important to realise at the outset that these rules are negatively expressed although their aim is positive. They are nothing more than a series of 'dont's': don't use fixed ropes, belays, pitons, a series of camps, etc. The purpose of these negative rules is essentially protective or conservative. That is, they are designed to conserve the climber's feeling of personal (moral) accomplishment against the meaninglessness of a success which represents merely technological victory.

Let us take as a concrete example the most complex game in the climbing hierarchy – bouldering. It is complex by definition since it has more rules than any other *climbing-game*, rules which prohibit nearly everything – ropes, pitons, and belayers. All that is left is the individual standing in front of a rock problem. (It should be noted that the upper belay belongs to practice climbing, that is, training for any of the *climbing-games*.) But why so many restrictions? Only because boulders are too accessible; they don't defend themselves well enough. For example, it would be an absurdity to use a ladder to reach the top of a boulder in Fontainebleau, but to use the same ladder to bridge a crevasse in the Khumbu Icefall would be reasonable since Everest defends itself so well that one ladder no longer tips the scales toward certain success. Thus the basic principle of a handicap is applied to maintain a degree of uncertainty as to the eventual outcome, and from this very uncertainty stems the adventure and personal satisfaction of climbing.

More generally, I discern a complete spectrum of *climbing-games*, ranked according to the complexity (or number) of their rules. The higher one goes on the scale, the more inaccessible and formidable become the climber's goals, and, in consequence, he need apply fewer restrictions to conserve the full measure of challenge and satisfaction inherent in the *climbing-game* he is playing. At the top of the hierarchy we find the expedition-game, which although complicated to organise and play, is formalistically speaking, the simplest game of all, since virtually nothing is forbidden to the climber. The recent use of airplanes and helicopters exemplifies the total lack of rules in the pure expedition-game.

While variant games have arisen in isolated and special circumstances in different countries, one can distinguish the following seven basic *climbing-games*.

1. *The bouldering game:* We have already discussed bouldering, but one should note that the basic bouldering rules eliminate not only protection but also companions. The boulderer is essentially a solo climber. In fact, when we see solo climbing at any level of difficulty it represents the application of bouldering rules to some other *climbing-game*. Aside from that, this game is found in every country where climbing exists, although the number of climbers who specialise in it is relatively small.

2. *The crag climbing game:* Crag climbing as a pure game form has doubtless reached its highest form of expression in the British Isles. It is practised on cliffs of limited size – routes averaging one to three pitches in length. Because of their limited size and the large amount of time at the climber's disposal, such routes are not imposing enough to be approached with the full arsenal of the climber's tools (though they may contain moves as hard as those of any climb). Fundamentally the game consists in climbing them free with the use of extremely well-defined and limited protection. The use of pitons is avoided or, in special cases, standardised at an absolute minimum. Pure crag climbing is scarcely practised as a game in this country except in areas such as Pinnacles National Monument, where the rock is virtually unpitonable. There are, however, a number of areas in the States, such as the Shawangunks, where the crag game could be played with more rigour.

3. *The continuous rock-climbing game:* This is the game that most California climbers know best. It differs from the crag game in allowing the full range of rock-climbing equipment to be used at the discretion of the climber as well as allowing the use of direct aid. Fundamentally this game should be played on longer, multi-pitch climbs whose length puts a kind of time limit to the mechanical means that a climber can employ and still reach the top. Shorter climbs should still be approached as more complex games with stricter rules.

4. *The big wall game:* This game is practised not only on the bigger Yosemite walls but in the Dolomites and elsewhere. It is characterised by the prolonged periods of time spent on the walls and by the fact that each member of the party does not have to climb every lead (e.g. different climbers may prusik with loads on different days but are still considered to have done the entire climb). The full technical and logistic equipment range is allowed. In the modern big wall game fixed ropes to the ground and multiple attempts to prepare the route are no longer allowed, and a rigorous distinction is still made between free and artificial moves and pitches.

5. *The Alpine climbing game:* In Alpine climbing the player encounters for the first time the full range of hostile forces present in the mountain

The continuous rock-climbing game exemplified on the rock wall of El Capitan in the Yosemite Valley.

and Maestri, and the first winter ascent of the Eiger North wall.

7. *The expedition game:* I have already mentioned the lack of rules in this game, but I wish to point out that there are still differences of personal involvement on the part of the players from expedition to expedition. For example, members of the Austrian Broad Peak expedition who packed all their own loads up the mountain were, in a sense, playing a more difficult game than the usual Himalayan expedition that moves up the mountain on the backs of its Sherpas.

It should be noted that the above ordering of *climbing-games* is not an attempt to say that some games are better, harder, or more worthwhile in themselves than others. One remembers that the very purpose of the game structure is to equalise such value connotations from game to game so that the climber who plays any of these games by its proper set of rules should have at least a similar feeling of personal accomplishment. Of course, each type of game will still have its own proponents, its own classics, heroes, and myths.

The real purpose of ranking climbing games into such a hierarchy, however, is not to make judgements about a game or its players, but rather to have a useful scale against which to discuss climbing ethics, since unethical behaviour involves a disregard of certain rules.

Within our new framework we can now clear up certain misconceptions about climbing ethics. Ethical climbing merely means respecting the set of rules of the *climbing-game* that one is playing. Conversely, unethical climbing occurs when a climber attempts to use a set of rules appropriate to a game higher up on the scale than the one he is actually playing (i.e. a less restrictive set of rules). Applying this idea to the bolt controversy that has animated ethical discussions among climbers for the last several years, we can see that there is nothing unethical about bolts *per se;* it is merely that their use is prohibited by the rules of certain *climbing-games* and not by others. In certain games the question becomes meaningless for, as Bonatti points out, on a major mixed face no amount of bolts can guarantee success, whereas an excessive number will ensure defeat through lack of time.

I have assumed so far that the rules for various *climbing-games* were fixed. Of course, this is not the case, as both the games and their rules are undergoing a constant, if slow, evolution. The central problem of climbing ethics is really the question: who makes the rules for these games? and secondly: how do they change with time?

On reflection, it seems to me that the rules of various *climbing-games* are determined by the climbing community at large, but less so by climbers approaching the two extremes of ability. One of these elements is composed of those fainthearted types who desire to overcome every new difficulty with some kind of technological means rather than at the expense of personal effort under pressure. The other group is

environment. In addition to problems of length and logistics he meets increased objective dangers in the form of falling rock, bad weather and extreme cold, and bad conditions such as verglas. All this leads to a further relaxation of formal rules since success in the game may often include merely surviving. In Alpine climbing the use of pitons is avoided wherever possible because of time loss in situations where speed means safety, but where pitons are used there is a tendency to use them as holds also. Thus the rules of this game do not require one to push all leads free. The restrictions upon the player are more determined by the nature of the mountain and the route than by a set of rules which he accepts in advance.

6. *The super-Alpine game:* This is the newest *climbing-game* to appear and is not yet completely understood. It rejects expedition techniques on terrain which would traditionally have been suitable for it. Its only restrictive rule is that the party must be self-contained. Any umbilical-like connection in the form of a series of camps, fixed ropes, etc., to a secure base is no longer permitted. This rule provides a measure of commitment that automatically increases the uncertainty of success, making victory that much more meaningful. Often the major Alpine routes under extreme winter conditions provide suitable terrain for super-Alpine climbs. Some of the early, classic super-Alpine routes were the South face of Aconcagua, the ascent of Cerro Torre by Egger

Left: two climbers on the International Himalayan Expedition of 1971 surrounded by a mass of complex equipment. The expedition game may be difficult to organise, but it is sometimes relatively easy to play because equipment and supplies are largely carried by Sherpa porters.

Below: a loaded climber on Everest. There are no 'rules' about the use or non-use of artificial aids, but different conventions apply in different places. In the Himalaya the odds are so weighted against the mountaineer that everything available—ladders, fixed ropes, oxygen, helicopters—is considered legitimate.

the small nucleus of élite climbers whose basic concern is not with merely ethical climbing but with minimising the role of technology and increasing that of individual effort in order to do climbs with better *style*. But before talking about style and the rôle of the élite climber in climbing evolution, I want to expand my idea that the majority of climbers are responsible for deciding the rules of a given *climbing-game*.

No matter what their origin a set of rules must be consecrated by usage and general acceptance. Thus the way good climbers have always done a climb becomes the traditional way of doing it; the rules become classic and constitute an ethical minimum for the climb, defining at the same time the *climbing-game* to which it belongs. But what of new climbs? At any moment there are relatively few members of the climbing community capable of doing significant first ascents; these will be members of the creative élite we have already mentioned. The question arises: should the style they use on a first ascent determine the rules for succeeding ascents? I think not (although their approaches and attitudes will of course serve as guidelines for following parties). Examples of cases where the first ascent has not set the pattern for succeeding ascents are almost too numerous to list. Just because Jeff Foott made the first ascent of Patio Pinnacle solo or because Bonatti soloed the South-west pillar of the Drus, following climbers have felt under no obligation to stick to the difficult rules of the first ascent; or just because the first ascent of the Eiger North wall was made in a storm, no one has seriously suggested that later parties wait for bad weather to go up the face. A kind of group prudence is at work here, rejecting individual solutions whose extremism puts them beyond the reach of the majority of competent climbers climbing at any given period.

What, then, is the rôle of the small minority of extremist climbers in the evolution of *climbing-games*? To understand it we must first develop the idea of climbing style. Style may be defined as the conscious choice of a set of rules for a given *climbing-game*. Thus, if a climber follows the accepted rules for a given game he is climbing both in classical style and ethically. Bad style and unethical climbing are synonymous and represent the choice of rules from a simpler (higher) game, such as Alpine climbing with expedition style. On the other hand, a climber can choose to climb with better style and still be climbing ethically by choosing rules from a game lower down in the hierarchy than that which he is playing. A fitting example would be the way John Gil has applied bouldering rules to certain crag climbing problems, doing extremely hard, unprotected moves high off the ground.

In this way the creative nucleus of élite climbers can express itself by climbing with better style than the average climber (like aristocrats playing a more demanding game than the democratic majority), which certainly provides enough room for personal expression, yet seems to avoid the traditional aristocratic rôle of leadership and direction. In fact, these climbers lead the majority only indirectly – their responsibility is not to determine and set ethical standards (rules) for the majority but rather to demonstrate the feasibility of new standards by climbing with consistently superior style. Thus, they stake out the possible directions for the evolution of *climbing-games*. And this, aside from suffering the wiles of equipment-mongers, is the only way that such changes can come about.

Let me give a concrete example. The most evident is the way in which the rules of the big-wall game have evolved in Yosemite Valley under the influence of the best climbers of the day whose primary concern was to do their own climbs in the best style possible rather than to impose an arbitrary set of rules on all climbers. After the feasibility of doing the bigger Grade VI walls without siege tactics had been consistently demonstrated, climbers were impressed enough to accept this approach as a basic rule to such an extent that today even strangers to the Yosemite climbing community (such as the two Frenchmen who did the Nose of El Capitan in the spring of 1966) follow it as a matter of course.

In a less dramatic way the rules of all *climbing-games* are changing constantly, becoming ever more restrictive in order to preserve the fundamental challenge that the climber is seeking from the inroads of a fast changing technology. The present laissez-faire of the uppermost games is disappearing slowly as the complexity of rules shifts up the spectrum. The eventual victim, of course, will be the expedition game which will disappear completely as super-Alpine climbing takes its place. This is not only the newest but, in a sense, the most creative *climbing-game*, since here the nature of the obstacles encountered is so severe that it will be a long, long time before technological advances even begin to encroach upon the climber's personal satisfaction. The possibilities, on the other hand, are immense. One can even visualise the day when, equipped with ultra-modern bivouac gear, a climbing party of two sets off to do an 8,000 m. peak just as today one sets off to do a hard route on the Grand Teton or on Mont Blanc.

Tejada-Flores has explained the underlying conventions which define style and good form, but nobody has yet explained why people climb. Because they enjoy it, of course; but why do they enjoy it and embrace climbing with such devotion and passion?

There are a multitude of climbing pleasures. The pleasure of physical action, of successful technique, of superb scenery, of escape, of exploration. Each of these can be found in other activities and none can account for the unique climbing experience. Even the sanction of damage and death is shared by steeplechasing, parachute-jumping and many other pursuits. Nor will pleasure in the mountain scene alone suffice, important as it is; climbing can still be enjoyed when visibility approaches nil. The importance of the mountain stage becomes clear when we consider that climbing on railway bridges, on buildings or in quarries is regarded merely as practice, happy exercise in preparation for real mountains.

So far we have only found that the joy of mountaineering is a synthesis of pleasures, each of which can be sought elsewhere. The whole is more, much more, than the sum of its parts; it is as with Browning's musician 'out of three sounds he frame, not a fourth sound, but a star'. We have lighted on nothing to account for the numinous quality which nearly all mountaineers and very many others have ascribed to mountains from the twilight of pre-history to the darkness of today.

Michael Roberts, poet and mountaineer, found the central secret of mountaineering in its absolute uselessness and this view is closely akin to my own.[3] Professor Fred Hoyle makes the related point that 'any purpose that can be precisely explained is always temporary. . . . the things in life that last indefinitely cannot be explained and defined.' What is a means to something else can be explained in terms of that objective, but what is a means to nothing (i.e. is useless) but is simply an end cannot be explained. The choice of an end is a value-judgement and as such cannot be proved or falsified; it can only be discussed in terms of metaphysics or poetry.

A history is not the place to delve into the mysterious pull and poetry of mountains. We can only note that notable agnostics like Leslie Stephen have been brought to the edge of prayer, stout materialists like Professor Tyndall have been forced to write very unmaterial passages and the prosiest people have tumbled into halting poetry.

Geoffrey Winthrop Young read his last paper to the Alpine Club in 1957 on the evening before he finally took to his bed in terminal illness. He said: 'What held us together for a century may, then, well guide, or condition, our future. Not personal prowess or competitive achievement. But the understanding of that which mountains – and mountains only – mean to us: the long harsh days of endurance and discipline, on deep snow; the hours of splendid sunshine, of glorious self-forgetfulness, and of movement as upon wings, into adventure, into beauty, and, best of all, into the unknown; the hours of blizzard, and of iced rocks, and of the little cat's-paws of fear, that die away again as fate is pushed back step by step and grip by grip. Most memorable – that hour before dawn, upon cold high glaciers, with darkness shifting frostily upon formless shadows, and the long sighs out of unseen space quivering through the suspense, that suspense we have all known among mountains at this hour, the cold craving for life which filled chaos before earth took form.

And then – the miracle of the coming of light, as it breaks only over great mountains. Light alive with a purpose, the assertion of new being; not merely the ending of darkness, but a light which creates everything anew at each dawn, calling all the peaks and glaciers about us into a new declaration of lovely forms and colours, and bringing out of dead matter and darkness a fresh resurgence of cleansing spirit, into which we ourselves are absorbed as we begin to climb, and in which we feel ourselves to have been newly refashioned.'

A view of the Hörnli ridge of the Matterhorn.

231

Appendix I
Alpine First Ascents

The following list of ascents of Alpine peaks includes only those over 13,000 feet. This approximately corresponds to the continental 4,000-er (4,000 m. = 13,124 feet). The list includes Grand Cornier and Ebnefluh, traditionally 13,000-ers, but now degraded to 12,999. It must be remembered that altitude is a poor measure of a mountain's merit, either of beauty, distinction or climbing difficulty. A big mountain can also be what the irreverent call a 'cow' mountain.

1775	Mont Blanc, Dôme du Goûter	14,121 feet	J. N. Couteran and three guides
1786	Mont Blanc	15,771 feet	M. G. Paccard, J. Balmat
1801	Monte Rosa, Punta Giordani	13,275 feet	P. Giordani
1811	Jungfrau	13,642 feet	J. R. II and H. Meyer with A. Völker and J. Bortis
1813	Zermatt Breithorn	13,665 feet	H. Maynard
1819	Monte Rosa, Vincent Pyramide	13,829 feet	J. N. Vincent
1820	Monte Rosa, Zumsteinspitze	14,971 feet	J. N. and J. Vincent, J. Zumstein
1822	Monte Rosa, Ludwigshöhe	14,243 feet	L. von Welden
1829	Finsteraarhorn	14,019 feet	F. J. Hugi's guides, J. Leuthold and J. Währen
1842	Monte Rosa, Signalkuppe	14,948 feet	G. Gnifetti
	Gross Lauteraarhorn	13,262 feet	E. Desor, Ch. Girard, Arnold Escher von der Linth, with J. Leuthold, D. Briger, Fahner, M. Braunholzer and J. Madutz
1848	Monte Rosa, Grenzgipfel	15,079 feet	M. Ulrich's guides, J. Madutz and M. Zumtaugwald
1850	Piz Bernina	13,285 feet	J. Coaz with J. and L. R. Tscharner
1854	Monte Rosa, Ostspitze	15,197 feet	C., J. G. and E. Smyth
	Strahlhorn	13,747 feet	C., J. G. and E. Smyth
	Fletschhorn	13,111 feet	M. Amherdt with J. Zumkenni and F. Klausen
1855	Monte Rosa, Dufourspitze	15,204 feet	C. and J. G. Smyth, E. J. Stephenson, C. Hudson, J. Birkbeck with Ulrich Lauener, J. and P. zum Taugwald
	Mont Blanc du Tacul	13,938 feet	C. Hudson
	Weissmiess	13,199 feet	J. C. Heusser, P. J. Zurbriggen
1856	Lagginhorn	13,157 feet	E. L. Ames, three other Englishmen, Curé Imseng with F. Andenmatten and three other guides
	Allalinhorn	13,213 feet	E. L. Ames with F. Andenmattèn
1857	Mönch	13,449 feet	Sigismund Porges, with Christian Almer, Ulrich and Christian Kaufmann
1858	Dom	14,912 feet	J. L. Davies with J. Zumtaugwald, J. Krónig and H. Brantschen
	Nadelhorn	14,197 feet	J. Zimmermann, A. Supersaxo, B. Epiney and F. Andenmatten
	Eiger	13,025 feet	R. Barrington with C. Almer and P. Bohren
1859	Grivola	13,022 feet	J. Ormsby, R. Bruce with F. A. Dayné, Z. Cachat and J. Tairraz
	Grand Combin	14,154 feet	C. StC. Deville with D., E. and G. Balleys and B. Dorsaz
	Rimpfischhorn	13,777 feet	L. Stephen, R. Liveing with M. Anderegg and J. Zumtaugwald
	Aletschhorn	13,763 feet	F. F. Tuckett with J. J. Bennen, Peter Bohren and Victor Tairraz
1860	Gran Paradiso	13,324 feet	J. J. Cowell, W. Dundas with M. Payot and J. Tairraz
	Alphubel	13,800 feet	L. Stephen, T. W. Hinchliff with M. Anderegg and P. Perren
1861	Weisshorn	14,780 feet	J. Tyndall with J. J. Bennen and U. Wenger
	Monte Rosa, Nordend	15,204 feet	T. F. and E. N. Buxton, J. J. Cowell with M. Payot
	Castor	13,866 feet	W. Mathews, F. W. Jacomb with Michel Croz
	Lyskamm	14,692 feet	J. F. Hardy, A. C. Ramsay, F. Sibson, T. Rennison, J. A. Hudson, W. E. Hall, C. H. Pilkington, R. M. Stephenson with J. P. Cachat, F. Lochmatter, K. Herr, S. Zumtaugwald, P. and J. Perren
	Schreckhorn	13,379 feet	L. Stephen with P. and C. Michel and C. Kaufmann

1862	Dent Blanche	14,295 feet	T. S. Kennedy, W. Wigram with J. B. Croz and J. Kronig
	Täschhorn	14,735 feet	J. L. Davies, J. W. Hayward, with J. and S. Zumtaugwald and P. J. Summermatter
	Gross Fiescherhorn	13,285 feet	H. B. George, A. W. Moore with Christian Almer and Ulrich Kaufmann
1863	Dent d'Hérens	13,685 feet	W. E. Hall, F. Crauford Grove, R. J. S. Macdonald, M. Woodmass with M. Anderegg, P. Perren and J. P. Cachat
1864	Les Ecrins	13,455 feet	E. Whymper, A. W. Moore, H. Walker, with C. Almer and M. Croz
	Zinal Rothorn	13,849 feet	L. Stephen, F. Crauford Grove, with M. and J. Anderegg
	Pollux	13,423 feet	J. Jacot with P. Taugwalder and J. M. Perren
1865	Grand Cornier	12,999 feet	E. Whymper with C. Almer, M. Croz and F. Biner
	Grandes Jorasses, Point Whymper	13,728 feet	E. Whymper, with M. Croz, C. Almer and F. Biner
	Aiguille Verte	13,524 feet	E. Whymper with C. Almer and F. Biner
	Matterhorn	14,689 feet	E. Whymper, C. Hudson, Lord Francis Douglas, D. R. Hadow with Michel Croz and the P. Taugwalders, father and son
	Aiguille de Bionnassey	13,295 feet	E. N. Buxton, F. Crauford Grove, R. J. S. Macdonald with J. P. Cachat and M. Payot
	Obergabelhorn	13,331 feet	A. W. Moore, H. Walker with Jakob Anderegg
	Grünhorn	13,265 feet	E. von Fellenberg with Peter Egger, Peter Inäbnit and Peter Michel
1867	Monte Rosa, Jägerhorn	13,026 feet	C. E. Mathews, F. Morshead with C. Almer and A. Maurer
	Gletscherhorn	13,068 feet	J. J. Hornby with Christian Lauener
1868	Grandes Jorasses, Point Walker	13,806 feet	H. Walker with M. Anderegg, J. Jaun and Julien Grange
	Ebnefluh	12,999 feet	T. L. Murray Browne with Peter Bohren and Peter Schlegel
1869	Hohberghorn	13,843 feet	R. B. Heathcote with F. Biner, P. Perren and (young) P. Taugwalder
1870	Lenzspitze	14,089 feet	C. T. Dent with A. and F. Burgener
1871	Mont Mallet	13,088 feet	L. Stephen, G. Loppé, F. A. Wallroth with M. Anderegg, J. Cachat and A. Tournier
1872	Combin de Valsorey	13,728 feet	J. H. Isler with J. Gillioz
1873	Aiguille de Rochefort	13,127 feet	J. Eccles with M. C. and A. Payot
	Monte Rosa, Schwarzhorn	14,177 feet	M. Maglioni, A. de Rotschild with P. and N. Knubel and E. Cupelin
1876	Les Droites	13,124 feet	H. Cordier, T. Middlemore, J. Oakley Maund, with J. Jaun and A. Maurer
1877	La Meije	13,068 feet	E. Boileau de Castelnau with Pierre Gaspard and son
	Mont Blanc de Courmayeur	15,578 feet	J. Eccles with M. C. and A. Payot. (First recorded, it is hard to believe that no Mont Blanc party had reached this point before)
	Piz Scerscen	13,016 feet	P. Güssfeldt with H. Grass and C. Capat
1878	Mont Maudit	14,650 feet	W. E. Davidson, H. S. Hoare with J. Jaun and J. von Bergen
1881	Dôme de Rochefort	13,173 feet	J. Eccles with M. C. and A. Payot
1882	Aiguille du Géant	13,150 feet	A., A., C. and G. Sella with J. J., B. and D. Maquinaz
		13,166 feet	W. Graham with A. Payot and A. Cupelin
1882	Calotte de Rochefort	13,044 feet	C. D. Cunningham with E. and J. Rey
1884	Bieshorn	13,622 feet	G. S. Barnes, R. Chessyre-Walker with J. Imboden and J. M. Chanton. (12 days earlier Mrs Burnaby, with J. Imboden and P. Sarbach, had climbed the eastern rock point)
1885	Aiguille Blanche de Peuterey	13,475 feet	H. Seymour King with E. Rey, A. Supersaxo and A. Anthamatten
1886	Ober Mominghorn	13,003 feet	H. Seymour King with A. Supersaxo and A. Anthamatten
1887	Stecknadelhorn	13,915 feet	O. Eckenstein with M. Zurbriggen
1901	Mt Blanc, Pic Luigi Amadeo	14,663 feet	G. B. and G. F. Gugliermina with J. Brocherel
1906	Mont Brouillard	13,350 feet	K. Blodig, O. Eckenstein with A. Brocherel

Appendix II
First Ascents of the Highest Mountains

This list is restricted to mountains over 24,000 feet (7315m.) for ease of handling. It does not imply that a mountain of this stature is a better mountain or a worthier objective than one less lofty. Since the first 24,000-er was not climbed until 1930, the list is preceded by a record of the five earlier ascents of mountains over 23,000 feet. Both lists are compiled from the fuller lists prepared by D. F. O. Dangar and published in the *Alpine Journal*. Mr Dangar has not only allowed me to make use of his work, but has kindly corrected all heights to the latest computations as given in G. O. Dyhrenfurth's *Verzeichnis aller bekannten Berge über 7300 Meter (23950 Fuss)*.

The first five ascents of mountains over 23,000 feet

1907	Trisul	23,360 feet	T. G. Longstaff, A. and H. Brocherel, Karbir
1911	Pauhunri	23,180 feet	A. M. Kellas, Sonam and another porter
1913	Kun	23,250 feet	L. Borelli, M. Piacenza, J. Gaspard, Ali Rahin and porter 'Carrel'
1928	Peak Lenin	23,383 feet	E. Allwein, E. Schneider, K. Wien
1930	Nepal Peak, S.W. summit	23,442 feet	E. Schneider

First ascents of mountains over 24,000 feet

1930	Jongsong Peak	24,518 feet	H. Hoerlin, E. Schneider
1931	Kamet	25,447 feet	R. L. Holdsworth, E. E. Shipton, F. S. Smythe, Lewa
1932	Minya Konka	24,892 feet	R. L. Burdsall, T. Moore
1933	Peak Communism (then Peak Stalin)	24,548 feet	E. M. Abalakov
1934	Sia Kangri	24,350 feet	H. Ertl, A. Hoecht
1935	Kabru II	24,076 feet	C. R. Cooke
1936	Nanda Devi	25,645 feet	N. E. Odell, H. W. Tilman
1939	Tent Peak	24,162 feet	E. Grob, H. Paidar, L. Schmaderer
	Nanda Devi East	24,391 feet	J. Bujak, M. J. Klarner
1950	Annapurna	26,545 feet	M. Herzog, L. Lachenal
	Tirich Mir	25,290 feet	P. Kvernberg (repeated next day by H. Berg, A. Naess, H. R. A. Streather)
	Abi Gamin	24,130 feet	G. Chevalley, R. Dittert, A. Tissières
1953	Mount Everest	29,028 feet	E. P. Hillary, Tenzing Norkay
	Nanga Parbat	26,660 feet	H. Buhl
1954	K2	28,253 feet	A. Compagnoni, L. Lacedelli
	Cho Oyu	26,750 feet	S. Joechler, H. Tichy, Pasang Dawa Lama
	Kangchungtse (Makalu II)	25,066 feet	J. Franco, L. Terray, Gyalzen, Pa Norbu
	Chomo Lönzo	25,558 feet	J. Couzy, L. Terray
1955	Makalu	27,825 feet	J. Couzy, L. Terray (repeated by the rest of the party on following two days)
	Kangchenjunga	28,208 feet	G. Band, J. Brown (N. Hardie, H. R. A. Streather repeated the ascent next day)
	Annapurna IV	24,688 feet	H. Biller, H. Steinmetz, J. Wellenkamp
	Ganesh Peak	24,299 feet	E. Gauchat, Mme C. Kogan, R. Lambert
1956	Manaslu	26,760 feet	T. Imanishi, Gyalzen (repeated next day by K. Kato, M. Higeta)
	Lhotse	27,923 feet	F. Luchsinger, E. Reiss
	Gasherbrum II	26,360 feet	S. Larch, F. Moravec, H. Willenpart
	Muztagh Ata	24,757 feet	Russo-Chinese expedition
	Qungur	24,920 feet	Russo-Chinese expedition
	Peak Pobeda	24,407 feet	V. Abalakov and ten others
1957	Broad Peak	26,400 feet	H. Buhl, K. Diemberger, M. Schmuck, F. Wintersteller
	Skil Brum	24,345 feet	M. Schmuck, F. Wintersteller
1958	Rakaposhi	25,550 feet	M. E. B. Banks, T. Patey
	Gasherbrum I	26,470 feet	A. J. Kaufmann, P. K. Schoening
	Chogolisa (N.E. peak)	25,066 feet	M. Fujihira, K. Hirai
	Haramosh	24,299 feet	F. Mandl, S. Pauer, H. Roiss
	Gasherbrum IV	26,000 feet	W. Bonatti, C. Mauri
1959	Kanjut Sar	25,460 feet	C. Pelissier
	Saraghrar	24,110 feet	F. Alletto, G. Castelli, P. Consiglio, B. Pinelli

Year	Peak	Height	Climbers
1960	Dhaulagiri	26,795 feet	K. Diemberger, P. Diener, E. Forrer, A. Schelbert, Nyima Dorji, Nawang Dorji (M. Vaucher and H. Weber made the ascent ten days later)
	Annapurna II	26,041 feet	C. J. S. Bonington, R. H. Grant
	Himal Chuli	25,895 feet	M. Harada, H. Tanabe (repeated next day by H. Miyashita, K. Nakazawa)
	Distaghil Sar	25,868 feet	D. Marchart, G. Staerker
	Masherbrum	25,660 feet	G. I. Bell, W. Unsoeld (repeated two days later by N. B. Clinch, R. J. Akhter)
	Trivor	25,328 feet	W. Noyce, J. Sadler
	Noshaq	24,581 feet	G. Iwatsabo, T. Sakai
1961	Annapurna III	24,787 feet	M. S. Kohli, S. Gyatso, Sonam Girmi
	Nuptse	25,850 feet	D. Davis, Tashi (repeated next day by C. J. S. Bonington, L. Brown, J. Swallow, Ang Pemba)
	Mount Ghent	24,280 feet	W. Axt
1962	Jannu	25,296 feet	R. Desmaison, P. Keller, R. Paragot, Gyaltsen Mikchung (repeated next day by seven others)
	Chamlang I	24,006 feet	S. Anma, Pasang Phutar III
	Saltoro Kangri	25,400 feet	R. Bashir, A. Saito, Y. Takamura
1963	Noshaq East	24,541 feet	G. Gruber, R. Pischinger
1964	Gyachung Kang	25,990 feet	Y. Kato, K. Sakaizawa, Pasang Phutar III
	Gosainthan (Shisha Pangma)	26,398 feet	Hsu Ching and nine others
	Talung Peak	24,112 feet	F. Lindner, Tenzing Nindra
	Momhil Sar	24,090 feet	R. Pischinger, H. Schell, H. Schindlbacher, L. Schlommer, R. Widerhofer
	Tirich Mir East	25,233 feet	R. Hoibakk, A. Opdal
1965	Ngojumba Ri II	25,086 feet	N. Uemara, Pemba Tenzing
	Gangapurna	24,457 feet	L. Greissl, G. Hauser, H. Köllensperg, E. Reissmüller, Ang Temba, Phu Dorje
	Pt. 7532m. (between White Wave and Kangbachen)	24,712 feet	L. Juvan, M. Humar, Girmi Dorje, Holung Dorje
1967	Tirich West I	24,564 feet	J. Cervinka, I. Galfy, V. Smida, I. Urbanovic
	Tirich West IV	24,075 feet	K. Diemberger, D. Proske
	Istor-o-nal	24,290 feet	J. M. Anglada, J. Cerda, E. Civis, J. Pons
	Roc Noir (Annapurna)	24,556 feet	R. Obster, P. Schubert, K. Winkler
1970	Peak 29 (Dakura)	25,705 feet	H. Watanabe, Lhapka Tsering
	Lhotse Shar	27,553 feet	S. Mayerl, R. Walter
	Churen Himal	24,184 feet	Claimed by a Korean party in April, but claim disputed by Japanese party that climbed both N.E. and S.W. peaks in October
1971	Khinyang Chhish	25,761 feet	A. Heinrich, J. Stryczynski, R. Szafirski, A. M. Zawada
	Dhaulagiri II	25,430 feet	R. Fear, A. Huber, A. Weissensteiner, Jangbu
	Malubiting West	24,451 feet	H. Schell and others
1973	Kangchenjunga West Peak (Yalung Kang)	27,668 feet	Y. Ageta, T. Matusuda
	Dhaulagiri III	25,312 feet	A German expedition

There is no objective standard by which to determine when a subsidiary summit should count as a peak in its own right. For instance, in 1971 a Czech expedition was on Nanga Parbat; J. Psotka, A. Puškaš and I. Urbanovic climbed the Vorgipfel (25,952 feet) and the S.E. peak (24,709 feet). These should perhaps be in the list above. If these two first ascents go in, should we include Evans and Bourdillon on the South Summit of Everest in 1953? A further classificatory problem is also illustrated by this same Czech expedition: I. Fiala and M. Orolin reached the summit of Nanga Parbat, was this the fourth or fifth ascent? This depends on whether you count each rope reaching the summit as a separate ascent or only each expedition. Two pairs of Germans climbed the mountain on consecutive days; was this one ascent by an expedition or were these two ascents by different ropes?

Notes

The *Alpine Journal* is abbreviated to *AJ*

1 Darkness to Dawn

1 Scholars dispute about Hannibal's pass: see, for example, Sir Gavin de Beer, *Alps and Elephants* (London, 1955); A. H. McDonald, 'Hannibal's Passage of the Alps', *AJ* LXI.93; J. Hoyte, *Trunk Road for Hannibal* (London, 1960); and A. R. Jolly, 'Hannibal's Pass', *AJ* LXVII.243.

2 London, 1860.

3 Note by Dr H. Dubi in G. Studer, *Uber Eis und Schnee*, 2nd ed. (Berne, 1896).

4 Thomas Blaikie, *Dairy of a Scotch Gardener at the French Court at the End of the Eighteenth Century*, ed. by Francis Birrell (London, 1931). See also Montagnier, *AJ* XLV.1.

5 Gersdorff's journal is given, both in the original German and in English, in T. Graham Brown and Sir Gavin de Beer, *The First Ascent of Mont Blanc* (London, 1957). This admirable and closely reasoned work is the result of much scholarship and research, and is fully documented.

6 Notably D. W. Freshfield, *AJ* XIX.341; Dr H. Dubi, *Paccard wider Balmat* (Berne, 1913); E. H. Stevens, *AJ* XLI, XLII, XLVI, XLVII and XLIX; C.-E. Engel, *A History of Mountaineering in the Alps* (London, 1950). The story is first correctly told in Mlle Engel's book but the complete demolition of the Bourrit-Balmat inventions was only finally achieved by *The First Ascent of Mont Blanc* seven years later, in which all the evidence is given.

2 Exploration of the Alps

1 Da Spescha's first ascents include Stockgron (11,214 feet), Rheinwaldhorn (11,149 feet), Oberalpstock (10,926 feet), Piz Uralun (11,060 feet), Piz Aul (10,250 feet), Piz Scharboden (10,250 feet), Piz Terri (10,338 feet) and Güferhorn (11,132 feet). He seems to have been curiously timid of glaciers, rarely setting foot on one. His ancient monastery at Disentis, believed to have been founded in 614, was burnt by the French general as a reprisal for the resistance of the local people; all its ancient and valuable archives, including da Spescha's own manuscripts, perished.

2 The summit may have been reached by the 1799 expedition, which certainly climbed the Klein Glockner. There is a painting of Salm's first expedition in the Landesmuseum für Kärnten in Klagenfurt. This was restored at the expense of Dr Monroe Thorington in 1964.

3 The chronology is:

Year	Peak	Height	Climbers
1788	Rock of Discovery	14,325 feet	Seven men of Gressoney
1801	Punta Giordani	13,275 feet	Pietro Giordani of Alagna
1817	Parrotspitze	14,643 feet	E. Parrot (Germany)
1819	Vincent Pyramide	13,829 feet	J. N. Vincent of Gressoney
1820	Zumsteinspitze	14,971 feet	J. N. and Joseph Vincent and J. Zumstein, all of Gressoney (a Vincent and a Zumstein were among the seven of 1778)
1822	Ludwigshöhe	14,243 feet	Ludwig von Welden (Austria)
1842	Signalkuppe	14,948 feet	Giovanni Gnifetti of Alagna
1847	First attack from the Swiss side by two Frenchmen, MM. Ordinaire and Puiseux. They reached the Silbersattel		
1848	Grenzgipfel	15,079 feet	Melchior Ulrich's guides (repeated 1851 by the Schlagintweit brothers)
1854	Ostspitze	15,197 feet	Smyth brothers; Christopher, James Grenville and Edmund
1855	Dufourspitze	15,230 feet	C. Smyth, J. G. Smyth, E. J. Stephenson, C. Hudson and J. Birkbeck
1861	Nordend	15,122 feet	T. F. and E. N. Buxton, J. J. Cowell with M. Payot

4 Doubt has been cast on this ascent. Both Coolidge (*The Alps in Nature and History*, London, 1908) and R. L. G. Irving (*The Romance of Mountaineering*, London, 1935) agree that there is no reasonable doubt that they climbed the Jungfrau, but Mlle C.-E. Engel (*History of Mountaineering in the Alps*) thinks that the peak gained was probably the Gletscherhorn.

5 Edinburgh, 1844.

6 J. D. Forbes, *Tour of Mont Blanc* (London, 1855).

7 Albert Richard Smith (1816–60) was the son of a country doctor and a qualified MRCS himself, practising with his father at Chertsey for nearly three years. He abandoned medicine to live by his pen and showmanship. He fell under the fascination of Mont Blanc as a child, but did not attempt to climb the mountain until 1851. The party consisted of Smith, three Oxford undergraduates—the Hon. W. E. Sackville West, C. G. Floyd and F. Philips—an Irishman, G. N. Vansittart, and a small army of guides. (Each traveller had to have four guides.) The Irishman gave up on the Corridor. Smith was in not much better shape; at the foot of the Mur de la Côte he faltered, but the guides urged him on. He was in no sort of training but his own efforts and the guides' traction landed him on the summit where he at once fell asleep. He climbed no other mountain. C. E. Mathews includes a sympathetic chapter on Smith in his *Annals of Mont Blanc* (London, 1898).

8 These figures are given in Graham Brown and de Beer (see Chapter 1, n. 5). The separation of Savoyards is due to the fact that Savoy only became incorporated in France in 1860 as part of the price exacted from the House of Savoy for Louis Napoleon's temporary assistance against Austria.

9 The Golden Age is often said to begin with Alfred Wills's ascent of the Mittelhorn peak of the Wetterhorn in 1854, supposed to be first 'sporting' ascent for fun only with no scientific or other ulterior motive. There had, however, been a great many earlier climbs which equally deserved this description. His guides led Wills to believe that his was a first ascent and many subsequent writers have fallen under the same delusion. But apart from his agreeable account of the trip, this particular climb has little historical importance. (I happen to have hit on the same year as the beginning of the Golden Age, but for a different reason.) Similarly there has been a tendency to close this epoch with the Matterhorn climb and disaster in 1865. I can find no logical justification for this either; there were still plenty of unclimbed peaks left in the Alps at that date.

3 The Golden Age

1 The first ascent of Mont Blanc du Tacul may have been made a week earlier by Sir J. Ramsay's party. See T. S. Blakeney's discussion, *AJ* LXXI.131.

2 The Bosses route was first taken by Leslie Stephen and F. F. Tuckett with Melchior Anderegg, Bennen and Peter Perren in 1861. The Bosses arête itself, from the Col du Dôme to the summit, had been traversed by Marie Couttet, called Moutelet, about 1840.

3 Leslie Stephen, *The Playground of Europe* (London, 1871).

4 John Tyndall, *Hours of Exercise in the Alps* (London, 1871).

5 Edward Whymper (1840–1911) has become the archetypal mountaineer in public opinion, largely through the long siege of, and tragic victory on, the Matterhorn and the evergreen popularity of his *Scrambles Amongst the Alps* (London, 1871). His father was in business as a wood-engraver and Edward, without enthusiasm, entered the business after leaving school early. Nevertheless, when he succeeded to the business, he carried it on with characteristic resolution and success until it was killed by cheaper photographic processes. It was through his early engravings that he first came to the mountains, in 1860. He made an extensive general tour, doing much wandering over glaciers and passes, often alone, discovering the theatre for his life. He returned in each of the next three years, climbing Pelvoux and making his first six attempts on the Matterhorn, but 1864 and 1865 were his great years. They included the first ascents of Mont Dolent (1864), the lower, western, peak of the Grandes Jorasses and the Aiguille Verte (1865). He was a lonely man, and the Matterhorn accident, or rather the inquiries, controversy and criticism which followed the accident, exaggerated his solitude; he was bitterly reluctant to explain and justify to the ignorant, yet he could never avoid the need to do so. See Mumm's *Alpine Register*, Vol. 1; C.-E. Engel, *They Came to the Hills* (London, 1952) and Frank Smythe, *Edward Whymper* (London, 1952).

6 J. P. Farrar, *AJ* XXXII, reprinted in the appendices to Tyndale's edition of *Scrambles* (London, 1936).

7 Edward Whymper, *Scrambles Amongst the Alps*.

8 A. W. Moore, *The Alps in 1864*, privately printed in 1867, but more easily available in E. H. Stevens's edition (Oxford, 1939). I quote Stevens's note to this chapter: 'This chapter, which was added by Moore as an appendix to his 1864 Journal, is a reprint of the paper he read to the Alpine Club on March 6th, 1866. This accounts for one or two references to his audience. A great judge (the late Capt. Farrar) wrote of it, "There are few alpine narratives to compare to this. For accuracy of observation, topographical clearness, and general interest it is almost unrivalled".'

9 W. A. B. Coolidge (1850–1926) was born in New York of an old American family. After a childhood illness, he was sent to Europe, accompanied by his aunt, Miss Meta Brevoort. His aunt fell under the spell of mountains and soon took the boy to the Alps. He never returned to America and after twelve years as a don at Oxford he settled in Grindelwald and devoted the rest of his life to the Alps. He was an indefatigable alpinist; no rock climber but what he lacked in agility he made up in resolution, stamina and the choice of good guides. His entry in Mumm's *Alpine Register* occupies 25 pages (he made 1,700 expeditions) and was obviously supplied to Mumm by Coolidge himself. Notable as was Coolidge's contribution to the exploration and climbing of the Alps, he is chiefly remembered as their historian and as a pioneer of winter mountaineering. His main works are *Swiss Travel and Swiss Guide Books* (1899), *Josias Simler et les Origines de l'Alpinisme* (1904), *The Alps in Nature and History* (1908), *Alpine Studies* (1912), but these are a tiny part of his multilingual output. He was editor of the *Alpine Journal* from 1880 to 1889, he edited Murray's *Handbook to Switzerland*, Ball's *Guide to the Western Alps* and countless other editions; he contributed largely to the Encyclopaedia Britannica and the Dictionnaire Geographique de la Suisse. He was, of course, joint author of the Conway and Coolidge *Climbers' Guides*. His contributions to British, Swiss and Italian mountaineering periodicals were countless. He was at least as cantankerous as he was learned; his quarrels would make as long a list as his alpine expeditions. See Mumm's *Alpine Register*, Vol. II, Sir Arnold Lunn, *A Century of Mountaineering* (London, 1957), C.-E. Engel, *They Came to the Hills*.

10 Translated from *Annuaire du Club Alpin Français*, 1877.

11 C.-E. Engel, *They Came to the Hills*.

12 Mlle Engel says he never climbed again, and no subsequent climb seems to be recorded but the *Bulletin* of the Club Alpin Français for 1879 mentions Boileau as one of the most active climbers of the year without particularising his activities.

4 High Summer

1 The text follows Professor Graham Brown's expert reconstruction in *AJ* LII and LIII.

2 Henri Cordier was a brilliant young French climber. In his third season, 1876, he made several first ascents and new routes, including Les Courtes and Les Droites with T. Middlemore and J. Oakley Maund. He was friend of Boileau de Castelnau. In 1877 he made the first ascent of Le Plaret and was killed on the descent; he was 21. Georg Winkler made a number of sensational climbs in the eastern Alps and the Dolomites, including the Winklerturm, the hardest of the Vajolet Towers. He made all his climbs solo; he compensated for his small stature (he was less than five foot tall) by using a grapnel *à la* Whymper. He disappeared seeking a new route on the Weisshorn in 1888; he was 19.

3 Cascades of stones falling down the couloir from Col Emile Rey prevented any ascent of the col from the Bouillard side until 1899, when it was achieved by the Gugliermina brothers. The first ascent of Mont Blanc by this route had to wait until 1933, when it was accomplished by V. Bressoud, R. Dittert, W. Marquart and F. Marullaz. The classic route to Mont Blanc over the Brouillard ridge reaches Col Emile Rey from the other side and is less dangerous; it was first taken by G. W. Young, K. Blodig and H. O. Jones with Joseph Knubel in 1911.

4 This is the figure given by L. Devies and J. Lagarde in the Vallot Guide. Graham Brown gives four repetitions, including two climbs by variations which Devies and Lagarde classify as separate routes.

5 London, 1895.

6 *Ibid.*

7 *AJ*, XI.72.

8 Trans. by H. E. G. Tyndale (London, 1934).

9 *Ibid.*

10 Geoffrey Winthrop Young, *On High Hills*, London, 1927.

5 The Alps Between the Wars

1 *AJ*, XXXV.

2 *Guide des Alpes Valaisannes*, Club Alpin Suisse.

3 Jacques and Tom de Lépiney, *Climbs on Mont Blanc*, trans. by Sydney Spencer (London, 1930).

4 Heinrich Harrer, *The White Spider* (London, 1959); Heckmair, Vorg, Kasparek and Harrer, *Um die Eiger Nordwand* (Munich, 1938). The latter had been taken over by Nazi press control and turned into propaganda; the publication ends, alas, with these stirring words: 'We were very proud. We had climbed the Eigerwand, over the summit to our Führer.' One hopes, with some assurance, that these words were not produced by the four climbers. Vorg was killed on the Russian front and Kasparek fell on Salcantay in 1954. Harrer is still active, having recently done some successful climbing and exploration in the Carstenz mountains of New Guinea.

5 In his book Harrer only counts 13 ascents in these 20 years. It is reasonable to add Uly Weiss and Heinz Gonda, who fell after climbing the wall but before reaching the summit of the mountain. When Harrer wrote his book nothing was known of the fate of Nothdurft and Mayer in 1957; in 1961 their bodies were found near the normal way down on the north-west flank mountain, so they must have completed the ascent of the wall before their accident.

6 *AJ*, LXVIII.

7 Giusto Gervasutti, *Scalate nelle Alpi*, 1947, trans. by Nea Morin and Janet Adam Smith as *Gervasutti's Climbs* (London, 1957).

8 Edouard Frendo, *La Face Nord des Grandes Jorasses* (Lausanne, 1946).

6 Further Afield

1 It is possible that Elbruz was ascended in 1829 by a Circassian, Killar Haschirow, but there is little evidence. See, e.g. *AJ*, LIX.460, LXXI.312 and LXXVIII.265.
2 Tom Longstaff, *This My Voyage* (London, 1950).
3 Vallepiana's party was: L. Gasporotto, R. Herren and R. Singer.
4 The four young men were: R. L. Beaumont, R. A. Hodgkin, J. R. Jenkins and M. S. Taylor.
5 Conrad Kain, *Where the Clouds can Go*, edited and with additional chapters by J. Monroe Thorington (Boston, 1954). (There is an earlier edition, hard to come by.)
6 The party was: Hudson Stuck, Harry Karstens, Robert Tatum, Walter Harper and two Indians, Johnny and Elias.
7 Whymper could not have made this mistake, it must be due to the reporter. The Carrels were Italian and the Val Tournanche is in Italy.
8 *AJ* XLV.
9 See W. S. Green, *The High Alps of New Zealand* (London, 1883).
10 Freda du Faur, *The Conquest of Mount Cook* (London, 1915).
11 Eric Shipton, *Upon that Mountain* (London, 1943).

7 Himalaya to 1939

1 Oscar Eckenstein (1859–1921) is a name that crops up in the Alps, the Himalaya, North Wales and in the development of technique. Although he contributed to the *Climbers' Club Journal* and wrote a rather dull book about the Conway Karakoram expedition, his career remains shadowy. His father was a German who, after the failure of the 1848 revolution, deemed it prudent to retire to England, where he married an Englishwoman. A railway engineer by profession, Eckenstein applied his mechanical knowledge to the problems of climbing technique. It was he who developed the principles of 'balance climbing', as Young testified when he expounded this technique in *Mountain Craft* (London, 1920). He was converted to crampons by his companion, A. Lorria, and went on to design a pair that was still the best when *Mountain Craft* was published. He also designed an ice-axe, much shorter than those then in use and with a much smaller head so that it could be effectively plied with one hand. He was thus a forerunner of much modern development.
2 Tom Longstaff, *This My Voyage*.
3 A. E. Crowley, Guy Knowles (British), H. Pfannl and W. Wessely (Austrian) and Dr Jacot-Guillarmod (Swiss).
4 G. L. Mallory in C. K. Howard-Bury, *Mount Everest: the Reconnaissance* (London, 1922).
5 Bauer's party was: E. Allwein, Peter Aufschnaiter, E. Beigel, J. Brenner, W. Fendt, K. von Kraus, J. Leupold and A. Thoenes.
6 Dyhrenfurth's party was: Professor and Mrs Dyhrenfurth, H. Richter, U. Wieland, H. Hoerlin (German); F. S. Smythe, G. Wood-Johnson, J. S. Hannah (British); Marcel Kurz, C. Duvanel (Swiss); and E. Schneider (Austrian).
7 This time Bauer took: Allwein, Aufschnaiter, Brenner, Fendt and Leupold as before, plus H. Hartmann, H. Pircher, H. Schaller and Karl Wien.
8 Smythe's group was: Wing-Commander E. B. Beauman, R. Holdsworth, Raymond Greene, Eric Shipton and Captain E.StJ. Birnie.
9 F. S. Smythe, *Kamet Conquered* (London, 1932).
10 Merkl's party was: Peter Aschenbrenner, Fritz Bechtold, Hugo Hamberger, H. Kunigk, F. Simon, F. Wiessner and the American, Rand Herron.
11 The 1933 Everest party were: Smythe, Shipton, Greene and Birnie, all of the successful Kamet team, E. O. Shebbeare, C. G. Crawford, J. E. H. Boustead, G. Wood-Johnson, P. Wyn Harris, L. R. Wager, J. L. Longland, T. A. Brocklebank and W. Maclean.
12 Merkl's 1934 party were: Aschenbrenner and Bechtold again, Wieland and Schneider of the 1930 Kangchenjunga expedition,

plus A. Drexel, W. Welzenbach, P. Mulritter, W. Bernard and a survey team of three.
13 Kenneth Mason, *Abode of Snow* (London, 1955).
14 Eric Shipton, *Upon that Mountain* (London, 1943).
15 In 1936 Ruttledge had with him: Smythe, Shipton, Kempson, Warren, Wigram, Wyn Harris and two newcomers, R. R. Oliver and J. M. L. Garvin, C. J. Morris was Transport Officer, the doctor was G. Noel Humphreys and W. R. Smijth-Windham was in charge of radio communications.
16 H. W. Tilman, *The Ascent of Nanda Devi* (London, 1937).
17 See Chapter 9 for an account of the Chinese expedition in 1960, which claimed to have climbed the mountain via the North Col and the north-east ridge.
18 This account, in Shipton's words, is included in H. W. Tilman, *Everest 1938* (Cambridge, 1948).
19 Houston's team was: R. H. Bates, R. Burdsall (who had climbed Minya Konka), W. P. House, P. Petzoldt, Captain N. R. Streatfield (the only British member) and six Sherpas.
20 Wiessner's five climbers were: C. Cranmer, D. Wolfe, E. Cromwell, G. Sheldon and J. Durrance.
21 For an analysis of the expedition see *Himalayan Journal*, 1940, and *American Alpine Journal*, 1940.
22 The party of four was: Aufschnaiter himself, Heinrich Harrer, L. Chicken, H. Lobenhoffer.
23 Heinrich Harrer, *Seven Years in Tibet* (London, 1953).
24 F. S. Smythe, *Kamet Conquered*.
25 Appendix to H. Ruttledge, *Everest 1933* (London, 1934).

8 Europe since 1945

1 Sir Charles Evans, D.Sc., FRCS. Valedictory address as President of the Alpine Club, *AJ* LXXVI.7.
2 It was much the same in Germany and Austria. Andreas Heckmair (of the Eigerwand first ascent) writes: 'In those early days of the 30s, many people had more than enough free time. In Germany there was mass unemployment. Instead of waiting for unemployment benefit, these men went into the mountains, earned enough for the basic essentials in the huts by cutting wood, and undertook such extremely difficult routes in the surrounding mountains that they soon belonged to the ranks of the finest alpinists.' *AJ* LXXIV.49.
3 Walter Bonatti, *On the Heights*, trans. by L. F. Edwards (London, 1964).
4 C. J. S. Bonington, *AJ* LXVII.111.
5 *Très difficile supérieur*, literally, hard very difficult, roughly equivalent to severe in guide books to British rocks. The French classification is based on that originally put forward by Willo Welzenbach.
6 Peter Gillman, *AJ* LXXI.256.
7 *AJ* LXXII.291.

9 Since the War, mostly America

1 M. A. Azéma, *The Conquest of Fitzroy* (London, 1957).
2 Guy Poulet, *AJ* LX (translation).
3 *AJ* Vol. LX.
4 Lionel Terray, *La Montagne et Alpinisme*, April 1957 (translation).
5 G. Magnone, L. Dubost, P. Gendreand, J. Soubis.
6 H. Carslake, S. Clark, C. Darbyshire, M. Gravina, J. H. Longland, K. Meldrum, R. Wathen.
7 It must, however, be recorded that doubts have been expressed as to whether Maestri reached the top; see, e.g. *American Alpine Journal* 1973 and *Mountain*, September 1972.
8 According to the 1970 New Zealand expedition, the mountain climbed by Shipton's party, although the highest in Tierra del Fuego, was not the actual Mount Darwin.
9 Don Whillans, *AJ* LXVII.
10 Chris Jones, *AJ* LXXIV.
11 Fosco Maraini, *AJ* LXVIII.
12 Dave Roberts, *AJ* LXXI.
13 F. S. Smythe, *AJ* LVI.
14 Yvon Chouinard, *AJ* LXXI.
15 Chris Jones, *AJ* LXXV.
16 Shih Chan-Chun, *AJ* LXVI.

17 The Chinese claim to have reached the highest point is challenged in the January 1973 issue of the *Bergsteiger*.

18 I. G. McNaught-Davis, *AJ*, LXVIII.

19 Malcolm Slesser's book, *Red Peak* (London, 1964) gives a good insight into Soviet climbing.

10 Himalaya, Post-War

1 Maurice Herzog, *AJ* LVIII.

2 See, for example, Michael Ward, *In this Short Span* (London, 1972), p. 125. Hunt discusses his plan on pp. 138-9 of *The Ascent of Everest* (London, 1953), but the logic still seems unclear. After conceding that the weather might not last long enough for a second attempt, he only allows a higher camp for the second attempt. He intended to follow the advice of Norton and Longstaff to put a camp at about 28,000 feet, but not for the first attempt which was the only one the weather might allow.

3 John Hunt, *The Ascent of Everest*.

4 Hermann Buhl, *Nanga Parbat Pilgrimage* (London, 1956).

5 H. R. A. Streather, *AJ* LIX.

6 They were Franco, Magnone, Bouvier, Leroux, Coupe and Vialatte.

7 George Band, *AJ* LX.

8 J. M. Hartog, *AJ* LXI.

9 Wilfred Noyce, *They Survived* (London, 1962).

10 Michael Ward, *AJ* LXVI.

11 The summit was reached by R. Desmaison, R. Paragot, P. Keller, Gyalzen, J. Bouvier, P. Leroux, A. Bertrand, Y. Pollet-Villard, L. Terray, J. Ravier and Wongdi. The last-named went to the summit without oxygen, although Terray insisted that he carry his apparatus and a full bottle with him. M. Lenoir was detained at Camp II on doctor's orders.
The successful party was the same as in 1959 except that Jean Franco and Guido Magnone had dropped out for personal reasons, and Keller, Pollet-Villard, Bertrand and Ravier had been added. The French claimed that Jannu was technically the hardest Himalayan summit climbed to that date.
In comparing it with, say, Ama Dablam, it must be remembered that Jannu is nearly 3000 feet higher but also how much greater were the human and material resources used on Jannu.

12 Norman Dyhrenfurth, *AJ* LXIX.

13 The party was: Bonington, Whillans, Martin Boysen, Mick Burke, Nick Estcourt, Tim Frost, Haston, Dave Lambert, Kelvin Kent, Ian Clough and Mike Thompson.

14 Dougal Haston, *In High Places* (London, 1972).

15 The party consisted of Bonington, J. O. M. Roberts, M. Burke, N. Estcourt, D. Haston, K. Kent, H. MacInnes, D. Scott, G. Tiso, D. Bathgate and B. Rosendale.

16 Dougal Haston, included in C. J. S. Bonington, *Everest South West Face* (London, 1973).

11 The One and the Many

1 *AJ* LXXVII.98.

2 This article first appeared in *Ascent*, the journal of the Sierra Club in May 1967.

3 Discussed in *AJ* LXXVIII.168.

List of Plates

Acknowledgements

The author's grateful thanks are due to the many who have helped him and particularly to D. F. O. Dangar, who has always given him the benefit of his unrivalled erudition, and to Douglas Milner, Ian McMorrin, Nea Morin and Charles Warren.

The author and publishers are indebted to the following individuals, libraries, museums, archives and organisations for permission to reproduce illustrations: by courtesy of the India Office Library and Records, jacket illustration, 123 top; Radio Times Hulton Picture Library, title page, 12 top, 24 left, 25 top, 30 bottom, 33, 39 bottom right, 59, 96 bottom, 98, 99; by courtesy of the Alpine Club Library, 6, 9, 12 bottom, 13 bottom, 14 top, 15 top, 16, 18 top and bottom, 21 top and bottom, 22 left and right, 23 right, 25 bottom, 29 bottom, 35 top and bottom, 36, 41, 65 bottom left and right, 90, 91, 96 top, 101; photo John Cleare, 8, 31, 38 right, 50-51, 54 top right, 67, 68, 71 top, 72, 77, 87, 134-135, 180, 194, 206-207, 208 top and bottom, 214, 221, 222, 223, 224, 229 left and right, 231; Royal Library, Windsor by gracious permission of Her Majesty the Queen, 10; Swiss National Tourist Office, 11 top and bottom, 14 bottom, 19 top, 23 left, 26, 28, 29 top, 32, 34, 38 top 'eft, right centre, bottom left, 40, 64 left, 65 top, 81; photo Jean Feuillie, 13 top, 57, 58, 69, 131 top; photo C. Douglas Milner, 15 centre, 54 top left, 56, 60 bottom, 71 bottom, 75; the Trustees of the British Museum, 15 bottom, 53 top and bottom; John Hillelson Agency photo George Gerster, 17 top left; Laing Art Gallery and Museum, 17 top right; the Tate Gallery, London, 17 bottom; Spectrum, 19 bottom, 133 bottom left and right, 205 bottom right; Popperfoto, 20, 27, 42, 45, 105, 115, 138, 139, 148 top, 153, 178, 181; photo Bradford Washburn, 23 top, 48, 78-79, 85, 95 top, 170-171, 172; Aldus Archives, from the *Roof of the World* published by Aldus Books, London, 1971, 24 right, 30 top, 52, 123 bottom; Picturepoint, 54 bottom, 133 top; the Alpine Journal, 60 top, 61, 70, 93, 155, 156, 163, 165, 167 top, 173, 174 bottom, 187; Bibliothèque Publique et Universitaire, Geneva, 63 left; Barnaby's Picture Library, 66, 131 below, 190; photo Leo Dickinson, 83, 136 top, 141, 161 top and bottom, 162, 166, 167 bottom; Royal Geographical Society, 88 top, 100 bottom, 104, 108, 109 top and bottom, 110 top and bottom, 111 top and bottom, 112, 113 top and bottom, 114 bottom, 116, 121 right, 125 bottom, 127 bottom, 128, 129, 196 top left, right and bottom, 197, 202, 204; photo G. C. Band, 88 bottom; photo V. Heckel, 89; photo Austin S. Post, 92, 176-177; Istituto Photographia Alpina V. Sella, 94; by courtesy of the Alaska Historical Society Library, 95 bottom; Brown Bros., Stirling, Pa., 97; by courtesy of the New Zealand High Commission, London, 100 top; photo Len Holland, 102; photo H. A. Cockburn, 103; Susan Griggs Agency, 106, 145 top left and right, bottom left and right; Archiv Deutsche Himalaya Stiftung, Munich, 114, 121 left; Ullstein GMBH/Bilderdienst, 119, 127 top; by courtesy of Captain John Noel, 124 top and bottom; photo Eric Shipton, 125 top, 159 bottom; photo R. Grandison, 132; photo Chris Bonington, 136 bottom left and right, 143 top and bottom, 147, 149 top, 164 top and bottom; photo Gaston Rebuffat, 140; Central Press, 142, 148 bottom, 149 bottom, 150 top and bottom, 151; photo Alfred Gregory, 157; Camera Press, 158 top and bottom, 159 top, 184, 185, 186, 188, 217 top and bottom; photo Tony Smythe, 174; Robert Harding Associates, 179; photo Warren Harding, 182, Keystone, 212; N.Z. Aerial Mapping, 189 top; N.Z. Herald, 189 bottom; Paris-Match/photo Ichac, 193; Deutsches Institut fur Auslandsforschung, Munich, 199; photo Fosco Maraini, 201; photo Ardito Desio, 203; David Moore/Colorific, 205 top; by courtesy of the National Art Gallery, New Zealand, 205 bottom left; photo H. W. Tilman, 209; Fédération Française de la Montagne, 211; photo Norman Dyhrenfurth 218-219; photo Tom Frost, 222; Mary Evans Picture Library, 238. The maps have been drawn by Harold Bartram.

The author and publishers would also like to acknowledge permission to reprint copyright material from the following books and journals:

M. A. Azéma, *The Conquest of Fitzroy*, London: André Deutsch, 1957

Walter Bonatti, *On the Heights*, trans. L. F. Edwards, London: Rupert Hart-Davis, 1964

Hermann Buhl, *Nanga Parbat Pilgrimage*, London: Hodder & Stoughton; *Lonely Challenge*, New York: Dutton, 1956.

Giusto Gervasutti, *Gervasutti's Climbs*, trans. by Nea Morin and Janet Adam-Smith, London: Rupert Hart-Davis, 1957

T. Graham Brown and Gavin de Beer, *The First Ascent of Mont Blanc*, London: Oxford University Press, 1957

Dougal Haston, *In High Places*, London, 1972

John Hunt, *The Ascent of Everest*, London: Hodder & Stoughton, 1953, *The Conquest of Everest*, New York: Dutton, 1953.

Conrad Kain, *Where the Clouds Can Go*, Boston, Mass.: Charles T. Branford, 1954

Julius Kugy, *Alpine Pilgrimage*, London: John Murray, 1934

Jacques and Tom de Lépiney, *Climbs on Mont Blanc*, London: Edward Arnold, 1936

Tom Longstaff, *This My Voyage*, London: John Murray; New York: Scribner, 1950

Kenneth Mason, *The Abode of Snow*, London: Rupert Hart-Davis; New York: Dutton, 1955

Wilfred Noyce, *They Survived*, London: Heinemann, 1962

Lito Tejada-Flores, *Ascent*, May 1967

Lionel Terray, *La Montagne and Alpinisme*, April 1957

Eric Shipton, *Upon That Mountain*, London: Hodder & Stoughton, 1943

F. S. Smythe, *Kamet Conquered*, London: Gollancz, 1932

H. W. Tilman, *The Ascent of Nanda Devi*, London: Cambridge University Press 1937; New York: Macmillan, 1939

H. W. Tilman, *Mount Everest, 1938*, London: Cambridge University Press; New York: Macmillan, 1948

Geoffrey Winthrop Young, *On High Hills*, London: Methuen, 1927

And from the following articles in the *Alpine Journal*:

George Band, Vol 60
C. J. S. Bonington, Vol 67
Philip Borchers, Vol 45
Yvon Chouinard, Vol 71
Ian Clough, Vol 68
Norman Dyhrenfurth, Vol 69
G. I. Finch, Vol 35
Kevin Fitzgerald, Vol 77
Peter Gillman, Vol 71
John Hartog, Vol 61
Maurice Herzog, Vol 58
Chris Jones, Vol 74
Chris Jones, Vol 75
I. G. McNaught-Davis, Vol 68
Fosco Maraini, Vol 68
Guy Poulet, Vol 60
Dave Roberts, Vol 71
Alessandro Sella, Vol 11
Shih Chan-Chun, Vol 68
F. S. Smythe, Vol 56
H. R. A. Streather, Vol 59
Michael Ward, Vol 66
Don Whillans, Vol 67

A Select Bibliography

Journals

The *Alpine Journal* (annually, formerly twice a year)
The *Himalayan Journal* (annually)
The *American Alpine Journal* (annually)
The *Canadian Alpine Journal* (annually)
The *New Zealand Alpine Journal* (annually)
Alpinisme, now *La Montagne et Alpinisme* (five times a year)
Les Alpes/Die Alpen (quarterly)
Rivista Mensile (monthly)
Osterreichische Alpenzeitung (monthly)
Mitteilungen des Deutschen Alpenverein (six times a year)
Alpinismus (C., monthly)
Mountain (C., ten times a year)
Berge der Welt (annually 1946–67; English version,
The Mountain World, 1953–67)
All the above are Club productions, except those marked C.,
which are commercial ventures, and *Berge der Welt*, which
was produced by the Swiss Federation for Alpine Research.

Books

General
1920 G. W. Young, *Mountain Craft*, London (4th rev. ed.,
1945)
1935 Dorothy Pilley, *Climbing Days*, London and New York
1940 W. Welzenbach, *Ascensions*, Paris
1943 Arnold Lunn, *Mountain Jubilee*, London and Toronto
Scott Russell, *Mountain Prospect*, New York
(London, 1946)
Eric Shipton, *Upon that Mountain*, London
1946 L. S. Amery, *In the Rain and Sun*, London
H. W. Tilman, *When Men and Mountains Meet*,
Cambridge (New York, 1947)
1950 Tom Longstaff, *This my Voyage*, London and New York
1954 Conrad Kain, *Where the Clouds Can Go*, Boston and
London (limited ed., 1934)
1956 *Les Alpinistes Célèbres*, Paris
Charles Evans, *On Climbing*, London and Woodstock,
Vermont
Miriam Underhill, *Give Me the Hills*, London and
Toronto
1957 Arnold Lunn, *A Century of Mountaineering*, London
(New York, 1958)
1959 Arnold Lunn, *And Yet So New*, New York
1963 Lionel Terray, *Conquistadores of the Useless*, Paris and
London (*Borders of the Impossible*, New York, 1964)
1964 Walter Bonatti, *On the Heights*, London
1966 C. J. S. Bonington, *I Chose to Climb*, London and
Toronto
1967 Joe Brown, *The Hard Years*, London and Toronto
Mario Fantin, *Alpinisme Italiano Extraeuropeo*,
Bologna

1968 Nea Morin, *A Woman's Reach, London* (New York,
1969)
David Robertson, *Mallory of Everest*, New York
(*George Mallory*, London, 1969)
1969 Eric Shipton, *That Untravelled World*, London (New
York, 1970)
Wilfred Noyce and Ian McMorrin, *World Atlas of
Mountaineering*, London (New York, 1970)
1970 Dennis Gray, *Rope Boy*, London
1971 Kurt Diemberger, *Summits and Secrets*, London
Tom Patey, *One Man's Mountains*, London
1972 Dougal Haston, *In High Places*, London (New York,
1973)

The Alps and Europe
1555 Conrad Gesner, *Descriptio Montis Fracti juxta
Lucernani*
1574 Josias Simler, *De Alpibus Commentarius*, Zurich
1716 J. J. Scheuchzer, *Helvetiae Stoicheiographia,
Orographia, et Orcographia*, Zurich
1742 A. von Haller, *Die Alpen*
1779-96 H. B. de Saussure, *Voyages dans les Alpes*, Neuchâtel
1828 W. Brockedon, *The Passes of the Alps*, London
1833 W. Brockedon, *Journals of Excursions in the Alps*,
London
1845 E. Desor, *Nouvelles Excursions dans les Alpes*, Geneva
1855 James D. Forbes, *Tour of Mont Blanc*, Edinburgh
1856 Alfred Wills, *Wanderings Among the High Alps*, London
1857 T. W. Hinchcliff, *Summer Months in the Alps*, London
1859 John Ball, ed., *Peaks, Passes and Glaciers*, London
1862 John Tyndall, *Mountaineering in 1861*, London
E. S. Kennedy, ed., *Peaks, Passes and Glaciers II*,
London
1871 Leslie Stephen, *The Playground of Europe*, London
John Tyndall, *Hours of Exercise in the Alps*, London
Edward Whymper, *Scrambles Amongst the Alps*,
London
1875 F. Crauford Grove, *The Frosty Caucasus*, London
D. W. Freshfield, *Italian Alps*, London
1885 Clinton Dent, *Above the Snow Line*, London
1887 C. D. Cunningham and Sir W. Abney, *The Pioneers of
the Alps*, London
1889 E. Zsigmondy, *In Hochgebirge*, Leipzig
1892 E. Javelle, *Souvenirs d'un Alpiniste*, Lausanne
1895 A. F. Mummery, *My Climbs in the Alps and Caucasus*,
London
1896 D. W. Freshfield, *Exploration of the Caucasus*, London
G. Studer, *Uber Eis und Schnee*, (new ed.), Berne
Edward Whymper, *Guide to Chamonix and the Range of
Mont Blanc*, London
1897 Edward Whymper, *Guide to Zermatt and the
Matterhorn*, London
1898 P. Gussfeldt, *Mont Blanc*, Geneva
C. E. Mathews, *The Annals of Mont Blanc*, London
1899 John Ball, *Hints and Notes for Travellers in the Alps*
(new ed.) London

Mrs Norman Neruda, *The Climbs of Norman Neruda*, London

1900 George Yeld, *Scrambles in the Eastern Graians*, London

1901 L. Purtscheller, *Uber Fels und Firn*, Munich

1902 A. W. Moore, *The Alps in 1864*, Edinburgh (privately printed 1867); new ed., Oxford, 1939

1904 W. Cecil Slingsby, *Norway, the Northern Playground*, London; new ed., Oxford, 1941

1908 W. A. B. Coolidge, *The Alps in Nature and History*, London

1912 W. A. B. Coolidge, *Alpine Studies*, London

1923 A. L. Mumm, *The Alpine Club Register*, London

1927 G. W. Young, *On High Hills*, London (New York, 1934)

1928 Mrs A. le Blond, *Days In, Days Out*, London

1929 Jacques and Tom de Lépiney, *Sur les Crêtes du Mont Blanc*, Chambéry (trans. *Climbs on Mont Blanc*, London and New York, 1930)
F. S. Smythe, *Climbs and Ski-runs*, London (Toronto, 1934)

1931 Thomas Blaikie, ed. Francis Birrell, *Diary of a Scotch Gardener at the French Court*, London (New York, 1932)

1932 E. R. Blanchet, *Hors des Chemins Battus*, Paris
C. Egger, *Die Eroberung des Kaukasus*, Basel
W. T. Kirkpatrick, *Alpine Days and Nights*, London
C. Klucker, *Adventures of an Alpine Guide*, London (trans. from 3rd German ed.)
Eleonore Noll-Hasenclever, *Den Bergen Verfallen*, Berlin

1934 Julius Kugy, *Alpine Pilgrimage (Aus dem Leben eines Bergsteigers)*, London

1937 E. R. Blanchet, *Au bout d'un Fil*, Paris

1940 Julius Kugy, *Im Göttlichen Lächeln des Monte Rosa*, Graz
Charles Gos, *Tragédies Alpestres*, Paris

1941 H. Pfann, *Fürherlosen Gipfelfahrten*, Munich

1942 André Roch, *Les Conquêtes de ma Jeunesse*, Neuchâtel (trans. *Climbs of my Youth*, London, 1949)

1944 T. Graham Brown, *Brenva*, London

1946 Edouard Frendo, *La Face Nord des Grandes Jorasses*, Lausanne
H. W. Tilman, *When Men and Mountains Meet*, Cambridge

1947 Jacques Boell, *High Heaven*, London and Toronto

1949 Armand Charlet, *Vocation Alpine*, Paris

1950 Claire-Eliane Engel, *A History of Mountaineering in the Alps*, London and New York

1953 Guido Magnone, *La Face W. des Drus*, Paris

1955 C. D. Milner, *Mont Blanc and the Aiguilles*, London

1957 Gavin de Beer and T. Graham Brown, *The First Ascent of Mont Blanc*, London and Toronto
G. Gervasutti, *Gervasutti's Climbs* (trans. from *Scalate nelli Alpi*) London

1959 Heinrich Harrer, *The White Spider*, London (New York, 1960)

1960 John Hunt and Christopher Brasher, *The Red Snows*, London

1964 E. Vanis, *Im Steilen Eis*, Munich

1965 Robert Tézenas de Montel, *Ce Monde qui n'est pas le Nôtre*, Paris

1966 Peter Gillman and Dougal Haston, *Eiger Direct*, London (*Direttissima: The Eiger Assault*, New York, 1967)

1971 A. Bernard, *La Grande Civetta*, Bologna

America

1899 E. A. FitzGerald, *The Highest Andes*, London

1900 F. de. Filippi, *The Ascent of Mount St Elias*, London

1903 H. E. M. Stutfield and Norman Collie, *Climbs and Explorations in the Canadian Rockies*, London

1905 A. O. Wheeler, *The Selkirk Range*, Ottawa

1913 Belmore Brown, *The Conquest of Mount McKinley* (new ed., Boston, 1956)

1914 H. Palmer, *Mountaineering and Exploration in the Selkirks*, London

1946 J. M. Thorington, *The Purcell Range of British Columbia*, New York

1948 Arnold Heim, *Wunderland Peru*, Berne
D. Munday, *The Unknown Mountain*, London

1950 H. Kinzl and E. Schneider, *Cordillera Blanca*, Innsbruck
Frank Smythe, *Climbs in the Canadian Rockies*, London (New York, 1951)

1952 G. Kogan and N. Leininger, *Cordillère Blanche*, Paris (trans. *The Ascent of Alpamayo*, London, 1954, New York, 1955)

1953 Pierre Ghiglione, *Nelle Ande del Sud Peru*, Milan
Bernard Pierre, *La Conquête de Salcantay*, Paris

1954 M. A. Azéma, *La Conquête de Fitzroy*, Paris (trans. *The Conquest of Fitzroy*, London, 1957)

1955 C. G. Egeler and T. de Booy, *The Untrodden Andes*, London (*The Challenge of the Andes*, New York, 1956)

1959 Simon Clark, *The Puma's Claw*, London and Boston

1965 Margaret Griffin, *Tiquimani*, Stellenbosch
Pietro Meciani, *Le Ande: Monografia geografico-alpinistica*, Bologna
David Wall, *Rondoy*, London

1966 Malcolm Slesser, *The Andes are Prickly*, London and Toronto

1967 Terris Moore, *Mount McKinley: the Pioneer Climbs*, Alaska

1968 Cesar Morales Arnao, *Andinismo en la Cordillera Blanca*, Lima

1971 Bradford Washburn, *A Tourist Guide to Mount McKinley*, Alaska

Asia

1896 W. Weston, *The Japanese Alps*, London
F. E. Younghusband, *The Heart of a Continent*, London

1902 J. N. Collie, *Climbing in the Himalaya*, Edinburgh

1905 C. Merzbacher, *The Central Tyan Shan Mountains*, London

1910 C. G. Bruce, *Twenty Years in the Himalaya*, London

1922 C. K. Howard-Bury, *Mount Everest: the Reconnaissance*, London

1923 C. G. Bruce, *The Assault on Mount Everest*, London

1924 C. J. Wessels, *Early Jesuit Travellers in Central Asia*, The Hague

1925 E. F. Norton, *The Fight for Everest*, London

1926 J. Visser-Hooft, *Among the Kara-Korum Glaciers*, London
W. R. Rickmers, *Alai! Alai!*, Leipzig

1930 F. S. Smythe, *Kangchenjunga Adventure*, London

1931 P. Bauer, *Um den Kantsch*, Munich (trans. *Himalayan Campaign: the German Attack on Kangchenjunga*, Oxford and Toronto, 1937)
Philip Borchers, *Berge und Gletscher im Pamir*, Stuttgart

1932 F. S. Smythe, *Kamet Conquered*, London (Toronto, 1936)

1934 C. G. Bruce, *Himalayan Wanderer*, London
H. Ruttledge, *Everest 1933*, London

1935 F. Bechtold, *Nanga Parbat Adventure*, London
R. L. Burdsall and A. B. Emmons, *Men Against the Clouds*, London and New York
1936 Eric Shipton, *Nanda Devi*, London and Toronto
1937 H. W. Tilman, *The Ascent of Nanda Devi*, London (New York, 1939)
1938 Eric Shipton, *Blank on the Map*, London (Toronto, 1939)
1948 H. W. Tilman, *Mount Everest, 1938*, Cambridge and New York
1951 F. Spencer Chapman, *Memoirs of a Mountaineer*, London and Toronto
Maurice Herzog, *Annapurna premier 8000m.*, Paris
H. W. Tilman, *China to Chitral*, Cambridge (New York, 1952)
1952 G. O. Dyrenfurth, *Zum Dritten Pol*, Munich (London, 1955); rev. ed., *Der Dritte Pol*, Munich, 1960
André Roch, *Everest 1952*, Geneva
Eric Shipton, *Mount Everest Reconnaissance Expedition*, London
H. W. Tilman, *Nepal Himalaya*, Cambridge
1953 G. Chevalley, R. Dittert and R. Lambert, *Avant Premières à l'Everest*, Paris
John Hunt, *The Ascent of Everest*, London (*Conquest of Everest*, New York, 1954)
1954 Ardito Desio, *La Conquista del K2*, Milan
G. O. Dynrenfurth, *Das Buch von Nanga Parbat*, Munich
C. Houston and others, *K2: the Savage Mountain*, New York (London, 1955)
K. M. Herrligkoffer, *Nanga Parbat*, London and New York
Wilfred Noyce, *South Col*, London (New York, 1955)
Bernard Pierre, *Une Montagne nommée Nun Kun*, Paris
1955 Paul Bauer, *Das Ringen um den Nanga Parbat*, Munich (trans. *The Siege of Nanga Parbat*, London, 1956)
Paul Bauer, *Kangchenjunga Challenge*, London
Charles Evans, *Eye on Everest*, London
Edmund Hillary, *High Adventure*, London and New York
Kenneth Mason, *The Abode of Snow*, London and New York
1956 Hermann Buhl, *Drüber und Drunter*, Munich (trans. *Nanga Parbat Pilgrimage*, London; *Lonely Challenge*, New York)
Charles Evans, *Kangchenjunga, the Untrodden Peak*, London
Jean Franco, *Makalu*, Paris
1958 Wilfred Noyce, *Climbing the Fish's Tail*, London
1959 Mike Banks, *Rakaposhi*, London and New York
T. Hagen, G. O. Dyhrenfurth, C. von Fürer, E. Schneider, *Mount Everest: Structure, Exploration and Population of the Everest Massif*, Zurich (trans. London, 1963)
Marcel Kurz, *Chronique Himalayenne, 1940–1955*, Zurich
1961 M. Eiselin, *The Ascent of Dhaulagiri*, London
Fosco Maraini, *Karakoram*, London and New York
1962 Wilfred Noyce, *To the Unknown Mountain*, London
1963 Marcel Kurz, *Chronique Himalayenne II*, Zurich
1964 M. Fantin, *I Quattordici '8000'*, Bologna
Malcolm Slesser, *Red Peak*, London and New York
1965 Jean Franco and Lionel Terray, *Bataille pour le Jannu*, Paris
1966 Thomas Hornbein, *Everest, the West Ridge*, San Francisco and London
1971 Christian Bonington, *Annapurna South Face*, London and New York
1972 Michael Ward, *In this Short Span*, London
1973 Christian Bonington, *Everest South West Face*, London; *The Ultimate Challenge*, New York

New Zealand
1891 G. E. Mannering, *With Axe and Rope in the N.Z. Alps*, London
1896 E. A. FitzGerald, *Climbs in the N.Z. Alps*, London
A. P. Harper, *Pioneer Work in the Alps of N.Z.*, London
1915 Freda du Faur, *The Conquest of Mount Cook*, London
1922 Samuel Turner, *The Conquest of the New Zealand Alps*, London
1939 John Pascoe, *Unclimbed New Zealand*, London and New York
1946 A. P. Harper, *Memories of Mountains and Men*, Christchurch
1959 John Pascoe, *Great Days in New Zealand Exploration*, Wellington and London
1965 Peter Graham, *Mountain Guide: An Autobiography*, London and Beverly Hills
1967 Paul Powell, *Men Aspiring*, Wellington
1968 Jim Wilson, *Aorangi: The Story of Mount Cook*, Christchurch
1969 Michael Gill, *Mountain Midsummer*, London and Auckland

Africa
1952 Bernard Pierre, *Escalades au Hoggar*, Paris
1957 Sir Douglas Busk, *The Fountain of the Sun*, London, Toronto and Chester Springs, Pa.
1966 R. M. Bere, *The Way to the Mountains of the Moon*, London
J. Burman, *A Peak to Climb, the Story of South African Mountaineering*, Capetown (Beverly Hills, 1967)
1969 Peter Robson, *Mountains of Kenya*, Nairobi (New York, 1971)
1973 R. O. Pearse, *Barrier of Spears*, Capetown

Britain
1894 W. P. Haskett Smith, *Climbing in the British Isles*, London
1925 H. R. C. Carr and G. A. Lister, *The Mountains of Snowdonia*, London (2nd rev. ed., 1948)
1941 C. F. Kirkus, *Let's Go Climbing*, London
1947 W. H. Murray, *Mountaineering in Scotland*, London (New York, 1948)
1952 E. C. Pyatt and Wilfred Noyce, *British Crags and Climbers*, London
1957 G. W. Young, G. Sutton and Wilfred Noyce, *Snowden Biography*, London

Index

Entries in italics refer to captions

247